MW00834956

PRELUDE TO GENOCIDE

STUDIES IN CONFLICT, JUSTICE, AND SOCIAL CHANGE

Series Editors: Susan F. Hirsch and Agnieszka Paczyńska

This series is funded in part through the generous support of the School for Conflict Analysis and Resolution at George Mason University.

PRELUDE TO GENOCIDE

Arusha, Rwanda, and the

Failure of Diplomacy

DAVID RAWSON

AN ADST-DACOR DIPLOMATS AND DIPLOMACY BOOK

STUDIES IN CONFLICT, JUSTICE, AND SOCIAL CHANGE

OHIO UNIVERSITY PRESS, ATHENS

Ohio University Press, Athens, Ohio 45701
ohioswallow.com
© 2018 by David Rawson
All rights reserved

To obtain permission to quote, reprint, or otherwise reproduce or distribute material from
Ohio University Press publications, please contact our rights and permissions department at
(740) 593-1154 or (740) 593-4536 (fax).

Printed in the United States of America
Ohio University Press books are printed on acid-free paper ⊗ ™

28 27 26 25 24 23 22 21 20 19 18   5 4 3 2 1

The opinions and characterizations in this book are those of the author, and do not necessarily
represent official positions of the United States Government.

Library of Congress Cataloging-in-Publication Data
Names: Rawson, David P., author.
Title: Prelude to genocide : Arusha, Rwanda, and the failure of diplomacy /
David Rawson.
Other titles: Studies in conflict, justice, and social change. | ADST-DACOR
diplomats and diplomacy series ; v. 65.
Description: Athens, Ohio : Ohio University Press, 2018. | Series: Studies in
conflict, justice, and social change | Series: ADST-DACOR diplomats and
diplomacy series ; 65th | Includes bibliographical references and index.
Identifiers: LCCN 2018031923| ISBN 9780821423325 (hc : alk. paper) | ISBN
9780821423332 (pb : alk. paper) | ISBN 9780821446508 (pdf)
Subjects: LCSH: Rwanda--History--Civil War, 1994--Diplomatic history. |
Rwanda--History--Civil War, 1994--Causes. | Humanitarian
intervention--Rwanda--History--20th century. |
Genocide--Rwanda--History--20th century. | Rwanda--Politics and
government--1962-1994. | Rwanda--Ethnic relations--History.
Classification: LCC DT450.435 .R39 2018 | DDC 967.571042--dc23
LC record available at https://lccn.loc.gov/2018031923

ADST-DACOR Diplomats and Diplomacy Series

Series Editor: MARGERY BOICHEL THOMPSON

Since 1776, extraordinary men and women have represented the United States abroad under widely varying circumstances. What they did and how and why they did it remain little known to their compatriots. In 1995, the Association for Diplomatic Studies and Training (ADST) and DACOR, an organization of foreign affairs professionals, created the Diplomats and Diplomacy book series to increase public knowledge and appreciation of the professionalism of American diplomats and their involvement in world history. David Rawson's account of the Arusha negotiations preceding the Rwandan genocide is the 65th volume in the series.

RELATED TITLES IN ADST SERIES

Claudia E. Anyaso, *Fifty Years of U.S. Africa Policy: Reflections of Assistant Secretaries for African Affairs and U.S. Embassy Officials*

Prudence Bushnell, *Terrorism, Betrayal, and Resilience: My Story of the 1998 U.S. Embassy Bombings*

Herman J. Cohen, *Intervening in Africa: Superpower Peacemaking in a Troubled Continent*

———. *The Mind of the African Strongman: Conversations with Dictators, Statesmen, and Father Figures*

Peter D. Eicher, ed., *"Emperor Dead" and Other Historic American Diplomatic Dispatches*

Christopher Goldthwait, *Ambassador to a Small World: Letters from Chad*

Robert E. Gribbin, *In the Aftermath of Genocide: The U.S. Role in Rwanda*

Brandon Grove, *Behind Embassy Walls: The Life and Times of an American Diplomat*

Judith M. Heimann, *Paying Calls in Shangri-La: Scenes from a Woman's Life in American Diplomacy*

Michael P. E. Hoyt, *Captive in the Congo: A Consul's Return to the Heart of Darkness*

Cameron R. Hume, *Mission to Algiers: Diplomacy by Engagement*

Joanne Huskey, *The Unofficial Diplomat*

Richard L. Jackson, *The Incidental Oriental Secretary and Other Tales of Foreign Service*

Dennis C. Jett, *American Ambassadors: The Past, Present, and Future of America's Diplomats*

John G. Kormann, *Echoes of a Distant Clarion: Recollections of a Diplomat and Soldier*

William Morgan & C. Stuart Kennedy, *American Diplomats: The Foreign Service at Work*

David D. Newsom, *Witness to a Changing World*

Raymond F. Smith, *The Craft of Political Analysis for Diplomats*

James W. Spain, *In Those Days: A Diplomat Remembers*

William G. Thom, *African Wars: Recollections of a Defense Intelligence Officer*

Jean Wilkowski, *Abroad for Her Country: Tales of a Pioneer Woman Ambassador in the U.S. Foreign Service*

For a complete list of series titles, visit adst.org/publications.

To Sandy, for her love, courage, and support in difficult days

CONTENTS

PROLOGUE

On the evening of April 6, 1994, a full moon shone on Kigali Hill across the valley from the American residence. My wife Sandra and I had just stepped in from the front porch when we heard a huge boom followed by a smaller explosion. Sandra, accustomed to small-arms fire and grenade explosions after three months in country, exclaimed, "That was not a grenade!"

Within minutes, the president's cabinet director Enoch Ruhigira called me from the airport. "They have shot down my president," he said in a broken voice.

"Who is they?" I asked.

"The RPF of course!" was his instant and grieving response.

We later learned that two air-to-ground missiles hit the Dassault Falcon jet bringing President Juvénal Habyarimana back home to Kigali from a regional summit in Dar es Salaam. Three months earlier, Habyarimana had been sworn in as interim president under terms of the Arusha Accords, signed August 4, 1993, between the then Government of Rwanda (GOR) and the insurgent Rwandese Patriotic Front (RPF).[1] When the president perished with all aboard that plane, the two contending parties returned to war instead of working out the arrangements of democratic governance and power sharing based on the Arusha principles. A Hutu extremist faction grabbed the reins of government and launched a genocide in which over eight hundred thousand victims were slaughtered within one hundred days.

International Humanitarian Intervention in Rwanda

What was the context in which the downing of the presidential aircraft engendered genocide? What was the role of the international community in structuring that context? This study looks at the international humanitarian intervention in Rwanda[2] and asks what lessons might be learned from the nearly four-year international effort to halt the conflict between the Rwandan government and the Patriotic Front, and to restore peace and security to Rwanda's people.

From the outbreak of civil war in October 1990, regional states and international partners sought to broker a ceasefire. Once a durable ceasefire was secured in 1992, international Observers accompanied political negotiations in Arusha, while diplomatic missions pushed the peace process in Kigali.[3] After the parties signed a peace agreement in August 1993, the United Nations Security Council deployed a peacekeeping mission, UNAMIR, to accompany the establishment of a transitional government with a peacekeeping force.

The international community took the signing of the Arusha Accords as warrant of the negotiation's success and guarantee of peace and progress for Rwanda.[4] But attempts to implement the accords revealed political chasms that international mediation had not bridged. Only Habyarimana had been sworn in as transition president; the organization of other institutions established by the accords was still in dispute. When the president's plane went down, the peace process blew apart in the renewal of civil war and the launching of genocide.

What seemed a model negotiation had fallen apart in endless political point and counterpoint. Within eight months of the peace agreement, the international community, including the largest part of the UNAMIR mission, was fleeing Rwanda, leaving in tatters a carefully knit humanitarian intervention. What went wrong? What lessons for other humanitarian endeavors might we learn from this well-intentioned but tragic effort?

Participant-Observer

As a diplomat of the United States government, I was a participant in those tragic events. My own encounter with Rwanda's political strife began in 1973 during my first overseas posting in Kigali, Rwanda's capital. As second secretary at the US embassy, I witnessed, in the spring of that year, the outbreak of ethnic violence, born out of passions stirred by the prospect of elections in the summer. On July 5, a committee of ranking National Guard officers, self-designated as "The Committee for Peace and National Unity," took power, abolished political parties, dissolved the government, abrogated the constitution, and named the chief of staff, Major General Juvénal Habyarimana, as chief of state.[5]

Before I left Kigali in August 1975 for onward posting to Bamako, Mali, Habyarimana had installed a largely civilian government and established the Revolutionary National Movement for Development (Mouvement Révolutionaire Nationale pour le Développement, or MRND).[6] Adoption by referendum of a new constitution in December 1978 and the election of Habyarimana as president that same month completed the transition to a single-party state.

Habyarimana was still in power in 1990 when exile forces, brought together in the Rwandese Patriotic Front, launched an insurgent movement from Uganda, seeking to overthrow the regime. Distant from Rwanda by postings in West and East Africa and at the Department of State, I was drawn back to the region as a discussant at a State Department conference in March 1992 that presaged a new policy toward Rwanda. Actively directing this new policy was the assistant secretary for African affairs, Ambassador Herman (Hank) Cohen, who, in August 1992, asked me to delay my next assignment and become the US Observer at the political negotiations in Arusha, Tanzania, following the establishment of a ceasefire between the contending parties. Although these negotiations lasted from August 5, 1992, to August 5, 1993, my own engagement ended in November, when negotiations stalled and headed into impasse.

In March 1993, President Clinton named me as his intended ambassador to the Republic of Rwanda, presumably to be accredited to a transition regime as structured in the Arusha negotiations. Arriving at post in January 1994, I found that only the president had been sworn in to his transition position under the Arusha Accords. Three months of intensive diplomacy thereafter could not bring the parties to establish the transitional government or national assembly. When the president's plane was snot down on April 6, Hutu extremists rushed to fill the power vacuum, launching war and genocide in their quest to hold onto power.

The Rwandese Patriotic Army (RPA) vanquished government forces and stopped genocide in four months of fighting. In the meantime, some eight hundred thousand innocents had been brutally slaughtered as states debated how to restore an international force within Rwanda. Having on April 10 evacuated Americans and closed the embassy in Kigali under orders from Washington, I was now asked on July 24 to establish the base for cooperation with the new government and to oversee the launching of a humanitarian airlift, in effect reopening the US mission. For the next eighteen months, our embassy was engaged in providing humanitarian relief, rebuilding infrastructure, promoting justice, and increasing the capacities of the new government. I passed these responsibilities to my successor, Robert Gribbin, on January 6, 1996, and went on to West Africa as the US ambassador to Mali.

From Memories to Documents

Memories abound, but they are often selective, sometimes inaccurate, and always circumscribed by one's personal experience. More reliable are observations refined and inscribed, fixed in the official record. Upon my retirement from the US Foreign Service in 1999, I was encouraged by the late Senator Paul Simon to write about US engagement in Rwanda—policies and actions in which he had taken a personal interest. His recommendation evolved into a proposal to the United States Institute of Peace to look at the documentary record of international humanitarian intervention of that period, especially the US classified documents that were accessible to me as a former presidential appointee. Following reinstatement of my security clearance, I began the perusal of those documents in the summer of 2002. Had I known how laborious it would be to sort through the thousands of documents covering the period from 1990, when the RPF invaded, to 1996, when the United Nations withdrew its peace mission, I might never have undertaken the task. Nor did I have any idea of how slow the process of getting critical documents declassified and available to the public would be.

CAUTIONS

The analysis that follows is made with a great deal of hesitancy. I am reminded of Claude Lanzmann's remark, when asked to describe Hitler, that any attempt to explain Hitler is obscene because you are led, whether you want it or not, to justification.[7] Similarly, to discuss state and interstate response to genocide in Rwanda may well be seen as an attempt to explain away failure or to diminish responsibility. Nor can one claim powerlessness or lack of jurisdiction. Genocide happened "on our watch"! The observation of Czesław Miłosz, made in the context of the Holocaust, is thus appropriate here, "There is no such thing as an innocent bystander. If you are a bystander, you are not innocent."[8]

There are, as well, the issues of historiography in the African context. Joseph Miller reminds us that "Africans have had, and have, distinctive ways of thinking of themselves and their worlds . . . alternative casts on the Modern Western imaginings that make up our reality. . . . A world history that evaluates Africans only in terms of their relations with others' worlds catches only the most fleeting glimpses of what they were in fact about."[9]

A particular difficulty with this study is precisely that it evaluates the advent of Rwanda's genocide from the perspective of the others' world— namely, that of the international community engaged in humanitarian intervention. There is a much deeper story here that must be included in any comprehensive narrative, and it must be told from African perspectives, and hopefully from more Rwandan ones. Such would be a signal contribution to "the multi-centric world history of complexity" that Miller invokes.[10]

A larger problem of historical craft and the human condition remains. Hannah Arendt argues that "action reveals itself fully only to the storyteller, that is, to the backward glance of the historian, who indeed always knows better what it was all about than the participants."[11] I was a participant and still must live with the consequences of my actions in that troubled time. My rendition of the "intentions, aims and motives," of the international community in its effort to extricate Rwanda from civil war is admittedly partial. I have sought to ground my narration in the documentary record of the time.

There are, nonetheless, personal aspirations that emerge from this study. One is the desire that the admittedly partial readings and insights of a participant who has access to the documentary record may bring some light on events and decisions that led to the tragedy of the Rwandan genocide. The second is the hope that this analysis might offer some lessons on the possibilities and limitations of international humanitarian intervention seen through the prism of the Rwandan peace process. The third is the ambition that the long process of declassification of hundreds of documents that are particularly relevant to this story will provide "useful source material in the historian's hands."[12] I can only hope that this perusal of the historical record will inspire future historians to evaluate more deeply and narrate more tellingly the events on which the documents report.

SECONDARY SOURCES

A word is in order about the sources I have consulted and how they are presented in this study. There are numerous books and monographs on the history of genocide in Rwanda. Some studies survey the story; some focus narrowly on particular events or dynamics. Some analyses attempt an even-handed evaluation, whereas others are openly ideological; some cite empirical evidence, and others seek theoretical confirmations. Some are autobiographies with stories of horror and triumph. The studies center around those written close to the events, those that take a longer look at middle distance, and those that, on second look and through different optics, challenge the previous record.[13]

OFFICIAL RECORDS

This is a study of official records of the international humanitarian intervention in Rwanda from the opening of civil war in October 1990 to the death of President Habyarimana in April 1994. An epilogue brings the action forward to the installation of a new government in July 1994. State actors in this drama were Belgium, Burundi, Canada, France, Germany, Switzerland, Tanzania, Uganda, the United States, and Zaire; intergovernmental organizations included the Economic Community of the Great Lakes Countries (CEPGL), the Organization of African Unity (OAU), and the United Nations (UN). What is known of the actions of Belgium and France is a matter of extensive public record brought out by hearings in the Belgian Senate and in the French National Assembly.[14] Germany largely focused on its two-year economic development plans for Rwanda rather than on any political agenda. Although present as an Observer at the Arusha political negotiations, Germany did not participate in political discussions on Central Africa, discussions that brought Belgian, French, and US policy makers together regularly in each other's capitals during the period under investigation. Canada and Switzerland had significant economic assistance programs in Rwanda and occasionally joined in diplomatic demarches through their resident development officers.

In contrast to Belgium and France, the United States Congress never held a hearing on the Clinton administration's policy toward Rwanda, even though that was strongly recommended both by leading human rights groups and, in 1999, by a panel of experts.[15] A critical behind-the-scenes player during the Arusha discussions and the leader in postgenocide reconstruction, the United States covered the role of its decision makers during those events in a blanket of documentary confidentiality.

A significant part of the US story became public record thanks to the tireless efforts of William Ferroggiaro while working at the National Security Archive from 1995 to 2003. His pioneering work has led to full collection of declassified documents at the archives. More recently, the State Department has collated and made available to the public a large number of documents, many of which were first declassified at the request of Mr. Ferroggiaro or myself in the course of this study (foia.state.gov).

UN documents are deposited in UN collections at various institutions around the United States or are available online. The key documents of the period have been collected in the *United Nations and Rwanda: 1993–1996*.[16] Internal UN documents are not available. For what was happening within UN institutions, within the OAU, or in African capitals, this study has relied largely on the reports of the US Mission to the United Nations in New York and the US embassies in Addis Ababa, Bujumbura, Dar es Salaam, Kampala, Kigali, Kinshasa, and Nairobi. I also drew information from conversations with key actors and from my own experiences at the time.[17]

Drawing from the documentary record, this study looks at international efforts at conflict resolution in Rwanda from 1990 to 1996, with an

emphasis on international engagement within the Arusha political negotiations of 1992–1994. As background to that narrative, I first review the
historic roots of the Rwandan conflict, look at structures of international
intervention that sought to mitigate that conflict, and anticipate the effect
of international humanitarian intervention.

ACKNOWLEDGMENTS

I must thank those who made this study possible. The United States Institute of Peace and Spring Arbor University gave grants of money and of time to pursue the initial research. Diplomats on three continents offered their time and insight in interviews. William Ferroggiaro graciously shared his documents to help kick-start my own research.

Honor is due the "Life Cycle" staff of the State Department's Office of Information Programs and Services, who worked my many requests for declassification through the complicated process that turns classified documents into public record. Those stalwarts included Behar Godaine, Connie Cook, Jane Diedrich, Alden Fahy, Margaret Hardrick, Erin McClinn, Sayo Obayomi, Omolola Oyegbota, Rosemary Reid, Alice Ritchie, and Margaret Scholl.

I pay tribute as well to the distinguished diplomats Charles Daris, Harmon Kirby, John Mills, and Norman Shaft, who read through these documents, appropriately releasing what the law allowed and excising what was still not open to public purview.

My dear wife, Sandra, brought to this lengthy exercise patience with my dithering, critical assessment of the text, and an eagle eye for gratuitous errors.

Margery Boichel Thompson, publishing director and series editor of the Association for Diplomatic Studies and Training (ADST), has shown patience and perseverance in finding an appropriate publishing house for this study. My thanks also go to ADST for adopting my book for its Diplomats and Diplomacy Series.

At Ohio University Press, Gillian Berchowitz, director and editor in chief, and Ricky Huard, acquisitions editor, had the courage to take on this project. Nancy Basmajian led the editorial staff in the difficult task of turning a belabored manuscript into a readable book.

Finally, I should recognize the unknown peer reviewers for the Association for Diplomatic Studies and Training and Ohio University Press for their encouraging praise and keen suggestions, which added depth and clarity to my efforts in telling the story of the Rwandan political negotiations, a prelude to genocide.

ABBREVIATIONS

APROSOMA   Association for the Social Promotion of the Masses
ARDHO   Rwandan Association for the Defense of Human Rights
CDR   Coalition for the Defense of the Republic
CEPGL   Economic Community of the Great Lakes Countries
CND   National Development Council (the Rwandan
           parliament, 1976–1993)
FAR   Rwandan Armed Forces
FDC   Democratic Forces for Change
GOR   Government of Rwanda
ICTR   International Criminal Tribunal for Rwanda
MDR   Democratic Republican Movement
MRND   Revolutionary National Movement for Development
OAU   Organization of African Unity
PADER   Rwandan Democratic Party
PARERWA   Rwandan Republican Party
Parmehutu Party of the Movement for the Emancipation of the Hutu
PDC   Christian Democratic Party
PDI   Islamic Democratic Party
PECO   Green Party
PL   Liberal Party
PSD   Democratic Social Party
PSR   Rwandan Socialist Party
RADER   Rwandan Democratic Rally

RPA	Rwandese Patriotic Army
RPF	Rwandese Patriotic Front
RTLM	Free Radio-Television of the Thousand Hills
SRSG	Special Representative of the Secretary General
UNAMIR	United Nations Assistance Mission in Rwanda
UNAR	Rwandan National Union
UNOMUR	United Nations Observer Mission Uganda/Rwanda

PRELUDE TO GENOCIDE

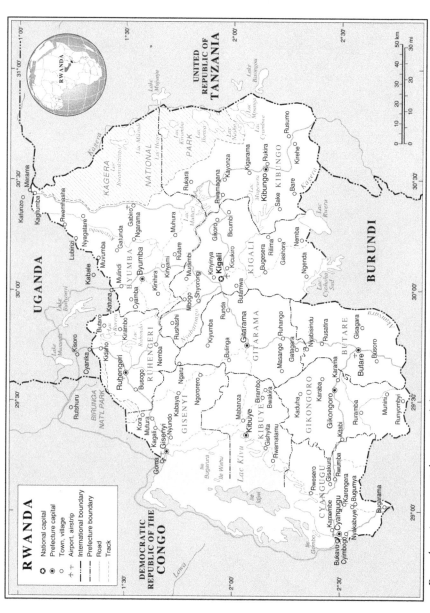

Rwanda, prior to 2006 change in subdivisions. Based on map by United Nations Geospatial Information Section, no. 3717 Rev. 7 December 1997

INTRODUCTION

Like most conflicts, the Rwandan civil war and attendant genocide are not easily confined within brackets of time. This study looks at the period of conflict in Rwanda from the incursion of the Rwandese Patriotic Army (RPA) on October 1, 1990, until the April 6, 1994 downing of President Habyarimana's plane. This event relaunched the civil war and opened the door to genocide, bringing the Arusha peace process to an untimely end. An epilogue brings forward the implications of this period for the genocide and subsequent events in Rwanda.

In this introduction, I review perspectives on the Arusha negotiations found in current literature, recount the antecedents of the Rwandan conflict, and pose the question of why humanitarian intervention failed. Subsequent chapters seek the answers to that question in a story that follows the international intervention against the backdrop of political negotiations in Arusha and political wrangling in Kigali. In that narrative, the arc of humanitarian intervention confronts questions that are customarily faced in international interventions as well as questions that reflect the peculiarities of the Rwandan context. A notation of conflict-resolution issues at stake and an inventory of lessons learned thus bookend each chapter.

What Do Folks Say about Arusha?

The conclusion of this study is that the Rwandan peace process, centered in the Arusha negotiations, helped set the dynamic context of genocide in Rwanda. Yet, in the voluminous reporting and analysis on the genocide in Rwanda, there is little systematic focus on the Arusha political negotiations, on the events leading up to those discussions, or on the effect of those negotiations on the outbreak of genocide. Few commentators stop by Arusha. Those that do intersperse occasional references to Arusha within their larger narrative. Most studies, with reason, concentrate on the breakout of genocide itself and its eventual suppression by the Rwandese Patriotic Front. Among the commonly cited references, the most comprehensive is Human Rights Watch's *Leave None to Tell the Story*, which mentions the Arusha negotiations in various places but only as a backdrop to growing internal political tensions.[1] Gérard Prunier's *The Rwanda Crisis* gives a chapter to the negotiations but similarly focuses on how negotiations played out within Rwandan domestic politics.[2] Grünfeld and Huijboom give numerous details about the situation in Rwanda during the period of negotiations, but little on the process of negotiations.[3] André Guichaoua's more recent work, full of behind-the-scenes details and excellent analyses of the ebb and flow of political contests within Rwanda, has but two chapters on the Arusha negotiations, and those are seen through the optic of the domestic political scene.[4]

Memoires of the period naturally deal with the moments when the writers were engaged in Rwandan affairs, most after the accords were signed. For example, in his excellent narrative on post-genocide Rwanda, Robert Gribbin, US ambassador in Kigali from 1996 to 1999, offers but a short chapter on the talks, noting, "I was not there and so cannot throw much light on the inner workings of the talks."[5]

Two Rwandan accounts from opposite sides of the conflict give useful insights into the Arusha negotiations. Dr. Theogene Rudasingwa, an officer in the Rwandese Patriotic Army and the Patriotic Front's representative to the OAU, was at the time of the Arusha negotiations RPF's secretary general as well as a member of the RPF negotiating team. He does not treat the negotiations chronologically or thematically, but his *Healing a Nation: A Testimony* does highlight RPF's ambiguity toward the peace process.[6] On the other side, Enoch Ruhigira, at that time the director of Habyarimana's presidential office, shows in his *La fin tragique d'un régime* how Habyarimana progressively lost the battle over the negotiating process as distance swiftly grew between the president and prime minister, between the presidential party and the internal opposition, and between the political elite in Kigali and the negotiators in Arusha.[7]

The most incisive analyses of the Arusha peace process and of its failures come from a key US policymaker of that time, Assistant Secretary Herman Cohen, and an academic and international consultant on peacekeeping, Bruce Jones. In a single chapter on Rwanda in his *Intervening in Africa: Superpower Peacemaking in a Troubled Continent*, Cohen, with pointed realism, faults US policy for its failure to understand the depth of hostility in Rwanda (an arena of low US interest), for being obsessed with the negotiating process, and for not realizing that "as the Arusha process unfolded . . . it inadvertently guaranteed the genocide."[8]

During the late 1990s, Jones, who is now a senior fellow at Brookings, wrote his doctoral dissertation on Rwanda. He published his *Peacemaking in Rwanda: The Dynamics of Failure* in 2001 on the basis of his doctoral work. His chapter on the Arusha negotiations analyzes the negotiations through the optic of their peacemaking objectives. Although his narrative contains errors on chronology, procedural details, and negotiating dynamics, Jones tells the larger story with insight into why the Arusha negotiations looked so good and failed so miserably.

In his conclusion, Jones highlights what went wrong with third-party intervention in the Rwanda crisis: undue pressure to democratize; drawbacks in the facilitation of negotiations; lack of community-level buy-in with the peace process; and failure to plan for violent opposition or to account for spoilers and losers.[9] I would agree with Cohen and Jones in their critiques of the Arusha process. But the social cataclysm that was the Rwandan genocide needs a more systematic explication of the international search for peace in Rwanda. That narrative begins with a look at what brought us to Arusha.

Antecedents

Like all Rwandan stories, this is a long one. Rwandan dynastic chronologies would push us back into the mystic past of the founding kings, Kigwa or Gihanga, depending on the legend. Some historians would credit stories about Ruganzu Bwimba, reputed to have built a kingdom in north-central Rwanda in the 1400s, only to have it fall apart in civil war five generations later. Others assert that it was rather Ruganzu Ndori who in the 1600s established the Nyiginya dynasty over the first Rwandan Kingdom of which we have reliable oral record.[10]

TRADITIONAL SOCIETY

Out of this ancient genesis, Rwandan social and political organization coalesced around descent groups. In Rwanda, heads of lineages formed alliances to build clans. "Being alliances rather than descent groups, clans were mutable . . . [and] the number of lineages composing a clan constantly varied over time according to the political adventures of the great families."[11]

As with many other emerging polities of the Great Lakes area, Rwandan leaders knit ties with clans having reputed ritual power and built clientage through distribution of land and cattle. By the beginning of the 1700s, the Nyiginya Kingdom was a fragile coalition of lineages in south-central Rwanda. By the end of the century, "it had transformed into a unified, centralized and aggressive entity."[12] Three factors brought about this transformation: the centralization of power at the court; the extension of clientage to bring all land and cattle under notional royal authority; and continuous expansion under armies by which sons of the ruling elite proved their valor and into which all Rwandan citizens were incorporated.[13]

During the 1800s, the reach of the state (king and court) deepened. Cyrimina Rujugira (1770), himself a usurper, structured succession to a cycle of four regnal names, expanded court ritual, and increased the number of armies. Around the 1840s, as population and demands on land and pasture grew, the court reserved pasture domains for royal use and disposition. It then appointed chiefs of "tall grass" to oversee pastures and herds, as well as chiefs of land to manage farmers and their obligations. Add to these the commanders of now-ubiquitous armies, and a tripartite system of bureaucratic control emerges, especially in the districts close to the court.

This system did provide a sort of check against arbitrary power at the local level where a client, whether herder or farmer, could seek the protection of one lord against the predations of another. Nonetheless, under a clientage system now triply bureaucratized, exactions necessarily increased, impoverishing farmers and herders. Two "social categories" came to define subjects of the king: those who had lineage links to power and privilege—the Tutsi; and those who by dint of circumstance fell into servile status—the Hutu.[14]

That was the Rwanda that the Europeans "discovered" in the late 1800s: a country ruled by a king newly installed by the 1896 Rucunshu coup and hemmed in by courtiers, ritual, and intrigue; a territory densely populated at the center with farmers competing with herders for land; and a militarized society in which each person belonged to an army and was a client of a superior both for land and cattle. An overlapping system of chieftaincies administered central lands; at the periphery, sons of aristocrats with new armies pressed against surrounding polities, making Rwanda one of the more powerful kingdoms of the region.

COLONIAL RULE

Rwanda's mountain fastness and warrior reputation had kept the outside world (including Swahili slavers and traders) at bay until German explorers crossed the land in the 1890s, with Count von Goetzen discovering Lake Kivu in 1894. Three years later, Hauptmann Ramsay offered the newly ascendant king, Mwami Musinga, a letter of protection. German forces and firepower helped Musinga consolidate his rule at the court and expand Rwandan control in Gisaka to the southeast and Bugoyi in the northwest.

In 1907, Germany's military protection changed to civil administration by indirect rule from a residency at Kigali. But in 1916, Belgian forces from the Congo pushed the Germans south out of Rwanda and beyond the rail center of Tabora. Belgium held its conquered territory provisionally until the Milner-Orts Agreement of May 30, 1919, ceded to Belgium the two German provinces of Ruanda and Urundi as the mandate territory of Ruanda-Urundi. At the Paris peace talks, the Mandates Commission approved the Belgian mandate and the Great Power Council of Five accepted the Milner-Orts Agreement on August 7, 1919.[15] In 1947, this mandate evolved into a trusteeship under the United Nations.

The Belgians, like the Germans, faced the dilemma of how to assert authority over a polity already endowed with a sovereign, an administration, and a society knit together by clientage relations. Under ideals of the League of Nations mandate, Belgium was to assure the uplift of the local population as well as the development of natural resources.[16] Belgium intended to meet these goals while administering the territory efficiently, with minimum investment and maximum gain from the territory's dense population and fertile lands. Tying into the Congo's physical and administrative infrastructure seemed the appropriate approach.[17]

Whereas in Congo, Belgian administrators ruled directly over respective provinces, in Rwanda, Belgium would follow the German approach of indirect rule. The goal, according to Colonial Minister Louis Frank, was to "associate the native princes with our plans and bring the indigenous ruling class into our service."[18] In 1919, the administration established schools for chiefs' sons to train the necessary cadre. Then in 1926, the administration began to rationalize and decentralize the tripartite chiefs system while setting contiguous boundaries for chieftaincies and subchieftaincies.

This streamlined structure was to uniformly administer the provinces throughout Rwanda, with chiefs trained first at Nyanza and other local schools and then at Butare. The new structure was also intended to relieve the "Hutu masses" of burdensome obligations to three different chiefs. However, the traditional system of clientage, both in land and cattle obligations, remained, now legally and efficiently enforced. Ignoring common social identities found in lineage and clan, as well as regional variances in social structure, the mandate administration saw Hutu and Tutsi as the overarching social constructs of personal identification and, in 1931, established identity cards classifying each person accordingly.[19]

In the name of progress, colonial policy discounted regional differences, reinforced clientage obligations, and crystallized identities along ethnic lines. Moreover, the colonial regime, through the local chiefs, assessed a head tax, required labor on public works, and enforced agricultural plantings in food crops and coffee. The burden of obligation to political elites weighed heavily on the poor, whether Tutsi or Hutu.

The Mandates Commission of the League of Nations might never have approved a policy of "indirect rule" that coercive and controlling were it not for the Rwakayihura famine of 1929–30 in which thousands of

Rwandans died in inaccessible parts of the country. Only ⸤
sures could build roads, increase harvests, and raise the tax⸤
country together.[20] With the exile of the recalcitrant King I⸤
the investiture of the more educated and compliant Rudahigwa in ⸤
Belgian mandate took root.[21]

TRANSITION TO TRUSTEESHIP

The League of Nations had been content to let Belgium administer the territory and send reports on social and economic progress to the Mandate Commission in Geneva, there to debate the merits of Belgian policy. Following World War II, however, the newly created UN Trusteeship Council actively pushed for political change, as well as for economic and social development. Regular missions began in 1947, reviewing progress on site. Although traditional autocracy had been legally grounded and administratively rationalized under indirect rule, the council's first visiting mission to East Africa was convinced that "political evolution has reached a stage when an acceleration of the movement would be justified without running any great risk of grave social upheaval."[22]

Grave social upheaval was precisely what occurred as Rwanda moved quickly toward independence in the late 1950s. By 1959, rural violence had broken out in northwest and central Rwanda, with massacres and hut burnings perpetrated by both Hutu and Tutsi partisans, while threats and intimidations harried Tutsi nobles into exile. In 1960, elected communal burgomasters and counselors replaced chieftaincies. As Reyntjens sums it up, "In less than two years [1959–1961], Rwanda had passed from a 'feudal' monarchy to a Hutu 'democratic' republic. . . . In 1952, the monarchist, fundamentally Tutsi regime was still solidly established, legally reinforced by 35 years of indirect administration. In 1962, Rwanda became independent under a republican, fundamentally Hutu regime."[23]

A SOCIAL REVOLUTION

Chrétien contends that "the 1959–1961 'social revolution' is the key event in Rwanda, one that shaped the country's politics for the next three decades."[24] Radical changes brought about by that event found root in several factors:

- The UN Trusteeship Council's interventions, which sought a rapid pace toward representative government and national autonomy[25]

- The monopolization of power, position, and privilege by the ruling Tutsi elite[26]

- The abolition in 1954 of *ubuhake* cattle-clientage without a concomitant reform of the land-tenure system[27]

- The emergence of Hutu intelligentsia, who challenged the legitimacy of traditional institutions and symbols and called for democratic governance[28]

- The death of Mwami Rudahigwa and the hardening of neo-traditionalist attitudes claiming right of conquest and superiority[29]

- The creation of political parties mobilized by individual leaders and ideologically centered on presumed Hutu and Tutsi identities[30]

Tensions built by these factors came to a crescendo on November 1, 1959, with the outbreak of violence around Kabgayi, center of the Hutu renaissance, and in the northwest, where clan leaders still opposed rule from the central court. By the time the violence abated, some three hundred Hutu and Tutsi were killed and twelve hundred were arrested, while the population of displaced burgeoned.[31]

To calm the storm, the Belgian administration installed Hutu chiefs and subchiefs in vacated chieftainships. They then implemented a previously planned administrative reform of replacing subchiefs with burgomasters and elected communal councils. A multiparty Provisional Council took over the legislative role of the High Council of State. After the failure of a reconciliation conference in early January 1961 at Ostend, Belgium, the Provisional Council called a national convention of burgomasters and municipal counselors. On January 28, these counselors deposed the "monarchy and all its symbols" and proclaimed a democratic republic.

Nine months later, under UN supervision but in an atmosphere of preelectoral violence and intimidation, legislative elections and a referendum on the monarchy confirmed the establishment of the republic and the parliamentary dominance of the Parmehutu Party. The elected legislators then set up the structures of the new republic, chose a government, and designated Grégoire Kayibanda as president. The "social revolution" thus gave birth to the government that took Rwanda to independence on July 1, 1962.[32]

FIRST REPUBLIC

Around the edges of this new, landlocked republic, monarchists in refugee camps plotted a return to power. Host country control and internal divisions within refugee leadership kept the attacks from being more effective; but with each attack, Hutu took reprisals against Tutsi still living in Rwanda.[33]

In December 1963, the monarchist UNAR party planned attacks from Congo, Uganda, Tanzania, and Burundi. While the other attacks were turned back, a refugee force from Burundi pushed to within twenty miles of Kigali before the Rwandan National Guard stopped the column. Tutsi opposition leaders were immediately arrested and executed without trial. Kayibanda ordered his ministers to organize civil defense in each prefecture; the national radio called for citizens to defend their country; some local officials urged the elimination of all Tutsi as the only solution. An orgy of hut burning and murder broke out, especially in areas of high Tutsi population. Some ten thousand men, women, and children were hacked to death.[34]

In 1964 and 1966, refugees again attempted cross-border attacks. Each was turned back and followed by an anti-Tutsi pogrom. The 1963 victory at the Kanzenze bridge brought pride to the National Guard, solidarity to the Hutu cause, and a template for handling the Tutsi threat. Given their political utility, attacks against persons and property went largely unpunished; impunity for ethnic crimes became an unwritten understanding.

As the outside threat receded, internal divisions increased. Parmehutu became a de facto single party coping with land tenure issues, tensions within the National Guard, intraparty struggles, and disputes with the Catholic church. At the local level, burgomasters and prefects recreated networks of clients, extracting dues for services just like subchiefs and chiefs under the monarchical regime. Mismanagement and malversation abounded.[35]

Hutu advancement remained at the core of the Parmehutu agenda, arbitrarily enforced in school admittances, civil service recruitment, and even checks on business payrolls. Hutu who fled the 1972 genocide in Burundi gave a further impetus toward Hutu identity. Ethnic solidarity became the watchword among Hutu intelligentsia and especially among politicians campaigning for elections in 1973. Vigilantism gave way to hut burnings and murders. The harassment and intimidation triggered yet another massive emigration of frightened Tutsi who had hoped to make their accommodation with the new regime.

SECOND REPUBLIC

In a situation of looming chaos, President Kayibanda finally called on the National Guard to restore order. On July 4, 1973, top ministers from the government attended the national day celebration at the US residence, then repaired to a nightlong meeting with President Kayibanda. In the early morning hours, the National Guard surrounded the meeting place and arrested all participants. A Committee for Peace and National Unity, made up of the National Guard High Command, had decided not only to restore peace but also to take over power.[36]

The committee declared martial law, displacing all institutions of the First Republic, including the party, the national assembly, and the Supreme Court. President Kayibanda and seven other top members of his regime received suspended death sentences at a court martial.[37] Coup leaders settled into high ministerial and administrative posts, with the newly promoted National Guard commander, Major General Juvénal Habyarimana, being named president and minister of defense.

In 1975, Habyarimana established the Revolutionary National Movement for Development (MRND) as a nationwide movement dedicated to unity and development. By 1978, Rwandans adopted by referendum a new constitution legitimizing the movement with Habyarimana as its president. Military committee members held onto their sinecures, but power and decision making flowed to the president, who instituted an ethic of punctuality and hard work focused on rural development.[38] A policy of balance in regional development and in ethnic quotas for admittance to schools or civil service initially reduced interregional and ethnic tensions.

Buttressed by connections to the president, some Tutsis prospered in the private sector, but others were denied access to higher schools or jobs.

Transition

The Kayibanda regime had held on shakily for eleven years, beset with attacks from without and social tensions from within; in contrast, the Second Republic constructed a system that lasted twenty-one years and projected an image of efficiency, economic growth, and national integration. Over time, however, Habyarimana's policies of ethnic and regional balance devolved into instruments for preserving Hutu hegemony or for channeling projects and perquisites to the regime's home areas of Gisenyi and Ruhengeri. The MRND single-party system, organized down to the ten-person "cellule," became a means for political mobilization and autocratic control at the national and local level.

CONSTITUTIONAL REFORMS

Whatever the achievements of the Habyarimana administration, thoughtful commentators would have agreed that, by the late 1980s, Habyarimana's one-party regime was losing its capacity to keep ahead of the political and developmental game. In response to political agitation and economic stagnation, Habyarimana promised constitutional reforms in 1990. These reforms were to establish political pluralism, to organize the eventual return of Tutsi refugees (after years of the regime's efforts to get them squatters' rights in neighboring countries), and to accept an economic structural adjustment program.

THE FRONT INVADES

Then, on October 1, 1990, the Rwandese Patriotic Army (RPA), the military arm of the Rwandese Patriotic Front (RPF), invaded from Uganda. Frustrated Tutsi in countries of asylum conceived the attack, which Hutu exiles' tales of corruption, human rights abuse, and incompetence within the Rwandan regime had incubated. The RPF's perception that Habyarimana and President Museveni of Uganda might agree to controlled repatriation midwifed the attack, which took disciplined, experienced RPF fighters deep into Rwandan territory. But they did not win the support they expected from Rwanda's restive population. Eventually, over one million Rwandans fled southward from RPF control. Meanwhile, Tutsis within Rwanda were subject to arrest, intimidation, and massacres; with the onset of civil war, the cycle of ethnic violence and social displacement spun out again.

STATES INTERVENE

Almost immediately, European governments (France and Belgium) intervened with troops to protect their citizens gathered in the capital city of Kigali. Meanwhile, neighboring African governments sought to arrange a ceasefire. As the two armed elements engaged in periodic combat, political representatives met under the auspices of neighboring chiefs of state. They signed agreements but never observed a ceasefire.

Finally, at Paris in June 1992, France, with the backing of the United States, facilitated a framework for ceasefire talks. In July, the talks moved to Arusha, Tanzania, where, under Tanzanian facilitation, the two parties adopted an operational ceasefire plan. In August, they opened negotiations on a transition regime. These negotiations, scheduled to last two months, went on for a year, punctuated by foot dragging in Rwandan political circles, massacres in Rwanda's north, and renewed fighting in February 1993. President Habyarimana finally signed the Arusha Accords with Rwandese Patriotic Front Chairman Alexis Kanyarengwe on August 5, 1993.

Nine months later, on April 6, 1994, someone shot down the president's plane with ground-to-air missiles. Murderous revenge immediately broke out against the president's political opponents and ethnic Tutsi. Embassies withdrew their personnel and citizens; the Security Council reduced the UN peacekeeping force to a small holding operation. Even as the Rwandese Patriotic Army and forces of a self-appointed Rwandan government contested for territory, extremist Hutu organized the genocide of eight hundred thousand innocents in just under one hundred days. The road to peace gave way to a policy of extermination.[39]

The Legacy

Rwanda's past casts an illuminating beam on the 1990–94 conflict in Rwanda. Evident traits of political culture have deeply rooted antecedents.[40]

Expanding borders and centralizing power have been Rwanda's leitmotif since the seventeenth century. While colonial agreements stopped territorial expansion[41] and rules of the Organization of African Unity prohibited change to colonial boundaries, each historic dynasty persisted in claiming territory and seeking to ingrate it into central institutions.

Regionalism was the flip side of centralizing power. The conquered periphery (Cyangugu and Kibuye to the west; Byumba and Kibungu to the north and east), once endowed with their own polities, resented the powerful center (Butare, Gikongoro) and the tributes it imposed. In the northwest (Gisenyi, Ruhengeri), former landlords still looked for ways to restore customary rights and political privileges. Regionalism, itself divided into loyalties (or enmities) built hill-by-hill, undercut attachments to the central state.[42]

Coercive violence has been a constant of Rwandan politics; the political elite brutally waged wars of conquest or battles for ascendency at court. Colonial invaders backed up the expansionary campaigns of the king (*mwami*), then imposed their own vision of "indirect rule," rationalizing and institutionalizing coercive force. Labor levies, clientage obligations, and taxes grew more egregious and heavy as ambitions of the elite (whether traditional or colonial) increased in size and reach. After independence, enforced development programs undergirded the structural violence of elite regimes.[43]

Clientage was the network that knit Rwandan society together.[44] Under indirect rule, clientage persisted as a legally recognized institution. Weighty burdens of this institution were at the root of the 1959 "social revolution." While the ideology of democratic representation might have challenged the monarchical system, the new republican order used clientage to enlist the support of the peasantry. Clientage, old and new, implied two things: the splendid isolation of the monarch (or president) who was always patron and never client, and networks of reciprocity and dependence from lords down to the lowliest peasants.[45]

Ethnic identity in Rwanda began with one's lineage; lineages built alliances and formed clans. Today one might identify with traditional clans or feel linked (obliged) to former classmates, military or professional associates, or party organizations. Overarching these ascriptive or attributive identities are social designators that since the 1800s had come to reflect linkage to the political hierarchy and status within the clientage system:

Tutsi and Hutu. Colonizers saw these as binary racial and occupational categories, born out of migratory patterns of conquest. Elites, struggling for power and place in the postindependence arena, used these designations to build loyalty and claim legitimacy. Amorphous categories became exclusive, hardened identifiers—matters of life and death.[46]

Profound psychological perceptions of superiority and inferiority underlay the interplay of these social categories.[47] This perceptual equation traditionally took on regional variances. Playing against this variegated background was the violence of modern Rwanda's birth. The Hutu revolution of 1959, Tutsi exile attacks with attendant reprisals in the early 1960s, and pogroms against Hutu in Burundi all accentuated notions of ethnic identity and solidarity. Ethnicity formalized on identity cards and entrenched by political competition became the passkey for Hutu entrance into the modern world and a barrier to advancement for Tutsi. Left out of the national equation were Tutsi harried into exile in 1959, 1961, 1973, and 1978. Some were allowed to return, but most lived abroad for thirty years, a people with a country that would not accept them back.[48]

International Intervention and Peacemaking in Rwanda

Eventually, the refugees did come back, not in the programmed return that the Habyarimana regime wanted, but in an insurgency led from Uganda on October 1, 1990, by the Rwandese Patriotic Front. What was to have been a quick overturning of a supposed weak and corrupt regime turned into an initial defeat for the RPF and then a protracted border war having all the elements of intractability.[49] States of the region and development partners rushed to quell the conflict and restore peace to the Rwandan people. But instead of a rapid settlement, a complex series of international interventions led eventually to the Arusha political negotiations and their result: the Arusha Accords of August 4, 1993. Within nine months, the negotiated peace went down with the crash of President Habyarimana's plane as civil war and genocide erupted.

Why were the hopes for peace set within the framework of the Arusha Accords so quickly crushed by political realities? This question drives our backward look over those events.

DIPLOMATIC PERSPECTIVES

A partial answer is to recognize that mediators, facilitators, and Observers involved in the international intervention did not fully comprehend the context of the crisis.[50] Our purchase on core dynamics was deficient in several regards.

We were too sanguine about African societies' vaunted capacity to endure. But the pressures of population growth, pluralistic politics, a deteriorating economy, and competition for power stretched Rwanda to its breaking point. In this context, pushing forward a peace agreement that required major structural change and redistribution of political and economic power brought not peace but civil war and genocide.

We misconstrued relations of force in a seemingly powerless country. The UN Security Council deployed a peacekeeping force of minimal size and mandate. When President Habyarimana's plane was shot down, extremist partisans quickly proved that the UN force had neither the mandate nor the materiel to counter determined opposition to the Arusha process.

We glossed over the emotional roots of conflict, which, in the Rwandan case, were fear and loathing—fear that the "other," once empowered, would be a perpetual oppressor, and the loathing that comes from devaluing one's neighbor. The contenders were caught in an emotional recreation of self-images generated by diminution and demonization of the other side.

We underestimated the will to power. Determination to control the political process brought an impasse to power-sharing talks; commitment to ascendancy brought disequilibrium to military negotiations; unwillingness to compromise blocked the installation of the transitional institutions. So when the president was killed, Rwanda was left without institutional authority, a void quickly filled by extremists who would hold on to power at all costs, even the slaughter of innocents.

As we reflect on the historical complexity of Rwandan society, so also we should consider the capacity of the diplomatic intervention to restore peace. The mediators were focused on democratic practice and power sharing; the negotiating parties were contesting for power. Diplomats proposed classic peacemaking devices for bringing the parties together; the parties negotiated out of deeply rooted cultural dispositions. Thus, deficient understandings of Rwandan culture and traditional peacekeeping modalities framed international intervention in the Rwandan conflict. As an Observer remarked at the time, "We are, after all, diplomats, not social psychologists."[51]

MODES OF REPRESENTATION

Interventions to bring peace to Rwanda moved through different modes.[52] At the start of the Rwandan crisis, states with representation in Kigali negotiated with the Rwandan government, often comparing notes among embassies and following similar approaches but keeping to a traditional, bilateral mode. Meanwhile, states represented in Kampala held separate discussions with leaders of the Rwandese Patriotic Front.

When political negotiations started in Arusha in August 1992, a parallel diplomacy emerged based on the conference principle.[53] Here the Observer group worked together in evaluating issues and jointly sharing their views with the Facilitator or with the parties themselves. As this study will show, the understandings arrived at in Arusha through this conference system were often out of touch with the bilateral discourse going on in Kigali, in Kampala, or in the capitals of concerned states.

In August 1993, the conference negotiations produced the accords that took the peace process back to Rwanda under the aegis of the United Nations Mission in Rwanda (UNAMIR). At this point, the conference was over and bilateral diplomacy was subsumed within a framework established by an international organization. The vital exchanges of bilateral negotiation and the collective wisdom of multilateral diplomacy became subservient to international collaboration in the project of implementing the accords and the "technical" program of peacekeeping as outlined and captained by the United Nations.[54]

This intervention on behalf of international peace and security and in the interest of rehabilitating the Rwandan state took on the cultural expectations of international diplomacy: giving status to arguments from both sides, seeking a middle ground, and urging compromise with a view to establishing an institutionalized agreement between contending parties.

However, this was not just an international diplomatic intervention to restore international peace and security. It was also a humanitarian intervention to save lives and comfort the hungry, sick, and homeless while protecting individual human rights on both sides of the conflict. The international intervention in Rwanda was driven by concern for the displaced and refugees, as well as by preoccupation with statecraft in Central Africa. The central question was whether the intervention could achieve its objectives in each domain. Obviously, it grievously failed in both regards.

Does "Humanitarian Intervention" Work?

In an insightful analysis, Anthony Lang has looked at international interventions taken for purported humanitarian purposes and found them wanting. Such interventions are, he finds, essentially self-serving, undertaken to heighten the image of those intervening rather than to succor the helpless. Echoing Hedley Bull's reflections on the ambiguous status of human rights within the state system, Lang concludes that humanitarian interventions concentrate more "on saving the state than on saving people."[55] Lang is not the only one to point out the failures of international humanitarian intervention; a plethora of recent studies take up the theme, many pointing to Rwanda as the demonstrative case.[56] However, Lang was one of the first in the genre, and he makes more explicit than most the connection between the failure of humanitarian action and the structural nature of state action.

Lang's thesis is that the space of international action is "the province of the states themselves," and that the language of international politics, including discourses on international humanitarian interventions, "is constituted and controlled by state interpretations."[57] Moreover, in humanitarian crises caused by collapsing state structures, intervening states are concerned with reestablishing the disintegrating state so as to repair the breach in the state system.[58] Once reestablished, a revived state also contests within the interstate arena.

Meanwhile, the interests of individual citizens, victims of the humanitarian crisis, are secondary to the playing out of initiatives designed to establish state identity and state persona (including that of human rights advocate) in the interstate arena. According to Lang, "State agents focus more on other state agents in an intervention rather than on people who need assistance."[59] The dynamics of state agency in an international crisis thus intrinsically conflict with the humanitarian aims of intervention. Nicholas Onuf echoes the theme: "The institutional machinery which governments have authorized for the protection of human rights greatly favors states over nationals; in effect, states' rights trump individual rights."[60]

A Look Forward

A glance forward at the record in this study will show that a state-centric agenda driven by a diplomatic ethos of negotiation, fair play, and power sharing prevailed over the claims of humanitarian intervention that would put the real needs of people first. Diplomats did seek policy responses that met human need. But they persisted in deferring to sovereign choice, in treating both sides as equal parties, in holding faith in power sharing, and in promoting democratic choice as the antidote to conflict. These approaches, reflecting the essential values of the twentieth century, obviously did not work.

Yet, internecine conflict was not new to world leaders, nor was the quest for peace.[61] Moreover, international peacekeeping had built up considerable experience and expertise since the Second World War. Thus, the unrolling of the Rwandan peacekeeping peace process as recorded in the several chapters of this book parallels similar endeavors in international conflict resolution.

First, parties in any conflict need to accept the reality of each other's presence on the ground and work through to a sustainable "ceasefire." Once the shooting has stopped, negotiations on the future order ensue: debates about fundamental "law," or negotiations on "power sharing." But negotiations about principles, structure, or power often come, as they did in Rwanda, to an "impasse." Getting past an impasse to a final settlement, an "endgame," is both an art and impelling goal of international mediation. A transition to a peaceful, secure future should then valorize provisions of a final agreement. Instead, in Rwanda's case, "things fell apart." In the Rwandan story narrated here, a brief analysis of conflict resolution issues at stake fronts each chapter. At the end of each chapter, I list the lessons we learned from that segment of conflict mediation, with specific insights into the tragic Rwandan experience.

Rwanda was a terrain where states and international organizations projected their own interests and identities; where peacemakers misjudged the depth of animosity between parties; and where the will to power of the contenders eventually overwhelmed the limited international project to hold the peace process on course. Customary modes of peacemaking and peacekeeping failed, and misjudgments of the peacemaking context contributed to the scenario that engendered genocide. Attitudes and habits of diplomatic actors, deployed in different arenas and within varying modes, did not mitigate the crisis. The Arusha political negotiations became a prelude to genocide and a tragic lesson in a failed international humanitarian intervention.

ONE

Ceasefire

On October 1, 1990, a military force moved from southern Uganda into northeast Rwanda at Kagitumba and headed down the eastern edge toward the tourist camp and police headquarters at Gabiro, the central entrance to Kagera National Park. The military force called itself the Rwandese Patriotic Army (RPA), the military arm of the Rwandese Patriotic Front (RPF). Major General Fred Rwigyema, formerly deputy commander of Uganda's National Resistance Army (NRA) and deputy minister of defense in Uganda's government, headed the invasion. A large part of the force was made up of Rwandan Tutsi from the Lweru triangle who had joined Yoweri Museveni's campaign to overthrow Milton Obote. Additional refugees had joined the NRA in 1986 to help put down a rebellion in northern Uganda. Now, the troopers moved out of barracks toward the Rwandan border under various guises. Major General Rwigyema told people that he was preparing for Uganda National Day on October 9. Recruits from within the Tutsi diaspora, as well as Hutu military leaders and politicians who had fled the regime of President Habyarimana, were part of the RPA corps.[1]

The exiles had carried from Rwanda stories of corruption, injustice, and economic bankruptcy in the Habyarimana regime. Expecting that a disenchanted population would join in revolt against the government, the RPF found that, instead, the people fled before them. Within three days of the invasion, General Rwigyema was killed at the front.[2] On October 23, Rwanda government forces ambushed the RPA, killing top officers along with scores of RPA fighters. After suffering additional losses, the RPA broke up into small mobile groups, seeking cover in the Virunga volcano forests and crossing over into Uganda by night. The initial RPA thrust had been broken; the Rwandan government declared victory.[3] But Major Paul

Kagame, head of Uganda's military intelligence, rushed back from training in the United States and revitalized the RPA forces, preparing for a drawn-out civil war.

The October 1 incursions quickly stirred an international response. Both President Habyarimana and President Museveni had gone to New York to attend the World Summit on Children and were about to journey on to meetings in Washington. Their precipitate return to their respective capitals highlighted both the surprise and the seriousness of the incursion.[4] Key donors, France and Belgium, dispatched forces to protect Kigali and the expatriates in it. The United States began to withdraw nonessential personnel from its embassy.[5] Neighboring presidents Mobutu of Zaire and Mwinyi of Tanzania called separate summit conclaves. All external parties wanted the fighting in this poor, overpopulated country to end quickly.

The journey to a ceasefire, however, went along a circuitous path. This chapter explores that journey by first looking at the issues that any search for a ceasefire confronts and then recounting the failed summitry of the first two years. After considering how cooperation between France and the United States and between the Organization of African Unity (OAU) and Tanzania ushered in a durable ceasefire on June 13, 1992, I ask what lessons we learned from the exercise.

Issues at Stake

Although the initial fighting in Rwanda had come to a temporary lull in October 1990, settling the conflict proved a lengthy exercise in diplomatic negotiation and political opportunism. The October hostilities presented a classic spectrum of questions.

What is the nature of the conflict? Was the 1990 RPF attack on Rwanda, for example, an invasion or an insurgency? An invasion across the border of a sovereign state is in international law "aggression" and a matter for UN Security Council consideration. The incursion into northeast Rwanda originated from Uganda with troops who had taken leave from Uganda's National Revolutionary Army. The Rwandan government characterized the incursion as a cross-border aggression sponsored by the Ugandan government, requiring a collective response by the international community.

But the Ugandan leadership insisted that the attackers left Uganda without the authorization or knowledge of Ugandan authorities.

If this was a cross-border attack, it was also without question an insurgency, a battle by Rwandans to find place and power within the Rwandan state.[6] Having launched the war, the RPF now sought to legitimize its status as an internal insurgency. The Rwandan government, however, was not interested in bilateral talks or a ceasefire, which would recognize the RPF as the opposite party and change the asymmetry of the government/rebel equation.[7]

Does a conflict warrant international attention, or should local wars be allowed to flame out?[8] In the Rwandan case, the care of refugees, the war-born impediments to trade and humanitarian aid, and especially this ethnic struggle for ascendency that found its echo in eastern Zaire, southern Uganda, and Burundi all constituted threats to regional peace and security.[9] The nature of the conflict also determined the applicability of international humanitarian law to the Rwandan case.[10] Thus, international interveners came to see the conflict between the Rwandese Patriotic Front and the Rwandan government as an internal insurgency with external repercussions that threatened international peace and merited an international intervention.

Who are the contenders and how cohesive are their organizations? It would seem at first glance that the battle in and around Gabiro was between the Rwandese Patriotic Army (RPA), fighting for the exiled Tutsi, and the Rwandan Armed Forces (FAR), defending the state of Rwanda and the people within it. However, the RPF/RPA was but one of many groups vying for influence among the Tutsi diaspora. Indeed, the RPF had launched the attack preemptively to forestall an agreement of exiles to a UNHCR plan for programmed repatriation.[11] In addition, expatriate Tutsi businessmen were attracted to possible business opportunities in Rwanda under a peaceful, negotiated return.[12] Early days of battle showed a force divided in terms of vision, strategy, and operations.

On the other hand, the Rwandan Armed Forces no longer represented a unified country. After over twenty years of one-party rule, Rwandan elites joined in demanding an end to autocratic control and an opening to a democratic, liberal order.[13] On July 5, 1990, the seventeenth anniversary of his coup, President Habyarimana promised a new economic and political order. A year later, under a new constitution, the legislature approved a law authorizing multiple political parties.[14] Some sixteen parties filed for recognition. Whatever their regional base or ideological perspective, the new parties sought to distinguish themselves from Habyarimana's rule.[15] Thus, even before the RPF invasion, an opening to multiparty politics brought to the fore the north-south chasm in Rwandan politics. Eventually, under a coalition government led by Prime Minister Dismas Nsengiyaremye of the opposition Democratic Republican Movement (MDR), Rwandan politics and the war effort became a contest with multiple stakeholders.[16]

Are parties external to the conflict part of the problem or part of the solution? Conflicts draw in interested partners. In this asymmetrical confrontation between an incipient insurgency and an established state force, each side could claim interested neighbors and external supporters.[17] France, Belgium, and Egypt had military assistance programs in Rwanda, while China was a regular supplier of arms. Libya built the Meridien Hotel and partnered with the government in joint enterprises. Zaire, linked formally to Rwanda in the Economic Community of the Great Lakes Countries (CEPGL) and impelled by close personal bonds between the two presidents, had responded to the October 1990 crisis with the immediate dispatch of several hundred troops from the Special Presidential Division.[18] Germany, the United States, Canada, and Switzerland all had significant assistance programs supporting a regime in a poor, small country that, during the early 1980s, was thought to model effective techniques of rural development.[19]

On the other hand, after a 1988 international conference, in Washington, DC, on Rwandan refugees, the RPF began to build up financial support among the Tutsi diaspora and moral support from sympathetic foreigners. Most important, in launching its adventure into Rwanda, the RPF had expropriated armaments from Ugandan army connections and continued to receive support from elements within the government sympathetic to the Front's cause, perhaps even from President Museveni. The smuggling of gold and diamonds along the Zairean border provided funds for weapons purchased on the international arms market. Thus, both contenders in the Rwandan crisis depended on support from states and third parties outside of Rwanda's borders.

Are the contenders ready for a settlement? Has a culture of peace prevailed over a culture of war? The 1990 incursion had quickly evolved into a rhetorical confrontation, with skirmishes along the border, but not into a "mutually hurting stalemate." Since both sides felt they could ultimately win, the conflict was hardly "ripe for resolution."[20] As the RPF tactics changed to guerrilla raiding, the conflict settled into a protracted, irregular war, all the more disturbing to external third parties who wanted to quickly restore peace.

If third party intervention becomes possible, who should mediate in the dispute? The Rwandan conflict was of immediate concern to neighboring states and a source of long-range anxiety for donors vested in large development programs and now burdened with humanitarian assistance within the Rwandan state. Who should mediate this troublesome conflict, and under what auspices? The Africans wanted an African mediation, but which personality or which state should lead?

Zaire's president Mobutu was a dominant figure among African chiefs of state but had hostile relations with Uganda's Museveni. As friend and protégé of Habyarimana, Mobutu would hardly be evenhanded in this matter. Finally, he was a sick man whose influence was fading abroad and whose rule was being challenged by "democratic" forces at home. Mobutu's capacity to sustain a mediation seriously engaging both sides was very much in question.

On the other hand, an insurgency launched and sustained from the southern reaches of Uganda into a landlocked neighboring state must have had Museveni's nod of approval. Moreover, Museveni and Habyarimana neither liked nor trusted one another. Museveni was in no position to mediate between the insurgents and the Rwandan government.

Burundi was the neighbor to the south whose history, politics, and social divisions mirrored those of Rwanda. However, Rwandans of all stripes considered themselves superior to their traditional enemies in Burundi. Additionally, by 1990, Burundi's military president, Pierre Buyoya, had recently put out the fires of a major ethnic blowup in Burundi's north and was too enmeshed in his own ethnic difficulties to provide mediation in Rwanda's conflict.

The country with the least vested interest or diplomatic liabilities among Rwanda's neighbors was Tanzania. While Prime Minister

Malecela and several within the ruling Tanzanian elite were friendly to-ward Habyarimana's regime, in 1990, both Tanzanian president Mwinyi and foreign minister Diria were from coastal Swahili backgrounds and had no affinity with either side. Moreover, conflict within Rwanda cre-ated insecurity on a distant western border. Tanzania had a vital interest in seeing peace restored.[21]

Regional Summitry

EARLY SUMMITS

Notwithstanding the inherent issues involved, neighboring chiefs of state rushed to bring the Rwandan conflict to a close. Within a fortnight of the October 1 incursion, Tanzanian president Mwinyi hosted a sum-mit with Museveni and Habyarimana at which the Rwanda government agreed to dialogue under OAU auspices and Tanzania and Uganda agreed to pressure the RPF to accept a ceasefire.

On October 23 and 24, the heads of state of the Economic Commu-nity of the Great Lakes Countries (Zaire, Rwanda, and Burundi), meet-ing at Mobutu's home in Gbadolite, proposed establishing a peacekeeping force and noted Mobutu's effort to facilitate dialogue between the Govern-ment of Rwanda and the Rwandese Patriotic Front. Two days later, a sec-ond summit convened at Gbadolite at which Museveni, now chairman of the OAU, confirmed Mobutu as mediator. The chiefs of state authorized a military observer group of officers from Rwanda, Burundi, Uganda, Zaire, and the RPF to be established under OAU supervision.[22]

When the military observer group convened November 12–19 in Goma, Zaire, to draft the terms of a formal ceasefire, they touched the foundations of the conflict's intractability. While it had agreed to dialogue with the Patriotic Front, the government of Rwanda would not accept that group as representative of the refugee community nor admit wholesale re-patriation of refugee populations. The RPF on the other hand wanted full recognition as an opposite in the negotiations, as an internal armed force whose interests had to be accommodated.

By this time, the Rwandan government thought it had repulsed the in-vasion; many of the insurgents had fled back to Uganda, and the rest were scattered along the frontier trying to pull together under Major Kagame's leadership. Neither side was particularly anxious to accommodate an international intervention and mediation. The OAU was not able to get the RPF and the Rwandan government to agree on terms of a ceasefire or on deployment of a military observer group. Mediation was instead being imposed by self-interested neighbors and patrons.

In a pattern that would be reiterated numerous times, this blockage led to military pressure from the RPF, which was countered by repression and ethnic violence abetted by the government. During the months of November and December, the Rwandan government pushed back RPF attacks along the Uganda-Rwanda border. In January 1991, the RPF returned to the attack along the northern border, briefly occupying the regional capital of Ruhengeri and freeing prisoners held in the local prison, including prominent political prisoners like former chief of security Theoneste Lizinde. In reprisal, the government, exercising state-of-emergency powers, arrested over eight thousand persons suspected of supporting the RPF. Attacks against Tutsi Bagogwe in the government heartland of Gisenyi/Ruhengeri area killed more than two hundred civilians.[23]

SUMMITS IN ZANZIBAR AND DAR ES SALAAM

Increased violence again drew in regional summitry. Meanwhile, President Habyarimana, having failed to stop repression at home, lost ground in regional discussions. On February 17, in a hurriedly convened minisummit on Zanzibar between the presidents of Tanzania, Uganda, and Rwanda, Habyarimana at last accepted the principle of a ceasefire.

Two days later, at a regional summit on refugees at Dar es Salaam (Burundi, Rwanda, Uganda, Tanzania, and Zaire attending), Habyarimana agreed in principle to the right of refugee return, and neighboring chiefs of state covenanted to facilitate naturalization for refugees who wanted to stay put. Significantly, the Dar es Salaam Declaration thanked Mobutu for instituting dialogue and urged him to maintain the momentum of dialogue "between the Rwandan government and the armed opposition." The declaration thus confirmed Mobutu as mediator and recognized the RPF without naming it as the opposite party in the conflict. The notion that Uganda was attacking Rwanda through its cohorts no longer held water with presidents of the region. With diplomatic optimism, the declaration held that dialogue would find "a solution to the problem facing the parties concerned."[24]

In March 1991, as ceasefire talks began at N'sele, Zaire, President Habyarimana announced his intention to offer an amnesty for those who had taken up arms against the Rwandan government.[25] But that initiative did not significantly change the dynamics of the conflict; the peace process was in its infancy. By March 29, Casimir Bizimungu, foreign minister of the Rwandan government, and now Major General Paul Kagame, vice president of the RPF, signed a ceasefire agreement, committing to ongoing dialogue and to the deployment of a military observer group under OAU supervision. Political dialogue was to start in fifteen days following the deployment of an observer group of the regional states of Uganda, Rwanda, Tanzania, and Burundi. But the military observer group did not get organized until May. When it deployed in Kigali, the Rwandan government restricted its movement around the country. The ceasefire, which was broken almost immediately by skirmishes along the Uganda border, turned into a stalemate between the Rwandan government's conventional forces and RPF bush warriors in a low-intensity civil war.

Meanwhile, the Rwandan government's position on internal politics seemed to soften. That March, the government, under pressure from the international community and from its own jurists, released eight thousand suspected RPF sympathizers who had been detained since January.[26] In June, the president promulgated a new constitution that allowed multiparty political competition. On June 18, the legislature, the National Development Council (CND), passed the Political Parties Law and the race to establish political parties took off.[27] By the end of the year, the CND finally passed two amnesty laws, one for refugees and exiles and one for persons within the country convicted of infractions of the law short of violent crimes.

THE OAU PROMOTES ANOTHER SUMMIT

At the OAU Summit in June, pressure built for another try at peacemaking. The OAU chiefs of state directed the secretary general of the organization to convene another regional summit to continue the mediation process. Accordingly, Mobutu hosted a meeting at Gbadolite to work out the terms of a new ceasefire. With the witness of the president of Nigeria, as new chairman of the OAU, the parties signed on September 16 a ceasefire agreement, seen as a revision of the understanding reached at N'sele six months earlier. The major change was in the makeup of the military observer group; this time it was to be composed of Nigerian and Zairean officers. Political dialogue was also initiated at Gbadolite, but the mediator broke it off in ten days, exasperated at RPF intransigence.

Absent a ceasefire reinforced by political dialogue, renewed fighting broke out in December and January, allowing the RPF to demonstrate its capacity to attack and leaving it with a permanent foothold in northern Rwanda, thus confirming its status as an "internal" insurgency. Back in Kigali, negotiations to install a multiparty government under the June constitution stalled; in frustration, a new government was finally sworn in on December 30, naming Sylvestre Nsanzimana as prime minister and including only one minister who was not from the president's party. In response to renewed fighting in the north, the government increased the size of the army fivefold, turning the usually balanced budget into deep deficit.

RESULTS OF SUMMITRY

A year and a half after the October 1990 RPF attack, the regional chiefs of state had little to show for their considerable efforts to stop the fighting and arrange a peace through summit agreements. Undertakings at the summits did move the parties closer to recognizing each other as antagonists with whom to negotiate. The chiefs of state laid out quite early the elements of a putative peace process: ceasefire, political dialogue, military observer group, and peacekeeping force. The implication was that goals of peace and security required an international intervention that was both political and military in nature.

But the summit discussions were based on faulty assumptions, namely, that the issues at stake were subject to presidential decision; that the contending parties ultimately wanted peace; and that ceasefires, military observer groups, or peacekeeping deployments could be created ex nihilo by spoken agreement. But neither the respective states nor the Organization of African Unity had the capacity to organize and operationally structure the peace process or ensure the compliance of the parties. Finally, intrinsic to summitry is failure continually to attend to the problem. Interveners responded to violent outbreaks rather than systematically addressing root causes of the conflict.[28] Clearly, if peace was to return to Rwanda, the levels of international engagement would have to be broadened.

Donors Respond

France and Belgium, the top two states engaged in assistance to Rwanda, reacted immediately to the October 1990 RPF incursion. President Habyarimana stopped by Paris and Brussels on his way home from New York and secured the promise of military assistance from President Mitterrand and King Baudouin. Both sent troops to Kigali, presumably to protect the capital city and the expatriates living there but obviously reinforcing the Rwandan military's capacity to carry the battle to the field. While France dealt directly with the Rwandan government and was an observer of the summit talks held under Mobutu's auspices, the Belgian approach was to send a high-level delegation to all capitals of the region to seek out regional African views and encourage a more vigorous African response to the crisis. Belgians seemed skittish about any direct engagement; the very fact that the Belgian foreign minister was visiting the region in regard to the Rwanda crisis raised an outcry in the Belgian press and in parliament. Once the situation on the front seemed stabilized and the capital city no longer threatened, Belgium withdrew its combat forces but left in place a military training mission working with the gendarmerie. By act of parliament, Belgian military assistance was limited to training, technical assistance, and nonlethal military materiel. Thereafter, Belgium settled into a watching brief, ready to demarche the Rwandan or Ugandan governments as interests required, but with no intention to mediate. Recognizing that the French, because of their troop presence in Rwanda, had the larger say and the larger headaches, Belgium tended to support French initiatives in the region.[29]

After the failures of regional initiatives, the French director of African affairs, Paul Dijoud, offered to mediate in August 1991, and in October he tried to bring the Rwandan government and the RPF together in Paris. Because high-level RPF representation was absent, Rwandan foreign minister Bizimungu declined to participate. In November, France sent an observer mission to the Rwandan-Ugandan frontier to assess the nature of cross-border incursions. As 1992 opened, Dijoud tried again to organize direct negotiations between the Rwandan government and the Rwandese Patriotic Front. By mid-February, the French foreign ministry admitted that the initiative had been a failure. The problem was twofold: first, the internal situation in Rwanda was "explosive and deteriorating," with Hutu hardliners in the president's entourage actively opposing moves toward democratization. Second, neither the Rwandan government forces nor the RPF had shown the capacity to prevail militarily, but the RPF seemed determined to fight on until Habyarimana was removed. In the French foreign ministry's view, the RPF would continue to secure supplies and establish safe haven north of the border; Uganda would not prevent the use of its territory as a springboard for RPF operations.[30]

VIOLENCE AND DIPLOMACY

The fragile internal situation became evident in March 1992 in another outbreak of ethnic violence, this time in the southeastern area of Bugesera, a region of new settlement that had attracted Tutsi pushed out of more populous zones to the west and north. The attacks occurred as political parties pressured Habyarimana for a coalition national government in Kigali and for changes in communal and regional (prefecture) governance. Although young thugs, presumably in political hire, led the attack, local authorities were slow to intervene, and some even encouraged the violence. Eventually the National Gendarmerie had to stop the fracas in which some one hundred persons died and twelve thousand were displaced from their homes.[31] France, Belgium, Germany (also representing the president of the European Community), Switzerland, Canada, and the United States joined in a vigorous demarche that reminded the Rwandan president of his government's responsibility to stop killings and destruction and to ensure peace and security.[32]

Both the donors and the government cast the demarche in the larger context of Rwanda's political evolution. The demarche called for the creation of a multiparty government "with the least possible delay" and urged moderation in media broadcasts. Inaction by Rwandan authorities, the ambassadors warned, could jeopardize the future of cooperative programs. The president said he shared the ambassadors' preoccupation but blamed, in part, the rabble-rousing rhetoric of opposition leaders. In his brief on the security situation, the interior minister noted that the onset of violence had left a vacuum in local administration, that is, local authorities did not counter the violence. He also argued that "the existence of multi-partyism by its very nature creates incitement."[33]

TOWARD A COALITION GOVERNMENT

Meanwhile, the Catholic Church sought to organize dialogue between the RPF and the Rwandan government. How many of these contacts were carried out informally, the record will not show. But by October 1991, one year after the RPF invasion, the church mediated a meeting in which the contending sides committed to common principles.[34] The church also sought broader political representation within the government through the establishment of a government of national unity that encompassed newly revived political parties. By February 1992, this effort had evolved into a ten-person *Comité de contact* of leaders from the Catholic Episcopal Conference and the Rwandan Protestant Council and brought together party leadership to work out their differences and seek a common future in the establishment of a coalition government.[35] In March, the church leaders met with RPF representatives, including Commissioner Pasteur Bizimungu, in Nairobi to determine the extent of the Front's commitment to negotiations with a broad coalition government.[36]

Even as talks moved forward on a multiparty government, new parties were proliferating. Some were based on sectarian loyalties, like the Islamic Party or the Catholic Christian Democrat Party. Others reflected aspirations of personal leaders. A significant party, the Coalition for Democratic Renewal (CDR), was based on the ideology of Hutu ascendancy. Formed by a charismatic but erratic Hutu civil servant who fell out with Habyarimana, the CDR became a party committed to preserving or enhancing the institutional stature of the Hutu majority, which the party saw as being jeopardized by negotiations with the RPF. Based in the president's homeland in northwest Rwanda, where Hutu chiefs had ruled in precolonial days, the CDR had links to the president through his wife's family. The party was not, however, invited to the dialogue that led to the signing of an interparty protocol on March 13 with a view to forming a multiparty "government of transition." After long negotiations with major party leaders, Habyarimana, on April 16, finally invited Dr. Dismas Nsengiyaremye, a leader of the MDR/Parmehutu party to head a new coalition government.[37]

THE UNITED STATES EXPANDS ITS ROLE

Political opening within Rwanda induced new international interest in resolving the conflict between the Rwandan government, now largely representative of internal political forces, and the Rwandese Patriotic Front, still harrying Rwandan government forces in the north. From the beginning, the United States had been concerned about the war in Rwanda. The foundations for US policy toward Rwanda were found in the inaugural address of George H. W. Bush and in his first State of the Union message, both of which emphasized democracy and human rights.[38] Thus, US policy viewed the conflict in Rwanda in terms of its larger international dimensions, namely, regional insecurity, refugee burdens and challenges to democratic governance, and fundamental human rights. But in an area where it had no significant stake, the United States deferred to regional players and to European partners with keener interests. As Mobutu, then other regional leaders and the OAU, and finally France moved to bring the parties together, the United States took a watching brief and played behind the scenes.

At the Department of State, Assistant Secretary Herman Cohen regularly received intelligence reports of the ongoing efforts to establish peace in the region. On learning of the RPF attacks on Ruhengeri in January 1991, he contacted President Museveni of Uganda by phone to ask Ugandan help in preventing the incursions and stopping the fighting.[39] The department then instructed ambassadors in Kampala and Kigali to proceed by urging Museveni to deny Uganda as a sanctuary for attacks on Rwanda and asking Habyarimana to accelerate national reconciliation within Rwanda, to intensify direct talks with the RPF, and vigorously to pursue a comprehensive refugee agreement. In addition to this bilateral approach, the United States tried to encourage a joint demarche with the European Community in order to have a common message from all Western donors to both Rwanda and Uganda. The European Community would agree only to a more modest parallel demarche, and even then it had to drag a reluctant Great Britain in its wake.[40]

In April 1991, Cohen convoked American ambassadors from the region to a meeting in Bujumbura. The chiefs of mission concluded that there were "no vital US interests at stake [in the regional crisis], either internationally or domestically." With regard to Rwanda, they recommended that the United States not assume a leadership role but, "in coordination with EC colleagues, exert influence selectively to uphold U.S. interests." They felt the United States should use the crisis to encourage movement on democracy and human rights interests, to tell the RPF that the United States supported its democracy and political equality goals, and to seek a durable solution to regional refugee problems. Following their deliberations, the assistant secretary articulated the fundamental US approach to the conflict in a news conference:

> We believe that the protection of refugees who return to their homes should be ensured by a democratic political system that provides to every citizen equal rights and defends human rights.
> We condemn any use of force to settle the problems of refugees and ask all governments in the region to prevent any use of their territory for military action against their neighbors.[41]

The assistant secretary went from that convocation to meet with President Museveni and with the Ugandan foreign minister, pressing the Ugandan government to interdict military supplies to the RPF and to move the RPF toward negotiations. Meanwhile, reports from the field outlined the distance between the two sides. In Kigali, US ambassador Robert Flaten reported that President Habyarimana was still blaming the war on Museveni and holding that "Museveni has not changed at all!" According to the president, political dialogue was possible if the RPF took its place as a party among other parties within a pluralistic environment. Automatic integration of RPF forces into the Rwandan army was totally unacceptable. The military observer group set up under terms of the N'sele Accord had not inspected RPF positions and did not appear truly neutral.[42]

In Kampala, the US chargé stated that the ceasefire was not holding, that artillery and small arms fire along the border occurred daily, and that a major escalation was eminent. Thousands of Ugandans were displaced by the war all along the border. According to credible reports, the RPA had taken over portions of Kisoro District in Uganda, and the National Resistance Army still connived with or acquiesced in RPA activity. During the lull in fighting, both sides had had the time to reorganize, train, and equip.[43]

After the June 1991 OAU Summit at Abuja put Nigerian president Babangida in the chairmanship and confirmed Zairean president Mobutu as mediator of the Rwandan dispute, the United States asked the OAU leadership to do the following:

- To request both sides to observe the ceasefire

- To mediate the GOR/RPF dialogue on an urgent basis

- To request that Museveni permit the OAU-sponsored military observer group (MOG) to operate in Uganda

- To reiterate to Museveni the need to deny the RPF operational support in Ugandan territory

- To urge Habyarimana to implement programs of democratization and national reconciliation[44]

Babangida proposed a mini-summit of heads of state in the Central/East African region. US ambassadors in the region were instructed to inform their host governments that the United States supported the OAU's renewed efforts to mediate the conflict. That same demarche also inferred Belgian and French preference for African mediation.[45] Having sought OAU leadership in resolving this conflict, the United States, nonetheless, pursued a bilateral initiative when Deputy Assistant Secretary of State Irvin Hicks met informally with representatives of the Rwandese Patriotic Front and the Rwandan government in Harare.

The US hope was that, without impinging on other mediation efforts, this meeting might help revive the peace process and "lead to an agreement on a cease fire and to the RPF's participation in the democratic process." That hope was quickly dashed in a spate of acrimonious charges. The government representative, Augustin Ndindilimana, said he had come to inform the participants that Rwandan government forces controlled all national territory, that pushing back against incursions from Uganda was permitted under ceasefire terms, that the RPF would not let the military observer group inspect their forward positions nor were they seeking to join in political dialogue as a recognized party, and that the presence of Western forces in Rwanda was a guarantee of a political process open to all Rwandans.[46]

The RPF representative, Pasteur Bizimungu, said that the Rwandan government had failed to respect the N'sele Accord. He brought as evidence the continuing presence of foreign troops, the incarceration of political prisoners, and the inactivity of the military observer group. Were it not for foreign troops, the RPF would have achieved military victory. Visits of the observer group had been turned back because the Rwandan military insisted on accompanying them everywhere. Hicks found the Rwandan government intransigent and the RPF legalistic. The Harare meetings, in sum, made "little progress."[47]

For all its early efforts in promoting the peace process in Rwanda, Washington policy focused largely on other trouble spots in Africa and deferred to Brussels and Paris on Rwandan issues. As spelled out at the Bujumbura chiefs of mission conference, US policy had been to "keep former metropolitan powers (including EC) out in front in solving the problem." Since France among European Community partners had troops on the ground and the most direct entrée to the Habyarimana regime, Washington policy makers determined to let the French take the lead.[48]

Three factors seemed to have occasioned deeper US engagement in the Rwandan crisis in early 1992. First, there was general admission among the tripartite partners—France, Belgium, and the United States—that the peace initiative mediated by President Mobutu in the context of the Economic Community of Great Lakes States or the efforts of the Organization of African Unity was not bringing the conflict to a close. Nor were differences among political groups within Rwanda being bridged. In short, there was little progress after over a year of effort by states from within the region.[49]

Second, the nongovernmental and academic communities began to highlight the continuing seriousness of the crisis. Roger Winter at the US Committee for Refugees had been urging greater US government attention to the plight of Banyarwanda refugees since the early 1980s.[50] Gene Dewey of the Congressional Hunger Committee had traveled to the area in March of 1991 and reported that Rwandans wanted help from the outside in resolving the crisis.[51] In March 1992, academic and government specialists met under auspices of the State Department's Bureau of Intelligence and Research. Invited as a discussant, I returned to Rwandan questions for the first time in nineteen years. Our panel recognized the increased corruption under Habyarimana's administration and attendant economic decline, the fragile political situation, and the ravages of civil war. As a counter, we recommended economic and political decentralization within Rwanda and "the creation of a political system in which both groups win, i.e., power sharing democracy."[52]

The conclusions of the "specialists" convinced the director of Central African affairs, Ambassador Robert Pringle, to push for a higher US government profile in seeking peace for Rwanda, thus bringing into play the third reason for US engagement: high-level policy activism. Assistant Secretary Cohen convened a Policy Coordinating Committee on Rwanda and Burundi. The committee's conclusions followed both the track set down in Bujumbura nearly a year before and the way forward envisioned by the panel of specialists: democratization and ethnic reconciliation through diplomatic pressure and program emphasis on these issues by USAID, USIS, and military assistance. The committee also concluded that "if a coalition government acceptable to the opposition is formed in Rwanda, *we should urge the French to restart the GOR-RPF negotiations*, offering to assist by urging the Ugandans to end their support for the insurgency and help bring the RPF to negotiate."[53]

The African affairs "front office" quickly engaged to implement the new approach. Deputy Assistant Secretary Robert Houdek visited Kampala in April right after the formation of a multiparty government in Kigali. He confronted Museveni with the outside world's perception that the RPF was operating from Uganda: "A definition of sovereignty is that you control your own territory." In Houdek's view, the Rwanda/RPF conflict was igniting "ethnic tinderbox situations in Rwanda and Burundi." The American envoy left Kampala with demurrals from the Ugandans and a plea from Rwandan ambassador Kanyarushoki that the United States get involved again in trying to bring the sides together.[54]

After Houdek's visit to "test the winds," Assistant Secretary Cohen followed up with a May visit to Kampala and Kigali. In Kampala, he heard an RPF plea for direct intervention in the peace process, the integration of RPF into the Rwandan army, guarantees of RPF safety, and internationally observed right of return for all refugees. From Museveni, he heard, but disputed, the usual demurrals about Ugandan complicity in the conflict. Cohen agreed to US participation (if all parties assented) as an observer in a French-led meeting to help along the democratic process and jump-start negotiations. He suggested the possibility of US technical assistance in setting forth the parameters of a viable ceasefire and in promoting democratization.[55]

The assistant secretary carried to Kigali assurances from the Patriotic Front that it was ready to negotiate and to work toward an observable ceasefire. Refugees should be able to return freely (a nonnegotiable demand) and the RPF should be integrated into the Rwandan Army. The RPF doubted, nonetheless, the capacity of the new Rwandan government to govern and to carry forward an effective negotiation. Museveni, for his part, was still insisting that the war was between the Rwandan government and the RPF. He continued to promise full citizenship to Rwandan refugees who did not want to return to their country and expected that most of them would want to remain in Uganda.[56]

Cohen proposed that the Rwandan and Ugandan governments negotiate a security pact that would "lock in" commitments of both sides to peace. The international community would guarantee such a "mutual security" agreement. Cohen found support for this notion within Ugandan leadership and from the foreign minister of Rwanda, but he met with initial resistance from President Habyarimana, who wanted to maintain the posture that Uganda was responsible for the RPF incursion. Cohen also suggested to his Rwandan hosts that the integration of armies and the demobilization of forces be linked and that the right of refugee return be included in an eventual peace agreement. He told the Rwandan government, as he had offered to the Patriotic Front, that the United States would be willing to participate as an observer in future negotiations and would provide US technical assistance in preparations for the talks, if all parties requested a US presence.[57]

The Rwandans welcomed a possible US participation as observer at negotiations with the Front. Minister of Foreign Affairs Boniface Ngulinzira told Cohen that Rwanda proposed a two-pronged strategy for resolving the war: political dialogue with the Rwandan Patriotic Front and normalization of relations with Uganda. It was significant to the diplomatic structure of the talks that the Rwandan government would no longer demand a mediating message carrier between the two parties but would seek "facilitation" of direct, face-to-face negotiations.[58]

As a follow-up to this approach, and after having checked with the French, Cohen had Ambassador Johnnie Carson in Uganda facilitate a face-to-face meeting between the Rwandan government and the RPF in Kampala. In late May, Foreign Minister Ngulinzira (accompanied by the interior minister and the minister for refugee affairs) traveled to Uganda to initiate talks with the RPF and with the Ugandan government. The talks, delayed a week by hesitations on both sides, were finally held on May 24.[59] Ngulinzira later asserted that Cohen's role had been indispensable in arranging the projected meeting.[60]

The French foreign ministry immediately followed up those talks with an invitation to the two parties to meet in Paris. The parties could set the agenda and determine the extent of French participation. The ministry also informed the parties that, in view of the recent visit made by Mr. Cohen in the region and the discussions he had there, France had invited the United States to be associated with the meeting.

To Arusha through Paris

As the Rwandan government and the Rwandese Patriotic Front prepared to meet each other again, this time in Paris, it was in the context of a dramatically changed peace process. For one, the conflict was lasting longer than either side had expected. The RPF had hoped for a quick victory and enthusiastic reception in 1990. Instead, it found a population that fled before it and a GOR military that eventually dealt it some losses. Initially, the Rwandan army thought they had won as the RPF forces withdrew to the mountains between Uganda and Rwanda. Yet a year and a half later, the sputtering confrontation of forces was taking on the characteristics of an intractable conflict.

Second, the internal situation within Rwanda had changed significantly as well. Since the incursion of October 1, 1990, the Habyarimana regime had released thousands imprisoned for suspected RPF sympathies, promulgated a new constitution allowing multiparty government, committed itself to the programmed return of refugees, offered amnesty to persons who had joined the RPF cause, and finally, after eight months of negotiations and an aborted first attempt, set up a multiparty coalition government to rule until the next elections. That government now included parties, such as the so-called Democratic Forces of Change, determined to replace the established regime through constitutional processes. The government's position in any two-party talks was thus greatly complicated, and Habyarimana's freedom of maneuver significantly limited.

For all of the changes on the political front, the war that impelled those changes had drawn to a stalemate. Despite a huge increase in recruitment and operational expense, the Rwandan government forces were not able to dislodge or push back RPF forces entrenched in the Virunga Mountains, or to protect front lines from lightning incursions. The RPF forces were not able, or not yet willing, to leave their mountain redoubts and advance southward.[61] What united politicians of all stripes within Rwanda was a desire to end the war that had depopulated large parts of Rwanda's fertile north, created over a million internally displaced persons, ruined the economy, and bankrupted the country.

Third, peacemaking had failed, whether under auspices of the Great Lakes Community and President Mobutu, the interventions of Tanzanian president Mwinyi, or the efforts of the Organization of African Unity. For all the presidential summitry, subregional and regional organizations had not been able to organize an international presence in Rwanda as a guarantor of the peace process. As Foreign Minister Ngulinzira was later to note, "Rwanda has had two unfortunate experiences with African observer forces, one ineffective, the other nonexistent."[62] The RPF and the government met and signed a ceasefire agreement at N'sele and amended it at Gbadolite, but these had not diminished hostile posturing or armed conflict along the border. By the admission of all sides, this "African" problem no longer admitted a purely "African" solution.

Finally, the position of donors had evolved. Belgium and France had both been active on the diplomatic front since October 1990, with France supporting Mobutu's efforts and Belgium favoring OAU initiatives. Now, in the wake of the Bugesera massacres, Belgium had been particularly strenuous in its condemnation of the Habyarimana regime, while French patience with the Rwandan army's performance was wearing thin. Both sought a more vigorous engagement as a way out of an apparent dead end.

The Rwandese Patriotic Front and the Rwandan government had entreated Assistant Secretary Cohen to lead a new mediation. The United States, with its usual proclivity for regional approaches in conflict resolution, first suggested the EC as an appropriate mediating institution.[63] The US government finally had agreed to provide some technical assistance to the peace process and to be linked formally to future talks as an "observer." Thus, the parties were coming to Paris with the peace process now being managed by donor partners rather than by African states.

Two things remained constant in this protracted history of political change and military stalemate: the willingness of the Habyarimana regime to countenance or connive in ethnic violence at times of acute political tension, and the proclivity of the Patriotic Front to use military coercion to enhance its negotiating posture. A prime example of the former was the Bugesera massacres, perpetrated just as the Habyarimana regime was resisting pressure to form a coalition government. A good illustration of the latter came as the principals were on their way to Paris. On June 5, the day that peace talks were to begin, the RPF launched an attack in the center north at Byumba. France brought in an additional company of troops to protect its citizens in Kigali. It looked like the logic of war was again to win out over the logic of peace. Yet, though somewhat delayed, the Paris talks went forward on June 6. The US embassy in Paris concluded that "as far as we can ascertain neither the June 5 RPF attack in northern Rwanda nor the French deployment of an additional army company had any direct resonance in the talks."[64]

THE UNITED STATES JOINS THE DIALOGUE

The United States accepted the invitation of the French government and the parties to be "present" at the Paris talks, sending Jeffrey Davidow, the senior deputy assistant secretary for African affairs. Davidow engaged both sides on the substantive issues facing the talks: the when and how of a ceasefire, the agenda for political talks, the relation between the process of democratization within the country and the RPF demands for inclusion within the polity, and how to deal with repatriation of refugees into an already overpopulated country.[65]

In the talks with Ambassador Davidow, the Rwandan government delegation reaffirmed its two-track approach, patching up relations with Uganda even as it initiated talks with the RPF. On the other side, RPF chief negotiator Pasteur Bizimungu held that "the transition government should be broad based and have the agreement of all parties, even those not included in it." Regarding the talks, Davidow predicted that "successes, if there are any, will be minimal."[66] That is why, in his meeting with French director for African affairs Dijoud, Davidow noted that the Rwandans could not solve their problem alone. He urged the French to consider a mediation role, perhaps in conjunction with the Tanzanians, who did not have the resources to go it alone. "It is more important that the mediator be powerful than that it be neutral," Davidow insisted.[67] As for the United States, it was willing to be present in the process but would have difficulty contributing manpower or money other than some technical advice to the negotiators and assistance for refugees.

WHAT WAS CONCLUDED AND WHAT WAS NOT

The Paris talks finally began on June 6, 1992. Except for a French and US presence at the opening and closing sessions, the three-day talks were direct and closed-door. The closing communiqué reaffirmed the mediation of Mobutu while reserving the right to face-to-face "facilitated" talks. The parties asked neighboring countries as well as the OAU, France, Belgium, and the United Sates to be Observers to the negotiations. As regards the implementation of a ceasefire, the parties "affirmed their political will to put an end to the war," reaffirmed the validity of the N'sele Accord of March 29, 1991, and asked the OAU secretary general to provide information on an OAU monitoring role. On a possible agenda for negotiations, the parties retained from the Rwandan government the question of national unity and the democratization process and from the Rwandan Patriotic Front the fusion of the two armies, a transitional government with an enlarged base, and political guarantees. The two parties agreed to meet again July 10–12 in Africa (either in Zaire or Tanzania) for substantive discussion on a ceasefire.[68] Less than a month later, direct talks between Foreign Minister Ngulinzira and RPF chairman Kanyarengwe at the OAU ministerial in the presence of the Senegalese foreign minister (Senegal had just taken over as chair of the OAU) firmed up these understandings.

What was not in the communiqué was the very large arena still contested by the two sides. There was no agreement on how refugees should be repatriated. The coalition government wanted to preserve the institutions that the 1991 constitution put in place and expand them to include RPF participation; the RPF wanted to dismantle the current government and rewrite the constitution. The government wanted to move forward to new elections that would provide the basis for multiparty participation in government; the RPF wanted to hold national elections at the end of the interim period but insisted on immediate local elections to replace officials named by the current regime. The government would accept token integration of RPA officers into the Rwandan army; the RPF wanted to demobilize the government army and integrate RPF troops into a new force at a 50:50 ratio. As for the critical issue of moving forward on a sustainable ceasefire, the Rwandan government wanted an interposition force, whereas the Patriotic Front wanted a truce line monitored by a small observer force.

The Paris talks reflected, as well, positions of the international actors in this crisis. France's role, solicited by the government and questioned by the RPF, was confirmed by the success, however limited, of the Paris talks. The United States, which had early staked out a middle ground on the crisis, was now being solicited by both sides as an honest broker. However, Ambassador Davidow had carefully delimited the modest role that the

United States envisioned.[69] His argument against an expensive interposition force, his urging of progress in democratization as the path to peace, and his enthusiasm for parallel interim institutions like a political military committee were positions to which the United States would continually return. Operationally, keeping the French forward in the peace process and keeping costs low became central planks in the US platform.

Senegal, by virtue of its presidency of the OAU, was assured of a voice at the table. Both France and Rwanda seemed to see Uganda as an essential part of the peace process, as witnessed by the border-assessment mission France had already deployed and the upcoming visit of Ugandan foreign minister Ssemogerere to Paris. The parties were ambiguous about potential African mediators. Neither side was particularly friendly with the Tanzanians. Both the internal opposition and RPF mistrusted Zaire. But both were determined that the ceasefire negotiations should move back to an African locale. Eventually, Arusha won out over Kinshasa, although the parties insisted on keeping Mobutu as mediator and the N'sele Accord as the founding document for the revived negotiation process.[70]

AN AMERICAN GAMBIT

Since the US policy review in March, the United States had been visibly active in the Central African region. An internal summation of the US position concluded that "with Hank Cohen's high visibility as the promoter of dialogue and without a vested interest in the area, the USG is seen as the most objective party."[71] Cohen's personal diplomacy had brought together the Rwandan government and the Front in Kampala. He had encouraged Museveni's positive participation in the peace process and had secured an invitation to the United States to be present at the Paris talks in May. Now the French had invited the assistant secretary to be in Paris during the visit of Ugandan foreign minister Ssemogerere on June 20. The ostensible purpose of the foreign minister's meeting was to be briefed on the French border survey. But Paris wanted Cohen's help in pressuring the Ugandans to stop assistance to the Rwandese Patriotic Front.

At the meeting, the assistant secretary found the foreign minister surrounded by Ugandan security officers and plaintively denying Ugandan engagement with the RPF. Cohen finally got Ssemogerere to the side and told him that the United States knew that Uganda was supplying the RPF. This war was destabilizing the region and costing the international community large outlays for humanitarian relief. The war must stop. If a ceasefire was not in place by October 1, Cohen warned, the United States would deduct from its aid to Uganda the amount of its costs for relief for displaced persons within Rwanda.[72] The foreign minister said that he personally welcomed this demarche and wished that President Museveni would have a chance to hear it directly.

Consequently, Cohen had Ambassador Carson deliver to President Museveni a letter in which Cohen noted that the fighting in the Rwandan conflict had intensified despite Museveni's commitment to help end the conflict, that the fighting was not necessary since the democratization process in Rwanda allowed the RPF the best chance to gain satisfaction of its legitimate grievances, that the fighting was draining international relief coffers, and that Museveni's government "bears a direct responsibility in the continuation of the fighting." The letter then reiterated the US position that if a peaceful settlement or firm ceasefire "is not in place by October 1, 1992, we will have no choice, given the burden the conflict places on U.S. resources, but to deduct what is needed for relief for Rwanda's displaced from the economic assistance we provide to Uganda."[73]

On Assistant Secretary Cohen's return to Washington, the staff sent up a decision memorandum proposing technical assistance to the ceasefire negotiations. The memorandum was based on the belief that the Rwandan conflict had reached a critical turning point where "the situation may deteriorate due to inertia and inexperience on the part of the GOR and the RPF," if the United States did not exert pressure to influence the outcome of ceasefire negotiations. The proposal would have legal expert John Byerly and military specialist Lt. Col. Charles Snyder meet with the government of Rwanda and the Patriotic Front, respectively, to discuss preliminary ceasefire proposals and conflict resolution techniques.[74]

If those talks were constructive, the experts would proceed to the negotiations as backup technical support to the US ambassador to Tanzania, Edmund DeJarnette, the official US Observer for the ceasefire talks. The memorandum also recommended that "we brief the French and the Belgians on what we propose to do" and that the United States raise the level of regular contact with the Patriotic Front to the ambassadorial level in Kampala, thus "increasing symmetry in our relations with the GOR and the RPF." Cohen agreed to the proposals under specific condition that the French and the Belgians not object to this modest US initiative. The French and Belgian embassies in Washington were called in for a briefing, and demarches were made in each capital.[75]

Snyder and Byerly had helped construct the Namibian peace agreement and brokered a truce in the Angolan civil war, and they were at that time deeply involved in peace negotiations in Mozambique. With Byerly's knowledge of texts and approaches and Snyder's understanding of military requirements, they constituted a formidable reservoir of information on strategies for conflict resolution. Snyder spent long hours with RPA leader Kagame and his cohort when they visited Washington, and Byerly went to Kigali to huddle with the Rwandan government negotiators. The Byerly-Snyder team forwarded texts from ceasefire agreements in Zimbabwe, Angola, El Salvador, and Nicaragua to both parties.[76]

The experts found two very different planning environments. Colonel Snyder met with Paul Kagame, a military leader who had demonstrated military prowess in the field but had yet to raise significant political support within Rwanda. Convincing Kagame and the RPF that they could attain their minimum goals through compromise within a political process was Snyder's goal. He found the RPF to be quick learners who assessed negotiating scenarios and expanded their options and analyses in preparation for the July 10 encounter. On the other hand, Byerly met with a Rwandan government discouraged about the war, divided on core principles, and competing with the president for power. Byerly had to rally the divided and dispirited members of the Rwandan government, convincing them to develop a common position and confidently to engage the RPF in negotiations.[77]

Finally, a Ceasefire

Despite the apparent success of the Paris talks, the success of the July ceasefire negotiations was by no means assured. Until late June, it was not known where the talks would take place, other than that they would be held in Africa, in keeping with OAU principles. Though the parties were loyal to Mobutu as mediator and to the N'sele and Gbadolite Accords as the foundation for future discussions, Zaire, preoccupied with its own internal problems, was not in a position to host the negotiation.

With customary caution, the Tanzanian government indicated its willingness to take on such a role, should both parties request it officially.[78] On June 26, Rwandan minister of interior Munyazesa asked the government of Tanzania to "arrange for direct GOR-RPF talks to take place in Arusha, July 10–12." But it was not yet confirmed what the Tanzanian role would be in those talks.[79]

As the ceasefire talks opened in Arusha, July 10, Ambassador DeJarnette noted the style of Foreign Minister Ngulinzira as conciliatory and flexible but that of RPF commissioner Bizimungu as rhetorical and demanding. Ngulinzira presided over a large delegation representing contentious political parties, the foreign ministry, and the defense ministry. Bizimungu spoke for a small team of experienced negotiators and one field commander.[80]

The sessions were beset by "confusion over tabled texts, a tendency by both delegations to score negotiating points rather than focus on substance." According to DeJarnette, "mutual suspicion and a tendency to lose sight of final objectives" characterized the Rwandan delegations. Long-winded interventions by Foreign Minister Diria and other African Observers "missed the mark more often than they hit it." The US delegation concluded that "it is at best an even proposition that they will succeed in reaching any agreement in Arusha and even less that the agreement will be workable." Although the United States had been engaged in the negotiating process with technical advice from the Byerly-Snyder team and networking by Ambassador DeJarnette, the delegation felt that the United States should not associate itself with an agreement that could not be expected to succeed.[81]

Yet, despite maladroit handling of issues, including dismissal of a hard-won agreement on a buffer zone, Minister Diria persisted. On the night of July 11, he kept delegations locked in discussions until fundamental agreement had finally been hammered out in the early morning hours. Technical framing from the Observer group, including the proposal of a "mixed commission" to oversee the peace process, contributed significantly to an early morning consensus. An agreement was in hand by July 12 and finally signed on July 13. Under its terms, a truce would take effect on July 19 with the full ceasefire to go into force on July 31. Political negotiations were to begin on August 10 and conclude no later than October 10 with the signing of a permanent peace treaty. Measures in the peace agreement were to be implemented by January 19, 1993.

The ceasefire agreement reestablished the Neutral Military Observer Group (NMOG) made up of contingents from West and Southern Africa and officers from the contending parties. The group would verify and control the ceasefire and report violations to the OAU secretary general and a Joint Political Military Commission (JPMC). This mixed commission, which Observers had pressed on the negotiating parties, would be composed of five representatives each of the opposing parties, with the OAU, neighboring countries, Belgium, France, and the United States invited to participate as Observers. The JPMC would follow up implementation of the ceasefire and of the peace agreement, once it was signed. Its first session was held in Addis within a fortnight of the ceasefire agreement, another meeting convened in Addis on September 25–27, and two more met in Arusha on October 25–26 and December 22–23. In those early days, absent the expected deployment of the NMOG and given the tough jousting of political negotiations, the JPMC became guardian of the ceasefire and a channel of dialogue between parties.

Under Article V of the agreement, the signatories accepted political principles whose "modalities of implementation" were to be specified during subsequent negotiations:

- establishment of the rule of law on national unity, democracy, pluralism, and respect for human rights
- formation of a national army of government forces and those of the Rwandese Patriotic Front
- establishment of power sharing within a broad-based transitional government[82]

The United States, which had wondered if there would be a ceasefire worth supporting, now wanted to buttress the first realistic ceasefire document in the war's nearly two-year history. In an official statement, the Department of State said it was "greatly encouraged" by the signing of the ceasefire agreement and gave credit to both parties, as well as to the government of Tanzania which hosted the negotiations, to the Organization of African Unity which would supervise the military observer group and to the government of France for its lead role in organizing the negotiations.[83] The Department of State immediately dispatched letters of congratulations to President Habyarimana, RPF chairman Kanyarengwe, and the chief negotiators.[84]

Residual Issues

CONCESSIONS AND COMPROMISES

A quick look at the simple language of this brief agreement shows how much is granted by both sides. At the Paris meeting, the RPF urged dissolution of the current regime and the constitution of a new order in which the RPF would be a major partner. The Rwandan government wanted to preserve the 1991 constitution and to insert the RPF as a political party within the emerging democratic process. The ceasefire called for an "enlarged, broad-based" interim government, suggesting deeper changes in established institutions than the government might have wanted. The RPF wanted the "dissolution of the Rwandan army and its reconstitution as a new entity with full integration of RPF soldiers." The Rwandan government was willing to accept only integration of select RPF officers. That the ceasefire formula called for "formation of a national army consisting of Government forces and those of the Rwandese Patriotic Front" implies that the RPF won the day on the military side. [85]

What is missing from the scope of the ceasefire principles is any mention of refugee return. After the June three-day, closed-door session in Paris, Foreign Minister Ngulinzira told Ambassador Davidow that there was still no real agreement on the refugee issue. The Rwandan government was prepared to permit the return of qualified professionals, but "a mass return of peasants without lengthy careful preparation would bring insurmountable problems."[86] At his news conference at the conclusion of the Paris meeting, Ngulinzira reaffirmed the Rwandan government commitment to the February 1991 Dar es Salaam Declaration on refugees. The Patriotic Front, however, did not want Rwandans' right of return contravened by any schema, whether Rwandan government or international. That is one of the reasons they launched the war.[87] Yet, the ceasefire agreement, other than mentioning the Dar es Salaam Declaration on refugees in its preamble, did not set forth the refugee issue as a matter of future negotiation.

PRESIDENTIAL HESITATION

There was as well a structural and political difference in this ceasefire negotiation. President Habyarimana or his cohorts had agreed to the two previous ceasefires. Despite the fact that one had been ineffective and the other nonexistent (to use the characterization of Foreign Minister Ngulinzira), the president had been engaged in the process. This time, the foreign minister, coming from an opposition party in the coalition government, negotiated the ceasefire. The agreed political agenda conceded ground that the Rwandan government had adamantly held on continuity of the government and on integration of forces. There was a question whether the president would accept the handiwork of the Rwandan government delegation.

Immediately following the ceasefire signing, President Habyarimana went off to Belgium. At his meeting with King Baudouin on July 20, Habyarimana seemed hesitant in his support for the ceasefire terms. But at his later meeting with Foreign Minister Claes, Habyarimana came out solidly in support of the ceasefire. What happened in between was that the US embassy tracked down the president in his hotel and delivered a letter from President Bush congratulating him on "his success in bringing Rwanda one step closer to peace." Having read the letter, Habyarimana gave his "personal and unwavering commitment to continuing the peace process" and asked that that oral response be conveyed to the president.[88] The Belgians saw the quick and unambiguous support of the United States for the ceasefire as the element that tilted the Rwandan president, publicly at least, in its favor.[89] Whether the president would buy into subsequent negotiations carried out by the coalition government remained a problem to the very end.

MUSEVENI'S ROLE

Perhaps pivotal to the success of this ceasefire's implementation was a new engagement by President Museveni. He had, heretofore, claimed innocence regarding the RPF incursion and had perfunctorily attended peacemaking summits. Now he called in the American chargé and told her that, although he "didn't know what was happening in Rwanda" and in view of the fact that he was being held responsible, he had asked his people (the NRA) to find out who was responsible for the fighting in June. He also sent a message to the RPF informing them of his strong support for the ceasefire. The president took the occasion to complain that the French were arming the Rwandan army with a new long-range gun, which French instructors had fired at the RPF. Museveni's positive support for the ceasefire, his apparent efforts to rein in the RPF, and his strong criticism of the French put the jinx on a joint French-US demarche to Museveni being proposed in the capitals. The chargé concluded, "This meeting would seem to make a joint French-U.S. demarche ... superfluous."[90]

NMOG IV

The text, mainly at the insistence of US technical advisors, contained a provision for establishment of a "neutral corridor" separating the two respective forces so as to facilitate monitoring of the ceasefire by the Neutral Military Observer Group (NMOG). This monitoring group was not a new idea; the Gbadolite Summit, the N'sele ceasefire agreement, and the 1991 OAU Summit outlined a monitoring group in different iterations.

At the Arusha discussion, the parties decided to reconstitute the fifty-officer Neutral Military Observer Group (NMOG) under direct OAU authority, giving it responsibility for verification and control of the ceasefire. The group was to be deployed on July 31, but the international community was not prepared to fund deployment of the force. Equipping of the NMOG was still being discussed between donors and the OAU secretary general on August 10 at the opening of the political negotiations. Only on October 13 could OAU deputy secretary general Mapuranga report that the six NMOG contingents were at last in Kigali and would be deployed to the "neutral zone" by the weekend. By this time, the first two parts of the Arusha Protocols had been negotiated, without any intervening force on the ground.[91]

KIGALI'S REACTION

Back in Kigali, Rwandan political forces did not universally welcome the ceasefire. Some were suspicious of the sincerity of the RPF in entering into negotiations, believing that it might use negotiations as a blind to cover rearmament and an enhanced field position. Others wondered if Habyarimana's trip to Europe was not a way of getting support for toning down provisions of the ceasefire. An insider from the Revolutionary National Movement for Development (MRND) said that many party stalwarts believed that the government had given away too much at the ceasefire talks. On his return from Europe, Habyarimana urged all Rwandans to support the agreement, and the president of the MRND accepted the principles of the agreement as long as they did not "call into question either the political system or the republican institutions already existing in the country."

The nascent CDR, however, came out categorically against the ceasefire, denouncing the agreement point by point and claiming that all concessions had been on the Rwandan side, that Uganda should be party to the agreement (in line with the thesis that the RPF was a Ugandan front), that the RPF should not have parity with government either in negotiations or in the Joint Political Military Commission, and that the CDR should be accepted in the government and participate in the next negotiations. Its rhetoric heightened in subsequent weeks as CDR leaders called for the prime minister's resignation and urged the creation of a new government that would protect Hutu interests.[92]

As a result of changes in internal administration, strife erupted between youth wings of the major parties.[93] The MRND Interahamwe showed its strength and connections to the security apparatus as the youth corps barricaded traffic in and out of Kigali under the benign eye of the Kigali prefect, gendarmerie captain, and the prosecuting attorney. Although the purpose of the demonstration was to protest intimidation by other youth militia against MRND incumbents, the fact of interparty strife accentuated the divisions within Rwanda even as the government sought to organize a united front for political negotiations.[94]

CHANGED PERSPECTIVES

The two days of disjointed but intense negotiations that constituted the Arusha ceasefire talks changed the dynamics of the peace process in two ways.

First, there was enough in the details of the agreement to offer promise of implementation through the Joint Political Military Commission, the Neutral Military Observer Group, and the Organization of African Unity's clear mandate for oversight. Second, whatever their ultimate goals regarding control in the country, the two Rwanda parties did commit to the logic of peace built around discussions on the rule of law, military integration, and power sharing, and to a warrant searching for common ground in subsequent talks.

Meanwhile, the context of international intervention had changed. Mobutu, the mediator, held on to his title but was too busy parrying with the Zairean National Conference by this time to give much thought to Rwandan negotiations. Instead, OAU secretary general Salim Ahmed Salim presided over the talks, while Tanzanian foreign minister Diria "facilitated" the negotiations with a certain heavy-handed determination that finally won concessions and agreement. Finally, under the able leadership of Senegal's ambassador Louis Pape Fall, the Observers gained cohesion as a group.

PERSISTENT PROBLEMS

For all the changed dynamics of the peace process, many things remained the same. The distance between the two parties was palpable in the tensions of the negotiations and in the rhetorical attacks of formal presentations. Both parties anchored their strategies in positions that seemed irreconcilable: radical change of Rwandan governing institutions on the one hand, or continuity and defense of those same structures on the other.[95] The exiles carried in their conceptual baggage long years of participation in Museveni's National Resistance Movement. The government brought thirty years of experience in governing or contesting for governance in Rwanda. The question was whether the parties—given their long, separate histories and contrary perspectives—would find common ground. The conflict that had settled into a stalemate now had a sustainable ceasefire, but was the crisis "ripe for resolution"?[96]

Lessons We Learned

The search for a durable ceasefire in Rwanda took over twenty-one months and involved states and organizations of the subregion, major partners, and international organizations. Lessons learned in this multi-stakeholder pursuit of peace include the following:

- *Outbreaks of international violence are seldom predictable.* Both President Habyarimana and President Museveni were playing on the world stage in New York when the Rwandese Patriotic Front attacked across their mutual border into Rwanda.

- *Conflicts between states and insurgencies usually need outside intervention to bring both parties to the negotiating table.* In Rwanda's case, it took a high-level intervention by France backed by the United States at a meeting in Paris to set up the eventual framework of the Arusha talks.

- *A willingness to talk comes out of a mutually hurting stalemate.* Parties will stop the fighting and pursue peace only when they see a greater long-term advantage in political dialogue than in continued armed conflict.

- *Along the path to a cessation of hostilities, return to fighting can be expected.* Contenders will use violence to demonstrate their capacity to harm before engaging seriously in negotiation. In Rwanda, the government abetted ethnic violence, whereas the RPF used unexpected strikes against strategic targets.

- *Failed attempts at a durable ceasefire have a certain utility.* In Rwanda, identifying the parties, drawing out their commitment to negotiations and to peace, mobilizing international concern, and outlining the elements of a peace process all came out of aborted ceasefire negotiations.

- *A carefully tailored agreement might not last if power holders are uncertain that the negotiation satisfies their interests.* In the case of Rwanda, Habyarimana almost backed out of the ceasefire agreement until reassured by a presidential letter from the United States.

TWO

Law

In a ceasefire agreement hammered out in the early morning hours of July 12, 1992, the Rwandan government (GOR) and the Rwandan Patriotic Front (RPF) decided that political negotiations should include the "establishment of the rule of law that is based namely on national unity, democracy, pluralism, and respect for human rights."[1]

International participants in the negotiations applauded the wisdom of this intention. After all, since ancient days, law has been linked to state founding, whereas in modern times, the rule of law has been seen as a fundamental building block of international peace and domestic tranquility. The Conference on Security and Cooperation in Europe (CSCE) built its ethos on the notion that "societies based on the rule of law are prerequisites for . . . the lasting order of peace, security, justice, and cooperation."[2] Boutros-Ghali saw the rule of law as intrinsic to peacekeeping. "There is an obvious connection between the rule of law and the achievement of true peace and security in any new and stable political order."[3] Kofi Annan considered the rule of law and fair administration of justice as essential to the consolidation of peace in a postconflict situation.[4] "A government of laws and not of men," John Adams's prescription for the Commonwealth of Massachusetts, has become a formulaic mantra of numerous governmental and nongovernmental agencies seeking to promote stability and order.[5]

This chapter will first review the issues confronted in negotiations on the rule of law. Since this was the first session of the political negotiations, I also look at the context of the policies and strategies being developed on both sides before considering the physical space across which the negotiations were conducted. For the international interveners buttressing the talks, the questions under debate took on curious twists of meaning, but the signing of the first protocol raised hopes for future success. However, postscripts to the talks—ethnic violence within Rwanda, diplomatic jockeying, and a signal lack of focused attention by international partners— were harbingers of difficult times ahead.

Issues at Stake

If there is anything in political negotiations that contending parties might agree on, it surely ought to be the creation of a regime of law that would channel conflict into peaceful, political engagement. It is seldom so simple. The issues at stake in negotiations on law entail several questions:

Should political negotiations first deal with foundational principles of law or brace into the complexities of power sharing and military integration? Can agreement on first principles generate a fundamental understanding on which to build subsequent negotiations?

What is the understood purpose of negotiated principles? Are these understandings to reform existing institutions, or are they to establish a revolutionary new order?

How do the perspectives on legal order that delegations brought with them affect the course of the negotiations? Do perspectives from different legal traditions and political circumstances lead finally to shared understandings, or do they cover over profound differences of view and approach?

What was the significance of the agreed principles? What did democracy, participation, rights, equity, or good governance mean to each party? The language in agreements usually comes out of different contexts and points toward different objectives.

Whose Rule? Which Law?

Like many descriptors in the public arena, the rule of law is a more complicated and ambiguous prescription than it seems.[6] Which legal order is being invoked? A legal system may be nothing more than the maintenance by accepted authority of traditional customs and sanctions.[7] It may be, in the continental tradition, a codification of fundamental principles, derived from a universal normative order. Or it may be the compilation of particular decisions of law courts using previous precedent to establish "common law."[8] Changing legal systems can radically restructure society. In transitional situations especially, law becomes an instrument of power rather than a hedge against it.[9]

The Rwandan government delegation was schooled in code law, a good part of it directly taken from Belgian criminal and civil law at the time of independence. The RPF's experience, at least for the leadership that came from Uganda, was in the common law tradition, combining precedent from British courts with local custom. Within Rwanda, Rwandan citizens had experienced the administration of law under a de facto single party from 1962 to 1973 and a de jure single party from 1978 to 1991. The president ruled, and the law was his instrument.

Outside of Rwanda, refugees and exiles that made up the RPF had lived in quasilegal status. Theoretically they were under the protection of the international refugee regime, but they were without guarantee of life or property and thus at the mercy of local and national politics. In 1982–83 for example, thousands were forced off land they had bought in southwest Uganda and harried back to refugee camps or into Rwanda with great suffering and hardship. Moving from one part of the host country to another was sometimes necessary to avoid local animosities. Under these conditions, law was arbitrary; refugees made up their own rules for survival. Security became the lodestar of any legal undertaking.

UNIVERSAL NORMS OR POSITIVE LAW?

In the particular case of Rwanda, it was also a question of what international understandings of law were at play. Was the Rwandan dispute a matter of international province or local jurisdiction? Emphasizing the external nature of the insurgency, the Rwandan government tended to appeal to international law on intervention, whereas the RPF generally held that this was an internal argument to be resolved between the parties themselves. Rwandan authorities believed that civic rights and social status were internal matters for the government to control, whereas the RPF appealed to universal standards of human rights.[10]

In its formulation, the amended N'sele ceasefire agreement described the rule of law in terms (national unity, democracy, pluralism, and respect for human rights) that bespoke late night wrangling over such differences of approach, bridged by a grab-bag definition of multiple and sometimes contradictory notions.[11] Could the rule of law undergird the national unity objectives of the N'sele ceasefire agreement? As Kritz points out, the rule of law is fundamentally a conservative principle, unless one is seeking to replace an existing legal system with another. The "respect for human rights," however, is a liberal principle, often challenging—on the basis of universal norms—the particular application of existing law.[12] Positive law and innate rights may often conflict.[13] In the Rwandan negotiations, the government tended to emphasize existing law and local custom, whereas the Patriotic Front appealed to immutable, universal rights.

WHICH FOUNDING PRINCIPLES?

The appeal both to democracy and pluralism had its ambiguities as well. As Aristotle long ago made clear, democracy has within it a bias toward anarchy or tyranny. His preferred option was a "mixed regime," incorporating the strengths of several political interests within the body politic. This view has its champions in contemporary proponents of pluralistic republicanism.[14] In Rwanda, since the revolution of 1959, Hutu elite had ruled under the banner of majoritarian democracy. But the Hutu regimes excluded, either arbitrarily under Kayibanda or by announced policy under Habyarimana, a significant part of the population from effective representation in the institutions of government and the occupations of state. The leadership of the RPF, on the other hand, had been trained in the "no party" politics of Museveni's National Resistance Movement, inclusive of various ethnic groups but holding to a vision dictated from the top, not to a consensual agreement on law. What would be the constitutional foundation underlying the establishment of political order in Rwanda?

A TRADITIONAL RWANDAN VIEW?

Was there, behind the scrim of these modern interpretations, a traditional understanding of judicial relations in Rwanda? There did exist in precolonial Rwanda a formal judicial mechanism mediated by the army system into which each Rwandan male was integrated. Assisted by his local military chief, every Rwandan had the right to appeal directly to the court of the king (*mwami*). In disputes with land chiefs or cattle chiefs, the army chief became the designated protector of his clients' interests.

Although the king was surrounded by guardians of ritual custom (*abiru*) and by a council of chiefs (*abatware b'intebe*), he ruled by virtue of his divine origins, gave account to no one, and passed judgment as he saw fit.[15]

The import of this traditional system of justice is fourfold. First, there was an institutionalized system of justice in precolonial Rwanda with a direct route from local grievance to the king's court. Second, the mediator for that justice was the local army chief, and thus justice was tied directly to military representatives of royal authority. Third, the king was not circumscribed in his right to judge; the system of justice was thus hierarchical and autocratic, untrammeled by institutional limitations. Finally, with the president's close control of the judicial system, the pattern of judicial administration under the Second Republic replicated in modern garb this traditional model. The first agenda item at Arusha—negotiations on the rule of law—implied a direct challenge to the prevailing judicial ethos and to a traditional Rwandan understanding of judicial administration. Would negotiations on the rule of law lead to a separation of powers and judicial autonomy, or would the old system of personalized but autocratic justice prevail?

If autocracy and autonomy, law and rights, democracy and plurality are problematic in any contemporary polity, how much more were they salient in troubled Rwanda?[16] The ruling regime, the newly established political parties, and the "armed opposition" all invoked the norm of "democracy" and the process of "democratization." All would have, as well, upheld a national unity that allowed some form of diversity. All would have, in principle, supported "human rights" as constitutionally defining the place of citizens within the national polity. All, no doubt, sought a regime in which "political relations between the state and its citizens feature broad, equal, protected and mutually binding consultation."[17] But what, concretely, did these ideals mean for determining the parameters of "law" and for structuring the other items on the negotiation agenda: "establishment of power sharing" and "formation of a national army"?

Preparing to Negotiate

The difficulties of answering that question became apparent in the weeks leading up to the opening of political negotiations in Arusha. Jockeying for advantage threatened to undo the goodwill and understandings that brought contenders to the arena. On the government side, the weakness of the negotiating team during ceasefire talks demonstrated the imperative of building a solidly reasoned government position that had the support of all major parties. In the face of significant political resistance to the ceasefire terms, this was not an easy task. On the RPF side, concern that the government might back away from positions already conceded led to a steady stream of media invective and continuing thrusts and parries on the battlefront.

As the State Department geared up for the upcoming negotiations, Assistant Secretary Cohen asked me to be the US Observer at the negotiations, which were to begin in Arusha on August 10, 1992, and conclude with a peace agreement on October 10. I would have to delay reporting to my next assignment and so arranged a short leave. Thus I would become the first of four US Observers in what ended up being a yearlong wrangle.[18]

GOVERNMENTAL DISCORD—THE ANTI-ARUSHA FORCES

My route to Arusha took me through Kigali, where I met with the prime minister, party leaders, and the team working on drafting instructions for the Rwandan delegation. They briefed me on the difficulties of bridging differences in Rwanda's fissured body politic. The problems were threefold. First, there was the split between the old regime represented by the president's party (The Republican Movement for National Development, or MRND) and the emerging political parties legitimized by promulgation of a new constitution and the Political Parties Law in June 1991. The MRND youth wing (Interahamwe) and party allies, especially the Coalition for the Defense of the Republic (CDR), had protested the terms of the Arusha ceasefire and led unauthorized demonstrations in an attempt to delay the peace negotiations.[19]

Nor was the protest to the course of peace talks confined to political demonstrations. As the Arusha talks commenced, the American embassy noted that "internal insecurity has increased in parallel with each significant step forward in the democratization and the peace processes and subsided as internal political forces reached a new level of common understanding."[20] The violence had included massacres in Bugesera, random land-mine explosions, interparty dustups, military mutinies, political as-sassinations, and grenade and car-bomb explosions.

Along the political track, MRND ministers had been boycotting sessions of the multiparty government over what they considered to be arbitrary decisions of the prime minister on internal administrative re-form. The MRND was less than enthusiastic about negotiating with the RPF and actively challenged the leadership of the coalition government; opposition leaders in turn looked to the negotiations as a means to ef-fect regime change within Rwanda. Bringing the broad-based coalition government together on a comprehensive negotiating strategy was a Sisyphean task.

GOVERNMENTAL DISCORD—THE MDR

Second, a split within the largest opposition group undercut the co-hesiveness of the government delegation. Prime Minister Dismas Nsen-giyaremye's party, the Democratic Republican Movement (MDR), was a revived successor to MDR/Parmehutu, the party that brought Hutu lead-ers to power in 1960. The party still suffered from a regional and ideo-logical split between those who favored a Hutu-centered polity and those who favored national reconciliation, those who were from the north and those who represented the center-south. Whereas the prime minister, who was from the center of the country in Gitarama, seemed to anchor the geographic and ideological core of this party, Faustin Twagiramungu, a businessman from the southwestern town of Cyangugu and son-in-law of former president Kayibanda, led the progressive wing. Donat Murego, a historian and renowned orator, led the northern, pro-Hutu faction. An-other Kayibanda son-in-law, Emmanuel Gapyisi, also from the central party stronghold of Gitarama, was another party leader.[21]

In the insecurity that surrounded the response to the Arusha ceasefire and the workup of political negotiations, Twagiramungu was accused by his political opponents of destabilizing the country. He had, they claimed, sought to capture the youth wing of his party, the Democratic Republican Youth (JDR), by stirring them up against elders within his own party and co-opting the appointment of new local mayors with newly minted MDR partisans of his own choice. For a while, Twagiramungu and the prime minister publicly encouraged the forceful takeover of mayoral offices in communes where the MDR was dominant. Twagiramungu worked closely with Justin Mugenzi, the fiery founder of the interethnic Liberal Party, in raising popular opposition to the Habyarimana regime.[22]

MDR politics thus complicated the position of Rwanda's chief negotiator, Foreign Minister Boniface Ngulinzira. A northerner, he was nonetheless of the Nsengiyaremye political clan, which drew its support from the center of the country. As foreign minister, he led the breakthrough to ceasefire talks by reaching out to the RPF, a move that won him enmity of the pro-Hutu right, even within his party. Moreover, Ngulinzira had replaced Dr. Casimir Bizimungu, a stalwart of the president's party, as minister for foreign affairs; having begrudgingly ceded this key post, presidential supporters could find little good to say about the new foreign minister. As leader of the government negotiating team, the foreign minister was developing networks and building a consensus among political leaders that challenged the "progressive" alliance that Twagiramungu had built with the Liberal Party. Thus, the Rwandan government's chief of delegation and principle negotiator was on ambivalent political ground within his own political party and fiercely contested from without.

GOVERNMENTAL DISCORD — THE CND

Finally, Rwandan polity was beset with an encumbering institutional oddity. When the new constitution and party law were adopted in June 1991, members of the national legislature, or the National Development Council (CND), voted themselves incumbency as a transitional legislature until new parliamentary elections could be held, presumably in April 1993. Members of the CND were all elected under the old single-party slate drawn up by the Habyarimana regime. While some had political and regional loyalties that made them favorable to a new political order, most were oriented toward the status quo. In the lead-up to the peace negotiations, Rwanda's only elective institution found itself sidelined; political negotiations were within parties, among parties, and between party leaders and the presidency. Nonetheless, after the government's negotiating strategy had already been drawn up, the CND belatedly made its views known, delaying finalization of the project.[23]

DISCORD OVERCOME

The regime establishment hardly wanted to negotiate, the opposition was badly split, and the people's representatives were making new claims on the policy process. What brought this inchoate mix of historic parties and self-appointed politicos together were two principle dynamics. First, the war was draining the nation's resources and the expanded army had stopped fighting. The people and their political leaders were tired of the war. Second, the forces of democratic change had swept over Rwanda. Within a couple of years, Rwanda had gone from a single-party system based on "democratic centralism" to a multiparty government with several centers of power. Opposition political leaders saw "democratization" as their key to political control. That was why the government delegation chose to negotiate "within the framework of existing laws and institutions."[24]

Continuity and evolution, not revolution, was the Rwandan government's negotiating strategy. Intrinsic to this democratic evolution was the prospect of nationwide elections, established by protocol as prior to April 16, 1993, when the terms of office of the CND would end. Parties would have to contest for legislative and mayoral offices, thus confirming for the first time their true political weight. The prime minister insisted on the agreed timetable. Difficulties that the communes were facing over appointed mayors prompted the foreign minister to comment, "Officials need the legitimacy of elections."[25] How to incorporate the Patriotic Front into the framework of the existing political process—to let it function as a political party and participate in a defining electoral tally—was the challenge of political negotiations as the Rwandan government saw it.

INSURGENT VISION

The Rwandese Patriotic Front did not accept the government's notion that existing institutions were sacrosanct or that the democratization timetable had explicitly to be observed. For the Front, "Peace, reconciliation and national unity are the overriding objectives which the RPF is determined to achieve."[26] There was a remarkable consistency to the position the RPF put forward in the years between its invasion of Rwanda and the formal opening of peace negotiations. National unity required the eradication of barriers to the return of refugees, to equal opportunity, and to full participation of all in Rwandan society and politics. Reconciliation of Rwandans to each other would come through the elimination of "sectarian and antagonistic regional divisions." In this process, democracy would gestate through grassroots change. Elections under conditions of instability and sectarianism would "throw the country into another wave of bloodshed."[27] In a presentation to the May 1991 African Leadership Forum, the Patriotic Front summed up its principles as follows:

- To bring about and cement national unity

- To institute a genuine democracy from the grassroots to the legislative level

- To promote an integrated and self-sustaining economy

- To eradicate corruption in all its forms

- To guarantee the security of persons and property

- To promote social welfare for the benefit of all the citizens

- To promote peace and cooperation between our neighbors and all the peace-loving nations of the world[28]

INSURGENT STRATEGIES

These goals implied a long-term process. In a March 8, 1992, letter to the Department of State, the RPF attempted to explain the failure of the meetings in Paris the previous January as a premature attempt by the French and the Rwandan government to put forward issues that were short-term and self-serving, such as the distribution of ministerial portfolios. The Front called rather for "a just and durable solution to the problem of peace," to be discussed after a ceasefire was in place and its monitoring was effective.[29] As RPF statements over time show, such a durable solution would include the right of return of all refugees, a constitutional and governmental revolution that ensured a democratic process and fostered national unity, the integration of the two contending armies, and a national debate on the future of the country, all before elections could take place.[30]

The same documents make it consistently clear that the RPF considered the Habyarimana regime to be oppressive, corrupt, and delinquent in upholding the rights of the Rwandan people. Already at the 1991 Kampala Forum, the RPF document noted that "President Habyarimana and his clique ... continue upholding the principles akin to Nazism of Germany."[31] On an interim basis, the RPF wanted the Habyarimana regime replaced by an organ of national will and action patterned after Museveni's National Resistance Movement. In its proposals tabled at the June 1992 ceasefire talks, the Front insisted that "there should be a national council which is broad-based and which has full executive and legislative powers. This national council should preside over the interim period."[32]

INSURGENT TACTICS—MILITARY INITIATIVES

For all its evocation of national unity and peace, the RPF pressed for tactical ascendency in field operations, media coverage, and negotiating positions. First, the RPF intentionally used the force of arms to make political points. The initial thrust into Rwanda came when the Habyarimana regime had accepted a UNHCR plan for the programmed return of refugees, a presumed RPF goal. But the RPF wanted an untrammeled right of return to a Rwanda rid of Habyarimana's control.[33]

Thereafter, the RPA punctuated negotiating strategy with military tactics: witness the January 1991 attack on Ruhengeri when Habyarimana stalled on ceasefire negotiations in Goma, the quick investment of Byumba right before the June 1992 ceasefire negotiations in Paris, the temporary RPF offensive immediately before the political negotiations opened in August 1993, and, especially, the February 1993 push toward Kigali after the government reneged on negotiated protocols.

The RPF claimed its actions were defensive. Its theme became, "We are not yet in a situation of ceasefire and we have only responded to offensives of governmental forces." As regards the attack on Byumba, the RPF explicitly laid the blame on efforts of the president and his party to block the peace process. "Thus, the investment of the city of Byumba by the combatants of the RPF was a response to the provocations trying to check the process of peace that had been initiated."[34] In fact, war tactics were the sharp instruments of policy, the means to negotiating preeminence.

INSURGENT TACTICS — MEDIA

In communiqués and press releases, the Patriotic Front fought for media advantage. In an increasingly sophisticated approach, RPA publicists used French and English according to the intended audience. RPA concern for the Visoke gorillas, for example, was published in English for an American audience.[35]

Where the government was claiming victory, the RPF claimed, on the contrary, the capture of strategic positions.[36] Press releases gave details on "defensive operations" in which government positions were overrun and government materiel captured.[37] After the Kibuye massacres that followed negotiations on the rule of law, a press release gave data gleaned from Rwandan human rights organizations and excoriated the shelling of an RPA position as a violation of agreements already reached.[38] A press release analyzing the "rout of governmental troops" claimed that "the ambition of Major General Habyarimana to resolve by arms the conflict which opposes the Rwandese Patriotic Front to the Kigali regime shows itself today to be an impossible mission."[39]

What for the RPF was the outcome of these back-and-forth raids? RPA commander Kagame, with a modesty that belied some press release claims, summarized the RPF battle strategy to a BBC reporter: "I do not think we have been fighting to capture territory. We have been engaging the government troops and we have done a very good job of crippling that army, and that is the army that is being used to keep the dictatorship in place. I think we can even use one square kilometer to do that job very successfully."[40]

Even as the Rwandan political complexion changed with the institution of a multiparty government, the RPF condemned it with faint praise. A press release noted that Prime Minister Nsengiyaremye's April 16 speech on the installation of the interim government "seemed to reflect a willingness and commitment to tackle the many problems facing Rwanda." But it also found that "despite the apparent goodwill, it is doubtful whether the prime minister has the means to effect the changes he envisages."[41]

INSURGENT TACTICS — NEGOTIATIONS

As Rwanda's coalition government staked out positions and engaged partners in between the meetings with the RPF in Kampala in May and in Paris in June, the Rwandese Patriotic Front returned to a negative and cautionary tone. A June 23 communiqué questioned whether the new government had changed its goals and whether a process of negotiation for a return to a durable peace remained on the agenda of the prime minister and the minister of foreign affairs. The RPF concluded that the prime minister and the ministers of the internal opposition, in general, "operate under the pressure of President Habyarimana, of the party-state MRND, and of the military forces of the regime."[42]

What had stirred the RPF riposte were calls from the prime minister to bolster Rwandan government troop deployments, presidential criticism of a Brussels meeting between the RPF and the *Forces démocratiques pour le changement* (FDC, the loose coalition of internal opposition parties), and open discussions by the foreign minister on modalities for carrying out the Paris agreements with France, the United States, and Belgium, including a Rwandan request for Belgian facilitation of the next meeting. As far as the RPF was concerned, the war continued until there was a ceasefire, and ceasefire talks had not yet taken place.

While the commitment to peace had been affirmed in Paris, the modalities of how to put it in place had yet to be discussed; the next meeting on African soil would initiate those discussions. In sum, the only acceptable discussions for the RPF were those that strictly followed the negotiating schedule and strategy that formed the basis of the Paris communiqué and had been buttressed by a sidebar meeting with opposition parties. Moreover, having drawn up the draft text that Facilitator Diria used as a working document in the July ceasefire talks at Arusha, the RPF had shown its superior strength in negotiating tactics. The Patriotic Front seemed to take negotiation as war by another means, and it was determined to win. Observers, noting RPF continuing dominance in the July ceasefire negotiations, counseled behind the scenes on a more flexible and compromising approach. This was a negotiation in which both sides should take away something of value, not a "winner-take-all" scenario.

Negotiating across the Divide

On August 11, a multicentered government delegation and a highly focused RPF team gathered on either side of the negotiating forum under

the eyes of international Observers and the guidance of Tanzanian foreign minister Diria as Facilitator.[43] Other than the distance across the
room, there was not a lot separating the parties, or so it seemed. Though
they spoke formally in English or French at plenary sessions and required
documents in both languages, the parties were, in fact, of the same culture, speaking the same language, sharing the same history, and given to
the same habits of life. Ethnic, regional, and physical stereotypes failed to
explain their separation at the negotiating forum. Observers, even African
neighbors, would have been hard-pressed to tell who belonged to which
supposed ethnic group.

More important, the parties had covenanted at the July ceasefire talks
on the logic of peace: "the cessation of all hostilities for the purpose of dialogue and serious negotiations between the two parties." They had agreed
on the structure of that peace: "establishment of the rule of law; formation
of a national army; and, establishment of power sharing within the framework of a broad-based transitional government." What remained for the
time allotted to political negotiations, from August 10 to October 10, was
to work out the "modalities" of the interim order.[44]

It was not to be that simple. The parties came at those principles from
very different perspectives. It was fundamentally a question of what kind
of change was necessary to build the Rwanda of the future and who should
control that change. Habyarimana and his cohorts in the MRND wanted
to preserve the institutions of state, a political culture that still in large
part reflected the ethos of the one-party state. They would accommodate
enough change to end the war and to secure the presidential and MRND
supremacy within the transitional order. In this regard, they were for
quick elections, before the party grip on the hinterland eroded.

The internal opposition wanted to use the democratic process and the
threat of RPF arms to break down MRND power and circumscribe the
president, to whose role each political leader no doubt aspired. The parties' role in the political game, however, was determined by the 1991 constitution and the interparty protocol of March 13, 1992. The institutions
and arrangements within those documents were intrinsic to their political
survival. As the Rwandan political parties had agreed in developing a common position for the political negotiations, the government would, at the

negotiating table, seek to preserve the democratic gains of the previous two years and negotiate within the framework of existing laws and institutions. As Foreign Minister Ngulinzira explained it to Kigali's diplomatic corps, "The RPF must accept to integrate into the existing system and into the democratization process already underway in Rwanda."[45]

The RPF, on the other hand, wanted revolutionary change. The constitution, the CND, the judiciary, appointments to the bureaucracy, and the pattern of local government all reflected the design and the power of the Habyarimana regime. Encamped on a small sliver of northern Rwanda, the RPA had repeatedly proved its capacity to move forward at will and to counter any effort to dislodge its positions. Observer states like France, which was training and supplying government forces, or Tanzania, which was the purportedly neutral Facilitator, recognized RPF military prowess.[46] The Front hoped to use its military capacities to force change and its political skills to win over the FDC to a radical remake of Rwandan polity. Thus, in spite of a common culture, a mutual commitment to peace, and an engagement in a diplomatic process of negotiation, the parties were deeply divided in perspective, purpose, and quest for power.

LAY OF THE LAND

The two contending parties were to gather at the old East African Community headquarters in Arusha along with the official Mediator of the ceasefire (Zaire), the Facilitator of the ceasefire talks (Tanzania), and the Convener of political negotiations (the Organization of African Unity, or OAU). Also present were representatives of the official Observer nations: Senegal (representing the chair of the OAU), Burundi, Uganda, France, Belgium, Germany, and the United States.

The Rwandan delegation came late, detained by last-minute internal discussions on their negotiating mandate. Contention over the agenda further delayed opening ceremonies. The Facilitator wanted to follow agenda points as they were ordered in the July 13 ceasefire agreement, namely, the establishment of the rule of law, the formation of a national army, and the establishment of power sharing within the framework of a broad-based transitional government. The Government of Rwanda agreed with this approach, but the Rwandese Patriotic Front wanted to go back to the communiqué of the preparatory meeting in Paris that listed the objects for general debate as the question of national unity, the democratization process, the fusion of the two armies in the conflict, the transitional government with an enlarged base, and political guarantees.[47]

Even with the delay, the opening ceremonies were finally held without clear agreement on future directions. Up on the third floor of the renamed Arusha International Conference Centre, the organizers had arranged the negotiating arena with the government delegation on one side and the Rwandan Patriotic Front, thirty feet away, on the other. At the head of the negotiating rectangle were OAU officials and the Tanzanian government. At the bottom of the arena were the Observers, with the representative of the OAU chair (Senegal), neighboring states, and France (as head of the Western group) having pride of place.

Behind the tables, a rat's nest of cables attached to antiquated headphones and microphones stretched out to the interpreters' cabins for simultaneous renditions in English and French. Although Kinyarwanda was the common mother tongue of the contending delegations, the Rwandese Patriotic Front spoke in French and English, and the Rwandan government delegations spoke in French. Both would insist throughout the negotiations on use of world languages and simultaneous translation in plenary sessions.

I had taken a plane to Nairobi and then caught an early bus to Arusha. Travel fatigue and a jump seat on the crowded minibus during the four-hour journey south hardly prepared me for active representation at the negotiations. Fortunately, Edmund DeJarnette, the US ambassador to Tanzania, was there to introduce me to the key personalities and hand off the Observer responsibilities he had held during the ceasefire negotiations.[48]

The delegations as well must have been tired at that late morning opening, for they had been up past midnight arguing over the order of the agenda.[49] Foreign Minister Diria contended that the June Paris communiqué had been incorporated in the later Arusha agreement and, in his opening remarks, tabled an agenda based on the July ceasefire.

In opening remarks, Foreign Minister Ngulinzira outlined the Rwandan government's desire to be open-minded and collaborative in the negotiations but underscored its commitment to the legitimacy of existing

Rwandan institutions and the democratic process already underway. Chairman Kanyarengwe echoed the rhetoric of Commissioner Bizimungu in Paris by harshly criticizing President Habyarimana and the MRND party. But he also declared that the "Revolution of 1959" was not in question in these negotiations. Since that revolution overturned the monarchy and established Hutu political dominance in Rwanda, this declaration seemed to alleviate the worst fears of some on the Rwandan government side.[50]

Immediately after the opening session, Kanyarengwe flew down to meet with President Mwinyi in Dar es Salaam. The Tanzanian president tried to convince the RPF chairman to be realistic in his expectations of negotiations; Mwinyi told Kanyarengwe that "results must be acceptable in Kigali to be considered a success." Both the OAU and the Tanzanian government felt that the Rwandan government had showed its weakness in the ceasefire negotiations. This time, the RPF had to understand that successful negotiation meant no losers.[51] ·

If the message got through, it was not obvious. Once the formalities were over, hardheaded negotiating tactics surfaced. Foreign Minister Ngulinzira had anticipated a general debate on principles of governance so as to elicit what the RPF really wanted from the negotiations and then to clear with Kigali authorities the terms of the government rejoinder.[52] The RPF wanted to get right to negotiation of agenda items, the first being the rule of law. It took two days of corridor wrangling before the formal sessions started in acrimonious general debate.

In plenary session, the negotiating styles of each side quickly became apparent. RPF negotiator Pasteur Bizimungu, adopting the manner of a trial lawyer, was aggressive and at times insulting, characterizing the political system in Rwanda as "dictatorial" and claiming that the coalition government he faced across the table was "neither democratic nor in charge of Rwandan administration."[53] In a bad-cop, good-cop routine, and after Bizimungu had totally exasperated the other side, RPF commissioner Patrick Mazimpaka might intervene and offer to take a look at government proposals.[54]

Foreign Minister Ngulinzira had to keep peace within his oversized delegation and was constantly consulting with its more prominent members. He generally held to straightforward presentations of the government's position. However, the Patriotic Front found his attitude (and no doubt, the position of his government) on refugees and power sharing to be condescending and patronizing. Observers had characterized the foreign minister's style at the July ceasefire talks as "diffident."[55] One month of careful preparation for political negotiations had, apparently, not changed that characteristic. In a moment of pique at RPF intransigence, Ngulinzira commented, "The government's commitment to democratic change is irrevocable; that process will go on with or without RPF participation."[56]

This "take it or leave it" attitude had the RPF wondering whether there was anything to negotiate. Clearly the hopes for quick and systematic negotiations of agenda items within the agreed timeframe were naively out of tune with the determinations and ambitions of each side. Reflecting back on that period, I later commented, "Under the intellectual discourse of that conference, one could sense the distrust and hostility, that pride and ambition which alienates brothers and divides peoples."[57]

THE OBSERVERS WEIGH IN

As the parties groped toward some common ground for discussion, Observers jumped into the fray with ideas, formulations, and suggested compromises, mediating in ways that no doubt exceeded their mandate but that both sides solicited. The Observer team was changed in several ways from that which buttressed the ceasefire talks in July. Among African Observers, Zaire had played a significant role in July by dint of the personal capacities of its ambassador to Tanzania. However, at the political negotiations, Zaire was represented by a chargé d'affaires who was seldom there and took no significant part. In contrast, the Senegalese ambassador to the OAU, Pape Louis Fall, the formally designated spokesperson for the Observers, gave remarks at the opening plenary and played a vital intermediary role throughout. At this negotiating session, Uganda was present only at the opening. However, Rwanda's southern neighbor, Burundi, sent its ambassador to Tanzania and the director of its foreign ministry's Africa section; both were experienced diplomats and effective message carriers.

Among the Western group, France was represented not by their ambassador but by the deputy chief of mission in Dar es Salaam, Jean-Christophe Belliard, a Swahili-language linguist with large experience in Africa and a real sensitivity to African perspectives. His lesser diplomatic title may even have increased his access to both parties; in any case, he was a most effective interlocutor and leader of the Western group. Belgium had intended to send its foreign ministry's director for East and Central Africa, Will Jannen, back into the fray, but he fell ill. He was replaced by his deputy, Rudolph Van den Maagdeberg, who understood his role in more traditional terms as a listener and supporter rather than as an activist. The Germans had been invited to join the Observer group by virtue of their large assistance partnership in Rwanda and their willingness to help fund the OAU's peacekeeping role in the Neutral Military Observer Group (NMOG). German diplomats from Dar es Salaam intermittently showed up at the negotiations.

On the US team, "Maitre" Byerly and Lt. Col. Snyder had gone from the ceasefire talks back to negotiations in Mozambique. I took over from Ambassador DeJarnette, who was soon to depart post. The embassy in Dar es Salaam did second their able political officer, Robert Bentley, who assisted as duties in Dar es Salaam permitted. We operated without limits on creative thinking or innovative approaches but under one clear instruction, namely, "Keep the French out front!" Given the weight of the United States as world leader and the tendency of Foreign Minister Diria to convene me for one-on-one discussions over breakfasts of millet gruel, it was not easy to keep a low profile. Good relations with Belliard, however, allowed us both to work toward our common interest in moving the Arusha process toward lasting peace.[58]

The success of the Arusha negotiations was predicated on close cooperation between the Organization of African Unity as Convener and the Tanzanian government as Facilitator. The good relationship between Secretary General Salim Salim and President Mwinyi made that possible. Salim Salim brought a thorough grasp of negotiation dynamics and an imposing presence to the talks, but he attended only occasionally. He was seconded at the negotiations by the scholarly Zimbabwean, Dr. Machivenyika Mapuranga, who was the assistant secretary general for Southern Africa at the OAU. Mapuranga had been detailed by Salim Salim for consultations with the RPF in the bush and with the Rwandan government in Kigali throughout 1991, as the OAU sought what role it might play. Most familiar with the ground-level dynamics of the conflict was the gregarious Joe Felli, a Ghanaian political officer on Salim's staff who had been similarly itinerant between the parties. Felli seemed to know everyone and everything about the state of play in negotiations, but he discreetly used what he knew to push the OAU agenda forward.

Tanzania's foreign minister, Ahmed Hassan Diria, a fellow islander with Tanzanian president Mwinyi and OAU secretary general Salim Salim, came to the August political negotiations with a reputation strongly enhanced by his having pushed the ceasefire talks to a satisfactory conclusion. But although both parties wanted a ceasefire, it was not clear that either party wanted to give much on their political agenda. Up against erudite language and bunker intransigence, Diria sometimes confused issues and misinterpreted intentions, as his maladroit handling of opening exercises illustrated. Fortunately, he was seconded by a veteran diplomat seasoned in Namibia/Angola negotiations; Ambassador Ami Mpungwe became the point man of the Tanzanian facilitation.[59] Since Foreign Minister Diria had to leave the first session of negotiations for OAU meetings, the Tanzanian government replaced him with the then minister for education and former foreign minister Ben Mpaka. So skillful was Mpaka's handling of the remainder of the negotiations that I extraordinarily requested his return for the second round.[60]

Questions at Large

Even with a de facto RPF acceptance of Foreign Minister Diria's agenda, namely, an initial discussion on the rule of law, it did not take long for the delegations to lock horns on what, to us, were arcane arguments. Foreign Minister Ngulinzira's hope for a debate on general principles of governance quickly gave way to an acrimonious argument over particulars: the right of return, the nature of democracy, and human rights.

THE RIGHT OF RETURN

To our surprise, the RPF strongly rejected efforts to qualify the "inalienable right of return" with the word voluntary. Voluntary return of refugees had been a cornerstone of international treaties on refugees and was part of the 1991 Dar es Salaam communiqué. The RPF's European representative, Dr. Jacques Bihozagara, who fled Rwanda to Burundi after his parents were slaughtered in Gikongoro in 1963, emotionally argued that, after thirty years living as a refugee in Africa and Europe, the unconditional right of return as a citizen meant infinitely more to him than any internationally guaranteed refugee rights. The RPF finally agreed to the phrasing offered by the Western observers, namely, that "they undertake not to hinder the free exercise of this right [of return] by the refugees."[61]

ELEMENTS OF DEMOCRACY

The RPF wanted the broad-based transitional government mentioned in the N'sele Accord charged with carrying out the agenda of democratic change. The government wanted the RPF to join in the democratic process already underway. Over this fundamental difference, the negotiations went into a two-day stall. The government apparently accepted a corridor compromise brokered by the Burundi Observers. But back at the table, the government added language that reemphasized the government's position. RPF negotiator Bizimungu called the negotiation to a halt. It took a phone call to the prime minister in Kigali (always a long and difficult operation) to get permission to drop the added language. Ambassador Fall finally came up with a formulation that was incorporated as Article 12 of the protocol.

> The broad-based transitional government provided for in Article V of the N'sele Agreement, as amended in Gbadolite, on 16 September 1991 and in Arusha on 12 July 1992, shall lead the country to a democratic system defined above.
>
> To this end, the two parties note that a political process has been initiated by the Rwandese people to ensure the progress of democracy and reaffirm the need to build together a society founded on the Rule of Law as stipulated in the present Protocol.[62]

Articles 5–12, which provided the definition of a "democratic system," were worked out in lengthy esoteric debate on the meaning of popular sovereignty, fair elections, multiparty governance, pluralism, and tolerance. Having been excluded for twenty years from rights of citizens by the Rwandan *politique d'équilibre*, the RPF wanted nothing in the document that hinted of group rights, whether it be majority rule, minority rights, or political distinctions based on regional or "sectarian" identity.[63] They chose rather to stake their political future on a strong affirmation of individual rights and of popular sovereignty.[64]

The government side did not have particular problems with the notion of individual rights or a commitment to the will of the people; those, at least for the opposition members, were building blocks for a better future. But the government delegation was concerned about a notion of national unity that expected all persons to be autonomous as well as equal. The hard-won rights to political pluralism implied the right to group affiliation and the political expression of group aspirations. Moreover, popular sovereignty was but a utopian chimera unless some sort of electoral process channeled the people's will. The RPF, however, saw elections as the culmination of a long process of transforming the popular will at the grass roots. The government would not, however, accept the RPF's formulations unless it also would commit to pluralism and to "regular, free, transparent and fair elections."[65] In its final rendition, the protocol had something for both sides.

Article 5: Democracy is founded on the idea that sovereignty belongs to the people. It is expressed, notably, through regular, free, transparent, and fair elections. Popular representation must be the authentic expression of the will of citizens.

Article 6: The two parties accept the universality as well as the implication of the following fundamental principles of democracy:

+ sovereignty of the people

+ government based on the consent of the people expressed through regular, free, transparent, and fair elections

+ separation of the legislative, executive, and judiciary powers

+ independence of the judiciary

+ guarantee for the fundamental rights of the individual as provided for in the Universal Declaration of Human Rights as well as in the African Charter on Human and Peoples' Rights, among others, freedom of speech, freedom of enterprise, and freedom of political, social, and economic association

- laws and regulations based on the respect of fundamental human rights

- equality before the law

- respect of laws and regulations by all

- a constitution that respects the principles enunciated above, organizes the state power, and defines the powers and limitations of the institutions of the republic

- multipartism, social and economic pluralism

Not satisfied with the principles detailed above or with subsequent provisions on "multipartism," development, elections, and democratic culture, the government fought for the inclusion of Article 13: "The two parties recognize that a democratic society is also founded on pluralism, which is the expression of individual freedoms and must respect national unity and the fundamental rights of the citizen." In the back of the government delegation's thinking was the specter of Museveni's National Resistance Movement, which in the interest of national unity outlawed all other political movements. Many in the government delegation had fought hard for freedom of association and the right to mobilize politically in parties. They were not about to give up "pluralism" for an ephemeral "popular will."

TOLERATION

In the discussion of "tolerance" (which the government promoted and the RPF rejected), Observers came to realize how ideas with deep resonance in the Western political tradition can come to mean something quite other in a particular African context. Hard-won after wars of religion, abrogated edicts and pilgrim migrations, tolerance came to be considered in the West as the communal glue that guaranteed the life of reason and held diverse societies together. From Pierre Bayle through Locke and Jefferson to J. S. Mill and the drafters of the UN Charter, Western political history has been a progressive celebration of the political virtues of "tolerance."[66]

The RPF, however, saw in tolerance the seeds of secondary status. Mere tolerance was intolerable. They did not want to be diminished by being put in a "tolerated" category, Commissioner Mazimpaka explained. Rather, they wanted full rights as citizens and universal recognition of those rights by all in society. The government had originally seen "toleration" as a guiding principle of the rule of law. The RPF saw in that a paternalistic condescension that they had felt as refugees in strange lands and an attitude that still, in their view, characterized the government's approach to refugee return. At the insistence of the RPF, all references to "toleration" were dropped from the protocol. "Intolerance," however, joined "ethnicism, regionalism, and integrism" as obstacles to national unity.[67]

HUMAN RIGHTS

In contrast to the extended debate on other subjects, negotiations on human rights went quickly, and its provisions were quite briefly inscribed in the protocol's chapter 4. Human rights were universal and their violation was declared to be matters of concern to the parties and to the "International Community" (Article 14). The Rwandan government accepted an RPF proposal to establish an independent National Commission on Human Rights charged with investigation of "human rights violations committed by anybody on Rwandese territory" and use its findings to sensitize the population and institute legal proceedings, where necessary (Article 15). The parties also agreed to establish an International Commission of Enquiry to investigate "human rights violations committed during the war" (Article 16). In fact, the government had already pushed through provisions setting up such organs, as Foreign Minister Ngulinzira, with a certain touch of one-upmanship, revealed in his concluding speech.

Noticeably absent from the document is any guarantee of group or minority rights. As with its views on democratic representation and on toleration, the RPF did not want any recognition of minority rights, something the government was quite willing to offer. They rather sought to avoid labels and categorization, basing their claim to rights on individual freedoms as human beings.[68] As Esman has noted, the cause of individual human rights based on universal claims of humankind has a strong appeal to human rights activists. On the other hand, states have found the evocation of group rights the easiest way to effect change in authoritarian regimes or to resolve conflicts over political entitlements.[69]

Be that as it may, the RPF wanted no part of a group designation that would allocate them to a minority position. Creating a level playing field for each individual was rather the RPF goal. In effect, this commitment to individual rights, finally agreed to by the parties and inscribed in the protocol, foreclosed on power sharing within a consociational model or on proportional representation of designated groups.[70] According to the protocol, the only lawful claim to power within the emerging democratic system was a claim to represent the people in some degree. That could be asserted not by group identity but by affiliation within a political party and endorsed, one assumed, by some kind of plebiscite.[71] The two parties agreed that "the Rule of Law is . . . first and foremost characterized by justice based on the recognition and full acceptance of the supreme value of the human personality and guaranteed by institutions providing a framework for its fullest expression."[72]

The result of these rather Byzantine negotiations was a surprisingly liberal document, although its affirmations, as we have seen, held some occult meanings. This declaration of basic human liberties and conditions of democratic governance, however common the language, was an outgrowth of each party's experience and vision. On reviewing the terms and tenor of the previous debate, I predicted, "The parties were still miles apart on how they conceive the next stages of negotiation. The central issue will be the RPF's hope for radical change against the government's championship of continuity."[73]

In his concluding remarks, Commissioner Bizimungu looked forward to that next stage. The RPF, he noted, would not sell itself for a few ministerial portfolios nor cooperate with the dictatorial system still in place. Since the next session was to consider power sharing in the broad-based transitional government, a sharing in which the regime in place expected to play a dominant part, the upcoming negotiations seemed headed into stormy weather. Nonetheless, the first negotiations on rule of law concluded with a sense of mutual achievement in a protocol signed on August 18. Foreign Minister Ngulinzira said the protocol was a solid document containing the principles his government wanted and drawing the RPF into the democratic process. RPF representative Dr. Rudasingwa said that the protocol of agreement reaffirmed the centrality of the transition period (hence an end to the current regime) and demystified allegations regarding the Patriotic Front's commitment to democratic principles.[74]

Postscript

Whether that sense of achievement was shared in Kigali political circles depended on whom I talked to as I passed through Kigali on my way home from the talks. Some were proud of the achievement and hopeful for further talks. Some wanted the initial protocol to have signaled greater change. Others were fearful that the high ideals deceptively covered over deep divisions that would surface in subsequent negotiations.

INSECURITY

The rule of law did not seem very much on the minds of party youth who were forcefully demonstrating for their demands to be heard. In a pattern evident since the RPF incursion in 1990, politically motivated violence again became a counterpoint to political change. The US embassy commented, "Throughout this year, internal insecurity has increased in parallel with each significant step forward in the democratization and peace processes and subsided as internal political forces reach a new level of common understanding."[75] On July 28, CDR demonstrations in Kigali against the Arusha ceasefire left three dead. On August 8–9, interparty violence in the northwest and southeast between MDR and MRND and in the southwest between CDR and Liberal Party left four dead and many injured. The issues were twofold: opposition to the whole course of the Arusha negotiations, which CDR and MRND youth considered to be surrender to the RPF; and "communal cleansing," the effort of MDR and PL parties to force out of office local mayors appointed by the regime and to replace them with their candidates.[76] Moreover, as the delegates returned from the rule of law negotiations, ethnic violence broke out in the east at Kibuye, with attacks on Tutsi homes involving several dead and many displaced.[77]

There were several dimensions to this recrudescent violence. The size and forcefulness of political action groups in the multiparty competition had clearly outstripped the ability of communal police to control them, but the gendarmerie was habitually slow to intervene.[78] Security officers in civilian dress were sometimes seen participating in political demonstrations. Upon a protest from the embassy, MRND leaders admitted that some reservists might have been involved in the Interahamwe youth movement but promised to tighten up procedures. Party president Mathieu Ngirumpatse decried CDR's policy of ethnic separatism and claimed the CDR posed a threat to party leaders. The minister of defense said that any active duty military found engaging in political activity would be disciplined.[79] Finally, stories were circulating of a secret group of forty-five prominent Rwandans allied to the Habyarimana regime whose purpose was to destabilize the country, blame the opposition or the RPF, and slow down the democratization process.[80] On the other hand, MRND officials charged opposition parties of collaborating with the RPF by engaging in a destabilization campaign.[81] Whoever was responsible, an atmosphere of insecurity prevailed and no one was brought to bar.

POLICY PERSPECTIVES

It was against this background of insecurity and impunity that the government evaluated the results of the rule of law and prepared to negotiate principles of power sharing. Foreign Minister Ngulinzira sounded out opinions of civil society and the political parties in a series of meetings. Justin Mugenzi, president of the Liberal Party, argued that, if the ideals of the rule of law protocol were to be upheld, parties like the Hutu-supremacist CDR would have to be disbanded and the constitution re-written. Political parties, not government leaders, should head the negotiation process.[82]

On the other hand, Mugenzi's putative political ally Faustin Twagira-mungu, just elected president of the largest opposition party, the MDR, said that "the Arusha negotiations were given full support in the MDR convention August 29 and 30."[83] He seemed perfectly satisfied with the direction and tenor of the negotiations, as well he might be, since the prime minister and the foreign minister, the two principal architects of the government position, were both from his party.

The presidency, for its part, believed that the negotiations ahead would be very difficult and rancorous. Enoch Ruhigira, Habyarimana's cabinet director and a drafter of the 1991 multiparty constitution, expressed "profound hope" that no one would insist on changing the constitution as a condition for further negotiations. The very narrow limits within which the government could negotiate were not "the result of CDR pressure or of Habyarimana's reluctance, but the result of the fundamental ethnic mistrust that pervades the society."[84]

Minimally, the political leadership within Rwanda seemed agreed on two things: the protocol that set up the interim government would have to be modified in some manner in order to allocate ministerial portfolios to the RPF, and admission to any revamped cabinet would not be open to the eleven recognized minor parties clamoring for a seat at the political table. Such an incipient political monopoly took scant recognition of the protocol's demand that "all citizens have equal opportunity of access to the political, economic and other advantages," or its recognition of "the aspiration of any Rwandese citizen to accede to power through democratic process."[85]

DIPLOMATIC ITINERARIES

Neither side was slow in picking up on the diplomatic implications of this agreement. The protocol's language won a favorable audience, particularly in Western capitals. Thus, the RPF sought follow-up meetings in Paris and Washington. The Rwandan government asked me for a briefing; I met instead informally with key leaders. After Kigali, I undertook consultations in Paris and Brussels, buttressing the good relations already developed at the talks. I found both capitals encouraged by the process but not particularly focused on how to broker future power-sharing arrangements. Meanwhile, back in Washington, with the Arusha talks presumably on track, the State Department focused on other African trouble spots: encouraging the South African negotiations to a successful conclusion, pushing along a power-sharing agreement and elections in Mozambique, and especially initiating within the administration a response to famine and anarchy in Somalia. Trilateral diplomacy between Washington, Paris, and Brussels was also in a watching brief. At Western capitals, except for the office directors directly concerned, the Arusha political negotiations were taking place in a diplomatic vacuum.[86]

THE OAU RESPONSE

The Amended N'sele Ceasefire Agreement signed July 13 included in its provisions that "the verification and control of the cease fire shall be conducted by the neutral military observer group under the supervision of the Secretary General of the OAU." This group of ten officers each from Nigeria, Senegal, Zimbabwe, and an African country to be determined, as well as five officers each from the Rwandan government and the RPF, was to be deployed on July 31, the date the temporary truce was to become a formal ceasefire.[87] By the end of the rule of law talks, there still were no monitors on the ground in Rwanda.

The ceasefire agreement also set up a Joint Political Military Commission of five officers each from the Rwandan government and the Rwandese Patriotic Front, along with Observers. The commission was "to ensure the follow-up of the implementation of the cease-fire agreement; [and] to ensure the follow-up of the implementation of the peace agreement to be signed at the conclusions of the political negotiations."[88] This group did meet as scheduled on July 26 at OAU headquarters, with another meeting planned for a month later.

In Kigali, on return from the rule of law talks, I searched out OAU's Mapuranga and Felli to let them know that the United States, having already funded OAU's peacekeeping office, was "impatient with the languor of OAU's deployment of the GOMN [NMOG]." To maintain credibility, the organization needed to get the military observers in the field immediately.[89] In the absence of any coercive international presence, the fact that the intermittent warfare had effectively stopped after mid-July 1992 was testimony to the will of both parties to pursue the logic of peace. The US embassy noted, "The continued observance of the cease fire is the baseline for the relative optimism of the peace process."[90]

Lessons We Learned

The ability of the parties to find common ground on principles after this intense debate on law pleased all participants at the negotiations. Only in retrospect did we come more fully to understand some of the lessons learned from this exchange.

- *The idea of starting negotiations on fundamental principles seemed to work.* It gave very bright minds a chance to spar over important principles before tackling power sharing and military integration. Ambassador

Mpungwe, the Facilitator's key person on the spot, later noted that
the negotiations were "forging ahead almost on a continuous basis and
building on the momentum gained on the way."[91]

+ *The fundamental question "whose rule and whose law?" remained.* Would the
basis of law and justice in Rwanda be the traditional order, with its
close link to executive control? Or would it reflect the broadened base
of rights and participation as established in the constitution of 1991?
Or would it be a transformed system founded on radical notions of
individual rights and general will? Inclusive crafting in the Protocol on
the Rule of Law signed at Arusha papered over deep differences.

+ *The erudite debate had its surprises.* We thought we knew what "national
unity, democracy, pluralism, and respect for human rights" meant, but
the parties each had their own interpretation. The final description of
democracy was more a grab bag of ideas than an operational definition. Behind the agreed language was a fundamental disagreement on
what kind of regime should structure the transition and beyond.

+ *An agreement may represent nothing more than views of the negotiators.*
While concluding speeches at Arusha welcomed the protocol, back in
Rwanda discord and violence greeted the protocol's signature. Prime
Minister Nsegiyaremye and Foreign Minister Ngulinzira, both from
an opposition party, had made the negotiating decisions. The Arusha
peace process was already becoming estranged from a major part of
the constituency back home.

THREE

Power Sharing

At Paris in June 1992, the Rwandese Patriotic Front and the government of Rwanda set an agenda for peace talks based on questions of national unity, democratization, the fusion of the two armies, a transitional government with an enlarged base, and political guarantees. During the Arusha ceasefire talks in July, these aspirations were conflated into an agenda for political negotiations: establishment of the rule of law, formation of a national army, and establishment of power sharing. In August, the parties resolved on the principles of "national unity, democracy, pluralism, and respect for human rights" that would undergird the rule of law. Now, the negotiators turned to the third agenda item: "establishment of power sharing within the framework of a broad-based transitional government."[1]

Those power-sharing negotiations at Arusha were held in September and October 1992 during two sessions, commonly called Arusha III and Arusha IV (counting the ceasefire talks as Arusha I and rule of law negotiations as Arusha II). This chapter opens with a look at issues entailed in these two negotiations, then reviews discussions during Arusha III, which constructed a framework for sharing power in cabinet, national assembly, and judiciary; and evaluates the negotiations of Arusha IV, which sought to fill in the framework with provisions for each institution. The chapter also assesses the interim between the two sessions and concludes with lessons we learned from these difficult negotiations.

Issues at Stake

Power, of course, infuses the whole agenda. These were, after all, "political negotiations," and politics, we are told, is about keeping, increasing, or demonstrating power.[2] As the contending parties negotiated how power was to be shared within state institutions, they faced common questions.

How is power to be defined, and once defined, how is that power to be shared? Hannah Arendt sees that "power is what keeps the public realm, the potential space of appearance between acting and speaking men, in existence . . . power springs up between men when they act together."[3] But is the binding power of human relations to be seen as hegemony, as control of resources, as regulation of the political environment,[4] or as engagement in "shaping, molding, or managing the social environment in which rules operate"?[5]

Who has the right to rule? Geertz poses the historic question, "How do some men come to be credited with the right to rule over others?"[6] Under international law, the UN General Assembly established the Republic of Rwanda on July 1, 1962. But three constitutions later and with an armed insurgency at the door, who was in charge or ought to be? Who was to say that Habyarimana must go and that internal opposition parties or exiled fighters should now rule?

Where is power to be located, and how does its control emanate across the state? In the Rwandan political culture, power was centralized, exercised by the *mwami* (king), the colonial resident, or the president. If that power was now to be shared, how would it devolve and to whom? How was authority to be both shared and exercised locally? And by what means was the consent of the governed, from whom governments derive their just powers, to be assessed?

Is power sharing a short-term, interim instrument in peace building, or a fundamental principle of democratic governance? Sharing power is a classic means of channeling violent confrontation into political competition during a transition period. This short-term objective is easily distorted by a long-term ambition: the determination of participants in the peace process to hold power after the interim. International interveners, on the other hand, generally seek some equitable sharing of power during the interim that could lead to durable power sharing in a future democratic order.

Arusha III—Laying the Groundwork

Despite the seeming consensus on the rule of law built up during the first negotiating session, the Rwandan government and the Rwandese

Patriotic Front came to power-sharing discussions with very different visions of what was to be shared and how the sharing was to be instituted.

The RPF, which had voiced a willingness to look at all options, opened the negotiations with a proposal for a super commission, a National Committee for Reconciliation, with broad executive and legislative powers to run Rwanda during the transition period. Commissioner Bizimungu, noting the continuing insecurity in Rwanda, argued that the current regime with its flawed constitution could not be entrusted with the transition. In response, the government queried whether the Patriotic Front intended to dissolve all existing state institutions, substitute a new agreement for the constitution, oust current administrative personnel, and rule through a self-appointed committee of limited membership and extensive powers.[7]

After the opening session, the Facilitator, Tanzanian foreign minister Diria, told our Observer group that the Front's proposal duplicated the roles envisioned for the Joint Political Military Committee (JPMC). The proposal would surely be unacceptable to the Rwandan government. In Diria's view, the Front's project, concentrating power in a commission, stripped away the legal basis for guaranteeing human rights, undermined authority of institutions, and pushed back the democratic process until the end of the transition.[8]

WHERE IS POWER TO BE SHARED?

In the subsequent session, Foreign Minister Ngulinzira clarified at length the government's position on power sharing and opened the possibility of constitutional change through legal channels.[9] After a day's pause in which to prepare a response, Commissioner Bizimungu detailed the Patriotic Front's position. "The old order must change," Bizimungu asserted. "The transition is from dictatorship to democracy."[10] The Front wanted not only to share power within the government (that is to say, the cabinet), but also to share the power that MRND exercised through the presidency, administration, and most of the institutions of state. The constitution—with its articles 50, 55, and 101—was against power sharing and should be suspended or radically amended. In an impassioned summation, the commissioner outlined the following RPF goals:

- respect for fundamental liberties

- an end to repression under the MRND government

- establishment of democratic rule[11]

The foreign minister gave a rather studious reply to particular points raised by the RPF. A previously appointed two-party committee tabled a working draft. Immediately, the sides locked horns on the meaning of "power" in the document's title. Diria stopped the debate and had OAU's Mapuranga explain how the working document was put together and highlight areas of agreement and areas of disagreement that needed negotiation. But the spadework, rhetorical exchanges, lengthy behind-the-scenes meetings, and prolonged breaks did not move the negotiations forward.[12]

Before the next plenary, Foreign Minister Diria convoked the Observers, asking us whether we had a common position on the negotiations that might constitute a fair settlement of initial issues. It was generally agreed that the Rwandan government was showing greater flexibility in trying to accommodate RPF demands. Even the Ugandan representative offered that the Rwandan demand for a "Supreme Council" and the exclusion of the MRND from it was untenable. I noted that some of the RPF's concerns about ensuring security and the guaranteeing of negotiated agreements could be addressed within the already established Joint Political Military Commission.

Remarking that a "broad-based transitional government" as now enshrined in the ceasefire accord was originally an RPF idea, Dr. Mapuranga suggested that Observers point the parties toward negotiation on specific institutions, hoping that the meaning of power sharing might be better understood in concrete arrangements. We agreed to meet with the parties behind the scenes and move the government and RPF toward discussion of specific changes needed in existing institutions.[13]

The next plenary did not, however, follow the game plan. The parties continued to debate the central operative point: whether power sharing was within the government or spanned the separate institutions of state. Exasperated, the chair harangued the parties, especially the RPF, accusing them of backing away from commitments made under the protocol on the rule of law. He then tried to define power sharing as being across the three governmental powers, precisely the interpretation held by the Patriotic

Front. For the government, however, power sharing was within the government (presidency and cabinet), with the possibility of reforms enabling the RPF to participate to some degree within other institutions. The parties then got into a tendentious debate over whether they were talking about power sharing between the government and the RPF or power sharing as a feature of the institutions of state. The Facilitator offered some commentary and an amendment that pleased neither side.[14]

In between plenary sessions, we met with both sides and urged compromise on definitional statements so the parties could discuss mechanisms of participation. At the beginning of the September 13 plenary, the two sides offered a two-part compromise formula on power sharing. The first part only reiterated agreement on the principle of power sharing as encompassed in the N'sele Accord. Article 2, part A defined the modalities of power sharing as "maintenance of the present structures of the coalition government with appropriate adjustments to be mutually agreed upon in this protocol with a view to making room for the participation of the RPF and other political forces in the country."[15]

THE GOVERNMENT PROPOSES

Having agreed on a formula, the parties then debated whether to proceed immediately to a discussion of particular institutions or agree on a common program for the transition. The RPF wanted to discuss structural particulars; the Rwandan government wanted to outline a general program. Finally, the government went along with the RPF's proposal, but wanted to begin the discussion of particulars with consideration of "the broad-based transitional government."[16]

The next morning, however, Facilitator Diria insisted that the parties adopt a program for the transitional government. Both sides got over the issue by agreeing to adopt a draft program as a "working document." Playing along with the erratic direction from the chair, the government said it was ready to present proposals but wondered if the RPF had any. It was also willing to adjourn talks for several days to give the RPF time. This turned the meeting into an uproar while we sought to convince both sides to keep talking. Eventually, the government side was convinced to present its proposals on a gamut of changes that envisioned the following:

- A constitutional amendment would give primacy to the peace agreement.

- President Habyarimana would retain his office but devolve powers to the cabinet.

- The RPF would join the cabinet, negotiating its portfolios with other parties.

- The cabinet would take decisions by consensus.

- The government would be open to all parties subscribing to the peace agreement.

- Ministers would be accountable to the prime minister.

- The prime minister was accountable to the president.

- A transitional national assembly with members elected by proportional representation would replace the current legislature, and the RPF would appoint its members and hold veto on legislation related to the peace agreement.

- Within the judiciary, the Council of State would be abolished and a Supreme Court would exercise legislative review as well as have the final word on judicial appointments.

- The transitional government would create commissions to deal with national reconciliation, pubic security, information and education, refugees, the constitution, and preparation for general elections.[17]

THE RPF DISPOSES

That evening, we heard the RPF spokesman accept the government's proposal as a basis for discussion, while scathingly underscoring the illogic of the government's position. The RPF countered with the idea of a tripartite presidency, a prime minister drawn from internal opposition seconded by an RPF vice prime minister, an appointed national assembly, and an independent judiciary that elects its own Supreme Council of Justice.[18]

Foreign Minister Ngulinzira took the floor, saying that he spoke for both government and the parties within it. He would welcome RPF amendments or changes to the government proposal. The RPF promised to make its formal proposals the following day. Thus, by the evening of September 14, a week after these discussions began, the government had finally outlined a structure for the transitional order, one that would set the course of future negotiations.

RPF rejoinders, however, demonstrated the deep disagreement on details. The RPF was not opposed to executive powers; its super-commission would have exercised untrammeled executive and legislative authority. But the RPF was opposed to an executive dominated by the president's party, the MRND. The Front had seemed to favor elections, but now it proposed a nominated assembly and accepted delays in local elections for communal mayors. The Front proposed an independent, self-perpetuating judiciary as a hedge against residual MRND power and its record of human rights abuse. In effect, the RPF wanted to change the old order and to claim a regular place in all the transition powers, with "strong protections for basic rights and the principle of equal access without quotas or special treatment."[19]

The following day, the RPF locked in the government proposals on participation in the government and institutions, especially the legislature, but stuck to its proposal for a presidential troika. By that evening, as the two parties met to tally areas of agreement and of disagreement, the presidential council had become a seven-person commission, with the chief of state as chairman. But the government wanted the presidential powers to devolve to the cabinet, not to some new executive commission. It was agreed that the two parties would finalize their lists and then work up a provisional protocol detailing progress to date before adjourning.[20]

INTERNATIONAL PERSPECTIVES

The first session on power sharing revealed varied outlooks in the international community, just as it uncovered the parties' contrasting positions. The French were for change, but change had to be legitimized by elections, which incumbents would no doubt dominate. The Belgians upheld the importance of seeking change within the existing framework and suggested a smaller working-group meeting in Kigali to define parameters. The United States concentrated on practical ways to move the negotiation process ahead, urging both sides toward a middle ground. I worked with both parties in suggesting a variety of ad hoc commissions that could build confidence in the interim period by collaboration on particular problems.[21]

None of the Observers, African or Western, felt that the RPF's idea of a transitional national commission (or its later iterations as a presidential troika or a presidential commission) could work. The idea of a separation of powers was too ingrained in Western thinking; the idea of an executive of co-chiefs did not fit the African hierarchical tradition. However, the idea of placing the powers of state in a collective executive for the transition period was not as far-fetched as the diplomats imagined.[22] It was not just an RPF echo of Museveni's National Resistance Movement. In precolonial Rwanda, executive control prevailed through monarchs surrounded by courtiers and ritual advisors. The colonial system at the provincial level made the "administrator" the executor, legislator, and judge of all. Moreover, the model in the mind of RPF's chairman, Col. Kanyarengwe, was not Museveni but the Committee for Peace and National Unity, which had managed a transition to a new constitutional order while ruling Rwanda for some ten months after President Kayibanda was deposed in 1973.[23]

The Facilitator and Observers were also unified in seeing the government as flexible and forthcoming and in characterizing the RPF as obstructionist and obdurate. This was due in part to the courtroom rhetoric of RPF spokesperson Pasteur Bizimungu, who was given to hyperbole, sarcasm, and castigation. How much of this was the RPF version of "shock and awe" and how much was just Bizimungu's style was hard to tell, but it stood in vivid contrast to the studious, careful approach of the Rwandan foreign minister. Observers felt that Bizimungu's rhetoric was not helpful to the negotiating process; it was simply not "diplomatic."[24]

PRELIMINARY AGREEMENTS

At the beginning of this session, the two sides were opposite in their views of power sharing; at the conclusion of these discussions, in the Observers' view, the positions were still at odds. We would have agreed with the assessment of Ambassador Mbapila, permanent secretary at Tanzania's foreign ministry, who commented that for all their negotiated language, the two parties were still far apart on what that language meant or how they would share the future of governance in Rwanda.[25]

Nonetheless, the parties had in eleven days worked through to suffi-cient agreement such that on September 18 they were able to sign a protocol defining power sharing and outlining a possible structure for the transition period. How power would be shared within that structure would be the subject of the next negotiating session.[26]

The Interim

THE GOVERNMENT'S "LAST WORD"

In between the two negotiating sessions on power sharing, Foreign Minister Ngulinzira traveled to Dar es Salaam to brief President Mwinyi on the talks. Ngulinzira's remarks closing the first power-sharing negotia-tions prefigured his talks with Mwinyi. The foreign minister had reminded the plenary that the very idea of sharing power "within the framework of a transitional government with an enlarged base" had been a major gov-ernment concession to RPF demands in the July 12 ceasefire agreement. Notwithstanding that concession, the government side had not been able to elicit from the RPF a memorandum on what it thought power sharing should mean in concrete terms. Moreover, he saw the RPF as intransigent, interested in "power sharing" per se rather than sharing power within the framework of the government. Indeed, the Front seemed to see itself as an entity outside of Rwandan society wanting to divide up state powers without regard to the will of the nation or people to whom government was responsible. Ngulinzira invited the RPF to drop its ideas about new and expensive structures based on failed models and instead to come par-ticipate in government to improve structures from within.[27]

It was a tough speech by the usually circumspect foreign minister, and it demonstrated his suspicion that the divide between reform and revolu-tion had not yet been bridged, even by the agreements conveyed in the concluding joint communiqué. He went to Dar es Salaam with this skep-tical assessment and with a message from President Habyarimana. That message was in fact twofold: first, it communicated that the Rwandan gov-ernment stood behind the offers it made at the last round of negotiations; and second, it informed President Mwinyi that "this was as far as it could go." The estimate of Ambassador Mpungwe, who attended the meeting, was that there was not much further give in the Rwandan government's position. President Mwinyi, in turn, invited RPF chairman Kanyarengwe to Dar es Salaam to relay the Rwandan government's position and to ask that RPF consider it seriously.[28]

JPMC CONVENES

Meanwhile, the Joint Political Military Committee (JPMC) met in its second session in Addis Ababa. This guardian institution of the ceasefire agreement attracted a full complement of Observers to this meeting, including Zaire, which had hardly appeared at the political negotiations, and Germany, which had been added by the consent of both parties as a major donor and supplier of funds for OAU's Neutral Military Observer Group (NMOG).[29]

Technical issues delayed the consideration of substantive questions: RPF's request for travel subsidies and group commander General Opalaye's request for more troops and UN-level per diems. Observers worked out a compromise on travel subsidies while the OAU finally decided to limit the food and lodging supplement to $10 a day. Since NMOG force levels had been set at fifty in the July 12 ceasefire negotiations, the matter of an increase in the NMOG's size was referred to future political negotiations.[30]

In the substantive discussions, the sides exchanged accusations of human rights violations, of mistreatment of prisoners, and of using foreign forces in the battle line. Many of these charges were being raised for the first time and were used by both sides as debating points. Lt. Colonel Tony Marley, the US Observer, remarked that "there was very little evidence of progress in national reconciliation" in the formal sessions and in the presence of Observers. Away from the formal meetings, however, members of the two delegations seemed to get along well, engaged in "relaxed conversations about world events, mutual acquaintances, contemporary Rwanda, and the ongoing peace process."[31]

Despite the rhetoric and posturing, the JPMC did provide an arena for venting complaints that might not be brought up in formal political negotiations. It also provided an opportunity to refine procedures of the JMPC and the NMOG, both novel organizations. Importantly, the setting offered an opportunity for the Rwandan parties to be together outside of the negotiating halls of Arusha and the physical and psychological distances of that arena.

The meeting also furnished two bits of corridor intelligence that prefigured discussions to come. The RPF political commissioners told Colonel Marley that they would be asking for a 50 percent share in the new integrated army, including command positions; the RPF's competence and discipline merited a coequal position. They were uncertain as to what they wanted to do about the gendarmerie. As a matter of policy, they wanted a small national military rather than a large one but had not given much thought to the process of demobilization.[32] Additionally, the RPF commissioners, while pressing for more concessions, told Ambassador Mpungwe that they might be able to accept the Rwandan offer tabled at the last session of political negotiations "pretty much as it stood."[33]

MEETING WITH MUSEVENI

With hopeful hints coming from the Patriotic Front, the Department of State sent me to Kampala to see President Museveni, get his views of the negotiations, and encourage him to keep the RPF moving toward accommodation. Ambassador Carson and I met with Museveni on the lawn of State House in Entebbe. Our assumptions were that Museveni's National Resistance Army had been supplying the RPF, that the RPF military and diplomatic strategy took a lot from Museveni's play book, and that the Ugandan president could have direct influence on RPF negotiating positions anytime he wanted.

The president demurred in all those regards, then launched into an analysis that showed him to be following Rwandan events with a keen eye. In Museveni's view, the RPF had, in effect, won on the battlefield and therefore could expect an even 50/50 sharing of positions in the integrated military. Moreover, the RPF needed that kind of military weight if they were to feel secure in their old homeland. Politically, however, Rwanda had, over the last thirty years, evolved into a complex social and political landscape. The peace agreement had to take into account that landscape, giving parties place according to their influence among the people. This included the partisans of the president's party, the MRND. The RPF must have a significant but not a dominant role in that political process. At the conclusion of this long analysis, the president said he would try to get in touch with RPF leadership and encourage them toward serious and realistic negotiations.[34]

Arusha IV—Devolution of Executive Powers

TALKING PAST EACH OTHER

Although the renewed session of negotiations was to open on October 5, the RPF delegation was delayed in Uganda because of problems with their travel documents. The next morning in the opening plenary session, Foreign Minister Ngulinzira, with details on the powers of the president and government, outlined how the government's previous offer would work.[35] In his response that afternoon, Commissioner Bizimungu went through the government's proposals point by point, finding them too vague or a duplication of the existing constitution. He proposed instead a "National Presidential Council," melding the RPF's National Reconciliation Council and presidential troika proposals. The Presidential Council would do everything from initiating legislation to exercising control over government and declaring war or states of emergency. The government would be left with proposing the budget to the Presidential Council and drafting decrees for the council's approval and promulgation. Such were the comprehensive powers and inclusive membership of the council that Bizimungu suggested it could be called "The Broad-based Presidential Council."[36]

In exchanges the following day, the government side amplified its proposals, while the RPF countered that it preferred sharing executive powers in collective decision making but could accept the transfer of these powers to other institutions. In the RPF's view, the government proposals echoed the 1991 constitution. Commissioner Bizimungu insisted, "We do not care to be offered the June 10 Constitution." To prove that the 1991 constitution had not changed much in Rwanda, Bizimungu referred to a letter of September 22 from Prime Minister Nsengiyaremye to President Habyarimana noting the ways in which the president under that constitution was blocking the actions of government.[37]

Ngulinzira told the plenary that the National Presidential Council was unwieldy, duplicative of existing institutions, and ambiguous as to its place in the hierarchy. The government's proposals on the other hand provided a series of amendments to make the governmental system work effectively. The point was to make sure that "the fate of the nation was not in the hands of one man."[38] So at the conclusion of the first plenary session, despite signals out of Dar es Salaam, Addis, and Kampala, the RPF was reiterating in new guise its shared executive proposal, and the government was sticking to its narrow interpretation of power sharing within the cabinet. The two sides appeared locked into their respective positions.

Caucusing on October 5, our Observer group once again concluded that the two parties held different definitions even of what they had mutually accepted. With similar phrasings, they were, in fact, talking past each other. Moreover, the Ugandan delegate suggested that the RPF was being encouraged in its proposal for a collective executive by opposition parties in Kigali, who wanted to use RPF pressure in breaking Habyarimana's control of national institutions.[39] Now in a meeting with the Facilitator, Observers agreed that "while we had more clearly defined the position of the two sides, little real progress had been made."[40] The RPF had told several Observers and intimated in the plenary that it would be flexible about the government's proposal, provided it could be amended to meet their concerns, but the Front's initial riposte suggested that it would fight over every clause.[41]

THE OBSERVERS ENGAGE

With the stalemate of the last session threatening to perpetuate itself, we huddled with both sides. Over breakfast with US and German Observers, the government's team leader, Ambassador Kanyarushoki, was blunt. The Front was demanding more executive powers than the government could possibly concede. However, RPF's concerns about the president being able to obstruct cabinet decisions were genuine. The government proposals addressed these concerns by making it impossible for the president to act without consent of the cabinet or national assembly. Pressed on what would happen if the president acted in defiance of the constitution or peace agreement, Kanyarushoki said that the president could be impeached.[42]

In informal meetings with Observers the same morning, RPF negotiators Bizimungu and Mazimpaka elaborated on their concerns about the government proposal. In their view, the government was simply repackaging the existing constitution with no means to prevent the president from abusing his powers or reneging on the peace agreement. They feared that the president would obstruct and frustrate the peace process, using terror tactics and his control of groups like the MRND youth to abort the transition.[43]

At the next plenary session, Foreign Minister Ngulinzira described how powers would devolve from president to cabinet. If the president sought to block implementation of government policies, the impeachment process offered a remedy. Surprised by the government offering the impeachment idea, the RPF side sought adjournment for private meetings with the Rwandan side. These consultations continued for the next two days. However, by October 10, Ngulinzira reported that an impasse had been reached in bilateral discussions. We asked that an accounting of points of agreement and points of discord be put before the plenary. The foreign minister, on behalf of the negotiators, went down a list of twelve items on which there was convergence, five items on which there was partial convergence, and ten items on which there was disagreement. The main issue was the role of the president in decision making. In Ngulinzira's characterization, the RPF wanted a total transfer of power from the president to the Council of Ministers; the government side, in contrast, was urging a semipresidential system, political efficacy, and separation of powers.

The RPF representatives said that they did not intend to exclude any party or any person from contributing to the transition; they wanted to make sure that no party or person could block the transition process. The mechanism of government should be efficient, transparent, and broad-based. The head of state might have prerogatives, but he should share his powers with other forces in the executive. The RPF urged the government to distinguish between the exercise of presidential power and presidential prerogatives.[44]

There was enough give in the two statements that I pressed the parties to meet again in head-to-head negotiations and pin down areas of commonality. Over the weekend, the parties worked out broad agreement on major issues. This time, Commissioner Bizimungu briefed the October 12 plenary on behalf of the negotiators: the parties had agreed that the incumbent president, Juvénal Habyarimana, would remain in power until elections at the end of the interim period, exercising certain prerogatives and participating in decision making, but that executive power would be exercised collectively in the Council of Ministers. The presidential "suspense veto" had evolved into an obligation to sign decrees and laws in ten days. The president would have the usual duties of appointing the prime minister and ambassadors as well as signing treaties, pardons, and orders to mint money. But the proposing of laws went to the Council of Ministers. Yet to be resolved was who would be the guarantor of national unity and judicial independence, who would get to address the nation, who was to be chief of armed forces, and who had the power to dissolve the national assembly. In effect, while the issues of assuring continuity of government had been resolved, the means of managing national crises had not.[45]

The negotiators went back into closed session. The following day, Foreign Minister Ngulinzira summarized further aspects of their agreement. The president would sanction and promulgate laws without right of veto. The "Government in Council" would safeguard national sovereignty, assure national defense, and organize the armed forces. War and peace would be decided by the council, authorized by the national assembly, and declared by the president. The prime minister would declare national emergencies. Key issues outstanding were what to do in case of presidential vacancy; how the national assembly might be dissolved; and who would name the prime minister, nominate judges, and authorize nominations to civilian positions, as well as who was responsible for drafting the "national program." Nor had it been agreed whether the president would remain commander-in-chief.

Once the principle of "Government in Council" had been accepted, the devolution of executive powers to the Council of Ministers had proceeded very rapidly. Observers cautioned that the notion could work only if authorities in Kigali agreed to both the concept and the pattern of devolution. I urged that keeping the president as commander-in-chief was vital for the functioning of the transition system and necessary in keeping Habyarimana committed to the peace process.[46]

Wrapping Up Arusha IV

On the evening of October 17, Commissioner Bizimungu informed the plenary that all matters regarding executive power had been decided except for the questions of presidential vacancy and who dissolves the national assembly. The president would be commander-in-chief. Authority to make judicial appointments would be vested in a new Supreme Council of the Judiciary, thus finessing the question of who would safeguard judicial autonomy. Decisions in government would be by consensus, but after a second reading, decisions would be by two-thirds majority. Questions of defense, security, and amending the peace accord would require consensus. Foreign Minister Ngulinzira told observers that the negotiated settlement had been endorsed by the Council of Ministers in Kigali with Habyarimana's MRND ministers present. The negotiators promised signature to a protocol by October 22.[47] RPF negotiator Rudasingwa told Observers that the Front was satisfied with the discussion on presidential power, the most critical area for them. There should be no major problems on judiciary or the national assembly. The RPF was concerned, however, to get the refugee issue back on the political agenda.[48]

RESIDUAL ISSUES

While the parties had finally negotiated the devolution of executive power, there were vital elements of power sharing still unresolved—namely, the structure of the judicial system, the naming of the interim prime minister, the composition of the broad-based government, and the formation of a national assembly. Dr. Rudasingwa's optimism as regards the judiciary was warranted. Both sides apparently welcomed the creation of an autonomous judicial organization that would make bench appointments. The parties seemed anxious to prove their commitment to the rule of law through a thorough reform of judicial structure.[49]

Rudasingwa's optimism was sadly premature on the other outstanding issues. Wrangling over the interim prime minister's slot split the existing coalition government and the main opposition party, the *Mouvement Démocratique Républicain* or MDR. Differences over the role of the national assembly and how it should be established persisted throughout subsequent negotiations. When and if elections should take place was hotly debated. In Kigali, there was widespread concern among the political elite over what negotiators may have ceded in the negotiations.

PRESIDENTIAL ANGST

President Habyarimana was quite negative on the results of the power-sharing negotiations. He complained, in a private meeting with US

Ambassador Flaten, that the foreign minister and prime minister were not keeping him informed on the concessions they had been accepting in Arusha. In particular, he saw power devolving from elected institutions (the presidency and the National Commission for Development, or CND) to appointed officials in the government and the transitional national assembly. In an unelected government or national assembly, the opposition could join forces with the RPF to override or even exclude from power the president and his party, which had the mandate of the people. Early elections were the only way to meet donor requirements for democratic progress. If negotiators concluded an unacceptable settlement, the president warned, the people would substitute a civil war for a war on the border.[50]

NAMING THE PRIME MINISTER

The power-sharing protocol had devolved presidential prerogatives to a transitional "Council of Ministers," but who would lead the council? The government team asked that the incumbent, Prime Minister Nsengiyaremye, be kept in office, as President Habyarimana had been. Observers saw this as a scarcely disguised ploy by the incumbent through his political ally, Foreign Minister Ngulinzira, to preserve his position and power by negotiation. The RPF response appeared to be procedural: the peace negotiations should not be used to confirm the current prime minister in his office. Observers again sensed that in this the Front might have been colluding with internal opposition that clearly wanted Nsengiyaremye out of the way.[51]

SHARING CABINET POWER

More difficult yet was the issue of how portfolios were to be allocated within the council of government. Initially, the government side seems to have been in favor of an early naming of ministers. But then it backed off and came up with a formula of dividing portfolios in tiers by function: national sovereignty, economics and development services, and social services. The government would offer the RPF at least one portfolio in each functional area and limit each party to but one portfolio in the national-sovereignty function and two portfolios in the other tiers. The RPF told observers that the formula was acceptable, but it insisted that specific portfolios had to be assigned to respective parties (without naming the officeholder) and incorporated into the peace agreement.

The Front, which had derided a narrow focus on distribution of port-folios, now pushed for conclusion on this matter. Spokesman Bizimungu made it clear that agreement on portfolios was necessarily antecedent to other discussions still on the table.[52] But the government backed off again; early distribution of portfolios might undercut the authority of ministers now in place. We sensed a disconnect between a negotiating team want-ing closure on power sharing and the government back home not wanting to be superseded by negotiations in Arusha. Moreover, the allocation of portfolios to parties by functional area would strip the MRND of key portfolios and reduce the party to 25 percent representation in cabinet, less than a blocking third.[53]

ESTABLISHING A TRANSITIONAL NATIONAL ASSEMBLY

There was even less progress in negotiations over the transitional na-tional assembly. Under the 1991 constitution, the existing assembly (CND) was to serve out its term and be replaced when a new multiparty assembly was elected. Negotiated protocols had mentioned an interim assembly but with no intimation on how it should be set up. The Observers weighed in with several scenarios for the parties' consideration, such as a bicameral house with the transitional assembly as the upper and controlling house, or an expanded assembly leaving the CND in place but countering their influence with appointed members (the Ugandan proposal).[54]

On the morning of October 23, Ngulinzira told us that the Council of Ministers in Kigali was discussing an entirely appointed assembly.[55] At plenary on October 24, the foreign minister said the government wanted a national assembly that was representative of the peoples' wishes. To that end, the government delegations had proposed direct legislative elections in three months, then offered indirect elections, an electoral college, a con-stituent assembly with seats reserved for the RPF, a nominated second house with special powers, or an expanded CND.

The Front accepted none of these compromise proposals. Commis-sioner Mazimpaka argued that the CND had been superseded by the gov-ernment's proposal of a transitional national assembly. Nonetheless, the negotiators were still looking for ways to set up a national assembly, and Mazimpaka promised, "We will find them."[56]

PUSHING TOWARD SIGNATURE

By October 27, the parties had agreed on immunities and an oath for the president, had transferred tourism and information from the presidency to newly created "offices," and had worked out the organization of judicial power as well as the attributes of the Supreme Court. There was, however, no progress on how and when government portfolios would be handed out or how the national assembly was to be organized. Recognizing progress in "peripheral matters," the RPF said it would wait for the government's proposals, but absent progress on these, it suggested a pause. Ngulinzira noted with asperity that the agreed matters were not peripheral and that the government had offered several compromise proposals on the assembly, but the RPF had offered nothing but its original idea of a nominated assembly.[57]

By October 28, Ambassador Mpungwe had informed Observers that President Habyarimana could not accept the RPF's idea of an appointed assembly and that the Council of Ministers in Kigali was deadlocked on the matter. The prime minister wanted the foreign minister to press ahead and get any deal he could, while the president insisted that Rwandans work out a common position. Both sides in Arusha then agreed to initial whatever had been agreed and take a pause. At the plenary, however, Minister Diria said that the two parties would sign a "Protocol on Power Sharing, Part One" and return in fifteen days to deal with refugees, the formation of the government, and the nature and functions of the national assembly. Foreign Minister Ngulinzira suggested instead first dealing with the formation of government and the assembly when talks reconvened, followed by opening up military integration issues, then pausing before returning to conclude military issues and refugee matters.[58]

Even as a protocol outlining areas of agreement and a joint communiqué were being drafted, the Facilitator was hoping for a breakthrough on the national assembly question. In conversation with Robert Bentley and me, Ambassador Mpungwe reviewed the alternatives. We pointed out that an elective process would move the current CND aside constitutionally.

Barring that, some way had to be found that included CND members in the peace process or they would undermine it from without. Moreover, the peace process should move quickly through to elections that would break political deadlocks and remove ambiguities of mandate. Mpungwe, supported by the Ugandan high commissioner, insisted that elections would be counterproductive in the Rwandan situation, a position that Foreign Minister Diria also held. We, nonetheless, stressed the importance of understanding why President Habyarimana was opposed to an appointed legislature and the value of working toward a deal that did not exclude any major political force.[59]

On October 30, 1992, the two parties signed a protocol on preliminary agreements regarding power sharing that devolved powers of the presidency to a Council of Ministers, reestablished an autonomous Supreme Court, and projected decision making in council by consensus with overrides requiring a two-thirds vote. Further negotiations were suspended until November 15.[60]

The Joint Political Military Commission—an Instructive Aside

Toward the end of the fourth set of negotiations at Arusha, the Joint Political Military Commission (JPMC) met for the third time.[61] The JPMC was supposed to be a central transitional institution charged with enforcing military and political agreements. The Facilitator, Foreign Minister Diria, and the Observers had urged that the commission actively engage on the questions of ceasefire violations and ethnic violence that had enflamed the rhetoric and slowed the process of political negotiations on the peace accord. Yet, at its third meeting, the commission did not live up to its mandate.

POST AND RIPOSTE

The opening remarks of Dr. Mapuranga, as deputy secretary general of the OAU, highlighted a core problem: OAU's monitoring group, which was to have been the international guarantors of the ceasefire, would only be fully deployed by October 23. Mapuranga also reported that the delimitation of the neutral zone between forces had only just begun. In other words, the ceasefire was tenuously holding all by itself, without international mapping or monitoring. Mapuranga noted that this was a "pioneering role for the OAU, hitherto outside the domain of the Organization's preoccupations." He hoped that the work of the JPMC and the experience of the NMOG "would be of immense benefit to the organization."[62]

Meanwhile, all had not been quiet on the northern front. The NMOG commander, General Opalaye, reported seventy-one ceasefire violations since the last JPMC, including a series of attacks and counterattacks around the northern town of Byumba. The JPMC report characterized the discussions on violations as "exhaustive"; it also found the debate on the withdrawal of foreign troops to be "lengthy and at times heated."[63] The chair and the Facilitator had to intervene to keep the discussions on track.

The issue of radio propaganda brought an admission from the OAU that it was not able to monitor radio broadcasts because they were in Kinyarwanda.[64] When the RPF raised the issue of human rights abuses, General Opalaye noted that NMOG had no mandate to deal with human rights violations per se.[65] Similarly, administrative questions met with bureaucratic referrals to heads of state, the Rwandan government, or a study committee.[66]

When the commission received a report from the Facilitator on the progress of the negotiations, the government side endorsed the brief, whereas the RPF blamed the slow progress of negotiations on Habyarimana and the MRND party. In the RPF's view, the government's negotiating team was not representative of the government or the political parties in Rwanda. This outburst, calling into question the negotiating process, brought rejoinders from the Facilitator, the commission chairman, Uganda, and Germany. Observers noted their confidence in "the eventual success of the negotiations."[67]

THE JPMC—AN ASSESSMENT

The October meeting of the Joint Political Military Commission started cordially enough. Some of these representatives had met before in Addis; some had fought against each other on the battlefield; there were embraces all around. In the meetings, however, postures were hostile. As usual, the rhetorical points went to the RPF, with the government representatives thrown on the defensive. Both courtesies and contestations belied the seriousness of the issues being considered.

The Patriotic Front's interventions showed two core concerns: the continuing power of Habyarimana as well as that of the MRND hierarchy, and the continual ethnic attacks within Rwanda, for which the RPF blamed the president. The government's liberality in suggesting an International Human Rights Commission did not mitigate the reality of local ethnic conflict, which the government was either unwilling or unable to control, and for which the OAU/NMOG disavowed any responsibility.

The facts that the NMOG was not able to monitor incendiary radio broadcasts, had not delimited the neutral zone three months after the ceasefire agreement, and was just moving out of Kigali to the field as an observer force all pointed to how poorly the OAU was prepared for the task at hand. The Joint Political Military Commission did serve a useful purpose in being a point of some convivial contact, a sounding board for complaints, and a channel for reporting ceasefire violations, but the ceasefire held because both sides wanted it to, not because of any international deterrent.

The Peace Process Flounders

Arusha IV closed down on October 31, 1992, with the promise of reconvening a fortnight later. Few of the government delegates returning from power-sharing discussions in Arusha were prepared for the political hailstorm that attended their return to Kigali. After all, the basic framework of transition institutions had been agreed to in Arusha III and confirmed by the Council of Ministers. Habyarimana had committed to "a battle of ideas rather than arms," and in a "Referendum Day" speech on September 25 he asked the RPF to do the same.[68] After angry exchanges of letters and apparent disarray in regime and opposition circles, the cabinet had on September 29 negotiated open-ended instructions for Arusha IV. Foreign Minister Ngulinzira took that mandate as a confirmation of his leadership and in Arusha negotiated within what he considered his parameters.[69]

During the long October negotiations, distance grew between the presidency and the government's negotiating team. Habyarimana several times complained to diplomats that the negotiating team had exceeded its authority.[70] Supporting the Arusha negotiations and calling on Habyarimana to resign, opposition parties organized massive demonstrations in Kigali on October 10, thus linking progress in Arusha with the end of Habyarimana's rule. Meanwhile, in Kigali, the Hutu supremacist party, the CDR, flexed its muscle in violent demonstrations over the arrest of party members suspected of politically inspired murders and in protest of the Arusha negotiations. On October 29, MRND ministers angrily protested biased coverage of the October 27 cabinet meeting by the opposition minister of information.

In a postnegotiations meeting, Habyarimana gave Ambassador Flaten and me a pessimistic assessment. He clearly felt that negotiations had gotten out of hand by going beyond the agreed terms of reference and not responding to presidential queries. The president detailed at length an offer he made to meet with his old companion-in-arms Alexis Kanyarengwe, now chairman of the RPF. A leak to RPF negotiators aborted the offer of a meeting. The president thought he should rather meet with General Kagame, the true power in the RPF. He was worried about the lack of progress in discovering a formula for the transitional national assembly and the uncertainties regarding allocation of seats in the cabinet.

Habyarimana was clearly having second thoughts about the derogation of his powers to a council that other political forces might control. And he was particularly sensitive that an elected parliament, the CND, might be replaced by an appointed assembly. The president felt that some electoral sanction on the transition process was needed, either through an elected assembly or a referendum on the negotiated agreement.

We tried to convince the president of the significant role he could still play: under the protocol on power sharing, he would remain chief of state and commander-in-chief, he still would name high government officials, and he could propose legislation and build coalitions to pass his program. The protocol of October 30 was but an outline of the interim order. With strong leadership, the president could seize the moral ground as peacemaker and provide substantive direction for the next negotiations. Habyarimana did not appear convinced.[71]

The Arusha political negotiations had stalled on the core question of power sharing. While the negotiating team had made major progress in coming up with power-sharing structures, it had failed to communicate effectively with Kigali authorities or to gain the adherence of the president, the MNRD, and more radical parties like the CDR to the provisions being negotiated. Moreover, political parties within the internal opposition were at odds as to next steps in the negotiating strategy.[72] Within a couple days of the protocol's signing, the suspension of talks was pushed to November 23. The understandings of Arusha on power sharing were now to be tested within the Rwandan political landscape.

Everyone had expected this to be a difficult negotiation; most understood that sharing of power was the keystone of the negotiations. The RPF said that devolution of executive power was the most important aspect of these power-sharing talks. That process had in fact progressed rather steadily with the apparent support of the Council of Ministers in Kigali. The negotiations had proceeded in a businesslike manner, with most of the debate going head-to-head in closed session. In the plenary, there was less of the rhetorical sparring that characterized both the ceasefire talks and the rule of law negotiations. Informal conversations with Observers were frank, with serious discussions of options. Yet, the talks were hung up; impasse loomed on the horizon.

Lessons We Learned

These two sessions on power sharing carried some hard lessons. The high plateau of constitutional principles gave way to a valley of contest and contrariety. International interveners took some valuable instructions in political conflict.

- *If you want a realistic projection, do not ask the negotiators.* Negotiators set October 10 as the terminal date of political negotiations. By October 30, negotiators suspended talks on agenda item two: power sharing. More was at stake here than the optimism of the negotiators suggested.

- *If politics is about keeping, increasing, or demonstrating power, then negotiations on power sharing are counterintuitive.*[73] At the end of the negotiating game, the contending parties want it all. We considered inclusive decision making and sharing of power to be intrinsic elements of a sustainable, democratic polity; the contenders did not see it that way.

- *Power-sharing negotiations get complex with multiple claimants to power.* In Rwanda, an entrenched regime, a newly birthed internal opposition, and an armed insurgency were all vying for a durable and dominant share of power in a tripartite tug of war. In fact, among government negotiators were some who wanted Habyarimana's regime out of the way. The RPF often pressed for positions of the internal opposition as well as its own.

- *You do not have to define power before negotiating it.* But once negotiations had devolved powers from the president to the broad-based transitional cabinet, the locus of power and the focus of negotiations were clear. The RPF's call for early allocation of portfolios in that cabinet stirred up a hornet's nest within the internal parties and undermined cohesion of the coalition government.

- *Politics is about numbers.* Initially, power-sharing negotiations in Arusha had the assent of the coalition cabinet; all ministers should benefit from the devolution of presidential powers. But when MRND ministers saw their dominance sliced back in the projected allocation of portfolios, they realized that they would be outnumbered, unable to achieve their political goals or even to defend their political future.

- *Why not elections; why not test the people's will?* Security and social disruption were the reasons given, but delegates at Arusha realized that the MRND would win any near-term election. Negotiators at Arusha were actually vying for place in an elitist arrangement of designated government portfolios and appointed parliamentary seats that could guarantee their influence over the transition.

FOUR

Impasse

President Juvénal Habyarimana was in a dour mood when Ambassador Flaten and I met him after suspension of negotiations on power sharing. According to the protocol just signed, the power-sharing agreement would devolve his executive powers to a multiparty cabinet. Initial negotiations on the makeup of cabinet posts suggested that his ruling party, the MRND, would be shorn of critical portfolios and assume a minority status. Moreover, the chance of gaining influence in interim institutions through elections for the national assembly now dimmed as the political elite gravitated toward the notion of a nominated assembly. All this was negotiated by a delegation out of reach in Arusha and through a foreign minister and prime minister who were not consulting with or reporting to the president. We tried to convince the president to get out in front of the negotiations and put his imprint on the interim structures. As subsequent events would show, the president instead let the temporary suspension of negotiations fall into a full-fledged impasse.[1]

In this chapter, I will again examine the issues at stake, review the period of formal suspension, dissect the solutions offered by the clergy contact group, and assess the roles of diplomats and the Facilitator in getting the peace process back on track. Resurgence of ethnic violence and renewed war on the front brought the impasse to its denouement.

Issues at Stake

For all the hope generated by the initial success of power-sharing negotiations, we should not have been surprised to find a barricade at the end of this road. The process of conflict mitigation often leads to "impasse," as

practitioners and analysts have attested.[2] Issues that occasion such blockages are multiple.

*Is power sharing a viable objective of conflict resolution in a deeply rooted
conflict?*[3] Power-sharing negotiations often end up being more about controlling power than sharing it. Neither at Arusha nor in Kigali was there
much focus on "a necessary shared future." The belief that "if we do not
dominate, we will be dominated" remained the leitmotif.[4] The first question then was whether a future for the contenders could be so constructed
that real power might be shared.

If communication is the key, who is talking to whom?[5] What appeared to
us Observers as improved communication in face-to-face talks in Arusha
was, in fact, indicative of the distance between understandings arrived at
in Arusha and politics in Kigali. Moreover, in the close-knit circles of
Rwanda's tiny capital, the breakdown of communication was patently evident. Communication breaks down and impasse creeps in.

*How do negotiators or interveners discern between opening bids and fun-
damental interests of the contending parties?* While basic human needs might
undergird the antagonists' positions, it may be sufficient to realize that respective parties saw their political future at stake.[6] At this point, the particular ambitions and visions of the parties become paramount and difficult to
unravel; solutions to the conflict also become particular, sui generis.

How does geographic distance affect the course of conflict resolution? Off-site
negotiation is a classic technique in getting parties in conflict away from
their usual haunts and focused on the common problem, but such isolated
negotiations begin to take on a dynamic of their own. Negotiators develop
a sense of empowerment and camaraderie; international interveners add
to the local feeling of importance.[7] Thus, returning to the domestic scene
is disruptive, especially if the achievements of the negotiation are frontally
challenged in the political marketplace.

Slowdown or Breakdown?

Did the suspension of November 1992 confirm the intractability of
the Rwandan conflict, or was this the proverbial "speed bump on the high-
way to progress"? Resistance in Kigali to the terms and direction of the

political negotiations was profound. Partisans of the pro-Arusha position confronted an anti-Arusha constellation. Denigration remained the mode for characterizing the other's position. The pro-Arusha "Concert for Peace" organized mass demonstrations deriding the president while the anti-Arusha Hutu extremists considered the pro-Arusha parties as "traitors."[8]

The profitability of continuing the conflict was questionable for either side; the war was bankrupting the Rwandan government, and President Museveni now was pushing the RPF to keep on the peace track.[9] Nonetheless, the costs of going ahead with negotiations on terms the other side could accept were unbearably high: either continued domination of the political process by the Habyarimana regime or revolutionary change of state institutions by the RPF and its allies. Thus, the impasse became a stable and self-serving stalemate.[10]

In retrospect, the second part of the power-sharing negotiations at Arusha failed in two ways. First, although the instructions for that session were flexible, some of the "creative" solutions put forward—especially an appointed national assembly and a classification of government portfolios by type—went beyond the negotiators' mandate. Second, the resultant distribution of portfolios in government, along with the proposed two-thirds voting override when consensus failed, were not realistic given the political landscape in Rwanda. It asked the presidential party, still dominant in all institutions and across the country, to give up its ascendency for a minority position where it could not protect its own interests. No wonder that Habyarimana started looking for "off-the-table" solutions.[11]

SUSPENSION DYNAMICS

Wanting a suspension but worried about a possible breakdown of the ceasefire and renewed armed conflict, Habyarimana hesitated to request a recess. At Arusha, however, the RPF, frustrated by the lack of progress, proposed the pause.[12] It remained possible that the disagreements and tensions that occasioned a suspension could crystallize into a hardened antagonism or that the two parties, relying on assumed goodwill, might fail to record achieved understandings.[13] The Tanzanian Facilitator, sensing the danger of an informal suspension, insisted on a formal initialing of the agreed points.[14]

According to US embassy reports, once the suspension of negotiations was decided, internal political discussions took on a rhythm and a seriousness that they had not seen in some time. The president and prime minister met October 30 to hash out their differences, the first meeting in weeks. Habyarimana's MRND agreed to meet and discuss differences with opposition parties; all internal parties agreed to meet with the president. Out of these meetings came two new initiatives. Both were efforts to break the negotiating logjam but, in effect, they sidestepped the negotiating process. With the newfound amity, the parties revived the notion of the parties in government meeting with the Front at some neutral spot and working through differences on power sharing. This would, in effect, take the political negotiations out of government control and out of the Arusha process.[15]

On the other hand, President Habyarimana, at his November 3 meeting with the political parties, broached the idea of inviting religious leaders, as representatives of civil society, to broker an equitable political solution.[16] This idea short-circuited the intraparty dialogue. All parties decided to wait and see what the church leaders would come up with before taking their own stance.

Even as church leaders met with political parties to open discussions on a common position for the Arusha negotiations, the debate over the Arusha process took on its usual manifestations. On November 4, at a meeting of the MRND National Committee, some delegates castigated the Protocol of Agreement on Power-Sharing of October 30 as a coup d'état in the making. Of particular concern were protocol articles 14, 21, and 46: article 14 gave the RPF veto powers over any expansion of the political field; article 21 provided for a two-thirds override in case consensus broke down in government; and article 41 called for the replacement of communal mayors without establishing criteria for the change. With no chance to expand representation in government, MRND leaders felt that proposed portfolio allocations would take away their ability to control national policy or influence local government.

While not specifically attacking the power-sharing protocol in the meeting's communiqué, the MRND leaders criticized the prime minister and foreign minister for their conduct of negotiations.[17] Moreover, four of the MRND ministers sent a letter to the prime minister "rejecting" the offending articles.[18] As if to assuage his party leadership, on November 15, President Habyarimana gave one of his more notorious speeches in which he characterized the Arusha protocols, in contrast to the institutions of the Rwandan state, as mere "pieces of paper." This drew an open-letter rebuttal from the prime minister and an opposition demonstration march in Kigali four days later in which some fifty persons were injured.[19]

Tanzania as the Facilitator had been active in the pause, receiving visits from President Museveni, Habyarimana's cabinet director Ruhigira, and RPF military commander Kagame. The Tanzanians twice convoked representatives of Observer states to discuss ways to get over the impasse.[20] In the November 20 meeting, the Facilitator and the Observers agreed that to preserve momentum and avoid endangering the ceasefire, talks would reconvene on November 23 as scheduled. The Rwanda government had proposed at the end of the last session that the talks open with discussions on military integration. This would give time for decision makers in Kigali to work out compromises on power sharing. The Facilitator was willing to put military integration at the top of the agenda but had not yet secured the assent of the RPF.[21]

So, on November 23, Foreign Minister Ngulinzira led his negotiating team back to Arusha. Since the talks had formally only been suspended, he was still theoretically operating under the instructions issued at the end of September. In reality, the foreign minister had already exceeded the parameters of his mandate at the end of the last session. He was now going back without a consensus about power sharing in the transitional cabinet or an agreement on how to constitute the transitional national assembly. Moreover, military integration did not lead the discussions. The RPF team insisted that political discussions be on the agenda as well. Formal negotiations opened November 25 but accomplished little as the negotiators awaited word on the church leaders' deliberations.[22]

The Bishops' Proposal

It had been President Habyarimana's intention to have religious leaders present at his first postsuspension meeting with the governmental parties on November 3. That did not happen; instead, Habyarimana informed the parties of his desire to engage church leadership in the search for an equitable solution. The first meeting between the clergy and political leaders could not be arranged until November 11, even as the clock was ticking on a return to the negotiating table.

A BIFURCATED PROPOSAL

After many informal and formal discussions, the bishops finally came forward with their suggestions.[23] Initially, the religious leaders outlined two options: one predicated on a percentage breakdown, and the other on a numerical allocation of seats. Under the first proposal the president's party, the MRND, would get 35 percent of the seats, the "Concert Parties" (MDR, PL, and PSD) 35 percent, the RPF 20 percent, and other parties 10 percent. The second proposal would have a government composed of three members each from the MRND, MDR, PL, PSD, and RPF, one member from the PDC, and three others from other parties. With an MNRD president and MDR prime minister, this would make a twenty-one-member cabinet.

Along with these possible formulas for the cabinet, the bishops proposed that article 14 of the October 30 "Protocol on Power-Sharing" be interpreted as encouraging the inclusion of other parties, hence the percentages of seats allocated to an unspecified "other." It also recommended that the national assembly be composed of members appointed by the "national conventions" of the parties, that it be named "The National Legislative Council," and that it be constituted of no more than forty members. Parties would decide distribution of seats in concert with the RPF. The bishops also recommended a code of ethical and institutional standards for party participation in government and the assembly.

The fruit of this consultation was noteworthy in several respects. First, the pattern of allocation in the first proposal gave the president's party, the MRND, an automatic block on hostile motions in government; in the second proposal, single parties would have at most four votes and need a coalition of seven to block the two-thirds override. The president liked the first option since it gave his party the protection against radical reform (not to mention punitive sanctions) that his regime so desperately feared. The prime minister from the MDR preferred the second since it ascribed equality among the major parties and gave the MDR, with the prime minister's seat, the same power in government as the MRND with its presidential vote.[24]

Second, the issue of inclusiveness (article 14 and the Code of Party Ethics) circled around a major problem, namely, the CDR (Coalition for the Defense of the Republic), a throwback to Hutu majoritarian politics of the Kayibanda regime and northern regional ascendency of the Habyarimana era. Since the RPF was obviously opposed to the CDR and its pro-Hutu ideology, the CDR seemed to many a barrier to peace and tranquility in a new Rwanda.[25]

Of parties not in government, the CDR claimed the largest political base and proved this in antigovernment, anti-Arusha demonstrations on October 18.[26] Although CDR leaders were intellectuals educated abroad, its cadre came from restless, landless youth given to thuggery. Some ranking officials in the MRND detested the CDR, but it was connected to the presidency through Habyarimana's wife's lineage.[27]

Third, the bishops' contact group and its proposals had no standing in the Arusha political negotiations. While their status as counselors to the domestic political process had a long tradition in Rwanda, in the context of political negotiations with an insurgent force, the president had, in effect, deputized them. The hard political questions were delegated to a religious committee rather than bargained out in the political market place. As chief representatives of civil society and institutions committed to civil peace, the religious leadership was bound to look for a solution that they felt would be salable to the greatest number within Rwanda's now fractured social and political order and would hurry the peace process along.

A FINAL PROPOSAL

Both the president and the prime minister asked the bishops to find a compromise between the two modes of allocating seats in government that they had initially put forward. The bishops met with party leaders to work out a synthesis while negotiators in Arusha waited for instructions.[28] While many expected a final proposal that would find a compromise between the two options, the church leaders' proposal tabled November 27 was a slight variant on the second option that favored the internal opposition. Three ministerial portfolios each would be allocated to the MRND, MDR, PL, PSD, and RPF, as well as two seats for the PDC and three for other parties. The Council of Ministers the next day hurriedly endorsed the proposal before the MRND ministers arrived at the meeting. The MRND ministers then announced that they would not participate in the transition government on the basis of that proposal.[29]

The presidential ploy to involve civil society in the negotiating process had backfired. The clergy had specified a formula that curtailed the weight of the president and his party in council with no apparent trade-off. The allocation of seats, if the "progressive forces" held together in coalition discipline, assured a two-thirds majority and a hammerlock on decisions in cabinet and an appointed assembly. The religious leaders' intervention, far from bridging party differences on power sharing, had in fact solidified divisions.

President Habyarimana would, over the next several months, articulate in various ways his deeply felt antagonism to the bishops' formula, even as he agreed under pressure to accept the proposal, at least as a framework for future negotiations.[30] He felt that the alliance of opposition parties intended to overthrow the president, not to share power. And he continued to hold that an electoral process, not arbitrary allocation of positions, was the only real way to tell who represented the people. Moreover, to be legitimate, any negotiated agreement should be sanctioned by representatives of the people or by referendum.

Diplomatic Engagement

The suspension of the Arusha talks and the failure of the Rwandan political elite to agree on a formula for power sharing in government brought the position of the diplomatic corps into heightened relief. Already the papal nuncio and dean of the diplomatic corps, Monsignor Giuseppe Bertello, was deeply engaged as chair of the clergy contact group and thus committed to their final recommendation. The inference was that the corps would line up behind the bishops' position. The ambassadors of Western states having "Observer" status in the Arusha negotiations, however, eschewed taking sides in the internal dialogue.[31]

THE WESTERN GROUP

In contrast to the Observers in Arusha who were daily buttonholing the representatives of the two sides, offering options, suggesting negotiating formats, or even proposing language for protocols of agreement, the ambassadors in Kigali took a more discreet diplomatic stance. As the Arusha process lost momentum and intraparty communication in Kigali dried up in October, the Western ambassadors concluded that "the parties need to find a mechanism for dialogue." Embassies could not force the parties to talk.[32] After the Arusha talks had been suspended, the Western ambassadors in Kigali decided to "continue to urge internal dialogue among parties but not to press any specific formulas to break the impasse."[33] As the arguments among political elite in Kigali grew in fervor, Ambassador Flaten concluded in mid-November, "I believe it is still too early for us to select a preferred plan. I will remain in touch with the other ambassadors to explore the possibility that a concerted effort by foreign diplomats might at some time be appropriate in breaking these difficult impasses."[34]

Once the bishops had presented a concrete proposal, the question then became what the Kigali diplomats should say about it. The nuncio felt that the president had no alternative but to accept the proposal he had asked the bishops to devise. Bertello wanted the Western ambassadors to join him in a demarche to the president supporting the proposal. The Belgian and French ambassadors were not that enthusiastic about the proposal but willing to go along with the nuncio. Moreover, the French ambassador warned that should the president refuse the proposal and try an end run around the Arusha process, France would, no doubt, have to reevaluate its support for the regime.[35]

In a personal initiative, Habyarimana's director of cabinet Enoch Ruhigira came to see Ambassador Flaten, recommending a demarche by the United States and possibly France to persuade the president to accept the bishops' proposal. He specifically discouraged a joint approach with the nuncio since many around the president were suspicious of the nuncio's role in the bishops' discussions. Flaten replied that instructions from Washington and consultation with Paris would have to precede such an approach. In his dispatch to Washington, Flaten recommended that, if there were an opportunity to see the president, diplomats should take "a general approach to President Habyarimana, urging him to work with the context of the bishops' proposal, but stopping short of endorsing its specifics."[36]

In Kigali, ambassadors, accredited to the president and carrying on state-to-state bilateral programs, were also dealing with multiple claimants to power in the personalities of party leaders. The claims and interests of the RPF were known in Kigali only from external reporting. In this context, a tilt toward any particular formula inevitably favored one side over the other in the internal debate and discounted RPF interests. As Ambassador Flaten noted, "There is a reasonable consensus among Western ambassadors that for the moment our role is essentially one of encouraging dialogue among internal parties."[37]

But success in bilateral diplomacy began to wear down when confronted with specifics of the Arusha negotiations. Relations with the president, well known as a champion of bilateral rural-development programs, became more challenging as diplomats promoted democratic opening and supported the Arusha process. Not only was the French ambassador beginning to question the value of French engagement with the regime, but the American ambassador was never sure of the Rwandan president's commitment to democratization.[38] Belgium, with a domestic constituency focused on human rights, had increasing problems with the presidency. Germany, which took an economic brief concentrated on its two-year development program, was drawn into the political fray by its advocacy of democratic ideals.

What propelled Western cooperation on the issues at Arusha was a common commitment to human rights and democratic governance, which were seen as constituent elements of true development. The governance/development nexus had become a mantra for all major donors. The diplomatic structure of this commitment was regular trilateral consultation among the governments of Belgium, France, and the United States on Central African issues and among the governments of Belgium, France, and Germany as members of the European Community. With their capitals closely coordinating from the same ideological orientation, cooperation and consensus amongst Western ambassadors in Kigali was natural and necessary.

TANZANIA DEALS BILATERALLY

On November 30, the president made an unannounced trip to Dar es Salaam to meet with President Mwinyi. While the presidency suggested that the visit had been in the works for some time, it seemed obvious that the president was looking for a means of not acceding to the bishops' proposal. However, the Tanzanian president apparently convinced Habyarimana to move forward in negotiations using the religious leaders' proposal as a basis for discussions, as long as no major political bloc was permanently marginalized.

On December 1, Habyarimana addressed the nation in a speech that seemed to incorporate this understanding. Negotiations must avoid giving any single political group a permanent majority; the transition assembly could be appointed, but only if the transition was a brief, twelve-month period; local administration officials should be chosen by an early election; and the accords should be approved either by the current legislature or by a referendum.[39] In a follow-up letter to the prime minister, Cabinet Director Ruhigira referred to the president's discussions with the political parties and with the religious leaders whom he knew to be supported informally by the diplomatic community, although the diplomatic community had in fact avoided taking a position on the religious leaders' proposal. The letter asked the prime minister to transmit instructions to the Rwandan delegation in Arusha based on principles that followed the guidelines of the president's speech.[40]

Despite the Mwinyi-Habyarimana understanding, as interpreted by Habyarimana's speech, the coalition cabinet in Kigali was not able to formulate any instructions to the negotiators. But back in Arusha, Foreign Minister Ngulinzira claimed in a November 29 radio interview that the (truncated) cabinet's November 28 adoption of the bishops' recommendation gave him the legal mandate to move ahead in political negotiations.[41] On December 2, Ngulinzira told Observers in Arusha that in accord with the president's speech the day before, he was ready to move ahead on discussions on a transitional national assembly while awaiting further clarification on the assignment of portfolios within the transitional cabinet. The government side did not want to reopen articles in the October 30 protocol but rather to discuss their implementation in such a way as to avoid "blockages on the one hand and marginalization on the other."[42] The RPF still questioned the delegation's authority, but they agreed to continue discussions.

Meanwhile, actions taken by the government, without MRND agreement or presidential sanction, so angered Habyarimana that he refused to meet further with Nsengiyaremye. The MRND cabinet members threatened not to participate in whatever might be negotiated in Arusha. The CDR and some fringe parties took this impulse to its extreme by disowning the Arusha process in its entirety. Thus, as Ngulinzira was pushing toward a power-sharing agreement in Arusha, the political atmosphere in Kigali became increasingly rejectionist.[43]

DIRIA COMES CALLING

As political gridlock in Kigali undermined discussions in Arusha, the Tanzanian foreign minister and facilitator, Ahmed Hassan Diria, paid a visit to the Rwandan capital on December 9 and 10. This, Diria's first visit since taking over as facilitator of the peace process, gave him a chance to burnish his credentials as mediator.[44] Moreover, Diria needed to know what the real positions of the president and the prime minister were, as well as those of the MRND (a major part of the government), on an appointed assembly, division of portfolios, and duration of a transitional government. Finally, there was a growing impression at Arusha, held insistently by the RPF but increasingly by the government negotiating team and by the Tanzanians, that the main obstacle to settlement of outstanding issues was President Habyarimana himself.[45] From his meetings with the president, Diria had to extract concessions that would let the negotiations go forward.

At the conclusion of the foreign minister's visit, the Tanzanian ambassador in Kigali informed her colleagues that Habyarimana had agreed to a flexible time frame for the transition, an appointed transitional national assembly, and elections of local communal officers after the transition government was in place. The president was still insisting on 35 percent representation for MRND in the transition cabinet. Diria told him that was too high, that the president had to work out a compromise with the prime minister. He also suggested taking issues on which the cabinet was deadlocked to the Joint Political Military Committee for arbitration.[46]

The foreign minister was obviously anxious to put the understandings arrived at in Kigali in the best possible light. But the president's agreement to an appointed national assembly was conditional on some accommodation with the interests of the current elected assembly (the CND), as well as on some electoral process (whether popular referendum or endorsement of the CND) whereby the agreements made in Arusha would become the law of the land. Similarly, the president always wanted a short transition whose endpoint would be elections for all national institutions. Habyarimana's concessions were all made in view of extracting the principal point—namely, 35 percent of the portfolios in the transition cabinet for the MRND. In other words, there was to be no marginalization of a major political player. President Mwinyi had agreed to nonmarginalization as a cardinal principle of future negotiations.

Now Foreign Minister Diria had declared that Habyarimana's formulation of that principle was asking too much; he should rather work out an equitable allocation with the prime minister (who wanted Habyarimana and his party marginalized). In other words, the foreign minister punted, leaving Kigali with the major issue to be resolved further down the field at a later time. The Tanzanian team was aware that it was playing for field advantage. Ambassador Mpungwe told the US embassy in Dar es Salaam that, despite their doubts, the Tanzanian government had decided to let the parties press ahead on the basis of assurances from President Habyarimana to President Mwinyi and from President Habyarimana and Prime Minister Nsengiyaremye to Foreign Minister Diria that they were fully committed to the Arusha process and would accept the results of negotiations.[47]

A DIPLOMATIC DEMARCHE

Meanwhile, the Western ambassadors in Kigali finally agreed to join the papal nuncio in a demarche to the president and prime minister. Rather than directly endorse the clergy's recommendation, they would inquire whether the president or the prime minister saw any difference between principles enunciated in the president's speech of December 1 and the religious leaders' recommendations. If so, what were the means of bridging differences? The diplomats finally met with the president on December 10 and the prime minister on December 11. Habyarimana refused to be drawn out on the clergy's proposal or to meet with the prime minister to discuss differences. He went back to the formula of one-third of governmental seats for the MRND and proposed a technical team that would work out various scenarios as the bases for political compromise and for developing a national consensus.[48]

The prime minister, who had fully accepted the clergy's proposal, felt that a technical study of the problem rejected the religious leaders' intervention and could be manipulated by the president. Nsengiyaremye wondered whether the president was willing to use the clergy's proposal as a beginning point for efforts to build a consensus. He finally agreed to ask the presidency and the clergy to resolve remaining differences. General discussions could proceed in Arusha, but negotiations on cabinet positions would await harmonization of differences at home.[49] Taking the clergy's proposal as a basis, the negotiators saw that the critical issue was how to fill the unattributed portfolios so that no political bloc had a two-thirds majority or no particular party had a permanent blocking third of the positions.[50]

The diplomats' hope for a speedy conclusion to subsequent discussions was not to be realized. Their intervention did stir up renewed contact between the presidency and the prime minister's office—and as a consequence, renewed dialogue among the political parties—but no consensus emerged. Political leaders bandied a number of ideas for breaking the impasse, all centered on allocation of governmental seats and looking to finesse the two-thirds controlling vote (article 21) issue.

THE UNITED STATES STEPS BACK

In view of the delay in the formulation of negotiating instructions and the chasm between Kigali and Arusha, US participation in Arusha negotiations came into question. By the time Foreign Minister Ngulinzira finally took his delegation back to Arusha in late November, my mandate as Observer had lapsed and I had gone on to another assignment. Lt. Colonel Anthony Marley, military advisor for the Bureau of African Affairs, stood in the wings in case Arusha negotiations opened with military talks. When the Front insisted on picking up on power-sharing discussions, Senior Deputy Assistant Secretary Edward Brynn prepared to take on the

Observer role. Meanwhile, the political officer from the US embassy in Dar es Salaam, Robert Bentley, a member of the US delegation in the September and October talks, went to Arusha for the opening of negotiations.[51]

But the embassy in Dar es Salaam was shorthanded, with Ambassador Raymond Ewing on temporary status as chargé d'affaires and due to leave in mid-December. He needed Bentley back at his regular duties. Moreover, it was clear that political, not military, matters would dominate the agenda, so in late November, the embassy in Dar es Salaam urged Ambassador Brynn to come out.[52] From Kigali, however, Ambassador Flaten suggested that Ambassador Brynn delay his departure from the United States until there was an agreed Rwandan government position in Kigali and clear instructions to Arusha.[53] By December 8, that consensus had not developed. Ambassador Flaten urged that Brynn delay once again and that Bentley remain in Dar es Salaam until the situation clarified. A matter of personnel rotation and a decision not to grace Ngulinzira's freelance negotiations resulted in the United States not having a presence in Arusha in critical December days.

The action shifted to Kigali, where Ambassador Flaten was deeply engaged in urging parties to dialogue and compromise. According to French and German Observers on site who kept Bentley informed, nothing much was happening in Arusha. But the lack of a US presence was keenly felt by the negotiators, who had looked to the United States for leadership in the construction of peace.[54] After the February recess and subsequent RPA offensive, RPA commander Kagame told Colonel Marley that "the apparent lack of US response to the events of January, and the failure to maintain (in permanence) an Observer in Arusha, led many Rwandans to fear that the United States had withdrawn from the peace process."[55]

A DIPLOMATIC CONTRETEMPS

Since the revival of international efforts to promote a ceasefire in the Rwandan conflict, the United States and France had worked closely on the peace process. Coordinated US policy called for keeping the French out front in "GOR-RPF negotiations."[56]

Now, even as diplomatic consultation and cooperation seemed to reach a high point with the joint demarche on the president and prime minister, tensions flared between Washington and Paris. It began in the field as French advisors helped Rwandan frontline troops choose and reinforce more defensible positions. The forward movement of the troops brought fire from the RPF side, with a riposte from government forces. The Neutral Military Observer Group (NMOG), finally in the field and by chance at this site, was caught between exchanges of fire. Whereas previous reports on ceasefire violations had detailed exchanges of fire or movements of frontline forces, General Opalaye, the NMOG commander, this time highlighted his concern about the activity of the French advisors.[57]

The United States saw this reported activity as a "blatant disregard for the cease-fire line," confirming in Washington's mind the reports of "French military involvement on the front lines." Ambassador Flaten was instructed to discuss the issue with his French counterpart, Ambassador Martres, to ask that such violations not be repeated and to suggest some symbolic gesture (like replacing the commander responsible) that would calm the situation. The US embassy in Paris was instructed to "signal our concern to the Quai" and to report that the US ambassador in Kigali had been told to discuss "damage limitation" with the French ambassador.[58]

The French, in Paris and in Kigali, did not take lightly to the US scolding. For one, NMOG had only recently been deployed amid great squabbling about salaries and per diem. In the French view, the peace that had held along the ceasefire line since June was wrought not by the NMOG presence but out of the parties' desire for peace, as well as French restraint on government forces and deterrence of the RPF. Instead of NMOG arranging a withdrawal from the front, as the ceasefire agreement had demanded, hostile forces still faced each other; thus, the French did not consider reinforcement of front lines to be a violation of ceasefire terms. Moreover, the French considered the Nigerian NMOG commander highly prejudiced toward his fellow Anglophone Africans, the RPF, and wondered why the United States took the commander's report without question. Finally, the United States, which had so strongly pushed the idea of conflict resolution through the Joint Political Military Commission (JPMC), was now bypassing that institution in a direct approach to the French government. Quai officials reminded their US interlocutors that ceasefire issues were matters between the Rwandan government and the RPF parties and were to be resolved in the JPMC.[59]

The RPF did not appear to be as concerned about General Opalaye's report as the Department of State was. When Colonel Kanyarengwe met with OAU secretary general Salim Salim on December 8, the RPF chairman was preoccupied with larger issues. Foremost was the fact that the human rights situation in Rwanda was deteriorating, putting innocent civilians within areas controlled by the government at risk. The chairman challenged in general terms the continued French support for the Rwandan government. He also accused the government team of dallying on important issues at the political negotiations, especially the attribution of government portfolios. In briefing diplomats on the meeting between Kanyarengwe and Salim Salim, RPF representative Dr. Rudasingwa did not mention Opalaye's report. Rather, he commented presciently that a "good soldier does not sit around and react when attacked, a good soldier preempts his attackers." The RPF, he said, was not positioning itself to take the offensive, but that option was a future possibility.[60]

Back and Forth in Kigali

Even as interveners sorted out their differences, opposition parties in Kigali finally recognized how much the clergy formula had marginalized the MRND. There seemed to be a growing awareness that working in lockstep with the Front to hem in the MRND had gone to the point of national schism, threatening the whole democratic enterprise. Suggested adjustments included adding another seat for the MRND, more seats for more neutral parties like the Christian Democratic Party (PCD), or seats for independents. Common to all discussions was a vision of the internal political scene in terms of political blocs: the internal opposition, now known as the "Concert for Change" (MDR, PL, and PSD), and the allies of the Habyarimana regime, now brought together under the banner of the "Alliance for the Reinforcement of Democracy" (MRND, CDR, PADER, PECO, and PARERWA). Intrinsic in the formulations was the search for an allocation of seats that would give the MRND enough cabinet votes to protect its interests. As the American embassy reported, "President Habyarimana is clearly in a very difficult position. Although he gives signs personally of wanting to work out a compromise, his party, his family and his loyal supporters of years are terrified of being marginalized, unable to defend themselves, possibly being persecuted or prosecuted or worse."[61]

SCURRYING FOR A SOLUTION

The discussions among the political elites in Kigali since Habyarimana's December 1 speech and Diria's visit had been intense. The president of the opposition MDR, Faustin Twagiramungu, and the president's director of cabinet, Enoch Ruhigira, met four times between December 11 and December 16. Proposals from the presidency and the MRND encompassed Habyarimana's wish not to vote in council, but to preside above the partisan fray.[62]

In addition to the calculus on government portfolios, Kigali politicians came up with a number of operational notions designed to make the allocation more palatable to all sides. The idea of an inner cabinet, with a single representative from each party, was first broached by the presidency and then taken up by the prime minister's office. Many proposals provided that ministers in the transition period would not be candidates for office in the post-transition regime. There was the proposal that parties establish their ethical commitment to Arusha principles with an oath of office that rejected ethnism [sic], regionalism, and violence—a pledge that, in the view of many Kigali politicians, would be as onerous to the RPF as to the CDR. MRND leader Bizimungu even raised the possibility that President Habyarimana might not seek reelection if the opposition would agree to an amnesty for the president and his family to protect them against politically motivated reprisals.

After the visit of the Tanzanian foreign minister, Habyarimana sent two special envoys to Paris in hopes that at least one of them might see Mitterrand and arrange a later audience for the president. On December 22, Habyarimana went to Bujumbura with Burundian president Buyoya and Ugandan president Museveni in an effort to shore up regional support.[63] And he accepted an invitation to the National Prayer Breakfast in Washington in the first week of February, always a good means of making high-level contacts in the United States.

PARALLEL PARTY NEGOTIATIONS

Both the party leaders and the Facilitator kept working at the idea of a party meeting parallel to the political negotiations at Arusha as a way of building confidence and breaking through the political impasse. Pushing this option were parties like the PL and PSD, which felt underrepresented on the governmental negotiating team. The MRND finally agreed to participate in such a meeting if the parties chose a chair to lead the discussion and adopted a common position before the meeting.[64] That, of course, went back to the initial problem—the lack of consensus among internal parties on power sharing in government.

Although the RPF had had meetings in Brussels with the "unarmed opposition" before the June ceasefire, it was reluctant to now undertake a "major parties" meeting, rejecting Kigali as a locale because of security and Arusha so as to avoid confusion with the formal negotiations. By the end of December, it was obvious that a five-party discussion was not going to take place. The president's cabinet director began talking instead of a direct meeting between the RPF and the MRND, a variant of his boss's desire to meet not with Chairman Kanyarengwe, whom he considered but a front man, but with General Kagame, who was calling the shots.[65] That neither a meeting between the leaders of the two sides nor RPF/MRND party talks took place suggests that the RPF was determined to avoid preempting with high-level talks the negotiations in Arusha, where it was most likely to achieve its objectives.

A PORTENTOUS PROPOSAL

It was in this context of political gamesmanship in Kigali, absence of the United States from the Arusha negotiations, contention among the Western Observers, and growing RPF impatience that another proposal emerged. On December 22, Prime Minister Nsengiyaremye briefed key diplomats on a modification of the clergy's plan: four cabinet positions would go to the MRND, four to the RPF, three plus the prime minister to the MDR, three each to the PL and PSD, two to other parties or persons, and one to the PDC. The proposal took into consideration the president's position that he would not participate in cabinet but stay above the political fray. If the negotiators could not agree on balancing parties to be seated in government, the prime minister was open to the naming of independent prominent persons to ministerial portfolios. He would work with the president to assure that the persons nominated for the portfolios were acceptable to both sides. Nsengiyaremye thought, as well, that an agreed governmental program of action would reduce areas of confrontation.[66]

Previously, Ambassador Flaten had concluded that the prime minister would not "press the foreign minister to go forward with negotiations on cabinet positions on the basis of the clergy proposals until there is further clarification."[67] Now Nsengiyaremye told Flaten that he would quickly negotiate with the MRND on this proposition and then instruct the foreign minister to begin negotiations. Flaten cautioned that the formula, however laudable an initiative, would certainly be questioned by the MRND and would require modifications before becoming the basis of negotiations with the RPF.

Suddenly, without either presidential agreement or a cabinet meeting, Arusha announced a breakthrough on negotiations, with both sides agreeing to a formula that closely paralleled the one described by the prime minister. Indeed, it is not clear that the proposal was the prime minister's. Ambassador Mapuranga, the OAU representative at the talks, told the US embassy in Dar es Salaam that he was surprised that this particular proposal was even under discussion in Kigali. It apparently had been put forward in Arusha by the Tanzanians as a means of pushing forward discussions, with a view to signing a protocol by Christmas. The agreement was indeed characterized in the Kigali press as a proposal made by the Tanzanians and accepted by the negotiating teams in Arusha.[68]

Never had the negotiating team in Arusha and the political realities in Kigali been further apart. As the US embassy reported, "There is no joy in Kigali at the announcement of agreement in Arusha, because everyone knows that the president's party (MRND) did not participate in the agreement and has not accepted it."[69] The MRND, in a party meeting on December 21, had approved a white paper detailing the weaknesses of the bishops' proposal and accusing the prime minister of being the main source of blockage in government and in the Arusha negotiations.[70] After the announcement of agreement in Arusha, the MRND, in a press communiqué, noted that it had no interest in a government where it could not influence events and expressed astonishment that the chief negotiator would accept an agreement in Arusha when parties in Kigali were locked in discussions on distribution of portfolios.[71]

The processes in Kigali and Arusha proceeded within their own dynamic; toward the end of December, each new day seemed to bring yet another idea about power sharing in Kigali and yet another report of an agreement about to happen in Arusha. Tensions grew with two bombs exploding in Kigali, one occurring in a crowded nightclub and injuring some twenty people. Ethnic clashes broke out in the northern regions of Gisenyi, leaving dozens hurt and numerous homes destroyed. Meanwhile, the RPF Radio Muhabura streamed a litany of charges against the French presence and "the obstructions of the president of the Republic and his party to the Arusha negotiations."[72]

A MULTIPARTY SOLUTION

The negotiating sides in Arusha had agreed that the unattributed seats in government would be filled by independent personalities because, in their view, none of the *non-concertation* parties fit the bishops' party ethic.[73] However, in Kigali, negotiations took a different tack. Party officials, like the president of PL, Justin Mugenzi, resented the quick agreement in Arusha, which sought to forestall ongoing discussions among party leadership in Kigali; he even conveyed "his apologies" to the MRND for the surprise action in Arusha. Interparty discussions in Kigali sought to balance out political forces in government by giving seats to smaller parties rather than to "independent" individuals. Central to these discussions was the question of giving a role to the CDR, which had a considerable political following, especially in the northwest, but also a reputation for engendering violence. By December 28, the president's director of cabinet had worked out with the MDR president a new variant that would have three independent seats in the government, one of which was to be the CDR; inner cabinet decisions would decide most issues.[74] In a modification of this proposal, the MRND offered an extensive analysis of the options and proposed a cabinet in which MRND seats would be held to a minimum proposed level, but the CDR would be given three portfolios.[75]

The United States, which was not present in Arusha but active in promoting discussions in Kigali, urged inclusion of all parties that would commit "to accept the Arusha process, eschew violence and renounce regional and ethnic politics," a formula equally applicable to the CDR as to

the RPF or any other party wishing to play a role in the transition period.[76] In Washington, when RPF chairman Kanyarengwe came calling,
Assistant Secretary Cohen told the RPF that the French by their presence
were helping prevent military hardliners from launching an offensive. He
cautioned the RPF not to ask President Habyarimana to commit political
suicide by leaving him no authority within the institutions. Specifically, as
regards the CDR issue, Cohen urged the RPF to reflect on the danger of
excluding an extremist group from the new government. As participants in
the system, the CDR members would have to commit themselves to government decisions and respect its rule. Excluded, they would have nothing
to lose by sabotaging the process itself.[77]

BLOCKED AGAIN

Back in Kigali, it looked like political leaders were moving toward a salable compromise. MDR president Twagiramungu concluded that "if the
Rwandans wanted to have real national reconciliation, they had to reach
out not only to the RPF but also to the Hutu supremacists in the CDR."
However, given his previous public position against the CDR, he wanted
someone else, perhaps the bishops, to recommend inclusion of the CDR.[78]
On the other side of the question, in a long letter to the prime minister, Habyarimana expressed a strong desire to see the Arusha negotiations succeed. True, he complained that negotiators were taking positions
in Arusha without consultation with government and without informing
him. He reiterated the principles of "arbitration" on the portfolio question
communicated in his letter of December 1. He "encouraged" the prime minister not to flee the interior debate or to leave the negotiators to adventures
that a large part of the national population would contest. But for all his
qualifiers and admonitions, Habyarimana reiterated a foundational desire
to see a peace accord signed at Arusha that would guarantee a real peace
and the return of displaced persons to their properties, as well as a definite
resolution of the refugee problem. The president favored any solution that
was based on frank dialogue without exclusion, looking essentially toward
national reconciliation and a solid peace in the country.[79]

There were, however, limits as to how far party leaders were willing
to go in including others. They were willing to consider another seat for

the MRND or a portfolio for another minor party, but most did not favor any representation in government for the CDR. In a long meeting on December 30, four top party leaders and Enoch Ruhigira (representing the president's office) met with Nsengiyaremye to establish a common position on cabinet allocations. Although the prime minister's chief of staff had previously signaled that the CDR might be seated if it committed to the Arusha process,[80] this time the prime minister did not follow Twagiramungu's new openness but continued to insist that the CDR could not be part of the next government. MRND national secretary Ngirumpatse again warned that the MRND would not participate in the new transition government without the CDR being part of it.[81]

When this interparty effort to keep the MRND from being marginalized within the context of the negotiations failed, the Alliance for the Preservation of Democracy went out in street demonstrations in Kigali and northern towns of Gisenyi and Ruhengeri on December 31 to prove their political strength. The demonstrations stopped all traffic and virtually paralyzed the country. An MRND communiqué after the demonstration claimed that the foreign minister in Arusha continued to commit treason in an effort to pass all power to the RPF and its internal allies. The communiqué denounced the parties who continued to support the RPF and called on the prime minister to give up the policies of assassination and murder that he had been using in the past.[82]

ARUSHA GOES AHEAD

Meanwhile, in Arusha, despite the presumed agreement of December 22, the issue of portfolios persisted. The RPF favored dividing the government among parties currently within it and was categorical in refusing a portfolio to the CDR. The government insisted, however, that no agreement could work if significant forces were excluded from participation.[83] Tanzanian facilitator Ambassador Mpungwe, in letters to both delegations, noted that negotiations over the distribution of portfolios had stalled over two unallocated portfolios and thus had threatened to derail the whole peace process. He reminded the negotiating teams that their objective was peace and that the transition was not an end in itself but an opportunity to prepare Rwanda for "a new order of national unity." The Facilitator called for flexibility and realism and pointed to the need to "work for a solution which allows for maximum cooperation by all political forces with due regard to the existing realities in Rwanda." Laying down the gauntlet, Ambassador Mpungwe told the delegations that if they were not able to find an acceptable solution by Wednesday, January 6, 1993, it would be advisable to the delegations to adjourn the talks for further reflection and consultation.

Faced with this deadline, the Rwandan government delegation decided to find a formula on portfolios. By January 6, the two sides reached an agreement and began drawing up a final protocol. In Kigali, President Habyarimana asked Prime Minister Nsengiyaremye to stop the signing of the protocol. A letter from Director of Cabinet Ruhigira drew Nsengiyaremye's attention to the consequences of the signature of an agreement "on which the head of state has not taken a position and on which there is no consensus concerning the implementation of such an accord."[84]

At the same time, the MRND held a press conference at which it reiterated its intention not to participate in a government in which it would not play any significant role. In its press communiqué, the MRND argued that the agreement at Arusha does not come from any national consensus, that the interest of a major political bloc had been ignored in both the allocation of portfolios and the attribution of seats in the national assembly, that the issue of CDR participation had not been given the kind of consideration recommended by the clergy, and that the prime minister and foreign minister had made the negotiations a personal affair. The communiqué pointed out that the government had not met on the issue in two months and, in effect, demanded the resignation of the prime minister.[85]

As signatures awaited translation and the production of documents, the US State Department called Ambassador Mpungwe to urge that the parties not sign a protocol but rather a communiqué that summarized their agreement, thereby leaving the door open for modifications later.[86] Mpungwe called back two days later to say the protocol was the best deal possible and failure to sign it now would make resumptions of negotiations impossible later on. Mpungwe reported that the parties would sign a protocol of eighty-five articles that gave five seats each to the MRND and the RPF, four to the MDR, three each to the PSD and the PL, and one to the PDC. Seats in the national assembly would be appointed, with eleven each to major parties, four to the PDC, and one each to eleven other registered parties including the CDR, so long as they conformed to a code of ethics based on the principles of the Arusha agreement.[87] The negotiating parties signed the protocol on January 9, 1993, after what was characterized as intense negotiations undertaken in an atmosphere of frankness and fraternity.[88]

Back in Kigali, where the reaction was reported as negative on all sides, party leaders acted as if no definite conclusions had been reached. The PL's Mugenzi said that the MRND would eventually see the reasonableness of the opposition position and that serious talks would continue in a couple of days. MRND national secretary Ngirumpatse, after a meeting with MDR president Twagiramungu, said that talks would continue on changes that seemed necessary. Twagiramungu in turn argued that article 21, covering voting in council, could be reopened. Even President Habyarimana seemed jovial and relaxed at a January 7 farewell dinner for French ambassador Martres. It was as though nothing of consequence was happening in Arusha, and political dialogue would continue in Kigali unimpeded. Nonetheless, the Western ambassadors reflected on the earlier warning of presidential counselor Ruhigira that Arusha negotiators, by presenting Kigali with yet another fait accompli, would this time not bring acquiescence but might engender violence. This possibility was so serious that the ambassadors agreed to collaborate in the event of a breakdown of law and order in the capital city.[89]

By mid-January, the president had convoked the ambassadors and summarized themes that had been the background of his speeches, letters, and meetings since late October:

+ The proposed division of power was not the result of real negotiations between opposing sides but discussions among friends who want to divide up power.

+ The alliance of opposition parties had as its intent to overthrow the president, not to work through constituted transition procedures.

- The existing party alliances under proposed allocation of portfolios gave the opposition a permanent blocking third.

- The configuration of the proposal thus offered to opposition parties and the RPF the opportunity to change everything: every mayor, every civil servant, and all who had worked in the Rwandan administration.

- Ultimately, elections were necessary so that one can really know who has how much power.

- In any case, the existing assembly or a popular referendum must sanction the final agreement if it is to have any legitimacy.[90]

The opposition wavered between wanting to cash in on the political chips they had taken from the negotiating table and a realization that they must somehow shuffle the president and MRND a better hand. The PL's Mugenzi and the MDR's Twagiramungu talked of firing the foreign minister and reallocating the portfolios he so glibly gave away in Arusha. They discussed acceding to a ratification process but rejected both a popular referendum and a vote within the CND, which was now hostile to an accord that would put them out of business. Most of the opposition was not amenable to giving a government portfolio to the CDR, whose hostility toward the Arusha process was growing more vocal each day. Despite opposition, both the prime minister and the foreign minister were determined to go ahead on the basis of negotiated protocols, noting the historically unpopular position of peacemakers. Yet, they rejected any notion that peace and reconciliation required reaching out to the president and the MRND to keep them in the process.[91]

The president of the Social Democratic Party (PSD) from the southern city of Butare, Félicien Gatabazi, analyzed the issue from a regional perspective. In a realistic assessment, he admitted that the opposition had "played the game thus far to weaken Habyarimana," but no one knew where it would end or what to expect from the RPF. Nonetheless, he would rather have a Tutsi from the RPF than Kanyarengwe as minister of Interior, given the possibility of collusion between the northern-based CDR and this Ruhengeri political figure. His party was willing to compromise on territorial administration and push for the notion of an inner cabinet, even though the RPF had rejected the idea.[92]

A Human Rights Imbroglio

As politicians dickered in Kigali, ethnic violence broke out in the president's home area of the northwest against the Bagogwe, who were traditional Tutsi pastoralists. By the end of January, some three hundred persons had been killed and over four thousand had been displaced. This was happening just after the International Commission on Human Rights Abuses, invited to Rwanda under terms of the Arusha negotiations, completed a two-week inquiry into the civil violence that had plagued Rwanda since the inception of the civil war. Having witnessed the tensions and intimidation that had become a daily part of life in Rwanda, and cognizant of the political debate being argued out during the time of its inquiry, the commission held press conferences in Brussels and Kigali and issued an interim report highly critical of the Habyarimana regime.[93] At the same time, the commission released a graphic video that included footage of skulls and skeletons unearthed by its forensic team during the visit. Shown on German, Belgian, French, and Canadian TV and rebroadcast on a French-language cable program in Washington, the video and press conferences quickly drew public attention to the commission's conclusions.[94]

The findings of the commission were not news to Western embassies. In its human rights report for 1993, the US embassy noted that "human rights abuses plagued the first quarter of 1993."[95] According to the report, the victims of these violations were minority Tutsi and opposition political party members. The embassy tied the human rights abuses to the ongoing political debate, namely, "the dissatisfaction on the part of the former sole party (MRND) . . . over the power-sharing arrangement agreed to on January 9 between the multiparty Government and the RPF."[96] Notwithstanding previous reporting on human rights abuses, the graphic revelation of human rights atrocities and the charges of government complicity changed the outlook of local diplomats and of their home governments.

Since the suspension of political negotiations in October, and especially since the signature of the January 9 protocol, the Western ambassadors had seen the once omnipresent and powerful MRND and the president outflanked by collusion between the internal opposition and the RPF. Keeping Habyarimana committed to the peace process and getting his opponents to recognize his interests was the diplomatic objective. Now the regime stood charged by an international commission with human rights atrocities that no Western government could ignore. The energies of the Western diplomats were now directed toward encouraging the president to deal with the human rights crisis rather than in getting him back to the negotiating table.

BACK TO POLITICS

In Kigali, however, it appeared to be politics as usual. On January 27, the five parties of the coalition government issued a communiqué proposing a parallel meeting with the RPF outside of Arusha to work out a compromise over the disputed articles in the January 9 protocol, implicitly agreeing that the protocol was nonbinding.[97] The RPF apparently accepted such a meeting in principle but did not favor a parties' conclave as an arena for negotiations. Meanwhile, Habyarimana asked that Minister of Defense James Gasana replace Foreign Minister Boniface Ngulinzira as head of the government delegation. This was in part because military matters were supposed to be the object of discussions and in part because the president and his party, the MRND, had completely lost confidence in the foreign minister. Ngulinzira's tactic of pushing forward negotiations and then presenting Kigali with the results had reached a dead end.

The RPF accepted the change in the government delegation but announced two preconditions to the resumption of talks: that the violence in the north stop, and that the outcome of the Arusha negotiations be binding on all political forces in Rwanda. At the first plenary, the RPF asked for guarantees that mixed near-term operational objectives (that perpetrators be brought to justice, for example) with strategic goals (that foreign troops be withdrawn or that the gendarmerie be placed under the prime minister.)[98]

Dr. Gasana said that he could not possibly comply with those demands, bringing negotiations at Arusha immediately to a halt. Observers (which now included the United States) agreed to work with both delegations over the weekend to look for points of flexibility and possible compromise. By February 3, according to information received from Arusha, the talks appeared on the brink of collapse. The Rwandan government delegation was preoccupied with interparty discussions in Kigali on the negotiating mandate. The RPF, vexed by communal violence in northwest Rwanda, refused further negotiations until the Rwandan government met its demands for security guarantees within the country. By focusing on different priorities, the two sides ended up talking past each other.[99]

International opinion began to build against the Rwandan government. Some Canadian and Swiss human rights groups were demanding a cutoff of aid. French statements from the Quai seemed to be responding to critiques of its large role in support of the Rwandan state. The Belgians let it be known that Habyarimana would not be received by anyone should he come to Belgium. Habyarimana canceled his trip to Washington and the National Prayer Breakfast. In the view of the US Department of State, "the bargaining position of the MRND and CDR has eroded along with their credibility. . . . It will be harder to elicit international sympathy for their fears of marginalization in the transitional government."[100] The department concluded that the president and Rwandan government would need to take some significant action to guarantee that violence would not recur.

That action was too slow in coming. Following the president's visit to the northwest on February 4, Habyarimana and Nsengiyaremye set up a commission to determine which local officials were responsible for abetting local violence and which had taken appropriate action. The report was to be submitted within one week. The government met in long session from February 3 to 5, apparently hammering out a mandate for Arusha. Among its decisions was the suspension of six administrative officers for presumed involvement in recent violence.

In Arusha, the RPF welcomed the suspension of the officials as a "positive first step" but insisted that more actions were needed. Meanwhile, the Tanzanians, who were hosting the OAU Liberation Committee in Dar es Salaam, called for a pause in the talks to permit their diplomats to return to the capital; US and European Observers joined the exodus from Arusha to Dar es Salaam. The RPF lost patience with the pace of negotiations and the slowness of the government's response to recurring violence against their kin in Rwanda. Despite assurances of its negotiating team to the contrary, the RPF broke the ceasefire and on February 8 attacked across the front line, quickly moving toward Kigali.

Understanding the Impasse

The Arusha peace process, solidified in the power-sharing protocol of October 30, had not taken on substance and dynamism in subsequent negotiations. The real negotiations moved to Kigali amid wrangling of major parties over who would get what in the interim government. President Habyarimana failed to lead the process forward; in Arusha, a negotiating team led by the foreign minister tried to override the Kigali debate by preemptive agreements. So the distance between leadership in Kigali and negotiators in Arusha brought a deepening impasse.

How did a speed bump on the road to peace become a roadblock? Ugandan president Museveni told me before the second power-sharing negotiation that the agreement in Arusha had to reflect "the political landscape of Rwanda" if it were to endure. At the same time, Museveni claimed that the RPF had prevailed on the battlefield and deserved a 50/50 split in the integration of security forces; the Front would need that kind of force structure to guarantee security to their people. Museveni had identified the two elements that seemed most missing in the Rwandan political discussions: realism about what was possible given Rwanda's political complexity, and security in the face of ethnic violence.

REALISM

Looking over this opaque history, one wonders why President Habyarimana let the peace process slip back into violence and war. There was a constant mantra from the presidency, his staff, and the MRND after the October power-sharing protocol: the internal opposition, in league with the RPF, intended to use the Arusha political negotiations to carry out a civil coup d'état against Habyarimana and the MRND. In retrospect, what seemed a rhetorical device was Habyarimana's perception of political reality. By law and decree in the interim period, the internal opposition parties intended to uproot the Habyarimana's regime and replace it with one of their own design.[101] The Front had the same ambition, albeit with a different regime in mind, and would make common cause.

At the initiation of the political negotiations, the president enjoyed full control of the central administration, local government, the army, and the gendarmerie, while the ministers of his party dominated the coalition government. He carried out his own diplomacy, using the foreign ministry for the most mundane of tasks. To ask him to give all this up for a ceremonial role as president, with his party in a position to be consistently outvoted in cabinet, was not realistic. To believe that most decisions would be taken by consensus and only extraordinary measures would need the two-thirds overriding vote was to deny the realities of Rwanda's fractious politics. If Habyarimana was right about the intent of the opposition to move him out, then it was vain to hope for an ad hoc coalition to protect the interests of the president and his party. Hence the need for the addition of minor parties amenable to working with the MRND. Of these, the CDR had the largest political base, with strong support in Habyarimana's home region and links to his wife and in-laws.

The internal opposition was notably hardened to the president's interests. Party leaders gloated over the quick vote in cabinet on October 28, which approved the October protocol before MRND ministers got to the meeting. Their attitude did not change much in the subsequent two months of parlaying. Any party, other than those of the *Forces de concertation*, was considered not suitable for government. The CDR, which had earlier indicated its interest in playing by Arusha rules, was again rejected by the prime minister in the December 30 party leaders' conclave. The internal opposition wanted a cabinet and agenda in the interim regime that they would control without MRND interference. And the MRND persisted in its October declaration that it would not participate in such a government. All the variations on the theme—internal cabinet, portfolios to neutral personalities, prior elaboration of a government program, or designation of subcabinet positions for minor parties—were efforts to get around the core reality, namely, the need for a mechanism that would induce the president and his party to play the game.

Meanwhile, in Arusha, the foreign minister was trying to create another reality, a negotiating process that would create momentum to draw in political acquiescence from Kigali. Operating off his loose instructions from early October, he agreed to positions favorable to the internal opposition and acceptable to the RPF while ignoring other political claims from Kigali. As he journeyed back to the negotiating table in early December,

Minister Ngulinzira told diplomats in Dar es Salaam that "some sort of amnesty or indemnification would be needed ... so that parties ... would not be threatened by the prospect of change."[102] This he offered not out of sympathy for amnesty as a peacebuilding instrument—a notion that had been decried by both sides during the rule of law negotiations—but as an indication that he intended to move ahead with a formula that would politically marginalize the president and his party; consequently, he needed to provide them with legal cover.[103]

By the end of December, the foreign minister did not yet have a negotiating mandate from the coalition government. In the highland isolation of Arusha, he was surrounded by a delegation that wanted to get on with the show. Very negative reaction from Kigali to the December 22 agreement on portfolios may have thrown a bit of reality into the process. Early January reports show the government delegation still arguing for inclusion of the CDR, for example.[104] Nonetheless, Ngulinzira determined to press ahead. The allocation of portfolios and the nominated assembly he agreed to in the protocol of January 9 had no sanction from the Rwandan government and hence rested on questionable legal authority. Yet the OAU, the Tanzanian facilitator, and the Observers present pushed for signature on power sharing and rapid consideration of the rest of the agenda. Only the United States, kibitzing from the margins, urged recording agreements rather than signing a formal protocol. Getting on with the process became the imperative of the day.

The most curious element in these deliberations was the role of the clergy contact group. That priests and preachers should make high policy strikes devotees of secular democratic government as odd indeed. In Rwanda, however, there had always been a close link in traditional politics between the court and ritual lineages or, in the modern age, between the ethos of church and state.[105] One might well understand religious leaders facilitating contact and conversation between contending groups; they are, after all, peacemakers by vocation and had previously played that role in informal meetings between the RPF and Rwandan political leaders. In this case, however, the contact group offered not hortatory advice but a numerical division of the cabinet. Once it came out, the bishops' formula was considered the "right" solution not because it was representative, inclusive, or a negotiated compromise (all operational virtues of a democratic order) but because the bishops had proposed it. However "right" it may have been, the formula was not realistic. It marginalized the MRND in ways that made it suicidal for that group to accept the proposal without modifying it.

SECURITY

So instead of moving forward into a new era of power sharing and coalition politics, Rwanda went back to politics as usual: a public discourse punctuated by the intimidation, coercion, and violence that have been part of Rwandan political history for as long as oral history can record.

The issue of security should seemingly have been part of conversations on the repatriation of refugees. However, as negotiations picked up again in November, the RPF insisted on finishing discussions on power sharing before addressing the issue of refugees. For them the problem was the creation of a new order in which those refugees would be secure and fully able to play their part. Indeed, the initial RPF attack in October 1990 was executed at that time in order to forestall implementation of an agreement between the UNHCR and the Habyarimana regime for the orderly return of refugees.[106] Free and untrammeled right of return had been emotionally claimed in the sessions on the rule of law. In the RPF view, before conditions were secure enough for that right to be exercised, regime change was necessary.

In this context, returning to the intimidation and violence that accompanied previous interethnic crises proved dysfunctional. First, the RPF was at the door with proven superior forces. Second, the international interveners, the internal opposition, and a good part of the president's own party wanted a durable peace in which the rights of all were secured. It is possible that President Habyarimana was complicit in the ethnic violence of December and January that broke out in his home region of Gisenyi as the MRND lost its quest for a blocking third in the interim coalition government; in this case he was not to be trusted. Hutu extremists whom the president did not control could have carried out the attacks; in such a scenario Habyarimana was not in charge even in his homeland. Elements of the president's administration could have supported the attacks with his acquiescence, in which case, Habyarimana was opportunistic.

The effect was the same: insecurity within Rwanda at this point in the peace process only supported the RPF's demand for a new political order that Habyarimana could not control. The RPF were clear on this; in every demarche during the period of impasse, they blamed Habyarimana for obstructing the negotiations and decried political violence within Rwanda. The implication was that to have a secure Rwanda to which refugees could return, the Habyarimana regime must go. Political negotiations had not brought this about, so the RPF resorted to their standard practice, a military attack with a political objective. Would that tactic lead to prolonged war or back to negotiations? Events in the next month would tell.

Lessons We Learned

At the end of the power-sharing negotiations, we could sense President Habyarimana's deep reluctance to move down the negotiated path. None of the interveners fully understood the impediments along that path. Looking back, we can extract useful lessons from this roadblock.

- *Sharing power was an oxymoron, both in the traditions of African political hierarchies and in the specter of winner-take-all democracy.* The parties did not want to look forward to a game of compromising or to coalition politics; the contenders wanted to control power all through the interim and beyond.

- *Negotiating off-table, a preeminent tool of conflict resolution strategists, can easily backfire.* Off-table initiatives included the president's call for intervention from the clergy, the parties' pursuit of an all-parties meeting, the staging of protest marches, the releasing of ethnic violence in the north, and the RPF attack in March. Each essay failed to move peace forward and greatly complicated the prospects for subsequent negotiations.

- *Both sides were counting on the process of attributing seats in the cabinet and the assembly.* The proposals for allocation left the president's party without a blocking minority against hostile decisions by the cabinet or the assembly. Corrective notions within the vague terms of the bishops' formula were all proposed in ways that would not diminish any of the internal opposition's newly devolved power.

- *Exclusion and control, not compromise and sharing, became the prevalent values.* Any outside party proposed under the bishop's formula was declared unfit by parties that already had a place in the cabinet. All efforts to seat the CDR in the cabinet or assembly, even by those who said they personally favored such a move, came to naught.

- *Moving the peace process forward was the international goal.* Getting agreement took precedence over clear-eyed examination of whether terms of the agreement were toxic. Unity on that objective was easier in Arusha in the conference mode than in Kigali, where bilateral diplomacy was encumbered by different national stakes and interests.

FIVE

Endgame

The new year opened with violence, ending the two-month debate over composition of the interim government. The process of peace had devolved into acts of war. Ethnic massacres in Rwanda's northwest looked like another effort to win through violence what had not been achieved in political negotiation. The attack by the RPF across the front lines was both a reprisal against the ethnic violence and a means of coercing agreement in negotiations.

This retreat toward war was not a surprise to the international Observers mentoring the Arusha peace process. Despite the Front's assurances, the political atmosphere in Kigali and the distance between positions in Arusha pointed toward a possible return to arms. In their conversations with the parties, the Observers emphasized the fragility of the ceasefire and the tremendous human and political costs should either side again resort to arms.

Meanwhile, investigations into the responsibility for the mid-January massacres in Rwanda's northwest proceeded glacially. On February 4, Habyarimana finally made a visit to the area. He and the prime minister agreed to set up a special commission whose report was due in one week. Prime Minister Nsengiyaremye was poised to announce the suspension of some officials and the arrest of some perpetrators.[1]

In meetings February 3–5, the government apparently agreed on an agenda for Arusha, whose terms were briefed to the diplomatic corps on February 6 and were to be announced to the nation in a radio address on February 7.[2] In Arusha, Minister of Defense Gasana briefed the RPF and Observers on progress in Kigali. The RPF's immediate response was that more action was necessary in punishing those responsible for the massacres.[3]

As talks stalled on this issue, the Tanzanians announced a pause so its officials could return to Dar es Salaam to host an OAU Liberation Committee.[4] European and American Observers joined in the exit to Dar es Salaam. While recognizing a pause in Arusha as "probably necessary," the American embassy in Kigali warned that a lengthy halt could lead to RPF military intervention. Ambassador Flaten suggested the possibility of a coordinated statement putting international pressure on President Habyarimana "in the next few days."[5] Both in Arusha and within the government in Kigali, decision makers apparently felt that there was time for due deliberation.

The Arusha negotiations were, thus, in a "pause" when, on February 6, the Rwandese Patriotic Army attacked. Rwandan government forces fell back in some places to within twenty-seven miles from the capital. But the insurgent forces did not press their advantage. Instead, they offered a truce on February 8. The government accepted the truce with the understanding that the ground the RPF had taken would become part of a neutral buffer zone.[6] While there were, from that date, movements and skirmishes along the line, neither side launched a major offensive. Diplomats urged both sides to cease hostilities and get back to negotiations.

The improbable story of this chapter is that a peace process ending in political gridlock and renewed hostilities was pushed back on the rails and to a successful conclusion five months later. The chapter opens with a review of issues at stake and details of French government initiatives to get the peace process restored. A summit in Dar es Salaam in early March successfully reinstated the ceasefire and restarted talks, while encumbering those talks with a secret codicil on French military presence in Rwanda. But the summit failed to determine who would police the new ceasefire: the OAU or the UN. Attempts to launch an all-parties dialogue with the RPF exacerbated the divisions among the factions. While talks on refugee matters were quickly concluded, disputes on military integration persisted to the last moment. On August 5, President Habyarimana and RPF chairman Kanyarengwe finally signed the series of negotiated protocols now known as the Arusha Accords. Lessons we learned along this bumpy road conclude the chapter.

Issues at Stake

How do you get back from a culture of renewed war to one of peace? This question, common to many peace negotiations, has several dimensions.

What is the relative weight and effect of international intervention in pushing forward a peace process? Two and a half years after the October insurgency, the combined efforts of neighbors, donors, and international organizations had not brought peace back to Rwanda. How might a concerted new effort succeed?

How does an international presence within the negotiating process affect the course of decision making? Contending parties may play to known interests of interveners; or antagonists may take the international presence as a safety net for their practice of negotiating brinkmanship. Both happened on the road to peace in Rwanda.

What can the role of great powers be in an international intervention putatively led by African mediators and facilitators? In a crisis moment, great-power pressure and presence may be the critical element in getting a peace process restarted.[7] But contemporary peacemaking requires multilateral approaches.[8] In the February crisis, it was France working bilaterally and a multilateral summit that got the peace process going again.

Can the push to conclude an agreement override analysis of the realities in place and judgment on the durability of an agreement? The desire for forward momentum toward an agreed framework for peace is a compelling motive in international humanitarian intervention. "Lock it in!" is the mantra. And, in a system of sovereign states, the diplomatic assumption is that if the parties agree, then the accord settles the problem (*pacta servanda sunt*). It proved to be quite the opposite in Rwanda's case.

Getting Back to Peace Talks

FIGHTING FAILS

For the international interveners, whether the Observer states, Tanzania as Facilitator, or the OAU as Convener, the question was how to return to the peace process. That the negotiations should have unveiled fundamental predispositions to violence rather than to peace was not surprising given the bumpy record of this peace-building initiative. A ray of hope was that the recourse to violence had not worked for either side. The International Human Rights Commission rushed to publish its report that implicated the Habyarimana regime in the January pogroms as well as in a long history of ethnic violence.[9] The United States and the European Union condemned the killings. Belgium canceled President Habyarimana's visit with King Baudouin and recalled their ambassador to Kigali. Violence had isolated the Rwandan government and alienated its best friends.

On the other hand, the Patriotic Front's move across the ceasefire line had triggered the deployment of three hundred additional French troops from Bangui to Kigali and the displacement of nearly a million internal refugees. Should the RPF have persisted in moving forward, it would have had to engage disciplined, well-armed French forces protecting the capital city and to subdue hostile, frightened people. So now, both sides accepted a truce and were willing to discuss terms. The question was: could the Arusha political negotiations develop a "breakthrough strategy" that would finally lead to an established peace?[10]

THE FRENCH INITIATIVE

The French government, recognizing the seriousness of the crisis provoked by the RPF attack, quickly engaged within the window of opportunity that the truce of February 9 offered.[11] France's top Africanists, Bruno Delaye from the Elysée and Jean-Marc de La Sablière from the Quai d'Orsay, hurried to the area. In Kigali, the envoys reportedly read the riot act to Habyarimana, telling him that he must pull his government together in the face of a military rout and a perpetual government crisis. France's continued assistance was contingent on Habyarimana's leading a united government. Under French pressure, the president and prime minister met together for the first time in two months and agreed on February 13 to a joint declaration.[12]

Convinced that RPF battlefield success would not have been possible without materiel support from Uganda, the French diplomats flew to Kampala to lodge their protest and to seek Museveni's help in getting a renewed ceasefire. The French, having bolstered the regime in Kigali by the deployment of two more companies, now wanted to be certain that the RPF was not being resupplied by Uganda. While in Kampala, they secured Ugandan agreement in principle to accept a UN monitoring patrol on the border of Rwanda and Uganda.

RISE AND DEMISE OF PARTY ACCOMMODATION

President Habyarimana apparently decided to listen to the French envoys. Perhaps he knew that the army was demoralized and could not be mobilized for an all-out assault. (The French assessment considered the Rwandan army to be only 40 percent effective at this time.) In any case, Habyarimana met with leaders of the key political parties for the first time in many months. He committed his own MRND party to participate in an all-parties meeting with the RPF if the parties could

- find a way to stop the fighting immediately;
- resume negotiations in Arusha;
- reach a quick agreement on peace; and
- return the displaced to their homes.[13]

The parties on their part agreed to urge the RPF to return to the lines of the previous ceasefire, to support continued French presence in Rwanda, to argue for maintenance of the gendarmerie within the Ministry of Defense, and to dismiss administrative officials only upon proof of wrongdoing. The parties' meeting with the RPF, in the air since the suspension of talks in November, was finally scheduled for February 23.[14] However, by this time, the Facilitator had, in view of the truce on the ground, invited the contending leaders to a summit meeting in Dar es Salaam. The parties believed their meeting with the RPF should come before decisions were made at the summit.

Through convoluted consultations, the parties finally agreed to accept Burundi's invitation to a meeting in Bujumbura; negotiations with a view to restoring the ceasefire and returning to the Arusha political talks were to be pursued later in Dar es Salaam. On February 20, the parties adopted a paper outlining their common position based on what had been agreed between the parties and the president and in the president's meeting with the prime minister.[15]

In turn, the RPF had given public notice of its positions. According to its Radio Muhabura broadcasts, the RPF wanted the government to sack all officials who took part in the violence and demonstrate the will to prevent future violence. French troops should leave Rwanda as soon as possible.[16]

THE BUJUMBURA MEETING

The parties were to have left by chartered aircraft for Bujumbura on February 22, but the meeting was delayed. By the time of departure, the hard-fought agreements of the "Party Paper" were in shreds and the MRND was once again on the outs with the other parties. The only parties to show up in Bujumbura from February 25 to March 3 were the MDR, the PSD, the PDC, and the PL. Without the restraint of an MRND presence, the internal opposition parties returned to form, using the all-parties meeting as a platform for denouncing the "racist, regionalist, warlike, and dictatorial policy of President Habyarimana, his party the MRND, and his entourage." The meeting's communiqué also asserted that Habyarimana's policy of systematically blocking the government program had not changed since the establishment of the multiparty government on April 16, 1992. The parties claimed that innocent blood had flowed in several regions of the country, transforming an organized terrorism into a true genocide. It was because of these killings that the RPF was drawn into renewing hostilities. The communiqué then called for an effective ceasefire, withdrawal of foreign troops, reprise of negotiations, and return of displaced persons to their homes.

Insisting that immediate administrative sanctions be applied in the areas where massacres took place, the communiqué considered that the protocols already signed were "untouchable" and called on political parties that were obstructing the Arusha negotiations to honor their responsibilities. At the end of the discussions, there was little difference between what the RPF was demanding and what the parties agreed to. In the process, they had deserted the carefully negotiated agreement with the MRND on a common position and turned on Habyarimana with an invective that rivaled anything the RPF might have said on its own.

The parties' reunion in Bujumbura had shredded the common understanding on how to proceed at Arusha. Nonetheless, the president could not return to stalling tactics. A truce was in place, but the RPF was quite capable of pushing ahead in an offensive that government forces could not withstand.[17] Moreover, France, with its forces protecting Kigali, demanded a return to negotiations. To turn the truce into a formal ceasefire, Habyarimana would have to send Nsengiyaremye to the summit in Dar es Salaam and find a way to reengage in political negotiations.

POSITIONING FOR THE SUMMIT

Thus, despite the dissolution of the newly minted party consensus, the president and prime minister continued to meet together to prepare for the summit. A communiqué from their meeting with the chiefs of staff of the army and gendarmerie announced the common determination to proceed with negotiations and with democratization, to defend the rights of all citizens, and to reject the call for removal of French troops. In a nonpartisan working session, President Habyarimana (MRND) and Prime Minister Nsengiyaremye (MDR) met with the minister of foreign affairs (MDR), the minister of interior (MRND), and the minister of agriculture (PSD). The communiqué from that meeting spelled out objectives for the Dar es Salaam summit: to consolidate the ceasefire agreement and to create a climate for pursuing the peace process.[18]

On that same day, the religious leaders got back into the fray by chairing a meeting of twelve political parties, including all the major ones. The position taken by the parties at this meeting was in glaring contrast to the Bujumbura communiqué that excused the RPF for having been "drawn into" combat. Now back home and under church auspices, the parties condemned the RPF effort to take power by force of arms, praised the armed forces, invited the government to organize the whole population in civil defense, supported the presence of French troops, asked the United Nations to condemn Uganda and control the frontier, and called for consensus within the government and agreement between the president and prime minister.[19]

The political bureau of the MDR met March 1 without the presence of its president, Faustin Twagiramungu, who was still in Bujumbura. In a communiqué published the next day, and despite the position of Twagiramungu at the parties' meeting in Bujumbura, the MDR came out in favor of the presence of French troops, which assured security for foreigners, did not interfere with the Arusha negotiations, reinforced the democratic process, and sustained the process of reconciliation. As if to square the circle, the communiqué reported the party was "convinced that the presence of French troops in Rwanda did not in any way have the effect of supporting directly or indirectly the dictatorial regime of the retired Major General Habyarimana," and "it reaffirms its determination to combat this regime with all its force."[20]

The MDR statement reveals the dissonance in Rwandan politics at this critical juncture. This largest opposition party was beginning to show deep division in its own hierarchy: witness the convocation of the politburo meeting in the absence of the putative party president. Furthermore, the communiqué's pro-French stance, confronting the clear RPF demand for French withdrawal, seemed to reinforce roadblocks to negotiation at a time when continuing political stalemate and ethnic violence had brought on renewed fighting. Having paraded its commitment to negotiations, democratic process, and reconciliation, the communiqué then took a swing at Habyarimana that would have made the RPF proud.

Dar es Salaam and After

A leader of the MDR party, Prime Minister Dismas Nsengiyaremye, now equipped with a position paper worked out with President Habyarimana, went to negotiations in Dar es Salaam with the president of the Rwandese Patriotic Front, Col. Alexis Kanyarengwe. These March 5–7 discussions did what everyone wanted—namely, they formalized the ceasefire on the ground as of March 9—and what everybody had hoped: they promised the return of the RPF to the former ceasefire lines. The agreement also had in it a major point on which the Front had been insistent—suspension or dismissal of those administrative officers deemed to have been "directly or indirectly" involved in the January massacres and "those who failed to prevent massacres or other forms of communal violence."[21]

In paragraph 4, the communiqué calls for the withdrawal of foreign (read French) troops and their replacement by a neutral international force organized under the aegis of the OAU and UN. The communiqué claimed that the main purpose of the force was a humanitarian mission under article 11 of the ceasefire agreement of July 12, 1992, namely, to allay the fears and ensure "the security of expatriate personnel wherever they may be." Most entrancing is paragraph 5 that follows: "The two parties agreed on the modalities of the implementation of the preceding paragraph. Those modalities are contained in a confidential document known to the Facilitator."[22]

According to French commentators, this confidential agreement gave a timetable for French withdrawal: first the reinforced company sent to Rwanda after the Rwandan Patriotic Front offensive on February 8, then the withdrawal to barracks in Kigali of the forces held in Rwanda since the October 1990 war. These would stay in Kigali until their replacement by a neutral international force. France would retain in Rwanda a few dozen officers who were training the government army.[23]

INTERNATIONAL REACTIONS

As the Dar es Salaam Summit moved toward putting the peace process back on course, the international community picked up the Rwandan issue again. At the Security Council session of March 5, Under Secretary General James Jonah briefed the Security Council on the first meeting of the goodwill mission that the secretary general had sent to Rwanda. The mission found the RPF reluctant to withdraw from their forward positions, the Rwandan government uneasy and demanding quick UN action, and the OAU Neutral Military Observer Group not helpful in explaining the situation on the ground. At the same meeting, France circulated a draft resolution that was intended to reinforce the Dar es Salaam agreement and support the resumption of talks in Rwanda. It included a proposal for a UN observer mission on the Uganda-Rwanda border. In presenting his government's draft, Ambassador Ladsous noted a desire to support the new effort of the secretary general. He also encouraged close UN-OAU cooperation in the peacekeeping effort.[24]

On March 10, the United States, France, and Belgium, in trilateral discussions of Central African matters in Brussels, concentrated their attention on Rwanda. The Belgian side reported that the ceasefire seemed to be taking hold across the front and expressed strong appreciation for the political and military effort undertaken by France to stabilize the situation. The American representation seconded the appreciation for France's role. France, in turn, said it would respect the terms of the Dar es Salaam agreement concerning the withdrawal of foreign forces, barring a breakdown of the ceasefire. Although the French resolution before the Security Council called on the secretary general to examine the possibility of an international force under UN-OAU auspices, the Belgians wondered about a clearer division of responsibilities. They would give the OAU, reinforced by UN blue hats, support for the peace process, including patrolling the demilitarized zone. Belgium also favored handing protection of civilian populations, especially around the capital city, to a UN force.

The American side contended that human rights violations in Rwanda had their genesis in generalized fear of Tutsi hegemony as well as in acts abetted by elements allied to the president; the way to stop the human rights attacks was to stop the combat.[25] France entirely agreed, and the French representative urged his colleagues to concentrate on ending the fighting before dealing with human rights issues. Belgium, on the other hand, before it would send its ambassador back to Kigali, asked the Rwandan government to stop arming civilians, to stop stirring up anti-Tutsi sentiment, and fully to meet its commitments in the Dar es Salaam agreement. It was also preparing emergency assistance for the more than one million victims of the fighting who were displaced.[26]

The summit agreement that foreign troops should withdraw from Rwanda created a new dynamic in the international intervention. Notwithstanding support from the Rwandan government and political parties, French forces would not be a permanent part of the peace process. Without article 5, worked out with French representatives as a side protocol, the RPF would not have signed an agreement to turn the truce into a ceasefire and withdraw to their original position. Indeed, it would seem that the French were looking for a way out of their heavy engagement with a state that could not defend itself on the battlefield, was embroiled in endless bickering on the political front, and had given up the moral high ground by conniving in ethnic massacres. The only official French comment on article 5 was the government's statement that it accepted the plan for withdrawal of its troops decided upon in the Dar es

Salaam Agreement on the condition "that the Rwandan Patriotic Front honor its commitments and withdraw from the regions where it took up position after 8 February."[27]

Who Should Keep the Peace?

The protocol and the new ceasefire agreement thus raised with urgent immediacy the question of an international monitoring and peacekeeping presence in Rwanda. Approaches of the major donor countries reflected their policy differences. The United States took a bureaucratic and human rights perspective, wanting a larger role for the UN High Commissioner for Human Rights, public review of human rights in Rwanda within the Human Rights Commission, and the appointment of a special rapporteur as well as a strengthened OAU presence. Belgium looked at the human rights dimension from an internal Rwandan purview, demanding that the Rwandan government clean up its act before the Belgian ambassador could return. France, with troops on the ground, took a military focus, wanting to stop the flow of arms to the RPF from Uganda, to find a way of keeping the belligerents on opposite sides of a new buffer zone, and to secure a reliable, internationally sanctioned replacement for its troops protecting the expatriate community in Kigali.[28]

SECURING THE BORDER

The idea of a monitoring force along Rwanda's border with Uganda had been implicit in the security agreement that Assistant Secretary Cohen had urged on the parties in May 1992 and that the parties had signed that August. But realization of that aim had been slow. The Rwandan government, for all its complaints about the Rwandese Patriotic Army being a de facto Ugandan force, had been caught up in canonical arguments about which side of the border a monitoring force would patrol. Uganda initially took the position that a monitoring force was an affront to its assurances that there was no operational link between the Ugandan government and the RPA.

French envoys to Uganda in February 1993 had apparently overcome Museveni's opposition to the idea. By the time of the March Security

Council discussions, Rwanda and Uganda had together forwarded notes requesting the deployment of United Nations observers along their common border.[29] France's draft resolution on Rwanda, among other things, invited the secretary general to examine the request of Rwanda and Uganda for the deployment of observers at the border between these two countries.[30]

Security Council discussions on the French draft resolution raised two curious but prescient points. Djibouti said it could support a peacekeeping force only if the Rwandese Patriotic Force withdrew to the frontier of Rwanda, a naïve notion given the alignment of forces on the ground, but one that highlighted the problem of a chapter 6 "monitoring" force interposed between two belligerent camps. Spain agreed with the resolution as a whole but noted that the contending sides had different visions of what kind of force would most effectively support the peace process: an OAU force or a UN-OAU force. Although the US mission at the United Nations characterized the Spanish intervention as "carping," in fact the Spanish representative had foreseen a major issue: Would peacekeeping in Rwanda continue to be regional, under the auspices of the OAU, or international, under leadership of the United Nations?[31]

PATROLLING THE DEMILITARIZED ZONE

The second optic for an international military presence arose from the withdrawal of the RPA to its previous positions, which created between the two forces a no-man's-land ten to eighteen kilometers wide. The American embassy in Kigali recognized immediately that the fragile cease-fire accord needed a credible interposition force to patrol this area and that the fifty-plus OAU observer mission could not quickly be geared up to this task.[32] The OAU had already been talking for months about reinforcing its observer mission, but nothing had happened. A complicating factor was that the February fighting had created nearly a million internally displaced persons who needed to return to their homes before the end of the rainy season and the beginning of harvest. Moreover, the OAU forces had done nothing to report on or deter the RPF attack, which led the government to question the NMOG's neutral role.[33] For lack of a better alternative, the embassy made an eloquent, well-reasoned argument for rapid deployment of a temporary UN force until a neutral international force under OAU auspices could take over.[34]

This recommendation of action by the United Nations in what had heretofore been an African-led peace process stirred the policy machine at the Department of State. Three principles informed the department's analysis: the plight of the displaced with the specter of another large-scale humanitarian disaster; the need to keep the initiative in African hands; and the difficulties of securing UN involvement. The department's summation also notes the fundamental difference between a border monitoring force and a ceasefire interpositional force.

What the State Department did not consider was a force that would restore confidence and protect the international community, the only force actually mentioned in the Dar es Salaam communiqué. In a classic use of diplomatic indirection, the department reported that "any suggestion of UN involvement in Rwanda will face resistance." The text does not suggest where the resistance might come from. Reporting from the US Mission to the United Nations (USUN) suggested that among the Permanent Five members, Russia and Great Britain were reluctant to consider UN involvement because of potential costs. China was opposed to larger peace-keeping roles for the organization.[35] In effect, the United States was taking the sovereign positions of other states into consideration in formulating its response to this humanitarian crisis. Moreover, the US government, then in the process of formulating the new Clinton administration's approach to UN peacekeeping, had its concerns, namely, the following:

- The UN is already overstretched financially and managerially.

- With similar situations existing elsewhere (Sudan and Zaire), member nations may not want to set a precedent.

- The UN is unable to move quickly, but a monitoring force is urgently needed now.

- It would be difficult to locate troop contributors.

- UN intervention requires clear evidence of a threat to international peace and security; this internal dispute will require convincing arguments to fit this criterion.[36]

Given the difficulties of getting the UN involved, the State Department concluded that the OAU should be urged to take the initiative, recruit additional monitors from African countries, and seek technical assistance and monitoring experts from the UN. But the initiative for any OAU involvement must come from the African parties to the conflict. "It would not be appropriate for the USG to take the lead."[37] A role for the United Nations, whether in border or ceasefire monitoring, would have to have the approval of the OAU, the Tanzanian Facilitator, and the RPF, as well as the Rwandan government.

The RPF had indicated that the border-monitoring force was a matter between the Ugandan and Rwandan governments. However, it would have to be consulted as regards areas on the border that it controlled. Moreover, the RPF wanted an enlarged OAU force to monitor the ceasefire, unless the OAU should prove incapable of handling the new job and requested UN observers. Though aware that the Rwandan government mistrusted OAU-NMOG neutrality and wanted UN forces, the Department of State, nonetheless, came down in favor of the OAU: "The OAU should be urged to take the initiative in the Rwandan conflict, to seek additional monitors from African countries and to provide better support and supervision to the existing operation." What drove this conclusion were the costs of burgeoning UN peacekeeping responsibilities, the desire to enhance the OAU's peacekeeping capacities, and the intent to keep conflict resolution in Rwanda under African control.[38]

COVERING BOTH BASES

In any case, when the first Security Council resolution on the situation in Rwanda (based on the French draft) came to a vote, it reflected a strong humanitarian concern for displaced persons and refugees, offered appropriate tributes to the OAU efforts to arrange a political solution, and invited the secretary general to examine the request of Rwanda and Uganda for the deployment of observers at the border between these two countries, as well as "to coordinate closely his efforts with those of the Organization of African Unity and to provide it with the necessary assistance to the peacekeeping efforts in Rwanda." In equivocal language, the resolution also invited the secretary general "to examine in consultation with the

OAU the contribution that the United Nations, in support of the OAU's efforts, could bring to strengthen the peace process in Rwanda, in particular through the possible establishment of an international force under the aegis of the OAU and the United Nations, entrusted inter alia with the protection of, and humanitarian assistance to, the civilian population and the support of the OAU force for the monitoring of the cease fire."[39]

The resolution thus opened the door not only to a UN border-monitoring force but also to some sort of UN interpositional force. The resolution suggests, ambiguously, that the UN force (under OAU approval or aegis) might operate on its own for the given objectives of civilian protection and humanitarian assistance, while supporting the OAU in its ceasefire monitoring responsibilities.

A NEW UN ROLE?

The reopening of the Arusha talks on March 16 brought a mixed reaction to a possible new role for the United Nations. The Rwandan government favored UN assistance to the OAU effort and a UN operation in Kigali to replace the French forces. Commissioner Bizimungu, speaking for the Front, claimed that the Rwandan government was attempting to encircle and strangle the RPF with a number of UN forces and demanded the retention of the OAU Neutral Military Observer Group (NMOG) as an interpositional force.[40]

Ms. Florence Pomes, special representative of the UN secretary general, was present at the plenary session as the political negotiations reopened. In her remarks, she noted that "the UN is ready to cooperate with and support the OAU efforts in Rwanda; it has neither the intention nor the means to replace the OAU in African affairs."[41] Ms. Pomes's remarks seemed designed to allay the fears of African participants that the UN would move in on the OAU effort. Only the Rwandan government and France seemed anxious for that to happen.

The special representative may also have been addressing US concerns, already voiced in Security Council discussions. After the plenary, the new US ambassador to Tanzania, Peter De Vos, discussed with Ms. Pomes the US position: the quickest way to stand up an interpositional force for the expanded demilitarized zone was to enhance the field capacity of the OAU's Neutral Military Observer Group, thereby developing as well "effective OAU capabilities in the area of conflict resolution." Moreover, early, effective intervention by the OAU could keep conflicts off the UN's plate, reduce the magnitude of the crisis, and diminish the scale of human suffering.[42]

Behind this position was the determination of the new Clinton administration, with its focus on multilateral diplomacy, to get some organizational grip on US involvement in peacekeeping initiatives. The bureaucracy in Washington, led by the Department of State, was in full process of drafting peacekeeping guidelines under Presidential Study Directive No. 13. Part of the new strategy was to find alternatives to expensive UN operations through peacekeeping by regional bodies. Since the United States had already invested in strengthening the peacekeeping office within the OAU, the Rwandan situation offered a chance for that office to get operational. Furthermore, a force made up of African contingents under OAU captaincy fit the guiding principle of US policy: "African solutions to African problems."[43]

The US position discounted the obvious deficiencies of the OAU monitoring operation. The ceasefire of June 1992 was to have come into force with the promised deployment of the OAU's Neutral Military Observer Group. The force was not in Rwanda until October and not really operational until November or December. Force leadership was more concerned about pay rates than effectiveness on the ground. The force was underequipped, undermanned, and underfunded from the start, despite funds held by OAU headquarters that could have been designated for this cause. The NMOG's reports on border confrontations during the chaotic December '92–February '93 events convinced the Rwandan government that it was not really a neutral force. Yet, the ceasefire held until February 8, in large part owing to the restraint of the two contending parties, but also because of the belated but dissuasive presence of OAU officers. Now after the RPF advance and then withdrawal under the Dar es Salaam agreement, there were much larger responsibilities, both of policing the demilitarized zone and of replacing the French military force in Kigali. There was little in the record to suggest that the OAU was up to those tasks, but the United States was not giving up on its "African" peacekeeping strategy.[44]

Back to Arusha

By March 15, international Observers, who had left Arusha February 6, were headed back toward the negotiations. The talks reconvened in the afternoon of March 16 in plenary session. Foreign Minister Ngulinzira (back leading the delegation) took the high road of conciliation, committing the government to full implementation of its responsibilities under the various protocols while stressing the importance of human rights and reconciliation. On the other side, the information commissioner for the RPF, Pasteur Bizimungu, picked up his customary attack. He listed past massacres of Tutsi, complained of government ceasefire violations, denied all allegations of RPF improprieties in the recent fighting, and claimed that the Rwandan government was holding the Rwandan population hostage for political purposes.[45]

With usual optimism, the revised schedule allocated ten days for military talks, five days for refugee matters, and a final three days for remaining political issues. A review of the events that led up to these resumed negotiations should have given all Observers pause over the possibilities of such a schedule, and concern over the portents of impending discussions.[46] Having been proved ineffective on the battlefield, the government entered into the new negotiations suing for peace. Habyarimana's side had gained nothing in the months of political bickering since October, except a cessation of renewed hostilities. The opposition envisioned a rapid devolution of power, if they could quickly accommodate RPF interests in refugee and military matters. Ironically, a MRND moderate, Minister of Defense Gasana, had chaired the aborted February talks that fell apart on "political" issues. Now that the Dar es Salaam summit had wiped out formal objections to the January 9 protocol, the MRND minister of foreign affairs Ngulinzira was to preside over renewed "military talks."[47]

KEEPING PACE WITH THE PEACE TALKS

As renewed talks entered this critical period, the Convener (OAU), the Facilitator (Tanzania), and Observer states geared up for the final phase of negotiations. The rapid return to the conference table caught delegations off guard. At the opening plenary, delegations from Senegal,

Uganda, Belgium, and Germany were absent. Four days into the talks, the OAU leadership had yet to appear, being detained in Addis for discussions with the Rwandan government over the makeup of a ceasefire monitoring group. This graphically illustrated the shallow bench on the OAU team and the challenge that the new peacekeeping opportunities presented to OAU leadership.

The Observer groups were in transition. The Belgian director of African affairs was ill, so Brussels sent in rotating second-level Observers or used their personnel from the embassy in Dar es Salaam. The Germans similarly rotated in Dar es Salaam personnel, sometimes the ambassador, sometimes lesser embassy officers. The French used either their ambassador in Dar es Salaam or, more frequently, the deputy chief of mission, Jean-Christophe Belliard, by this time the most experienced of the Observers.

The State Department put high premium on pushing the renewed talks along. Assistant Secretary of State Herman Cohen, in a message to Ambassador De Vos in Dar es Salaam and Ambassador Flaten in Kigali, noted, "We attach great importance to this final (we hope) round of talks. Serious delays or a complete breakdown could result in renewed fighting that could prove tragic for both sides. We want to provide to the peace process the greatest support we can. I have therefore made the difficult decision to allow AF/RA sole military adviser at the moment, Lt. Colonel Marley, to remain in Arusha to observe the military talks until the first week in April."[48]

To move that process along, Cohen picked a particularly skilled team. In addition to Col. Marley, Cohen asked Kigali to send Deputy Chief of Mission (DCM) Joyce Leader, who had deep experience in refugee affairs and had represented the United States at the Dar es Salaam refugee conference. She was to observe the refugee part of the negotiations. Finally, Cohen asked Dar es Salaam to send political officer Robert Bentley to observe at the concluding political discussions and offered up his legal advisor, John Byerly, to assist in the last part of the negotiations, if there were constitutional issues to be resolved.

But meanwhile, there was a changing of the guard within the State Department. The newly elected Clinton administration was gradually settling in. Ambassador George Moose, who had served on the Clinton transition team, would take over from Hank Cohen as assistant secretary of state. Virtually all of the policy makers who had been working the Rwandan issue, excepting the desk officer, Kevin Aiston, would move on to other things. Reflecting the new administration's interest in global issues, Moose gave his former DCM in Senegal, Prudence Bushnell, a new portfolio for global affairs, regional conflicts, and peacekeeping. As members of the new team at the State Department worked out details of policy management, it fell to embassies of the region to assure a US presence at the Arusha talks and the Observer in Arusha to promote US perspectives and interests.

Military Integration

Serious discussions at Arusha started right after the plenary, with high hopes for rapid progress to the conclusions of the talks. Since the agreement on the coalition government in Rwanda was to expire on April 16, the parties wanted the negotiations concluded and transition institutions ready to install before then. Almost immediately, the two sides went into face-to-face bilateral discussions, canceling the scheduled plenary sessions. Observers finally asked for a plenary session so they would know what progress was being made and would be able to report to their capitals. Amid mutual accusations of ceasefire violations, the plenary began with discussions of the mission and principles of the armed forces, the participation of military in civil society, and the relative virtues of a national gendarmerie or a national police.[49]

Unfortunately, initial high hopes and apparently productive face-to-face sessions gave way to intractable conflicts over the notion of a gendarmerie, percentage of RPF representation in the officer corps and ranks, and the nature and mission of a "neutral international force." By the time Colonel Marley left on April 20 and DCM Leader replaced him, none of the critical issues of military integration had been resolved. The proposed April 8 date for signing the Arusha agreement was long past. The Facilitator was pushing for "early agreement" on the gendarmerie issue but recommending that force proportions be deferred until the end of the military talks. The Arusha negotiations appeared stalled again.

Meanwhile, OAU military observers in Rwanda were essentially hanging around waiting for a new order. Absent an effective OAU plan for monitoring the ceasefire, the two parties proposed a high-level meeting in Kigali between RPF chairman Kanyarengwe and Prime Minister Nsegiyaremye, to be advanced by technical talks on the regime of the demilitarized zone. The purpose of the meeting would be to work out a plan for providing security to the buffer zone so that displaced persons could return to plant their fields and participate in elections to set up local government. The parties suggested that forces on each side field teams under NMOG supervision within each commune. On all other matters of security, the talks were deadlocked.[50]

AN INTERNAL SECURITY FORCE

Since independence, Rwanda had cared for its internal security with communal police, who reported through authorities of local government to the Ministry of Interior, and with a national gendarmerie, which had the classic mission of protecting public facilities and highways as well as public order and reported through the minister of defense. The army was theoretically deployed for territorial defense, although under the Second Republic, its leaders had devoted themselves to running the country. This was the institutional form of security forces that the government negotiators sought to perpetuate. The Rwandese Patriotic Front, on the other hand, took its vision from its experience with the national police force in Uganda, the National Revolutionary Army, as well as the Ugandan intelligence services.

Three issues found the parties on opposite sides. The first issue was efficacy: the history of ethnic violence within Rwanda, often abetted by local police and with hesitant reaction by the gendarmerie, made the RPF question whether the Rwandan model was up to dealing with the increased tensions of the transition period. As a reserve reaction force, Rwanda's gendarmerie had a sorry record of slow response; the RPF wanted an active, engaged, constraining police force. Yet, the Rwandan government could hardly imagine a secure state without a paramilitary gendarmerie to defend the public interest.

Bureaucratic oversight of the gendarmerie was a second issue. Under the January protocols, the RPF was to hold the interior portfolio, and the

MRND, their prime political opponent, would hold the Ministry of Defense. The RPF wanted the control of internal security within the Ministry of Interior. The Rwandan government did not want to cede an armed force to a ministry that had always had an administrative rather than a coercive role. The government also saw the possibility of two competing security forces, each under politically opposite ministerial authority, as a recipe for continuous internal conflict. Even the internal opposition parties wanted the Ministry of Defense to oversee the gendarmerie, which is why the parties were still arguing about the issue one month after the start of military talks.

Finally, institutionalization of the new security organization during the transition was an issue. A new national police organization would put the two parties on level ground, each having to be trained into the practices and principles of the new organization. Although there was nothing in the ceasefire agreement requiring that the gendarmerie be integrated, if the RPF accepted a gendarmerie, it wanted it to undergo the same process as the army: disarmament, confinement to assembly points, and remobilization by training within an integrated force. The government was opposed to demobilization and integration, wondering how security would be provided for the transition without an active gendarmerie. The RPF thought the neutral international force would provide internal security during the reintegration process. Obviously, command responsibilities and force-level issues devolved from whether one would be integrating outside forces into an existing institution or creating a new organization.

By April 21, the talks were still stalled on the issue of the internal security force. Observers heard from the RPF that the major issue was not oversight of the force but its function and role. Later that day, the Facilitator, represented by Ambassador Mpungwe, convened a meeting with the parties and the Observers to express concern over the slow pace of negotiations. The parties explained that it was not a matter of bad faith in negotiations but the "need to discuss issues in depth." They agreed to consult with the Facilitator on a target date to end military talks.[51]

Four days later, the parties had reached an agreement in principle. The RPF dropped its proposal for a national police force in return for a commitment from the Rwandan government that the gendarmerie would shift its focus from paramilitary intervention to regularized protection at the communal level. Coordination mechanisms between the two ministries would be improved and civilian control over operations of all armed services assured. Having etched the outlines of that agreement, the parties then turned to other military issues: the composition and use of the neutral international force, force proportions, force demobilization and integration, and the security status of Kigali.[52]

INTERNATIONAL FORCE INTERVENTION

How February's ceasefire would be monitored and the transition processes upheld remained a disputed issue. Despite US enthusiasm for the OAU taking on a larger monitoring role through an expanded NMOG reinforced by UN expertise, the NMOG contingent remained largely what it had been before the February hostilities. OAU secretary general Salim Salim had stopped by the talks on April 4 and promised an operationally expanded NMOG by April 15, but all the OAU had managed was a survey mission to determine the needs of an expanded presence. According to its findings, the OAU would have to deploy a battalion-sized OAU force until the UN force came in.[53] The OAU pled a lack of personnel and resources necessary to the task despite the fact that Senegal, Tunisia, Zimbabwe, and Nigeria had tentatively agreed to provide troops for an OAU demilitarized-zone force. By late April, France, Belgium, and the United States had presented a demarche to the OAU in Addis and in New York urging the organization to accelerate its efforts. The United States pointed to $400,000 of a US contribution to OAU peacekeeping the previous year that had yet to be spent and urged rapid deployment of forces with monies at hand as well as a simultaneous fundraising session among concerned "Friends of Rwanda."[54]

Observers in Arusha envisioned an evolving international force: an OAU monitoring force assisted by the UN would police the demilitarized "buffer" zone until the peace agreement was negotiated. After the parties had signed the agreement, a UN peacekeeping force assisted by the OAU would bolster the peace process and help implement its military provisions. But, the contending parties did not share this vision. The Rwandan government was not impressed with the neutrality of the existing OAU force. Although it had agreed to a larger NMOG, the Rwandan government had also requested a UN force on the ground in Rwanda immediately. The Rwandan Patriotic Front, satisfied with the NMOG and its light observer presence on the ground, feared an overweening buildup of UN forces that would encumber the peace process (and override the RPF's field advantage).[55]

Immediately after the two parties had briefed observers on their breakthrough agreement on the gendarmerie, Ambassador Mpungwe convened the two sides to review progress in implementing the March 5 Dar es Salaam agreement. His government was concerned that nonimplementation of the agreement might be used as provocation by one side or the other to resume hostilities. The parties agreed to quell doubts by formally reiterating their request for an expanded NMOG and their interest in a continuing OAU role in the Rwandan peace process.[56] Most significantly, the OAU notified the two sides that the UN secretary general categorically turned back the OAU's request for technical and financial assistance, even though that request had been supported by a trilateral demarche by France, Belgium, and the United States on April 30.[57]

GETTING INTO THE ACT

Despite Boutros-Ghali's reticence, the United Nations' presence in the region was growing. The secretary general's goodwill mission to the region in March had set the stage for a follow-on survey team in early April to look at requirements for a possible UN force on the Rwandan-Ugandan border. That was after all a classic UN responsibility: interposition between two sovereign states. In conversations with Ambassador Flaten in Kigali, the survey team leader, General Baril, invited comments on the possible makeup of a buffer-zone force.[58] Nonetheless, Observers in Arusha were led to conclude that there was no chance of a UN role within the Rwandan peace process until the Arusha Accords had been signed.

Having foreclosed on the possibility of military assistance in Rwanda, the United Nations then began to modulate its position. For one thing, the Rwandan government was still pressing for a UN force on the ground as soon as possible, an objective for which Habyarimana sought the help of newly installed US assistant secretary for African affairs, George Moose, in their May 27 meeting in Gabon.[59] Moreover, the trilateral partners refused to take "no" for an answer. At a May 11 trilateral meeting, France, Belgium, and the United States agreed to reopen with the secretary general the question of UN support for peacekeeping in Rwanda. The partners put the best face on Boutros-Ghali's initial refusal, attributing it to misinformation on the Ugandan position regarding a border force.[60]

In late May, UN assistant secretary general Iqbal Riza told Secretary Moose that the UN would send experts to Rwanda to help the OAU plan for the introduction of a peacekeeping force into the demilitarized zone. According to Riza, the secretary general had also approved a report recommending eighty-one military observers with twenty-five support staff for the Rwanda-Uganda border. A report on deployment in other areas would be presented after the Arusha talks concluded.[61] Three and a half months after the demilitarized zone had been set up by the Dar es Salaam agreement, the peacekeeping bureaucracies were still in the "early planning" stage. By June, international partners of the Arusha process were still debating the authority, mission, and staffing of a neutral international force in Rwanda.

PATROLLING THE BORDER

Only the plans for a UN monitoring force on the border between Rwanda and Uganda seemed to be going forward. On this the French had become quite insistent. They had inserted the notion into their draft Security Council resolution, which sought to bolster conclusions of the March summit in Dar es Salaam. Having secured the agreement of Uganda and Rwanda to the idea, France then lobbied hard in the Security Council and among its trilateral partners for support. Other than arguing for a clear delimitation of international security roles in Rwanda, the Belgians were quite willing to go along with the French proposal.

The United States, on the other hand, raised a series of procedural objections and initially said it could not, without further clarification, support France's idea. Giving the UN a direct and immediate role in Rwanda countered the US effort to promote OAU peacekeeping. It also added another costly ad hoc UN peacekeeping operation just as the new US administration was trying to outline a policy for limiting and rationalizing international peacekeeping. Eventually, a high-level political and military mission came from Paris to New York and Washington to hash out differences. France largely conceded to US operational nitpicking. The United States decided to go along with France on border monitors in hope of French support for an expanded NMOG in the buffer zone.[62]

FORCE PROPORTIONS

The discussions about the gendarmerie's function and role and the nature of the international peacekeeping force were but sideshows in the military negotiations. The real issue was integration of the army. The ceasefire agreement of July 13, 1992, had set as one of its objectives the "formation of a national army consisting of Government Forces and those of the Rwandese Patriotic Front." Within a week after the reopening of talks in Arusha, Colonel Marley reported that "the Facilitator and both Rwandan parties have grasped the nettle and initiated negotiation of the integration ratios of the new Rwandan Army." The nettle stung! Even though the Facilitator decided to treat force ratios with "shuttle diplomacy" rather than face-to-face talks, RPF spokesman Bizimungu treated Rwandan government proposals with such ridicule that the Facilitator decided to defer discussions on force levels until the negotiators had come to agreement on other military issues: cantonment and assembly points, demobilization, and the status of Kigali, as well as the nature of the international force.[63]

The original positions of the two parties on force levels were far apart. The Rwandan government's initial conception of the negotiations was to include the Rwandan Patriotic Front as a political element within the existing multiparty government. The army would remain as it was instituted. Even the notion of integrating a few RPA officers into command positions was hard for Rwandan leadership to swallow. At the beginning of military talks in March, the Rwandan government was willing to offer an eighty-twenty split, a proposal the Front found risible.[64] Yet, by May 3, the Rwandan foreign minister said he did not expect a major problem in this area, although he did not elaborate on the basis for his optimism.[65] Certainly, his president a fortnight later characterized the discussion of percentages that would be integrated into a unified army as "sensitive and complex."[66]

The Front, early in the negotiations, talked in general terms of a fifty-fifty split in integration levels.[67] This position was buttressed by President Museveni's candid assessment that the Rwandese Patriotic Army (RPA) had proved its military superiority on the ground and, given its concerns for the security of Tutsi in Rwanda, had a right to an equal share in security responsibilities. The RPF were certainly aware of Museveni's views, and that he had forcefully shared those views with Arusha Observers and their governments.[68] In the military talks, the RPF again raised the idea of a fifty-fifty split between the two forces. When Colonel Marley suggested that different ratios be applied at different command levels, the RPF proposed a fifty-fifty split in troop levels and in command functions down to the company level.[69]

The Facilitator did not feel that the "conference diplomacy" of Arusha provided the appropriate means to resolve the sensitive issue of force proportions. So the Tanzanians took the issue off the table and dealt with it by a message-carrying facilitation. But the talks stalled with only the slightest movement on proportionality. Proximity talks with the Tanzanians brought the government bid to 75 percent for the government and 25 percent for the RPF. The RPF, however, stuck to a proposal for 55 percent for the government and 45 percent for the RPF.[70]

Tanzanian minister of defense Kinana joined the facilitating team carrying messages between Arusha and Kigali.[71] On May 11, Ambassador Mpungwe returned to Arusha after discussions with Tanzanian foreign minister Rwegasira and President Mwinyi with a strategy for negotiations on force proportions. As the US Observer Joyce Leader dryly commented, "He did not advise Observers on the substance of his discussions or his strategy."[72] Minister Kinana was to arrive shortly to assist in the negotiations. Thus, force proportions had become the preserve of the Tanzanian Facilitator, and agreement on those ratios was not quick in coming.[73]

While the Tanzanians pursued their shuttle diplomacy, the two sides met to consider outstanding issues they could resolve among themselves, such as the timetable for force integration and military discipline. They produced a document on "Proposed Confidence Building Measures" and asked that the twinned issues of an enlarged NMOG and a neutral international force be put on the agenda of the upcoming high-level meeting in Kigali.[74] The Observers met with the parties to discuss issues on which they requested advice: disengagement and demobilization, incorporation of the RPA into other security services, and the international force. Leader reported that as of May 23, "The Rwandan peace talks continue to turn around pending military issues without getting to key issues of force proportions and participation of the RPF in the gendarmerie."[75]

When the Tanzanians finally came up with a formula that they considered fair and sensible, they tabled it with authority. On May 31, Ambassador Mpungwe, "on instruction from President Mwinyi," laid before the parties a proposal that would have RPF participation of 35 to 40 percent. Subsequent negotiations were to work out how that applied to various ranks.[76] The following day, during follow-up consultations with the delegations, RPF told Mpungwe that it would not negotiate on that range and asked for a new proposal from the Facilitator. Mpungwe suggested that the RPF go back to its authorities for new instructions.[77]

In a later briefing of Observers, Ambassador Mpungwe said the RPF rejected the proposal "with contempt and arrogance." He suggested that the RPF was stalling to buy time for "other things" and questioned the Front's commitment to the peace process. The Ugandan and OAU Observers endorsed the Tanzanian view and urged maximum pressure to "bring reality home to the RPF." Belgian and US Observers sought to keep the sides talking. That evening, the RPF boycotted a Tanzanian government reception honoring the opening of refugee negotiations. To keep their pique over force proportions public, the RPF representatives at refugee talks made confrontational interventions even though the RPF had few changes to suggest to the draft refugee protocol that the Rwandan government had tabled. Joyce Leader concluded that given the atmospherics, "the year-long peace process could come to an abrupt, premature end."[78]

Having failed to move the RPF in Arusha on the force proportions issue, the Tanzanians then sought to move the argument to the leadership of both sides in Rwanda. On June 7, the Tanzanian prime minister, foreign minister, defense minister, and Ambassador Mpungwe with staff flew to Kigali to sell the plan to the Rwandan government and then drove to the Mulindi Tea Plantation to discuss it with Chairman Kanyarengwe and Vice Chairman Kagame of the RPF. At the conclusion of the meetings,

Prime Minister Malecela expressed optimism but was otherwise closed-mouthed. But Rwandan government sources reported that the Tanzanians were trying to secure the Rwandan government agreement to a split of sixty (GOR) to forty (RPF) in the army and a fifty-fifty split in the gendarmerie. The officer corps would be split fifty-fifty, but at what command level was not clear. The Tanzanians were also trying to sell a new tight schedule for concluding the talks, with signature of a peace agreement by June 12.[79]

On his return to Arusha June 9, Ambassador Mpungwe convoked the Western Observers and asked their help in convincing President Habyarimana that the sixty-forty split was "the most realistic solution for integrating both the army and the gendarmerie." Mpungwe said the force ratio was the best deal he could get from the RPF. President Mwinyi had called Ugandan president Museveni to ask his help in getting the RPF to accept a lower figure, but the Ugandans apparently had not got through to RPF leadership by the time of the Tanzanian delegation's visit on June 7. The French and Belgian Observers said that their governments would accept a ratio of sixty to forty but cautioned about taking the fifty-fifty officer ratio too far down the command structure. Joyce Leader recommended US acceptance, but Ambassador Flaten in Kigali demurred, believing that this was not a matter for the United States to decide.[80]

Trying to Wrap It Up

It had been eleven months since the Tanzanians had started facilitating the ceasefire talks under the chairmanship of then foreign minister Diria. Ambassador Mpungwe had warned the two sides on April 21 that the continuing lack of agreement was a threat to the possibility of peace. The Tanzanian government was running out of resources to continue to host and facilitate the talks.[81] On May 25, Defense Minister Kinana, speaking on behalf of the Facilitator, called on the government and RPF delegations "to demonstrate their continued commitment to the peace process by picking up on the pace of negotiations."[82]

Kinana contended that there sometimes seemed to be deliberate attempts to stall the talks and urged both sides to respect the advice of the

Facilitator's representative as "sincere, honest and objective." While the Rwandan delegation seemed to take the minister's advice on board, RPF commissioner Bizimungu resisted Kinana's contention that the Facilitator's word should be final. The negotiations were "between the two sides which should take expert views into consideration in reaching their own decision.[83]

A JUNE SIGNING?

By the end of May, the Facilitator's shuttle diplomacy had failed to bring closure on control of storage depots, demilitarization of Kigali, integrating the RPF into the gendarmerie, and the timing for installation of the broad-based government. "The question of force proportions is not yet under discussion," Leader reported. In the meantime, the uncertainty over the nature and timing of a neutral international force deployment to Rwanda was complicating discussions on all other issues.[84]

The Tanzanian effort had by all standards been heroic, evenhanded, and artful in pushing forward the boundaries of a possible agreement. With the annual OAU meeting now looming, the Tanzanians were pushing hard to wrap up the talks. After a weekend of intense discussions, the Tanzanian defense minister told the Observers on June 13 that June 19 had been set as the date for concluding the negotiations and signing the agreement. President Mwinyi was extending invitations to high levels of Observer states and international organizations.[85]

The package of remaining contentions was bigger than the Tanzanians wished to admit. The duration of the transition, the constitutional articles to be revised, the naming of the transition prime minister, and RPF participation in "other security services" all held hidden blockages. For example, Defense Minister Kinana considered the naming of Prime Minister Nsengiyaremye as transition prime minister a done deal. However, that nomination was engineered by the prime minister himself and was hotly contested by government ministers back in Kigali. The defense minister may have been right in holding that neither side in Arusha wanted popular or parliamentary ratification of necessary constitutional changes or of the overall accord; but the demand for popular ratification remained President Habyarimana's position and that of a significant part of the Rwandan body politic. US Observer Leader wondered if the Tanzanians were serious about the proposed date for signing or were trying to bluff the parties into speedy agreement. Given the track record on military discussions, the problems remaining to be resolved were not likely to be negotiated in five days.[86]

Back in Kigali, it was also evident that the Tanzanian deadline could not be met. The Tanzanian mission had stirred local political forces to address the peace process. Initially, the government wanted a better force ratio, but the internal political parties formally accepted a 40 percent figure for the RPF participation in security services. The Rwandan cabinet decided to accept the Tanzanian integration range of 35 to 40 percent for the RPA, in effect making a sixty-forty split acceptable. The cabinet did reserve on the notion of making Kigali a demilitarized zone or moving the transition government to some demilitarized location. While the Facilitator had told Observers in Arusha that the fifty-fifty ratio for officers should apply to the top ten command positions, the RPF claimed that the Tanzanians proposed a fifty-fifty ratio down to battalion command as part of the package it was asked to accept. The process of integration in the gendarmerie also remained at issue.[87]

The idea that inconsistencies between the Arusha Protocols and the constitution should be worked out in Arusha was not acceptable to the Rwandan government. Nonetheless, in a new initiative, Habyarimana had requested an opinion from the National Commission for Development (CND), parliamentarians elected under the one-party regime, on the Arusha process. The resulting two-day, closed-door debate essentially provided advance acceptance of the protocols and such constitutional changes as they might require. This process put to rest the demand for a popular referendum on the accords. However, the cabinet insisted on its right to review the completed texts, and the CND wanted to see the final document for a final approval.[88]

Even as the Tanzanians were trying to tie up military issues, party and government circles discussed the important question of who was to be the transition prime minister. While he had the backing of his party cadre, Nsengiyaremye had angered many of his cabinet colleagues by his lack of coordination and his practice of government by fiat. The cabinet asked the MDR to name another person. But the MDR political bureau confirmed Nsengiyaremye as their choice and reiterated their right under the current constitution and power-sharing protocols to make that decision.[89]

The American embassy in Kigali, usually cautious in pronouncements on the peace process, believed that there was enough accord on fundamentals that an agreement could be signed within a week or so of the Tanzanian visit. However, negotiators in Arusha failed to accept the Tanzanian proposal on proportions in command functions. The Facilitator blamed the RPF for reneging on an agreement; the RPF, in turn, claimed it had neither rejected nor accepted the Tanzanian package but needed further instructions from headquarters. Moreover, the RPF delegation said they understood the Tanzanian deal to be a fifty-fifty command split down to the company level, while the Rwanda government believed that the compromise ratio was fifty-five to forty-five down to battalion level. Having failed to meet the signature deadline, the Facilitator suspended talks, the Tanzanian and Rwandan foreign ministers went to the OAU summit in Cairo, and President Mwinyi promised to pursue the peace process there.[90]

WHO IS TO BLAME?

While Foreign Minister Ngulinzira was quick to blame the RPF for the suspension, he also faulted the cabinet for interfering in the designation of the transition prime minister and President Habyarimana for not personally negotiating the last elements of the accord. The US view was that "the Tanzanians may have pushed too far too fast in an attempt to arrive at the OAU summit with a peace agreement."[91] The effort to keep the decision making in Arusha or in closed-door shuttle diplomacy had in fact complicated the process. The cabinet was still insisting on final review. A deal the Tanzanians apparently cut with Chairman Kanyarengwe on force proportions seemed to have been overturned by RPF militants, hence the Arusha delegation's "lack of instructions." Moreover, the MDR persisted in its nomination of Nsengiyaremye despite cabinet objections. Hopes for the Arusha negotiations had once again become disconnected from political realities in Kigali and in Mulindi.[92]

The Politics of Negotiation

COOPERATION

Since the ad hoc reestablishment of a truce on February 9 and the confirmation of a ceasefire by the Dar es Salaam Agreement of March 5, the political mood in Kigali had fundamentally changed. The rhetorical opposition of the Bujumbura parties' meeting gave way to cooperation as the internal opposition parties began to work with the MRND. The cabinet moved ahead on the nagging problem of cleaning up local administration, holding elections in thirty-one constituencies. The opposition parties drafted a thirteen-page memorandum to outline a common position for a meeting with the MRND on extension of the current transition government and on Arusha issues.[93]

The president and the prime minister met more often in the two months after February 9 than they had since the coalition government was established in April 1992. As they worked on a common strategy for Arusha, the usual mutual recrimination seemed a thing of the past. Indeed, when Nsengiyaremye engineered his own nomination for transition prime minister, the opposition came not from the president and his MRND party but within the MDR and others of the internal opposition parties who resented the prime minister's high-handed rule. In his speeches, the president gave unequivocal signals of his willingness to accept the Arusha Accords. Habyarimana's March 21 speech in Bujumbura was considered the clearest statement yet of his commitment to peace. He also set a consistent track record of accommodating the political opposition, finally even accepting the naming of PL leader Justin Mugenzi as minister of commerce in the renewed coalition cabinet, a move the president had opposed for months.[94]

On the human rights front, the president and cabinet on April 7 jointly issued a largely positive *Response to the Report of the International Commission on Human Rights*. The commission's interim findings had previously been defensively dismissed for methodological errors. While insisting that the human rights abuses took place in the context of an ongoing war, the *Response* acknowledged the abuses detailed in the report, admitted the deficiencies of the government and undisciplined members of the armed forces, and pledged to take appropriate measures "against authorities who failed in their duties."[95] The Western ambassadors agreed that the most important aspect of the *Response* was the cooperation between the presidency and the government in producing the report. Its major failing was the lack of institutional arrangements to enforce its commitments.[96]

CONTENTION

If cooperation was increasing within the Rwandan government, the newly established political parties were having difficulties. Fissures within the body politic began to show up in the communal elections. These elections, the result of continuous pressure by the internal opposition to get rid of MRND loyalists in the local administration, showed the fragility of the opposition base. The Liberal Party (PL) president Justin Mugenzi was furious at his political allies within the PL and in fellow parties for not supporting the candidates he had preferred. Although the Liberal Party was created as an interethnic party, these elections began to show local solidarity along ethnic lines, with Tutsi winning in significant numbers. In the MDR, the split between the old-line politicians carried over from the MDR Parmehutu and the newer players in the field led by party president Twagiramungu became readily apparent in contention over communal nominations in MDR strongholds. Immediately after the elections, the party-political bureau held an all-day session trying to restore cohesion in party leadership and ranks.[97]

The April 1992 protocol establishing a multiparty coalition government for Rwanda was to have lasted one year, or until the establishment of the transitional institutions. One year later, as Arusha negotiators failed to wrap up their discussions, the protocol was extended. On July 16, with crucial issues still outstanding in the negotiations, the parties negotiated a new protocol extending the mandate of the coalition government but dismissing Prime Minister Nsengiyaremye. Minister of Education (and a Twagiramungu ally) Agathe Uwilingiyimana moved from the Ministry of Education to the prime minister's post.[98] The immediate reaction of the MDR political bureau was to suspend both MDR president Twagiramungu and the new prime minister. Ms. Uwilingiyimana was sworn in as prime minister on July 18, but an extraordinary MDR Party Congress asked her to resign her post. Under pressure, she initially agreed but then announced to the nation on July 24 that as a "patriot" she would remain in her post and exercise her responsibilities as prime minister. Twagiramungu, meanwhile, challenged the legality of the congress since he, as president, had not been involved in convening it.

Meanwhile, the split between Prime Minister Nsengiyaremye and Twagiramungu crystallized over their contest to be named prime minister of the interim government. The cabinet rejected Nsengiyaremye, and the MDR kept renaming him.[99] This standoff intensified as Arusha talks picked up again after the OAU summit. Initially, there was speculation that the cabinet would have Ms. Uwilingiyimana stay on as prime minister under the Arusha Accords, but the political play came to its denouement when Twagiramungu arranged to get cabinet endorsement.[100] The RPF appeared willing to accept the cabinet decision. What remained was for the MDR to accede to the new situation. On July 28, with the possibility of signature of the accords in sight, mediators met with Twagiramungu and Nsengiyaremye and sought the help of the diplomatic corps in pressuring Nsengiyaremye to face the facts. Western ambassadors encouraged reconciliation, but none were willing to "take a position on the merits of the case."[101]

Pushing toward Signature

Even as Rwanda's second largest party was in full turmoil, negotiations continued. On the very day that the Tanzanian foreign minister arrived in Kigali to continue his shuttle diplomacy on outstanding issues, he was confronted with a new team: Foreign Minister Anastase Gasana was taking instructions from the newly installed cabinet led by Prime Minister Agathe Uwilingiyimana. The cabinet had designated Faustin Twagiramungu, without the support of the majority in his party, as the transition prime minister.

What remained to be decided was RPF acceptance of the designated interim prime minister, force levels and command positions within the armed forces, and details on power sharing, especially provisions for impeaching the president and the place and timing for installation of the interim institutions. The parties decided to bring negotiations to Rwandan soil and meet again in the demilitarized zone at Kinihira, where technical talks had previously taken place on the regime for the demilitarized zone.

Negotiations stalemated early, but holding delegates in intensive sessions (until 2 a.m. on July 24 and 3 a.m. on July 25), the Facilitator achieved what was called a breakthrough but was actually a capitulation to RPF demands. The command of the gendarmerie would go to the RPF. The officer corps of the gendarmerie down to the prefecture level would be split fifty-fifty. The command in the army went to the government, and command positions would be split fifty-fifty down to the battalion level. The transition government would be installed in Kigali; to protect RPF personalities in the transition government, a battalion-level RPF force would be stationed in Kigali until the security forces were integrated.[102]

The RPF accepted Twagiramungu as transition prime minister. Although Twagiramungu was suspended by the MDR Political Bureau on July 17 and expelled from the party by an MDR Congress on July 23, he was challenging both procedures in the courts. As the US embassy commented, he was "clearly the choice of all parties in the current government and the future one, except his own."[103] The RPF also agreed to a compromise that would require a two-thirds vote in the transitional national assembly for impeachment proceedings against the president and prime minister. Additionally, the impeachment against the president could not proceed without consultation with the Joint Political Military Committee and with the international Observers of the Arusha process.

The Kinihira agreement called for security in Kigali to be provided by a "neutral international force" under UN command. In the interim, security would be provided by an expanded NMOG under UN command. OAU authorities had previously argued that charter provisions would never permit OAU forces to serve under UN command; operations of the forces of the two international institutions, whether in monitoring the demilitarized zone or patrolling the peace process, would have to be separate.[104] But it was clear that the Rwandan government would not accept a capital city force without UN control. Nor would the French leave under terms of article 5 of the Dar es Salaam agreement until a reliable (i.e., more than OAU) international force was prepared to take their place.[105]

Moreover, the OAU had shown itself incapable of responding to its new responsibilities in a timely way, even in the demilitarized zone. After months of talking about expanding its forces, the OAU Neutral Military Observer Group (NMOG) was expecting its first reinforcements from Senegal on July 31. Nigerian, Egyptian, and Tunisian contingents were also "promised," with arrival dates uncertain.[106] Even with an augmented force, the mandate under which the military observers were operating did not permit the kind of security operations that were being asked of them, whether in the demilitarized zone or in Kigali after signature of the accords. The OAU's Mapuranga had earlier made the argument that the final signature of the Arusha Accords would make the NMOG redundant. Thus, just as the much-heralded expansion was about to occur, and on the eve of final agreement on political negotiations, signals coming from OAU's headquarters on the NMOG's role were highly ambiguous.[107]

The US embassy in Kigali concluded, "The RPF squeezed a little more out of this last round than they had a right to expect."[108] This was particularly true with regard to command-authority and command levels in the gendarmerie and to the admission of RPF troops into the capital city. There may have been two reasons for this. One was that the negotiating team on the Rwandan side was new, not fully aware of the implications of past debates and wanting to show success. Certainly, the Tanzanians, especially in the person of Foreign Minister Rwegasira, who had been working the traces in Kigali since July 16, were pressing hard for agreement. Then the political crisis within the second main party and the resultant cabinet changes left the Rwanda government looking unstable and hardly in a position to dig in its heels.

A second factor was the heightened sense of insecurity brought about by the abrupt resignation and departure from Rwanda of Minister of Defense Dr. James Gasana. Gasana was an MRND loyalist but from Cyangugu rather than the northern heartland. As Rwanda's first civilian minister of defense, he earnestly defended the government position. But he was always a reliable interlocutor and a proponent of the peace process. In his cautious departure statement, Gasana said that a radical vigilante group called the "Akasu" had threatened his life and that of his family. Rumor had it that Gasana had learned that elements of the army were training and arming

militia and that he had tried to stop them. An MRND stalwart had commented, "If Gasana is not safe, then no one is."[109] The tenuous security
environment seemed to justify the RPF demand for an enlarged command
function within the gendarmerie and their own protection force in Kigali.

Endgame

The Arusha Peace Accords had been scheduled for signing on June 19,
June 24, June 25, July 15, and July 22. Now with agreements reached in Kinihira, the negotiations seemed truly to be at an end. In an extraordinary session, the cabinet, meeting under chairmanship of President Habyarimana
and in the presence of Prime Minister Uwilingiyimana, on Sunday, July 25
approved the negotiated conclusions. Then the foreign minister returned
to Kinihira to initial the protocols.[110]

An early August signing looked possible. In fact, a larger part of the
work on the agreements had already been prepared. Lawyers had worked
long hours in the run-up to the OAU summit trying to get protocols in
shape for signature.[111] As the intended signing date of June 19 eased by
and principles hurried off to the Cairo OAU summit where they were to
continue discussions of remaining major issues, teams from both sides at
Arusha met in direct discussions to tie up loose ends: the staging of gendarmerie training, the duration of the transition, and the relation of the
peace accord to the constitution. A draft of the final agreement had been
faxed to Habyarimana and to the cabinet. Working groups were putting
final touches on the protocol on military affairs and on outstanding political issues. A June 24 signing seemed possible.[112] Now a month later,
remaining issues seemed, at last, to have been resolved. With confidence,
the Rwandan government convoked the diplomatic corps to Arusha on
August 4 for the final signature.[113]

On August 4, as planned, President Habyarimana and Chairman
Kanyarengwe signed the Arusha Peace Agreement, declaring, "The war
between the Government of the Republic of Rwanda and the Rwandese
Patriotic Front is hereby brought to an end."[114] President Mwinyi called
the agreement the "first fruits of African conflict resolution," showing pride
in the accomplishment of the peacemakers that other African speakers

shared. Habyarimana said that all Rwandans were winners in this accord and committed himself to its implementation. Recognizing that the accord was not perfect, the president warned all Rwandans not to even think about rejecting it. Kanyarengwe called the accord an important first step. He joined many other speakers in seeing the deployment of the neutral international force as crucial, adding that an enlarged NMOG would be helpful and prodding Egyptians to send troops as promised. The US embassy reported, "The mood was serious throughout the ceremony and moved to self-congratulatory warmth afterwards . . . there was excellent mixing between the Rwandian [*sic*] delegations."[115]

Of the players at the signature scenario, President Habyarimana was generally deemed the most reluctant. In arranging a quick review of the texts by the CND and a stagy cabinet approval on the Sunday following the Kinihira talks, the president, in fact, seemed anxious to wrap up the negotiations. His endorsement of the Arusha Accords had the ring of personal approval. Nonetheless, Habyarimana could not have been happy about the final product. He had wanted a cabinet in which the MRND would not be marginalized, but the marginalizing formulas for government decision making had been retained and no balancing parties admitted to the magic circle. He wanted a national assembly that had the approbation of the people, but he now would deal with an appointed assembly whose make-up could prevail against his intentions.

Habyarimana had reluctantly agreed to the integration of security forces, but only on an eighty-twenty proportion; now the ratios were in essence the fifty-fifty allocation that the RPF had sought all along. He had wanted national elections so the people could decide who should rule, but elections had been delayed for the two-year interim period. In that period, both the internal opposition and the Rwandese Patriotic Front would certainly seek to transform his regime or bring him down by indictment.

In the euphoria of the moment, few observers worried with the US embassy about RPF dominance of the negotiating process. Optimism was the rule of the day. The negotiation had been long, well structured, and keenly argued on both sides. Most importantly, the Arusha political negotiations opened the door to the prospect of peace. As a French diplomat observed, "Arusha is a hard-earned agreement, and we cannot let it die."[116]

Lessons We Learned

Eight months later, ground-to-air missiles blew up President Habyari-mana's aircraft. In that fiery crash the hopes of the Arusha Accords perished as well. A sad and chastening retrospective would instruct us that:

- *Successful negotiations must deal with core interests.* The government's dilatory response to ethnic violence in the north demonstrated a signal lack of concern for a key RPF interest: the safety of the Tutsi people. The result was an unyielding RPF demand for a larger share of the security apparatus.

- *Successful negotiations must structure equity for key stakeholders.* The insistence on signing the Arusha IV power-sharing protocol against the president's protests showed a deep disinterest in the Habyarimana regime's concerns or prospects. That power-sharing protocol provided no means to adjust the agreement to the realities of the Rwandan political landscape and to assure the president of some purchase on policy or process.

- *In international intervention, power matters.* France's deployment of another reinforced company, stern dealings with the president and prime minister, and vigorous demarche to the Ugandans on border supplies made possible a successful summit in Dar es Salaam on March 9 and a return to the negotiating table at Arusha.

- *Putative issues may camouflage central objectives.* Discussions on refugee return, delayed at RPF insistence to the end of negotiations, were wrapped up in a week. The regional refugee conference of 1990 may have paved the way, as did an agreement for unrestricted right of return in the rule of law protocol. For all its invoking of the refugee cause, the RPF was more interested in winning on military integration than on belaboring refugee questions.

- *Changing horses midstream of negotiations is a bad idea.* In the push toward the end of negotiations, the government team, president, and prime minister were finally working together. But the split in the MDR, the change of government, and the deploying of a new negotiating team brought inexperience and naivety to the fore. In the wrap-up negotiations, this new team gave way to critical RPF demands that left the agreements unbalanced militarily and politically.

- *Bluffing works.* Having won out on acceptance of the power-sharing protocols, the RPF promised quick conclusion to power-sharing talks but in fact dug in its heels, turning back Tanzanian mediation with an invective that left Tanzanians wondering about RPF intentions. In the interest of concluding the talks, the Tanzanians and the international partners as well as the new Rwandan government gave way.

- *Does geography matter?* It is ironic that critical talks on the peace agreement were brought back from Arusha to Rwanda's demilitarized zone: first in April to set up the administrative structures of the zone, and then in July to wrap up the talks. Could an expanded international presence (OAU or UN?) have made the zone an island of peace and negotiation after the Dar es Salaam summit, rather than returning to Arusha, with its failed history?

Historical hypotheticals leave us with a lot of "what ifs" in the lead-up to the renewal of civil war and the launching of genocide in Rwanda. The reality at the time was a signed agreement after a year of hard bargaining and a euphoric enthusiasm for a return to peace. That something so carefully built and widely hailed should so quickly disintegrate is the sad story with which this narrative concludes.

SIX

Things Fall Apart

The international community became engaged in confronting armed conflict in Rwanda immediately upon the incursion of the Rwandese Patriotic Front (RPF) onto Rwandan territory in October 1990. Numerous bilateral and regional attempts finally produced a somewhat durable ceasefire in July 1992. Political talks began a month later. One year after that, following intense debate and heavily facilitated talks, punctuated by renewed conflict and a return to negotiations, the contending parties finally signed a peace agreement in Arusha on August 4, 1993. But four months later, the accords were still not implemented. Indeed, the peace process seemed to be falling apart.

What happens when agreements about power sharing so carefully debated and finally signed do not get initiated? What are the levers of suasion when the political parties, the units of power sharing within the transition institutions, break apart in internal contests for power? What are the ramifications when the euphoria of accomplishment and the spirit of cooperation, induced by the peace agreement, give way under subsequent events to pessimism and suspicion?[1]

In this chapter, I look at how the contending parties in Rwanda and the international actors supporting the search for peace sought to install interim institutions as outlined in the Arusha Accords. I begin with a review of the issues facing the implementation of the peace accords under the aegis of an international humanitarian intervention and an assessment of the particular challenges in Rwanda at this historic juncture. I then look at the recrudescence of violence, intraparty negotiations on the edge of the abyss, the negotiating seesaw that nearly broke the impasse, and finally the determined interventions of the United Nations and bilateral partners in the weeks of February and March 1994. But on April 6, someone shot down the president's plane, and the Arusha peace process dissolved into civil war and genocide.

Issues at Stake

Could the carefully knit tissue of the accords envelop Rwanda's divided polity? Could the accord's unraveling be stopped? Answers would have to engage these issues.

What is the role of external force in any peace process engaging the intervention of international actors? How critical is the coordination of negotiating initiatives with appropriate deployment of military observers, border monitors, or an interposition force?[2]

How do changing modes of diplomatic intercourse impinge on the effectiveness of international intervention? Which works best, bilateral suasion from near neighbors, bilateral demarches from development partners, conference negotiations in the presence of the above, or a full-fledged UN mission with accompanying peacekeepers? Or did we need all three at different stages in the conflict?[3]

What is the constraining power of a peace accord, negotiated by two hostile parties and certified by neighboring states and regional bodies? A cardinal principle in international politics is that an agreement once entered into will be kept.[4] But what if the agreement does not represent major parts of the body politic, which was the case in Rwanda?

When in an implementation mire, should international interveners change tactics to get out of the mess? Once engaged, can interveners disown a peace process? The common assumption in resolution literature is that mediators go into a conflict with a commitment to see it through.[5] But should mediators change strategies or tactics if negotiated formulas are not working?

What are the limitations to diplomatic suasion or coercive inducements in an intractable conflict? If interveners have to use heavy pressure to gain nominal adherence to an agreement (a signature on the sly), is a durable solution within sight? When is a move from peacekeeping to peacemaking in order? Should UNAMIR have come in more heavily loaded?[6]

The Danger of Failure, the Challenge of Success

There was no gainsaying the stakes involved in moving through Rwanda's transition process. It was not simply a matter of setting up a government, where executive power was to rest, or installing a national assembly, where the laws establishing the new order were to be adopted. The institution of a transitional presidency, when Juvénal Habyarimana was sworn in as transitional president under the Arusha Accords on January 4, 1994, did not guarantee success of the peace process. Failure to complete installation of the transition institutions was but symptomatic of a larger danger. Any turn away from the Arusha process would entail violent confrontation. It was also true that the very dynamics of the political situation in Rwanda pointed toward the possibility of civilian targeting, using mass atrocities as an instrument of war. The situation in Rwanda in many respects matched what scholars had established as a profile for genocidal potential.[7]

Since the advent of the insurgency and civil war in 1990, Radio Mille Collines and other Hutu media had fed hatred and suspicion between social groups by defaming Tutsi as "cockroaches" and "the enemy," while the RPF Radio Muhabura continually demonized the Habyarimana regime. The push toward multiparty politics increased anxieties among established elite who saw their power and privilege challenged. Furthermore, under the Habyarimana regime, the state dictated law and monopolized justice; but the development of indigenous human rights organizations threatened that monopoly and the traditional pattern of executive justice.

After twenty years of rule, the Habyarimana regime had lost its capacity to control the course of politics. But, notwithstanding the democratic rhetoric of emergent civil society and the advent of multiparty politics, opposition factions and the RPF were reluctant to ground their negotiated agreement in any election, popular referendum, or exercise in consensus building. The people were left out of the Arusha equations; the accords were self-serving arrangements among elites.

Diplomatic Observers were cognizant of these fault lines. One could not participate at negotiations in Arusha or talk to parties in Kigali without sensing the deep animosities and mistrust that were subtexts of the talks. During the heated discussions on power sharing at Arusha in October 1992, I had reminded both sides that the alternative to accommodation and compromise could well be a take-it-all attitude accompanied by genocide, the effort to eliminate the other. The Belgian and French diplomatic missions, with intelligence networks on the ground, were privately pessimistic about the possibility of peace but publicly totally committed to multilateral support for the Arusha peace process.

Even the Convener (OAU) and the Facilitator (Tanzania) voiced doubts about intentions on either side. During the post-accords implementation efforts, the Observers continually argued that backing away from peace would bring disastrous war and great human suffering. Installation of the Arusha institutions seemed like the only way to avoid social cataclysm.

There were hopeful signs. The parties had negotiated a power-sharing agreement in apparent good faith; had begun to plan the disarmament, demobilization, and integration of hostile armies; had jointly appealed for international help to accompany their peace process; and were at the very point of starting the transition. In Rwanda, interveners would ignore the worst-case scenario—social disintegration leading to genocide—and press forward toward the best option, namely, peaceful installation of a viable transition regime.[8]

GETTING TO UNAMIR

Those accords called for an international neutral force that would accompany the peace process. But the accords did not specify who would field that force. The United Nations was noticeably absent from both the July 1992 ceasefire arrangements and the follow-on political negotiations. The OAU secretary general did not inform the UN secretary general Boutros Boutros-Ghali of the ceasefire agreement and the subsequent Joint Political Military Committee meeting until a fortnight after the events. For his part, Boutros-Ghali was content with a note of congratulations to the parties, citing "the constructive approach that has been taken at the regional level and the important agreements which have resulted."[9] The UN would continue to stand aside until early 1993, when a governmental stall on negotiations and ethnic violence against Tutsi in Rwanda brought an RPF attack along the ceasefire line. As the RPF moved to within forty kilometers of Kigali, France reinforced its contingent and, with high-level diplomacy, convinced Habyarimana to return to the political negotiations. The UN sent a mission to urge the Front back to the conference table.[10]

At the March 5 summit meeting in Dar es Salaam, the RPF agreed to return to their former lines if the Rwandan government would negotiate in good faith and if French forces were withdrawn in favor of a "neutral international force." Parties and donors debated the nature and provenance of that force. The Rwandan government, upset by the Neutral Military Observer Group's (NMOG) failure to deter the RPF attack, favored a UN-led force.[11] The RPF felt that the NMOG had been doing its job adequately and only needed reinforcement to patrol the now-expanded de-militarized zone.[12] France wanted an expanded force in the demilitarized zone as soon as possible and a reliable, robust force in place in Kigali before it would honor its commitment to withdraw.[13] Belgium, having withdrawn its ambassador in January in protest of the Habyarimana regime's human rights violations, was focused on protection of civilian populations, which meant "blue helmets."[14] The United States strongly favored reinforcing the OAU contingent with UN experts and expanding the NMOG's moni-toring mandate to include security functions.[15] Such action would use the Rwandan experience as a training ground for OAU peacekeepers, support "African solutions to African problems," and keep peacekeeping costs down.

UN officials, engaged in the Rwanda crisis for the first time at the March 5 ceasefire meetings in Dar es Salaam, repeatedly affirmed that the United Nations had no intention of supplanting the OAU in this peace process. However, the UN was being dragged in the back door. In March, France proposed to the Security Council an international monitoring force for the Uganda-Rwanda border. Having secured a request from the gov-ernments of Uganda and Rwanda for such a force, French diplomats fi-nally convinced the United States to go along with the idea. Thus, under instructions from the Security Council, the secretary general had a good-will/reconnaissance mission in the area as political negotiations at Arusha resumed. By June 22, France won Security Council approval of its reso-lution proposing the United Nations Observer Mission Uganda-Rwanda (UNOMUR).[16]

Neither the United Nations nor the OAU was enthusiastic about a partnership in promoting the peace process within Rwanda. In early April, UN Secretariat officials, like General Baril, were openly contemplating modalities of UN assistance to the OAU. On April 30, however, Secretary General Boutros-Ghali turned back a trilateral demarche of the French, Belgian, and US ambassadors for accelerated UN cooperation with the

OAU. The secretary general characterized the OAU as "inexperienced, corrupt, incompetent, and lacking in funds." He later refused "to send a single observer" to Rwanda until the Peace Agreement was signed or even to launch a reconnaissance mission.[17]

On the other hand, OAU secretary general Salim, after the March 5 agreement renewing the ceasefire, campaigned for UN funding and technical assistance for an augmented OAU presence in Rwanda. But, he was not willing to have the OAU operating in Rwanda under a UN mandate and was "categorical in rejecting UN command of the OAU Neutral Military Observer Group."[18] However, the OAU's inability to expand its role in Rwanda was obvious to all; despite continuing pleas, there was no significant augmentation of the OAU observer force until late July. By that time, high OAU officials were seriously considering disengagement rather than expansion.[19]

As political negotiations in Arusha inched their way toward a conclusion, parties to the conflict transmitted to the United Nations on June 14 a request for stationing of a "neutral international force" in Rwanda upon the signing of a peace agreement.[20] There was still disagreement about the size and mission of the force. The RPF wanted a modest force designed to monitor the peace process, assist in integration of forces, and facilitate humanitarian assistance.[21] The government wanted, as soon as possible, a robust force that would provide the same kind of security the French troops were giving.[22]

Among concerned partners, France most vigorously promoted UN engagement in the peace process. The Belgians were agnostic on details, convinced of only one thing: Belgium should not participate in the force structure. Both the United Kingdom and Russia questioned the necessity and the expense of a UN force.[23] The United States, as usual, wanted to keep the costs down, the numbers low, and the Africans involved. As policy makers in Washington were deliberating, they wanted most to know what the UN Secretariat and the permanent members of the Security Council were thinking about the issue.[24]

The UN plan, drafted by General Roméo Dallaire a month after the Arusha peace agreement had already been signed, called for a progressive deployment of peacekeepers up to a full contingent of twenty-five hundred troops. The force structure was to include a mobile company in Kigali, with twenty armored personnel carriers and four helicopters, capable of reacting quickly with decisive force. Force operations called for continuous patrolling of the capital city to keep Kigali as a weapons-free zone.[25]

Although the State Department had pressed hard for an early deployment of the Dallaire reconnaissance mission and a quick report from the secretary general, the US government continued to hedge on a full-fledged UN peacekeeping mission. Wedded to a mixed OAU/UN peacekeeping presence, US bureaucracies also debated whether a mission to Rwanda met the criteria for international peacekeeping being developed under presidential directive (PRD13/PDD25). In early September, the RPF and the Rwandan government launched a joint mission to New York and Washington pleading for an early deployment of the neutral force. In a coordinated effort, the Belgian foreign minister wrote Secretary Christopher and the French president wrote President Clinton urging US support of a UN force. But it was not until October 1 that Ambassador Albright could tell French foreign minister Juppé that the United States was "prepared to be supportive of the Rwanda resolution."[26] The UN Security Council finally voted to establish the UN Assistance Mission in Rwanda (UNAMIR) on October 5, 1993.[27]

This resolution brought together the three components of an international peace intervention in Rwanda: UNOMUR observers on the Ugandan-Rwandan border, the OAU observers in the demilitarized zone, and the security contingent soon to arrive as a "neutral international force." The secretary general appointed General Dallaire as commander of the integrated force and former Cameroonian foreign minister Jacques-Roger Booh-Booh as special representative. Meanwhile, after the signing of the Arusha Accords on August 5, OAU secretary general Salim Salim, to the chagrin of the United States, considered the Rwandan problem to be "in the lap of the UN now" and sought to pull the OAU entirely out of the peace process.[28]

A Crescendo of Violence

As this study has demonstrated, politically motivated violence has been a counterpoint to the issues central to political control and ethnic division in Rwanda since before its independence. The failure to bring to justice those who perpetrated that violence had created within Rwanda a "culture of impunity." Moreover, the short-term success in using violence to intimidate social and political opponents throughout Rwanda's history underscored its utility in achieving political objectives.

A TENTATIVE CALM

Once negotiations were restored by the March 5 summit, however, the period from then to the signing of the accords was a relatively quiescent one. There were no significant party demonstrations; the usually rambunctious CDR was holding its tongue, and street violence seemed to fall away. There were, however, two assassinations that stirred the internal peace. The first was that of Emanuel Gapyisi of Gitarama, a leader in the MDR and son-in-law of the party founder, President Kayibanda. He had lost out in the 1992 election for party president to his brother-in-law, Faustin Twagiramungu, but had organized an interparty forum, Peace and Democracy, dedicated to opposing both the Patriotic Front and the presidential regime. In May, he was assassinated by automatic weapons as he left his house. In August, Felix Rwambuka, a former burgomaster, was killed by a grenade thrown in his house. The perpetrators in both killings were never identified, despite the government protests that they were developing good leads. Rumors varied: some blamed the RPF, some talked of revenge killings for financial dealings, and some suggested the elimination of political rivals by others within the MDR, possibly even the prime minister-designate.[29]

After the Arusha Accords were signed, Rwandans lived for a while within a euphoric culture of peace, hoping for the rapid institution of a new order. By mid-August, the US embassy was reporting that political youth were quiet; the Hutu extremist CDR party had kept a low profile since the RPF's February offensive, even though "the availability of guns and grenades does nothing to reduce anxiety on this point."[30] MRND president Ngirumpatse was assuring embassy officials that the party youth, the Interahamwe, were now under control. He did not anticipate "any further violence at their hands."[31] Meanwhile, while the MRND was holding together as it named ministers to cabinet and deputies to the national assembly, splits within the MDR and the Liberal Party deepened. As usual, the RPF showed strong cohesiveness as it planned to become an internal actor in cabinet and legislature.[32]

By early September, when decisions on a neutral international force were stalled, the government and the RPF decided jointly to carry out some international diplomacy, pushing for the force's early deployment.[33] On September 22, leaders of the Rwandan Government Army and the Rwandan Patriotic Army met under the chairmanship of Minister of Defense Bizimana in an important "confidence building" measure seeking to maintain the momentum of the Arusha Accords. The leaders planned more meetings and interforce sporting events.[34] But, by the end of the month, through its spokespersons in Kampala, the RPF expressed concern about keeping the post-Arusha peace process on track, arguing that President Habyarimana, by encouraging intraparty splits, was undermining the spirit of the accords.[35]

RESHUFFLING THE DECK

On October 21, Tutsi military officers in Burundi assassinated the newly elected Hutu president, Melchior Ndadaye, and attempted to take over the government. The Burundian assassination and attempted coup quickly changed the political atmosphere in Kigali. Meetings in Kigali decrying the event were, by their very nature, rallying calls to ethnic identity. Street demonstrations brought out politically active youth groups, who took advantage of the crisis to sack and pillage. Although the MRND and CDR refused to support an early November demonstration by MDR hardliners, the US embassy concluded that "it's still too early to judge whether this aborted confrontation will lead to renewed efforts at reconciliation . . . or more confrontation."[36]

Party divisions contributed to insecurity. Having failed to make more political capital out of the Burundi crisis, CDR officials sent open letters on November 4 and November 8 to the president protesting the choice of Belgium as one of the troop contributors to UNAMIR. Meanwhile, MDR hardliners sent a letter to the president threatening chaos if he did not remove Twagiramungu as prime minister-designate, challenging RPF's right to bring troops into the capital city, and calling for a reopening of negotiations on Arusha articles before the broad-based government was installed. The US embassy concluded,

> There is a determined group of Hutu supremists [*sic*] whose fear of potential Tutsi domination is the . . . only political factor of significance. These people have been unreconciled to the Arusha Accords from the beginning and now are groping for an effective means of derailing the Accord which offers an honorable place for Tutsi in Rwandan society. First, they tried to exploit the Burundi tragedy to unite Hutus behind them in Rwanda. . . . Now the tactic was to go after the Belgians hoping to exploit post-colonial antipathies. . . . Should they succeed in substantially delaying UNAMIR, they may have a chance to unravel the whole process.[37]

Concrete acts of sabotage were not far behind. On November 16, the public prosecutor of the Kigali Appeals Court, Alphonse Nkubito, was attacked with grenades as he returned home. He managed to get behind a door and suffered only grenade fragments to his back and legs. His car was destroyed and windows in his home shattered. As usual, speculations about the reason for the attack varied. Nkubito was the founder of Rwanda's first human rights organization, ARDHO, and president of the Human Rights Consortium, CLADHO, both of which had been active in publishing reports of human rights abuses and making interventions on behalf of victims. As prosecutor, he had played a significant role in getting Tutsi detainees released from prison in 1991. Shortly before the incident, Nkubito had ordered preventive detention of Colonel Sagatwa's protégé, a chauffeur accused of fraud in the diversion of relief foods. The chauffeur was thought to have known details of the unresolved 1988 death of a senior government officer, Colonel Mayuya, which might have reflected badly on the presidential household. In all instances, the attack could have come at any time. Its perpetration just as elements of the accords were coming together suggested "a renegade effort to derail the peace process by persons resisting the power-sharing arrangement so central to the Arusha Accord."[38]

TROUBLE IN THE DEMILITARIZED ZONE

On November 17, an attack in localities within the demilitarized zone just south of the RPF lines took the lives of some forty persons, several of them recently elected local officials. The attack was carried out with automatic weapons, all the victims dying from bullet wounds. This time the minister of defense offered a helicopter to the newly arrived UNAMIR force commander General Dallaire so he could fly out to investigate the incident. Dallaire reported that the raid had been well planned, coming at four locations within two hours and leaving no witnesses as whole families were wiped out. But Dallaire reported no leads as to perpetrators.

Once again, the attributions for the raids varied widely. President Habyarimana told Ambassador Flaten that he was convinced the RPF had carried out the raid and claimed the victims were MRND loyalists. RPF commander Kagame denied RPF involvement, as did the RPF radio. RPF coordinator Tito Rutaremara claimed the victims were RPF sympathizers and blamed the MRND, who he said had been blocking local elections and had an interest in insecurity in the zone.[39]

As General Dallaire set up a commission to pursue the investigation into the massacres, the minister of defense, who only a month and a half before had proudly presided over joint sessions of the two armies, on November 21 announced the suspension of all meetings and joint commissions with the RPF. While firmly asserting the massacres had been carried out by the RPF, the communiqué somewhat inconsistently demanded the immediate formation of the broad-based government, punishment of those guilty, and an international inquiry into the incident. The communiqué also reaffirmed the commitment of the Rwandan armed forces to the peace process and its support for the mission of UNAMIR.[40]

On November 23, the prime minister announced that the government would resume joint sessions with the RPF. In a hotly debated meeting, the government had voted unanimously to overturn the minister of defense's unilateral communiqué. The minister seemed to take being overridden in good grace, but shortly afterwards, MRND ministers disassociated themselves from the government position and refused to participate in talks with the RPF. Meanwhile, the original charges that the victims were MRND loyalists murdered by the RPF drew increasing skepticism in Kigali. MDR officials in the foreign ministry suggested the perpetrators might have been from the CDR, hard-liners from the MRND, or members of Inter-ahamwe, "suspected of having presidential guard and gendarmes secretly among its ranks."[41]

On November 25, Prime Minister Uwilingiyimana convoked the dean of the diplomatic corps, Monsignor Bertello, and requested that the Western diplomats make a demarche to the president "to take steps to lower tensions both in the army and in the country." The diplomats agreed that the security situation was deteriorating but that "rapid formation of the next government was the key to improving the security situation." The head of the EEC delegation offered to use the occasion of a call on the president during a high-level visit from Brussels to underscore concerns of humanitarian agencies about insecurity in the DMZ.[42]

No sooner had UNAMIR announced its "Committee of Inquiry" into the Ruhengeri atrocities than a nighttime firefight broke out at Kabatwa north of Mutara near the Visoke (mountain gorilla) Park and outside the demilitarized zone. The government blamed RPF aggression, while the RPF said the government was trying to provoke an incident. UNAMIR commander Dallaire went north to investigate the incident, as did government authorities. While there had clearly been troop movements on both sides in the area, it remained unclear what the firing was all about. Meanwhile, a Belgian Red Cross truck hit a mine, killing driver and passenger and stopping Red Cross assistance deliveries in the demilitarized zone. A Rwandan health agent of Médecins du Monde was murdered near Byumba, which prompted the removal of that agency from the north. A booby-trapped franc note was set off in a schoolyard, killing seventeen children; in a nearby school, a grenade was found and defused by the military.

The intimidation and arrest of persons considered to be RPF supporters continued. A Tutsi judge of the Kibungu regional court received several death threats in December. During the week of December 22, the public prosecutor released five persons whom the military had put in the Kigali prison. Arrests and beatings reportedly took place in the north among the traditional Bagogwe herdsmen who pastured their cattle near the area of the November massacres. Some in the military were apparently continuing to prosecute the war after the peace agreement had been signed.[43]

In the capital, however, officials did not reflect the insecurity and anxieties that these incidents caused in the north and west; planning by the government and the RPF on demobilization went ahead as scheduled, as did donor meetings with both camps on the same subject.[44] What did make the capital nervous were UNAMIR's preparations to bring into Kigali an RPA battalion to protect RPF officials. In late July at Kinihira, final, hurried negotiations had agreed to the presence of an RPF defensive battalion in Kigali. By mid-December, the location for this battalion was still up in the air. UNAMIR proposed Camp Kami, seven miles out of town, but eventually the government agreed to put the RPF force in the hotel complex connected to the CND, the national assembly. But Radio RTLM conducted a "man in the street" interview in which "people" reported that "they considered housing the RPF in the national assembly complex a threat to democracy and to the independence of the legislature."[45]

Finally, rumors were rife of party youth becoming militarized. Party officials denied that MRND youth, the Interahamwe, were engaged in "counterproductive activities," but human rights groups claimed that the Interahamwe were being deployed throughout the country and creating a climate of insecurity. Human rights advocates also asserted that the Rwandan military were training Interahamwe in remote military camps.[46] While other party youth had been responsible for thuggery and intimidation on behalf of their presumed cause, the Interahamwe was now being seen as a quasi-official third force. As spokespersons kept promising the installation of the new government, there emerged an autonomous and violent substructure, which the government could not control (witness the prime minister's appeal to Western ambassadors) and which the president chose not to deter. If neither the cabinet, with its respective ministries, nor the presidency could insure security for the transition, then the neutral international force in the form of UNAMIR would have to do it.

THE UN RESPONSE TO SECURITY CHALLENGES

On December 13, the special representative of the secretary general, Jacques-Roger Booh-Booh, convoked the diplomatic corps to hear UNAMIR force commander General Dallaire, Kigali sector commander Colonel Marchal, and the UN security officer discuss security and outline plans for UNAMIR deployment. General Dallaire reported that twelve hundred troops would be in Rwanda when the broad-based government was installed. Working-level negotiations on rationalizing the demilitarized zone, on troop assembly points, and on heavy weapons cantonment were to begin in two days. Colonel Marchal said that UNAMIR would establish an arms-secure zone in Kigali and the surrounding ten-kilometer radius "by controlling the movement of all arms and ammunition within the zone." Both sides were to notify UNAMIR of numbers of personnel, types of weapons, and troop movements. In response to questions, the officers admitted that security for the international community was "a concern but not top priority for UNAMIR." UNAMIR would be making random patrols twenty-four hours a day, and police monitors would be working with local gendarmerie units. UNAMIR's focus was on "reducing tensions of any kind."[47]

In a December 17 meeting with embassy security officers, UNAMIR staff expanded on their plan of action. Effective December 20, all weapons in the "Kigali Weapons-safe Area" were to be under direct UN control. Within this zone, eight hundred peacekeepers and eighty military observers would be responsible for security matters. The contending forces were not to move around the city or maintain roadblocks anywhere in the city. Movements of more than ten soldiers were to be under UN escort. UN observers, escorted by peacekeepers, would rove the city and monitor ammunition and weapons stockpiles. According to Colonel Nazrul, the UNAMIR operations officer, peacekeepers could fire if anyone seriously threatened bodily harm to them or the observers but not if the attack was against another Rwandan party. Colonel Marchal reported that UNAMIR was not taking the place of the gendarmerie or police but would work with them to assure that they responded to calls in an appropriate manner.[48]

The colonels agreed that they were "under no illusion that weapons had been cached by both the GOR and RPF as well as by the civilian population."[49] UNAMIR would gather intelligence on weapons caches; the biggest concern was not weapons held by the military but those in civilian hands, especially youth groups like the Interahamwe. The government had sent out a circular to all military commands and prefectures asking that all weapons be turned in, but few had been collected. The government had also recently tried to buy back grenades, but the black market in grenades continued to boom.

While UNAMIR's plans for dealing with insecurity in the capital city and around the country were well designed, effective implementation at the local level depended on UNAMIR's interface with the national gendarmerie. This force was poorly trained, slow to react, and politically suspect. In addition, UNAMIR needed better communication, more troops, and more materiel. Sector commanders did not have telephonic links with each other. Telephone contacts with patrols in the demilitarized zone were almost nonexistent. All public inquiries or requests for assistance had to go through the overstretched central at UNAMIR headquarters in the Amahoro Hotel. Peacekeeper numbers would not be at the desired level until the end of December, and that with troops completely unfamiliar with the Rwandan physical and social terrain. Only half the observer force was in place; some were being redeployed from the fragile demilitarized zone to bolster security in Kigali. Only two of five helicopters for air patrols and about half of the vehicles for mobile patrols had arrived. At that date there were no armored personnel carriers in country, and the reaction company had yet to be formed. The officers, in part, blamed these deficiencies on budget administration in New York. The Rwanda mission did not have high priority; headquarters gave attention to other peacekeeping operations like Somalia and Yugoslavia.[50]

At the Edge of Chaos

As the year drew to a close, both government (through the foreign minister) and the UN special representative were announcing the installation of the transition government on December 29. The prime minister-designate had met two times with the president to discuss details of the transition ceremonies. One of the issues was who would certify the correctness of the lists presented by the parties or by party factions. The Arusha Accord was not clear on that point, nor could the two leaders come to an agreement. Diplomats were skeptical that the institutions could be put in place. Long meetings and innumerable informal conversations failed to break the impasse in the Liberal Party and in the MDR. Within the

Liberal Party, for example, two separate lists of deputies held only one name in common, and different candidates were named for the ministerial slots. Particularly contentious was Justin Mugenzi's determination to make his colleague, Agnes Ntamabyaliro, the new minister of justice. The other side of the party considered her a hard-nosed Hutu supremacist; having her in that office would deny Tutsi the new day of equity and justice they had so desired. Mugenzi pointed out that Ms. Ntamabyaliro was the most experienced civil servant within Liberal Party ranks and deserved the prestigious seat.

Within the MDR, there were some differences in the choice of deputies, but the main fight was over ministerial seats. The prime minister-designate called for party reconciliation first before ministerial slots were handed out; reconciliation obviously meant that party leaders would accept Twagiramungu back into the party as president and agree that he was legitimately designated as interim prime minister. Twagiramungu intended to eliminate from the government not only the MDR hard-liners, like Murego and Karamira, but also party leaders who had the political base to challenge his authority, such as former minister of foreign affairs Ngulinzira and Twagiramungu's personal rival, former prime minister Nsengiyaremye. Diplomats could not see how Twagiramungu could install a government that excluded all the potential ministers in the Nsengiyaremye faction of the prime minister's own party.[51]

STALEMATE

The diplomats were right. December 29 came and went without an installation ceremony. On January 5, however, perhaps remembering the warning of the EU delegation about the UN Security Council review, the installation ceremonies began when President Juvénal Habyarimana was sworn into office as the president for the transition period of two years. But when the ceremony was held for installing the interim national assembly, prior to swearing in of the government, chaos broke out. Two sets of deputies showed up. Police providing security for the event admitted some but not others. Finally, the president of the Constitutional Court cancelled the ceremony. Neither side had been able to bluff its way into an ad hoc acceptance of its lists.[52]

A day later, my wife Sandra and I arrived in Kigali, where I was to take up my duties as the next US ambassador to Rwanda. I was met, not by the usual protocol officer, but by Habyarimana's political counselor, Ambassador Juvénal Renzaho. He explained that indeed the new transitional order had been launched with the inauguration of the president, but that there had been some "slight problems" with the establishment of the assembly and the government. I suggested that no doubt Rwandan political genius had found ways to create obstacles and that same genius would find a way around the obstacles.

Thus began a period of most intense diplomatic engagement in trying to pressure all sides into installing the institutions agreed upon in the Arusha Accords. The diplomatic community now engaged fully in rescuing the Arusha peace process. The activity took place around three groups: the papal nuncio leading the entire diplomatic corps; the Western Observer group of France, Belgium, the United States, and Germany, sometimes associating Switzerland and Canada as major donors; and the continuing efforts of representatives of the Tanzania Facilitator, often working in tandem with the UN political office.

The difficulties facing diplomatic initiatives became apparent on Saturday, January 8, when young gangs, intending to stop a second try at installing the assembly and government, blockaded a major crossroads between central Kigali and the airport. Depending on party or ethnic identity, some drivers were allowed to pass, whereas others, including prominent personalities of the opposition, were stopped and turned around. In some cases, occupants were taken from their cars and beaten, and the cars were trashed. The ability to obstruct this intersection just below the RPF headquarters and right by the presidential guard camp demonstrated the potential of street power. Witnesses claimed that military personnel in civilian clothing were among the "protesters." Neither the gendarmerie under the titular authority of the seated prime minister nor the UNAMIR forces were able to clear the area for several hours. Due at the government house for presentation of my credentials to President Habyarimana, I had to be extricated from our residence by presidential guards in a speeding convoy. Clearly the country (or at least its capital city) was headed for chaos.[53]

Efforts through the government, the prime minister's office, the presidency, and the prime minister-designate failed to reorganize the installation ceremonies. Once again, as he had done in the November–December crisis in 1992, the papal nuncio took a lead role. He divided the diplomatic corps in teams. Some were to go to the RPF, some to the president, some to the current prime minister, and some to the prime minister-designate. Each team listened to the point of view of its interlocutor on the current crisis and then, in common language, urged dialogue, compromise, and an early establishment of the institutions. The president asked that, when the diplomatic round-robin was complete, the group might return to give him a readout on what it had found.[54]

THE MILITIA THREAT

Even as the diplomats were completing their rounds, UN special representative Booh-Booh convoked the French, Belgian, and US ambassadors and asked our support on a security demarche that, on instructions from UN headquarters, he was to carry to the president. General Dallaire gave us the background. The prime minister-designate had put him in touch with an informant, a member of the MRND Interahamwe militia. The informant's role was to pass out arms from a cache in Kigali. Tired of his subversive task, he wished the UN to know where the arms were kept and how they were being distributed. The informant also wanted the UN to know that during the January 8 roadblock, demonstrators "were to have roughed up Belgian soldiers responding to the event as a way of further disturbing the peace, provoking an RPF reaction, and launching a militia-led counter-reaction." Sensing the possibility of a diplomatic or military trap, the UN officers had sought guidance from headquarters.[55]

The guidance from headquarters was clear. General Dallaire was to take no action before Booh-Booh met with the president. Booh-Booh was to review his demarche with the ambassadors prior to delivering it and seek their subsequent support in bringing the issue to the president's attention. In his demarche, the special representative of the secretary general (SRSG) was to do the following:

+ Apprise the president of the UN's concern over solid evidence that guns were being distributed to party militia within Kigali.

- Note that distribution of arms violated the Arusha Accord and its establishment of an arms-secure zone in Kigali.

- Ask that the president within forty-eight hours inform the United Nations of how he intended to retract the arms distributed and dismantle the militia apparatus within Kigali.

- Record that any violence carried out in Kigali would be fully reported to the Security Council and publicized in the world press.[56]

The ambassadors agreed to seek instructions from their governments and, if so instructed, make a joint demarche on the president on security issues. The diplomats urged that the forty-eight-hour ultimatum be couched in a larger context of expected Interahamwe demonstrations on January 15. The president should be forcefully reminded of the Arusha provisions for an arms-secure Kigali and told that Interahamwe demonstrations undermine current effort to bring about peace by implementing the accords.[57]

DIPLOMATIC RESPONSE

The Department of State agreed that the UN demarche merited support and found the proposed language of the joint demarche "right on the mark," except that the third point was broadened to note that "security can best be achieved if all parties work together and abide by the peace accords and leave security to the UN and, ultimately, to the integrated security forces." With instructions in hand, the ambassadors sought a meeting with the president.[58] Meanwhile, the papal nuncio, having reviewed with the diplomatic corps the political situation in light of the demarches made on the major parties, decided to visit the president again, this time to impress on him the urgency of the security situation.

In the meeting with Habyarimana, the nuncio reported on the diplomatic round-robin and urged the president to play his role as leader of the transition institutions in breaking the impasse. Then, the nuncio presented on behalf of the entire diplomatic corps the elements of what was to have been a Western demarche. Each of the three Western "Observers" added a point of emphasis: the French chargé called for a public statement renouncing violence and calling for reconciliation; I noted how political competition was now erupting outside of any framework and threatened the destruction of state legitimacy and control; the Belgian ambassador summarized concerns about the distribution of arms and the militarizing of youth organizations. The president expressed surprise at the diplomats' allegations and said he would see what he could do. Then he called in his director of cabinet and whispered some instructions.[59]

Meeting to review the situation, the Belgian and French ambassadors and I agreed that our demarche, while not trilateral, had more effect for being carried out within a broad-based diplomatic presentation. Since any further representations to the president would be counterproductive, we would wait and see if the president kept his promise to deal with the situation. In a follow-on meeting with the UN SRSG and force commander, we learned that the UN informant proved his bona fides as an insider by reporting back the content of the SRSG's meeting with the president, and by giving specific details on arms locations and on orders to hurry up distribution.

However, General Dallaire reported that his current orders would not allow him to carry out any operation against those caches. SRSG Booh-Booh said that the president "had promised to set up an investigation into the security question, especially the distribution of arms and report back." If Habyarimana failed to do so, Booh-Booh would so report to the secretary general, who might then apprise the Security Council. The secretary general had made his own pitch to the president in a telephone conversation in which he expressed deep concern over the security situation as well as the lack of progress in installing the Broad-based Transitional Government.[60]

In a follow-up to these initiatives, the UN decided to brief Security Council members on what had been transpiring. As Western ambassadors in Kigali were being asked to take the lead in pressing for a political solution, UN Peacekeeping Office's Hédi Annabi gave UN political officers a less-than-accurate account of the political stalemate and militarization of youth groups. Annabi reported that, in response to the reports that President Habyarimana's militia were receiving arms, "General Dallaire planned a very aggressive demarche to the president; UN officials, however, convinced Dallaire that a more subtle approach might be more effective at this time. Accordingly, a few weeks ago, Dallaire simply discussed his concern with the president. Although the president denied involvement in such events, apparently he noted and was impressed by the General's concern."[61]

In this innocuous brief, Annabi dissimulated regarding a direct challenge to UNAMIR authority in Rwanda and a major imbroglio within the UN peacekeeping office. He then requested that the "Friends of Rwanda" (Belgium, France, and the United States) take a more active role in brokering the current stalemate, and "thereby avoid having to bring it to the Security Council."[62] All this might seem regular enough. After all, there was nothing extraordinary about General Dallaire raising concerns with President Habyarimana (except that it was SRSG Booh-Booh who did so); and Dallaire had not proposed an aggressive demarche but a raid on an arms cache. There was, moreover, nothing unusual about resident diplomats weighing in on the peace process (they had been doing that for two years), nor about resolving crises at a local level without contentious Security Council debate (except that it was precisely the Security Council's role to hear of this crisis and review UN actions in that regard.) The briefing rather covered over the failure of the UN first to address the security issue, then to get anything more than a commission of inquiry out of President Habyarimana, and finally to have no political strategy for moving forward in installing the institutions. The bilateral diplomatic leaders, who had been on the sidelines since the UN took the field, were now being asked to take over the play and push the ball forward.

Lessening of street violence and a renewed dialogue between the president's men and the other parties seemed to be the result of the mid-January demarches by the SRSG and the ambassadors. On January 26, however, violence had again raised its ugly head. At a provocative demonstration in front of the CND where RPF forces were headquartered, someone fired shots. No one was injured, and the source of the firing was not confirmed. This demonstration seemed to be related to similar demonstrations on January 23 and 25, all thought to be by "Interahamwe-related" youth. Things then calmed down for almost a month. But on February 20, an MDR-Hutu power faction blocked from holding a demonstration turned to rioting; the next day the CDR protested its lack of access to the Arusha Code of Ethics in front of the foreign ministry and offices of the high court.[63]

A MINISTER ASSASSINATED

That night, gunmen, waiting in ambush, assassinated the minister of public works and president of the PSD, Félicien Gatabazi, as he returned to his home from a political meeting. The brutal elimination of a high-level political personality shocked the Kigali community. Moreover, because he played a swing role in the internal opposition and was thought to be disenchanted with the RPF's stonewalling as well as with Twagiramungu's leadership, he was a possible target of the political right, the political center, and the RPF. The Radio Mille Collines blamed Twagiramungu for organizing the assassination, which immediately led some to suspect a death squad in the pay of Hutu extremists, possibly the CDR. Others claimed that only the RPF had the skills and weapons for such a well-executed ambush. UNAMIR, which was supposed to be protecting political personalities, could come up with no leads.

Meanwhile, the founder of the CDR, Martin Bucyana, was on the road north from political campaigning in Gikongoro through Butare back to Kigali. North of Butare, in PSD heartland, he was recognized by PSD partisans. As if to demonstrate that the right had no monopoly on violence and bloody mindedness, the incensed PSD crowd lynched the CDR president. In reprisal, CDR gangs went out against PSD sympathizers in Kigali and against Tutsi neighborhoods. Local authorities imposed curfews; UNAMIR forces, working with the gendarmerie, were finally able to restore order two days later.[64]

On February 23, Rwandan clergy and government officials conducted Minister Gatabazi's funeral service in solemn dignity. High-level representatives from all political parties, the RPF, the presidency, and the chiefs of mission of France, Belgium, Switzerland, and the United States attended the funeral mass in the southern university town of Butare. Organizers, smoothly handling an overflow crowd, demonstrated Rwandans' capacity to do things right if they so desired. The ceremony also showed how much of Rwandan society remained intact. As I reported, "The gendarmerie smartly performed its policing role, the army provided an honor company, politicians of all stripes participated in the ceremonies. The mass was led by a Tutsi bishop who had been Gatabazi's teacher many years ago and spoke of him as a son."[65]

Uphill and Down

We go back in this story to the failed installation ceremonies of January 5, 1993, which stirred embassies to incessant meetings with party officials and formal diplomatic interventions with leadership on both sides. Headquarters of Observer states were concerned as well. At a trilateral meeting in Paris on January 23, George Moose, the assistant secretary of state for African affairs, reviewed events in Central Africa with Lode Willems, chief of cabinet in the Belgian prime minister's office, and Jean-Marc de La Sablière, director of African affairs at the Quai d'Orsay. The officials agreed that implementation of the accords had been blocked by "political squabbling"; strong internal divisions within the parties further complicated the process. The representatives expressed concern that the stalemate might well exacerbate ethnic tensions; the assassination of the Hutu Burundian president in October at the hands of Tutsi military had weighed heavily on President Habyarimana's mind and circumscribed his strategy. Habyarimana was concerned as well that "the Liberal Party will reopen questions about past government human rights abuses, especially if it receives the post of Minister of Justice in the transition government."[66] It was agreed that the three countries would again consider approaching the Rwandan government, the parties, and the RPF, "urging that they accelerate efforts to resolve their differences." Assistant Secretary Moose suggested having the Tanzanian ambassador, in his country's role as Facilitator of the Arusha talks, bring the parties together to iron out differences. Others noted the importance of not undercutting SRSG Booh-Booh's effort.[67]

A NEW DEMARCHE

By January 28, the Department of State had issued instructions for a trilateral demarche to the president, the RPF leadership, the prime ministers, and leaders of all major parties.[68] Other headquarters followed suit with similar talking points. It was February 11, however, before the chiefs of mission of the three states and the German ambassador (one of the Observers and chairman for six months of the European group) could jointly meet with President Habyarimana.

In the demarche, the German ambassador spoke for the Europeans in saying that the time was long overdue for setting up the institutions; if the Liberal Party could not get its act together, it should step aside. The French ambassador inquired why the "Code of Good Conduct," which Habyarimana had wanted as a complement to the accords, was never even tabled by the president's party. I reported a new flexibility on the part of the RPF as a result of Chairman Kanyarengwe's meetings in Washington and urged that the opportunity for compromise be seized. I also noted that most other parties were willing to go ahead with the installation, even without a common Liberal Party list; the MRND seemed to be the only recalcitrant voice and was being seen as such by the Rwandan people and outside observers. The Belgian ambassador reinforced previous comments and noted that former Belgian prime minister Maartens, now visiting Rwanda, would be pressing on the RPF the "same urgency, tolerance, and openness to compromise that the ambassadors were urging on the president." Habyarimana questioned whether most parties did, in fact, favor going ahead with installing the institutions and gave a detailed explanation of the schisms within the Liberal Party. He recognized the pressure to install the institutions on February 14 but said he wanted to have issues settled first and avoid the circus atmosphere of the last failed installation on January 5.[69]

In the week of February 8, SRSG Booh-Booh had brought together the contending parties in marathon sessions on Tuesday and Thursday; there were negotiations as well within the Liberal Party on Tuesday and Wednesday. While Booh-Booh had characterized the meetings as "constructive," presidential cabinet director Ruhigira said the meetings were intense and confrontational. The meetings did not, however, lead to installation on Sunday, February 14, as Booh-Booh had hoped. Rather, perhaps stirred by the ambassadors' prompting, the MRND had presented to the SRSG their draft of a "gentlemen's agreement" that it wanted all parties to sign as a prelude to installation of the interim institutions. Booh-Booh distributed the draft to the parties and convened a meeting at 3 p.m. on Sunday. By 5 p.m. only part of the parties had showed up. In frustration, the SRSG curtly dismissed the meeting with a sound scolding of those present for their dilatory approach to peace.

On Monday, party leaders nursed bruised egos in their several camps, and the RPF said they were willing to discuss the "gentlemen's agreement" if all other issues were put aside. They invited Observers to a meeting convened by the prime minister-designate on February 16. Other diplomats were reluctant to grace a meeting convened outside the UN framework and with an uncertain agenda, but I argued for supporting the prime minister's efforts.

Meanwhile, I had invited all party and faction leaders to a breakfast at the US residence on February 15 to hear the South African evangelist Michael Cassidy talk about the South African peace process, in which he had played a vital role. The breakfast produced lawn conversations between the RPF and the MRND, between factions of the MDR and the PL, and among other parties. Later that morning, both factions of the Liberal Party contacted me regarding elements of a compromise in the deputies and ministerial lists. Discussions on this compromise went on throughout the afternoon, with the parties separated by one deputy and one ministerial seat.[70]

On February 16, I found I was wrong about supporting the prime minister-designate at his morning meeting. There was no sign of new beginnings: no MDR members were present other than the two prime ministers, Mugenzi and his cohorts were missing, and the MRND did not show. Despite the ambassadors' request for an unpublicized event, television cameras were there, and those engaged in this exercise tried to promote a public condemnation for those not attending. The ambassadors withdrew, and the "all parties" meeting became a closed-door caucus. On the evening of February 16, the parties finally met. The RPF tore apart the MRND proposal for a "gentlemen's agreement," claiming that all its provisions could already be found in the Arusha Accords. Presidential counselor Ruhigira held his own in four hours of debate, claiming that the parties need to know that each was going to play the "Arusha game" straight before acceding to the installation of institutions. Its provisions on amnesty were but a way of clearing the deck for participation of all, including the outlawed "armed opposition," in the new state institutions.[71]

A US ASSESSMENT

By this time, I had been five weeks in country. As the parties argued, I gathered the country team for a review of the situation. The team agreed on three guidelines that should orient our future diplomatic efforts:

+ The final solution to the impasse must be all-Rwandan and inclusive of major political forces. SRSG Booh-Booh's effort to force installation on February 14 backfired because he did not have support from a major part of the political landscape. The "all-party meeting" on February 16 in fact represented a minimal electoral base. Any solution that did not include the president's party and the prime minister's opponents in the MDR was a nonstarter.

+ There must be cohesion in the international community. The Rwandans had tried to split the bilateral Observers from the UN effort. While multilateral demarches lose that special personal touch, which is often the diplomat's key to persuasion, the formal weight of a combined international voice far surpassed any tactical benefit of individual bilateral approaches.

+ The pace of political compromise and acceptance must somehow catch up with the speed of the international timetable. The peace process was moving slowly forward as politicians got to know each other's concerns and ambitions; the UN presence had established a transition atmosphere, and the security situation was generally calmer. But the country was out of money, international financial institutions were out of time, and reassessment of the UN mission was looming.[72]

In the light of these principles, the embassy team discounted the possibility of professional facilitation, an all-parties' retreat, or renegotiation of Arusha elements—there was not time. Similarly, tailored demarches to different persons might convince a particular party but would suggest a divided international agenda and would not lead to a comprehensive solution. The embassy did recommend support in the margins for the visit of the Belgian foreign minister and the minister of international cooperation, for a telephone call from Assistant Secretary Moose to the president and prime minister-designate, and for the initiation of informal diplomacy by nongovernmental facilitators.[73]

PROGRESS FORESTALLED

Even as we reviewed our strategy, side negotiations began to break down hard lines within the parties. By February 17, elements of a general compromise were in the air; the prime minister would offer two ministries to persons in the MDR faction that opposed him (which positions and to which persons was not clear). The Liberal Party factions were down to haggling about a seven-to-five or a six-to-six split in the national assembly and an argument about which ministerial portfolios each faction would get. The MRND would drop its demand for prior commitment to a "gentlemen's agreement."

Understandings worked out in these small group meetings were formalized at an all-parties' meeting on February 18. It was still not clear whether the RPF would accept compromise within the Liberal Party lists as Chairman Kanyarengwe had assured authorities in Washington. The public formulation was that of the RPF's Sendashonga: the RPF considered the September list the democratic option but would accept whatever the Ndasingwa faction agreed to. It was rumored that core RPF policy makers were not that flexible. In any case, there was consensus in the February 18 parties' meeting that the two factions should work out the exact number of national assembly deputies going to each and the number of portfolios within government that each would accept. The parties' meeting also called for installation of these institutions on February 21. After months of arguing over national assembly lists, Liberal Party differences now seemed to revolve around cabinet seats and whether the minister of justice would be Agnes Ntamabyaliro, Mugenzi's protégé, or a Tutsi from the Ndasingwa faction.[74]

It was in the context of these hopeful signs of forward movement that the minister of public works, Gatabazi, was assassinated just outside his home. The assassination froze any progress in breaking the five-month political impasse and brought back the climate of fear and distrust that had dissipated in previous weeks of serious negotiations. Clearly someone did not want the interim institutions established and sought to stall the process permanently.

Gatabazi's death, the revenge killing of Bucyana, and the subsequent two days of ethnic violence in Kigali bestirred President Habyarimana to an active intervention in the party disputes that he had hitherto eschewed. On their return from funeral services in Butare, diplomats heard that the president had convoked all the internal political parties to discuss remaining differences and to plan an installation ceremony. All parties and factions were represented in a two-day conclave.[75]

Initial word was that a possible result of the parties' meeting would be the setting up of a new government that would be more effective in managing the political scene than had been the government of Prime Minister Agathe Uwilingiyimana. On hearing of this gambit, I telephoned the president's legal advisor and his director of cabinet, warning them that setting up any government other than that provided for under the Arusha Accord, especially since the transition process had already begun with the swearing in of the president, could be construed as a coup against a legitimate government with attendant consequences for US assistance to any government thus established. The fact that both interlocutors tried to argue against my points suggests that such a ploy was in fact in the works. I then called the SRSG to inform him of my ad hoc demarche. Minister Booh-Booh said he would take a similar approach and reported on a telephone conversation between the president and UN secretary general Boutros-Ghali in which the secretary general, in strident terms, told the president to get on with the Arusha process.[76]

A new government was not formed. Instead, presidential cabinet director Ruhigira read a communiqué on the radio February 27 detailing a party agreement on a formula for installing the Arusha institutions. According to the communiqué, in return for accepting some of Mugenzi's candidates for the national assembly, the Ndasingwa faction would get another deputy minister post in government and a chance at the national assembly presidency. There were two problems with the meeting's conclusion: first, it had never been clear that agreements made by leadership in camera would be honored in public or accepted by party rank and file; and second, the RPF had not been part of the meeting.

THE RPF DEMURS

On February 22, the Front had already issued a statement reserving the right to reply "appropriately" to the ethnic violence that had broken out in Kigali. This violence, according to the RPF, was not a consequence of a lack of government but an exploitation of violence by authorities to intimidate and wring concessions from opponents while keeping the transition government from forming. More explicitly, on February 27, an RPF communiqué linked recent violence to "previous massacres at Kibilira, Bigogwe, Bugesera, Kibuye, Ruhengeri, and Gisenyi." These targeted massacres initiated at each political impasse constituted, in the Front's view, a "strategy of dissuasion by the Habyarimana regime designed to impose a series of induced concessions on the RPF."[77] The RPF saw no need for an alternative approach to conclusions worked out on February 18 and would not accept conclusions of a meeting that Habyarimana had no authority to convene.[78]

Despite our pleas that it consider carefully the results of the February 25–27 all-parties' meeting, on March 1, the Front formally stated that it would not participate in a government whose terms were adopted in a climate of terror imposed by Habyarimana. Up at his headquarters in Mulindi, RPF commander Kagame hinted that he might have no option but to return to war. RPF leaders in Kigali explained to the UN that they opposed any alliance that might give President Habyarimana the ability to block acts of the new government. The very marginality that the MRND was trying to avoid through a variety of proposals was what the RPF was determined to impose.[79]

Diplomatic Initiatives

Following Minister Gatabazi's assassination and attendant ethnic violence in Butare and Kigali, the diplomatic community pushed with increased urgency for implementation of the Arusha Accords. While the United Nations retained its leadership of the negotiating process, the Western Observers (Belgium, Germany, France, and the United States) met regularly to review events and suggest initiatives, while each sought to weigh in bilaterally on the process with high-level delegations from headquarters. The Tanzanian government as well took on a renewed engagement in trying to bridge the differences. These initiatives all went forward in the face of a diminishing capacity of the UNAMIR mission to influence the situation.

THE UNITED NATIONS

The ceremonies did not go forward as planned on the morning of March 2, bringing to yet another impasse the continuing effort of the United

Nations to support the Arusha process. Behind the glosses of international discourse, the ninety-day "Report of the Secretary General" on UNAMIR (30 December 1993) had already forecast the problems ahead: "recent signs of mutual intransigence" among the parties and the existence of a well-armed and ruthless group operating in the DMZ intending to disrupt or even derail the peace process. Nonetheless, the report cited the goodwill and cooperation of the parties and, despite logistical problems, held that UNAMIR had on the ground "a minimum viable force which can respond to the most pressing needs in Kigali."[80] In accepting this report, the Security Council questioned at length UNAMIR's viability. The January 6 Security Council resolution urged the parties to cooperate fully in furthering the peace process and establishing a broad-based transitional government at the earliest opportunity. It stressed that "continued support for the Mission will depend on the full and prompt implementation by the parties of the Arusha Peace Agreement."[81]

In a January 27 response to a letter from President Habyarimana, Secretary General Boutros-Ghali noted that "this persistent impasse can only have a negative effect both on your country's internal political situation and on your commitments you have made to the international community." The secretary general appealed for a compromise that would allow prompt establishment of the transition institutions and put Rwanda on the path toward peace, reconciliation, and reconstruction.[82]

Three weeks later, the Security Council endorsed a presidential statement on February 17 that expressed deep concern "by the delays in establishing the Broad-based Transitional Government." Taking note of the fact that Habyarimana had already been sworn in as the interim head of state, it encouraged him to continue efforts for speedy installation of other transitional institutions. It called on all parties concerned to overcome their differences and cooperate fully with UN and OAU representatives. In rather blunt language, the presidential statement reminded parties of their obligation to respect the weapons-free zone established in and around the city and "calls the attention of the parties to the consequences for them of noncompliance with that provision of the agreement."[83]

The official record does not tell the whole story. Though initially reluctant to involve the UN in the Rwandan peace process, Secretary General

Boutros-Ghali had become deeply engaged in making this UN effort a success. He followed the process with personal messages to President Habyarimana and telephoned him several times. After a phone call on February 24 in which the secretary general excoriated the president for holding up the peace process, Habyarimana sent Minister of Transport Ntageruka all the way to New York to set the record straight. The minister traveled on to Washington, where US officials made strong representations on moving the process forward.[84] SRSG Booh-Booh characterized the secretary general's personal interventions as the last straw in the UN effort, but international initiatives under UN leadership persisted during the month of March.

By the end of March, the secretary general's second progress report on UNAMIR detailed the many failed efforts to install the interim government and the national assembly, and it noted that "the prolonged delay in putting the transitional institution in place has not only prevented UNAMIR from carrying out its tasks in accordance with the implementation schedule approved by the Security Council, but has also contributed to a deterioration of the security situation in the country and posed a threat to the peace processes."[85]

The UN tactic for dealing with the impasse had shifted from facilitating talks and cajoling parties forward to threatening termination of the UN effort. The secretary general reported that he and his special representative had stressed to the Rwandan political leaders that without the early establishment of the institutions, "it would be difficult to affirm that sufficient progress has been made in the implementation of the Arusha peace agreement to warrant the continued support of the international community."[86]

In many ways, the military picture looked more promising than the political one. Military targets of UNAMIR were being met; troop strength was at peak strength of the twenty-five hundred troops envisioned by the plan of deployment. Force headquarters and sectors of deployment were deemed "fully operational." The deployment of engineer, logistics, and medical units was complete. The report did note that a dramatic deterioration in the security situation in Kigali had "severely overstretched the resources and capabilities of the national gendarmerie." It recognized that disturbing security incidents could seriously hinder the full and effective implementation of the Arusha peace agreement and found the situation particularly worrisome because "the national gendarmerie, which is responsible for maintaining law and order, is severely handicapped in terms of personnel, equipment and training." The secretary general sought, in consequence, an increase of forty-five civilian police monitors above the authorized level of sixty policemen. Under the category of "Military Aspects," the report mentioned the efforts of the SRSG to "express his serious concern about increasing reports regarding the distribution of weapons to civilians, which constitutes a serious threat not only to public security in Kigali and elsewhere in Rwanda but also to UNAMIR personnel."[87]

Despite his negative assessment, Boutros-Ghali concluded that progress in negotiations gave hope that a compromise could be reached on transitional institutions. He noted that parties have maintained the process of dialogue, and that the United Nations should continue to support that dialogue with a view to completing phase one (establishment of the government) and moving into phase two (disengagement, demobilization, and integration of the armed forces.) He recommended that the Security Council should extend the UNAMIR mandate for six months, with a mandatory review in two months if institutions were not installed.[88]

BELGIUM

In the Security Council, a January evaluation of UNAMIR had already drawn a strong critique of the Rwandan political performance. In early April, a vote was due on the renewal of the UNAMIR mandate. Friends of Rwanda were becoming deeply concerned, Belgium perhaps the foremost. The Belgian government had been part of the peace process from the very beginning. Immediately after the RPF invasion, in October 1990, Belgium sent troops to protect the capital and Belgian expatriates in it. Having helped promote a ceasefire under the mediation of General Mobutu at Gbadolite, Belgium withdrew its combat forces, while keeping in place a small military training mission and continuing Belgian diplomatic and assistance efforts. Now, with an act of good faith in the Arusha Accords, the Belgians had deployed 420 troops as the core contingent of UNAMIR. Deeply vested in a peace process going wrong, Belgium began a series of high-level diplomatic initiatives.

In January, former prime minister Eyskens, a longtime friend of Rwanda, came to Kigali to urge implementation of the accords and institutionalization of the peace process. In February, a heavyweight diplomatic team led by the Belgian foreign minister and the minister of cooperation came just in time to witness party bickering and observe the effect of Minister Gatabazi's assassination. Foreign Minister Claes was very direct in his private meetings with the president, prime minister, and prime minister-designate in which he described the seriousness of the situation, the impatience of the international community, and the importance of the Rwandans taking up their responsibilities. He was similarly blunt in a meeting at the Belgian ambassador's residence to which all party leaders were invited. At a reception for the diplomatic and political community, Minister Claes spoke forcefully of the need to reach out and work together in the cause of peace. Although Belgium was seen in Rwandan political circles as favoring the RPF, the Front chose not to attend the all-party gathering or reception, seeking instead a last-minute meeting with Claes at the airport. On arrival in Bujumbura, Mr. Claes sent out a most pessimistic assessment and asked his ambassadors in France, the United States, and the United Nations to tell their contacts that things were going very badly. On his return to Belgium, the foreign minister met with the UN secretary general in Europe and requested that the UNAMIR mandate be strengthened and troops on the ground reinforced so that they could deal with a deteriorating security situation.[89]

FRANCE

The local situation for Belgium and France was now reversed. Previously, France had had troops on the ground with the purpose of protecting the expatriate community and undergirding prospects for the Arusha negotiations. Now, Belgium had troops in Rwanda as the core contingent of UNAMIR in support of the Arusha Accords. Moreover, France had turned down a Rwandan government request that its troops be part of the UNAMIR operation and had quickly removed its troops as soon as the Belgian contingent deployed to Kigali. As the impasse lengthened and the chance of a new conflict between forces increased, France had been categorical that its troops would not return to Rwanda to restore peace.

Peace was now the responsibility of the Rwandans and of the international community.[90] While playing its part in the several demarches of the Western Observers, France also sent out to Rwanda the vice-minister for social affairs and the minister for international cooperation. The message was the same that Willy Claes brought: the Rwandans had to move ahead in the peace process, or political and social chaos could ensue.

THE UNITED STATES

High-level diplomacy was a tool the United States used as well. During this period, the United States sent to Rwanda the assistant secretary for international organization affairs, Douglas Bennet, and a deputy assistant secretary for African affairs, Prudence Bushnell, along with the director of Central African affairs, Ambassador Arlene Render, and, late in March, the deputy assistant secretary of defense, Pat Irvin.

Rwanda had recently been elected to a rotating African seat in the Security Council and hence was a focus country for Assistant Secretary Bennet. His representations on Security Council matters were, however, quite pro forma: the Rwandans had usually been cooperative in the United Nations and had no problem working with the United States in the Security Council. But Bennet's main message was "the great sense of urgency with which the United States government viewed the current situation in Rwanda."[91] President Habyarimana told Bennet that the impasse was caused by a lack of confidence among political leaders and a lack of political will to press forward on the peace process. Nonetheless, he felt that Rwandan political leaders wanted peace; he was prepared to seek compromises so that the peace process would go forward.

Habyarimana assured Bennet of his full support for the accords and his recognition of "scheduling constraints which required early installation of the government and the national assembly." Habyarimana then revealed his preoccupation with regional dimensions of the problem, whether in Rwanda, in Burundi, or in eastern Zaire. It was important to confront ethnic problems and deal with them rather than to claim they did not exist. He wanted mutual assurances in this period of "transition to democratic elections" so that distrust among contending parties and ethnic groups might diminish. Bennet argued that Rwanda should not wait for the problem to be resolved in other parts of the region but step forward by transcending ethnic conflict to "become a pole of stability, the standard around which others in the region might rally."[92]

The mid-March visit of Prudence Bushnell took place during an internal debate within the US foreign-policy establishment regarding the utility of the UN peacekeeping program in Rwanda. President Clinton had featured the US approach to peacekeeping (based on "Presidential Review Directive [PRD] 13") in his address to the United Nations at the previous General Assembly. Although the Somali debacle delayed public rollout of Presidential Decision Directive (PDD) 25 until May 1994, everything about the Somali experience seemed to confirm the wisdom of peacekeeping criteria developed under PRD 13. By March 1994, the UNAMIR intervention that our mission at the United Nations had acclaimed as one of the best-planned peacekeeping operations in recent years was neither meeting its objectives, keeping deadlines, nor staying within budget. To the great chagrin of the State Department's Africa Bureau, US diplomats at the United Nations were openly talking to the UN Secretariat about "pulling the plug" on UNAMIR.[93] Clearly some high-level effort to get the peace process back on track was needed. As the deputy assistant secretary holding the conflict-resolution portfolio for the Bureau of African Affairs, Bushnell's mission was to get the Rwandans moving.

Moreover, the actual issues on the table did not seem beyond resolution. Taking "the cautious assumption" that special missions from the European Union and from the Tanzanian foreign ministry would not achieve a breakthrough, I had outlined in mid-March possible US initiatives:

- Urge PL factions to a six-to-five deputies compromise and a two-to-one portfolio distribution.

- Urge the prime minister-designate to accept two ministers from the ten names given him by his party's political bureau.

- Keep RPF focused on political goals, the forward-looking issues they will be treating as members of government.

- Document broadcasts from Radio RTLM and Radio Muhabura that violate Arusha principles and complain to their sponsors.

+ Seek resolution of issues that might exclude the CDR from the national assembly on technical grounds.

+ Point out to all levels of government the costs in US assistance from further delays in setting up the government.[94]

During their March 19–23 visit, DAS Bushnell, Ambassador Render, and I met with top ranks of Rwandan political society, urging speedy installation of a transition regime, noting US consternation over increased violence in Rwanda and detailing the cost to the Rwandan people of each delay in forming a government. The visitors warned that the United States was seriously assessing peacekeeping operations around the world and was quite prepared to say "no" to ones that could not achieve their objectives. Rwanda could be a model of conflict resolution. The vote on UNAMIR was coming up on April 4; an interagency group would decide the US position on renewing UNAMIR within the next couple of weeks. The international community could not make the Arusha process work for Rwanda. Bushnell said she needed a good word to take back to Washington and that good word should come fast. She asked Rwandan leaders to "take responsibility for the future by acting to resolve the impasse, to chart a transition to glory rather than to chaos."[95]

Reactions to the visitors' demarche were, in many ways, set pieces. Habyarimana said that he supported the Arusha Accords and would continue to do so. He was disquieted by the lack of confidence, respect, and good faith in the current political atmosphere. As usual he talked about the regional dimensions of the problem and particularly about the effect the events in Burundi had on attitudes in Rwanda. The prime minister blamed the impasse on the president and said that the new lists prepared by the prime minister-designate and herself "allowed all factions of all parties to participate in the national assembly and government and represented the 'last compromise.'" She saw no reason for keeping the CDR out of the national assembly (even though her list of deputies did not have a CDR name on it); she wanted them not only to sign the "Code of Ethics" but also make a public declaration of support for the Arusha Accords. She said that, since 1992, the president's party had blocked every decision it did not agree with; the new transition government must be able to take decisions for change. She was examining how to control Radio RTLM; the president had asked that Radio Muhabura be controlled as well.[96]

The US delegation met with RPF leaders gathered at their up-country headquarters at the Mulindi tea plantation. Chairman Kanyarengwe said that the current political impasse was in no one's interest. The Front had agreed to changes in the Liberal Party lists but had a hard time accepting decisions imposed by violence. Now other bizarre issues had emerged as obstacles. The RPF held that someone was purposefully creating the current impasse. "The international community should assume its responsibilities by identifying that person and helping the Rwandan people remove the impasse."

When the US delegation argued for inclusion, Minister-designate Sendashonga claimed that the CDR was not an acceptable party. RPA commander Kagame said the CDR was a security issue and would be dealt with as a security issue once the institutions were in place and the security services integrated. DAS Bushnell reminded the Front that the international community could not put the institutions in place for them. "They would have to work out some arrangement that would let the government be set up and they had better do it fast. Time had become finite. The failure to reach accommodation could result in tragedy for all Rwandans."[97]

The United States made one more high-level effort to push the parties to agreement. The deputy assistant secretary of defense for humanitarian assistance and refugee affairs, Patricia Irvin, visited Kigali March 24 and 25. Her purpose was to lift visions to what might be: the challenge of bringing a better life to war-weary Rwandans, the possibilities of joint humanitarian efforts if the transition government were installed, and the possibility of yet making Rwanda an example of a successful peacekeeping effort. In Irvin's visit, President Habyarimana promised her that ceremonies for installation were scheduled for the next day. The only problem remaining was the CDR's exclusion from the assembly. Habyarimana planned to be there at 9:00 the next morning.[98]

THE TANZANIAN INITIATIVE

Encouraged by the Observer group and determined not to have its efforts in the Arusha Accords come to naught, the Tanzanians continued dialogue in Kigali through their ambassador. The two parties to the negotiations also recognized Tanzania's stake in the peace process. On March 2, a high-level RPF delegation went to Dar es Salaam to brief President Mwinyi on their versions of events in Kigali and to ask his intervention. President Habyarimana followed suit on March 4 and with the same intent.[99] In return, President Mwinyi sent Foreign Minister Rwegasira to Kigali on March 11 for discussions that turned into a weeklong marathon of talks with all parties and factions.

The foreign minister left without seeing the institutions set up but with a clear idea of where the blockades were. Rwegasira found it unacceptable that a power struggle within the Liberal Party should hold the process hostage. As long as he respected the lists presented to him by the parties, the prime minister had the right to name the government. The RPF's rejection of compromises made within the Liberal Party was also improper. The foreign minister recognized the problem of including the CDR in the national assembly as an issue to be resolved.

Pushing for Installation

On the morning of March 25, as diplomats filed into the CND assembly hall, they learned that the ceremonies were still confronted with two lists; the president's list for the national assembly differed from that of the prime minister in that it had different names for deputies from the Islamic Party and the MDR and an added name for the CDR. The prime minister hustled observers into a side room, where representatives of the presidency, the RPF, and the major parties engaged in four hours of recrimination over efforts to establish the institutions. Eventually, it was agreed to let the differences over the PDI and MDR candidates be resolved by the courts. The RPF was adamant, however, that it would not accept immediate installation of the CDR in the national assembly. That party would have to prove its good intentions and be judged by the assembly on a three-fifths vote at an appropriate time. RPF representatives did agree to meet later that afternoon with CDR leaders and discuss their differences. Coming out of the four-hour meeting, I encouraged RPF representatives to work for any formula that would meet the concerns of both sides.[100]

The prime minister announced a swearing-in ceremony for the morning of March 28. Only parties loyal to her attended. Failure to install the institutions brought the process up against two other datelines: Easter weekend, celebrated from Good Friday through Easter Monday in Rwanda; and a regional summit on the situation in Burundi called by President Mwinyi for April 4. By Good Friday, it appeared that "the sides are inching towards each other, but afraid to make the final offer." The internal opposition told me that if the president were clearly to declare that admission of the CDR to the national assembly was the last obstacle, they would lobby for CDR admission. The RPF told Ambassador Tambwe that, if the CDR was clearly the last issue at stake, they would take another look at their position. Meanwhile, a CDR youth leader was assassinated, but CDR leadership urged its partisans to be patient. Kigali remained relatively quiet with traffic at usual levels, even though unexplained grenade explosions and gunshots punctuated the night of March 31. Reportedly, youth taunting guards at the presidency drew their fire and suffered one casualty.[101]

When I contacted three different high-level personalities in the president's camp to elicit their views, each had a slightly different view of the state of play. Director of Presidential Cabinet Ruhigira told me that the CDR was the last substantive issue for the president, but he did not control party sentiment. The president's legal advisor said installation of the national assembly turned on whether or not Justin Mugenzi, the president of the Liberal Party, was successful in getting his candidate, former minister of justice Mbonampeka, elected as national assembly president. Minister of Transport Ntageruka (and recent presidential envoy to Western capitals and the UN) said all would go well with the national assembly once the CDR was admitted, but outstanding questions might trouble the installation of the government. I told him that the international community saw the installation process to be one and indivisible.[102]

The tactical details were not on President Habyarimana's mind when he convoked me on April 2. Rather, he was focused on the RPF's intransigence on the CDR inclusion when all the internal political parties and the international community thought the CDR should be in the national assembly. Habyarimana took it back to the RPF's original intentions: "They were a terrorist organization seeking to take power by force." They tried and failed in a classic military attack and in guerrilla warfare, and now the plan was negotiations accompanied by political assassination to destabilize the internal political order. He wondered why the internal opposition tried to undermine the office of the president, which still had a functional, stabilizing role to play under the Arusha Accords. Habyarimana mentioned recent RPF radio broadcasts calling him a traitor, but obviously he had in mind as well recent criticism by the prime minister. Finally, the president revealed his real concern, which was the US vote in the Security Council on the renewal of UNAMIR. Would the ambassador plead with authorities in Washington for a positive vote on extension?[103]

I noted that the international community's position had three elements: equity in the inclusion of all recognized parties, quick formation of a watchdog commission to make sure all parties kept to the principles of the accords, and no further intraparty delays in installing the institutions. This meant that all major players—the prime minister, the president, the high court, the political parties, and the Front—should agree on a single list before ceremonies were announced. As regards terrorism, the RPF and the CDR accused each other of all the violence in the country. Virtually every political group in Rwanda had lost some personality to such violence. The answer to such sabotage was to put institutions in place and let the UN work with the new law enforcement service to find out who perpetrated these acts and stop them. As for the renewal of the mandate, a call to Washington the previous day had confirmed that the US position was still being debated internally. I would obviously immediately communicate to Washington the president's plea for a positive US vote on UNAMIR renewal.[104]

Easter weekend passed in an unusual calm, punctuated by a UN reception and the usual church services. The majority of the RPF political representatives in Kigali had left their CND headquarters to return to Mulindi for a top leadership meeting. UN special representative Booh-Booh shuttled between Mulindi and Kigali trying to push the process forward. It seemed obvious that no further progress on setting up the institutions would be possible until Habyarimana's return from the regional summit in Dar es Salaam on the situation in Burundi. The Rwandan crisis was also expected to be on the summit's agenda.

Meanwhile, an international peacemaker and friend of the president came to town. Mr. Rudolf Decker, a German engineer and senator in Baden-Württemburg, had been doing "track two diplomacy" in the Great Lakes area for nearly eight years, meeting individually with presidents and bringing them together for informal meetings to encourage confidence in the possibility of peaceful and friendly relations. Invited to a personal and completely private meeting with Habyarimana, Decker found Habyarimana deeply troubled by the insecurity and political chaos over which he seemed to have little control. Nonetheless, Decker emerged from the meeting convinced that President Habyarimana intended to go ahead with the establishment of the Arusha institutions once he returned from Dar es Salaam.[105]

Was Peace Possible?

Was the calm of Easter Weekend the harbinger of a better day, or a pause before another imbroglio? In retrospect, it is easy to see the looming storm clouds; at the time, we were looking for hopeful rays of light. It had been eight months since the two parties had signed the peace accords in Arusha. The parties were now cheek by jowl in Kigali, with the presidential guard and RPF battalions only a mile apart. Meetings within parties and between parties went on endlessly. Yet, there was no real compromise in sight. The factions of the MDR were not reconciled, with the prime minister-designate still determined to name his own people to the government and national assembly. The Liberal Party was as split as ever, with failed talks building hostility between the camps. The presidential side, the MRND—plus whoever was calling the shots at the presidency—had put forward several ideas that would minimally protect its interests: an amnesty, a gentlemen's agreement, or the seating of the CDR in the national assembly. The internal opposition had given only recalcitrant, conditional responses to all these initiatives, and the RPF, after positive signals in Kigali and foreign capitals, had stonewalled all proposals from Habyarimana. Although talks between armies on cantonment and disarmament were going forward under the leadership of General Dallaire, the gendarmerie and police, backed by UNAMIR, were unable to prevent weapons distribution, contain unauthorized demonstrations, or prevent assassinations of key personalities. Violence was growing, as was the rumor of renewed war. Peace seemed far away.

Should diplomats have pushed the parties to seize the ever-receding day of installation for transition institutions? Or, did this long delay in implementation signal something so wrong with the agreements that they could not be implemented and a new approach was needed? What were the alternatives to more meetings, more endless discussion and no progress? As we had concluded at the US embassy back in March, alternative strategies included a return to discussions at Arusha, an all-players retreat, a summit meeting of the leadership and top military, or use of professional facilitation or mediation. But the embassy rejected these options because there was no time. The six-month evaluation of UNAMIR was coming up in early April. Parties needed to install the institutions before then. The reality of that upcoming Security Council vote drove the last diplomatic ploy, with all diplomatic missions jointly tabling a proposal with a take-it-or-else ultimatum.[106] But concerted diplomatic pressure seemed only to crystallize established positions. Could more creative negotiating strategies and more patience have won through to a structure of institutions acceptable to all?

There were two main perspectives on the deadlock. One was that Habyarimana was masterminding the divisions within the parties and the arguments over positions in the national assembly and government. That perspective, insistently pushed by the RPF and increasingly believed by many in the international community, left but one recourse with two options: deal with or deal out the president. Indeed, in the last days of March, top-level official and informal diplomacy had focused on Habyarimana. But the RPF wanted more than diplomatic pressure. The tenor of their argument was that, in order to let the rest of the parties move forward to the installation of the institutions, it was necessary to isolate or remove the president. The president, however, still held the largest political support throughout the country, the loyalty of most of the army, and the control of local administration. Getting Habyarimana out of the way as an impediment to progress would have required more leverage than the international interveners had at their disposal and a change of mandate for UNAMIR from that of a "classic peacekeeping operation" to that of a peace enforcer with a plan of action, equipment, and forces sufficient to match the mission.

The other perspective saw the wrangling over the institutions as a contest for power among Rwanda's political elite, each group hoping to use representation in the government and national assembly to ensure continued control during the transition process. The president and the MRND wanted a blocking vote in the institutions to ensure that they were not completely marginalized and pushed to the side by the end of the transition. Various elements of the internal opposition wanted a voting pattern that would keep the president powerless to influence the transitional agenda and put themselves in a controlling position. The RPF, already with military equity but with no significant political base in the country, needed a structure of representation within the institutions that would build its political position and guarantee its interests throughout the transition. Each contending faction calculated the arithmetic of representation in institutions at the beginning of the transition in such a way as to have political control at the end of the transition.

From the US point of view, shared broadly among development partners, the issue was not personalities or numerical ascendency but principles: the Arusha principles of power sharing, inclusiveness, compromise, and accommodation. Coalition building around issues, not perpetual control, was the ideal. It was in this context that the issue of the CDR had such saliency. In the early days of the multiparty government, the CDR—with its considerable political following in the northwest and Kigali—asked for a ministerial seat. The other parties refused, keeping the multiparty government an exclusive club. In negotiations on the transition government, only members of the multiparty government were allotted portfolios. Now the CDR, admittedly a bumptious actor with an ethnic attitude, wanted the seat in the national assembly accorded it in the peace agreement, and it was willing to sign on to Arusha principles to get it. International Observers had long argued for inclusiveness; representation of the CDR in the transition institutions was a way of co-opting political dissent.[107] But the internal opposition parties put up procedural barriers to keep that from happening; they did not want a party likely to support Habyarimana inside the institutional tent. Moreover, the RPF considered the CDR to be not a political issue but a security problem that would be handled once institutions were in place.

These entrenched positions regarding a seat in a ninety-member national assembly should have been a signal to Observers that exclusion was still the lodestar of Rwandan politics. The power-sharing ethos of Arusha had not taken root in elite political practice. A transition that fully reflected Arusha principles, incorporating diverse points of view and competition in the political marketplace, was an ephemeral hope. The diplomatic corps' demand for immediate institution of the cabinet and a legislature with the CDR within it might well have been a "bridge too far."

But this was not, as had been reported, the final issue. The split in the MDR remained; late lists conceded little to Twagiramungu's opponents. The Liberal Party grew more deeply divided, with no consensus on who should represent the party in the institutions. Any ceremony of installation at that stage might have made a good report for the Security Council, but it would have papered over profound fault lines that certainly would have resurfaced in the course of governing.

Holding fractious politicians on course in a transition that kept to Arusha rules would have required a forceful UN political presence and the power to back persuasion. Already in January and February, Observers had underlined the need for a more effective, forceful UN presence. I had urged UNAMIR to undertake its responsibility in keeping Kigali a weapons-free zone. In February, the Belgian foreign minister urgently demanded that the UN secretary general immediately reinforce the UNAMIR contingent. France consistently called for a vigorous and effective defense of the peace with competent "blue hats." Yet, neither the UN Secretariat nor the Security Council made any change in the equipping or staffing of UNAMIR forces.

Indeed, when conflict broke out, UNAMIR's chapter 6 rights to self-defense and responsibilities to protect civilians were downgraded by the Secretariat's instructions "not to fire unless fired upon."[108] Thus the international presence that was to accompany the peace process had neither the political capacity nor the military force to open the way to transition.

By April 3, Easter Sunday, these factors were not fully appreciated. The international community was optimistically looking for any formula that would get the institutions in place and validate the Arusha Accords. Rwanda's political leadership was hunkered down in quest for the power that would issue from controlling the institutions. We will never know whether, in time, the ambitions of either could have been realized. The analysis above speculates in the "what-ifs" of history.

The historical fact is that on a moonlit night of April 6, we were startled by a large explosion, followed by a smaller one. Someone using ground-to-air missiles had shot down Habyarimana's French-piloted jet as it approached Kigali airport on return from the Dar es Salaam summit. President Habyarimana, President Ntaryamira of Burundi, their presidential, military, and diplomatic counselors, and the French crew were killed in the crash.[109] With President Habyarimana's death, the only transitional institution initiated under the Arusha Accords came to an end, as did the Arusha process itself. Extremist politics and renewed civil war rushed to fill the vacuum. Genocide was soon to follow. To this, the Arusha political negotiations proved to have been a tragic prelude.

Lessons We Learned

In Rwanda, interveners had earnestly followed the devices and desires of their hearts, namely that the Arusha Accords could usher in a peaceful transition to a secure future. They got instead the tragedy of war and genocide. Some realizations extracted from this tragedy might include the following:

- *An enviable peace accord not grounded in political realities may have a short life.* The assassination of President Ndadaye in Burundi brought back the deep enmities within the Rwandan body politic that euphoria in signing the accords had temporarily masked. Implementing the Arusha Accords in that changed political environment was difficult and perhaps not possible.

- *A negotiated agreement must quickly show positive gains in security, economy, and governance.* Momentum, considered so vital in the early stages of negotiation, was just as important in the last stages of implementation. The stall really began with slow UN action in setting up and deploying the political leadership and peacekeeping force called for in the accords. By the time the United Nations had a minimal presence on the ground, things had begun to fall apart.

+ *Effective diplomatic pressure is vital to the success of an international intervention.* In Rwanda, the UN political leadership was erratic and feckless, presiding over counterproductive confrontations between parties and often falling back on bilateral representatives to carry the ball.

+ *Credible military power is likewise necessary; when outliers challenge the process, peacekeepers must be quick footed, decisive, and firm.* In Rwanda, General Dallaire would deserve high marks on this index, but the UN Secretariat countermanded plans to go after arms caches, downgraded the rules of engagement, and at the end forced peacekeepers into barracks.

+ *Interveners should be prepared for the unexpected.* Two "Black Swan" events upset the playing field and changed the game after the accords were signed: the October assassination of President Ndadaye in Burundi, and the April assassination of President Habyarimana. The former gave ascendency to voices challenging the Arusha Accords; the latter ushered in renewed civil war and genocide. In depth of commitment or resources, the international interveners were prepared for neither.

+ *Time moves on inexorably; setting unachievable deadlines complicates the peace process.* As we moved into April, Security Council votes on the renewal of UNAMIR were imminent. So the diplomatic corps united in demanding an end to party palavers and immediate establishment of the institutions. Meanwhile, President Habyarimana flew to the summit at Dar es Salaam to be similarly pressured by neighboring chiefs of state. Did something in those post-Easter pressures cause someone to change the game by ordering the president's plane downed?

+ *Common goals unite; common danger divides.* High goals of bringing peace to Rwanda and restoring security to the region brought states and international organizations into a vital partnership in international humanitarian intervention. With the renewal of war and the launching of genocide, the partnership melted; each state and organization turned to saving its own citizens or staff. Except for a brave residual UN mission led by General Dallaire and the intrepid work of the International Committee of the Red Cross, Rwandans were left to their own nefarious devices.

EPILOGUE

Juvénal Habyarimana, who had ruled Rwanda since July 5, 1973, was sworn in on January 5, 1994, as president for the twenty-two-month interim stipulated in the Arusha Accords. Four months later, missiles downed the presidential aircraft on its return from a summit meeting in Dar es Salaam, killing President Habyarimana, his colleague from Burundi, President Ntaryamira, their staff, and three French crew.[1]

That plane crash brought to an end the Arusha peace process that had been brokered and sustained by the international community seeking to bring peace between the Rwandan government and the Rwandese Patriotic Front (RPF) and to restore security to the Rwandan people.[2] The president's death rekindled civil war between a self-proclaimed Rwandan government of Hutu extremists and the Front. In an atmosphere of renewed conflict, political crisis, and social cataclysm, revenge quickly turned to genocide that targeted Tutsi civilians and partisans of the internal opposition. Some eight hundred thousand innocents were brutally slaughtered in one hundred days. Thus, an international humanitarian effort to restore peace to Rwanda had instead ushered in a great human disaster.

The story of the genocide has been recounted by numerous participants, analysts, and historians. In this epilogue to the narrative on the Arusha political negotiations, I review the more important contributions to this literature, then give my understanding of the major events in this story of national implosion and international failure. Finally, I look at lessons from the tragedy that could illumine our understanding of the Rwandan conflict and that might buttress future efforts to intervene on humanity's behalf.

Recounting Genocide

The many narratives of genocide in Rwanda divide along a timeline: those written in the immediate aftermath of the event, those written at middle distance and filling in dimensions of the picture, and more recent revisionist histories calling into question the standard interpretations. I mention below the more notable works that focus on the genocide per se (full citations are given in the bibliography).

One of the earliest comprehensive studies, *Rwanda: Death, Despair, and Defiance,* was published in September 1994 by Africa Rights. Rushed to press with documentation provided by the RPF, the text established in the literature a convincing description of the April–June events as a genocide planned by Hutu extremists who shot down Habyarimana's plane, took over government, and intentionally mobilized the military and militia to eliminate the Tutsi from Rwanda.[3] A more scholarly and comprehensive study, Human Rights Watch's *Leave None to Tell the Story,* is based on detailed fieldwork and well-documented interviews initiated immediately after the genocide. Stories and timelines in the study confirm the role of the so-called interim government and extremist militia, as well as local killers. The last chapter, however, also records the RPF atrocities.

Other early works include the summary history by Colette Braeckman, *Rwanda: Histoire d'un génocide,* and a study of the genocide's launching by Filip Reyntjens, *Rwanda: Trois jours qui ont fait basculer l'histoire,* based on his extensive network of informants among Rwandan political and military elite. Rony Brauman, then president of Doctors without Borders, in *Devant le mal: Rwanda, un génocide en direct,* initiated what became a series of soulsearching NGO reflections on humanitarian action in a war zone. Alain Destexhe, then secretary general of Doctors without Borders, weighed in with *Essai sur le génocide au Rwanda* to insist that the massacres in Rwanda were indeed genocide, one of three in the twentieth century. Fergal Keane's *Season of Blood* gives a journalist's on-the-ground truth about the early days of the genocide. Most accessible and useful of the early studies is Gérard Prunier's *The Rwanda Crisis: History of a Genocide*. A longtime scholar of Central Africa, Prunier also had a liaison role between the French and the RPF, which gives his story a participant's cachet.

Later studies published by participants include reflections of the military, such as UNAMIR force commander General Roméo Dallaire's *Shake Hands with the Devil*; Kigali sector commander Colonel Luc Marchal's *Rwanda: La descente aux enfers*; and a more recent memoir, *Rwanda 1994 and the Failure of the United Nations Mission*, by Captain Amadou Deme, a Senegalese officer of both the OAU Neutral Military Observer Group and UNAMIR. For a ground-level account of genocide's terror, there are the stories by survivors or their families: Paul Rusesabagina's *An Ordinary Man*, Immaculée Ilibagiza's *Left to Tell*, or Marie Umutesi's *Surviving the Slaughter*. In this same category are the now-classic essays by Philip Gourevitch based on accounts of survivors and gathered under the title *We Wish to Inform You That Tomorrow We Will Be Killed with Our Families*.

At middle distance from the events, we find a number of careful assessments. Jean-Pierre Chrétien and associates analyze a damning collection of pictures, cartoons, and media pronouncements in *Rwanda: Les médias du genocide*. The Canadian International Development Research Centre, hosting a tenth-anniversary symposium on media, published the symposium's results as edited by Allan Thompson, *The Media and Rwanda Genocide*. That same year, Linda Melvern produced a hard-hitting, well-documented critique in *Conspiracy to Murder: The Rwandan Genocide*. The sifting of a research symposium and the editorial work of Howard Adelman and Astri Surke turned the Nordic-funded, five-volume *Evaluation of Emergency Assistance to Rwanda* into *The Path of a Genocide: The Rwanda Crisis from Uganda to Zaire*. Mahmood Mamdani's *When Victims Become Killers*, while elucidating the regional context, also offers theoretical and anecdotal insights into the meanings of identity, race, and political violence in Rwanda's genocide.

Most of these studies accepted the standard scenario: that genocide was born out of enmity for Tutsi and planned by Hutu extremists who brought down Habyarimana's airplane, took over the government, mobilized the masses by media invective, and organized military and militia to lead the people in carrying out genocide.

Three books derived from pregenocide social analysis and postgenocide fieldwork began to challenge that scenario. The first out was Peter Uvin's *Aiding Violence: The Development Enterprise in Rwanda*, published in 1998. Uvin had taught in Rwanda and served on development missions there before the civil war and genocide. After a thorough examination of scholarly literature on genocide (chapter 10), he argues that the genocide in Rwanda emanated not just from elite manipulation and coercion but from a long history of social violence abetted by the development process and a pervasive social attachment to racist values.

In 2006, Scott Straus published *The Order of Genocide*, which was derived from a field inquiry that sought a framework that would explain the killing. His conclusions from interview data were that war, state power, and ethnic categorization drove the genocide. But situations mattered; Rwandans killed not out of long-standing hatred, deprivation, or greed but because, in given situations, they calculated that compliance was less costly than opposition.

In 2009 Lee Ann Fujii, in *Killing Neighbors: Webs of Violence in Rwanda*, draws similar conclusions, not from a nationwide survey but from her interaction with villagers in two different Rwandan regions. There and in prison interviews, Fujii found that ethnic hatred or ethnic fear does not explain genocidal violence. Rather, state-sponsored violence acted as a script in which social ties or group dynamics mediated local performance. Genocide emerged from social interaction at the local level, which exerted powerful pressure to join the violence and powerful identities for continuing the genocide.

A frontal challenge to the standard scenario came in 2005 from Abdul Joshua Ruzibiza, an RPF commando and key witness in the judicial inquiry of Judge Bruguière. In *Rwanda: L'histoire secrète*, he claims that, after the 1990 invasion, Paul Kagame and Tutsi extremists perpetrated terrorist acts across Rwanda, including shooting down Habyarimana's plane. Some of Ruzibiza's story has been seconded by a high RPF official. In *Healing a Nation*, former RPF executive secretary Theogene Rudasingwa directly asserts that RPA commander Kagame ordered the downing of President Habyarimana's plane. Presidential counselor Enoch Ruhigira in *Rwanda: La fin tragique d'un régime* portrays Habyarimana not as a despot but as a leader trying to hold the political factions of his country together. Captain Deme's book, *Rwanda 1994 and the Failure of the United Nations Mission*, questions the standard view on the famous January informant and whether Hutu extremists did indeed down Habyarimana's plane.

Over the last ten years, documents released and testimony given during French investigation into the downing of the aircraft and during the procedures of the International Criminal Tribunal for Rwanda (ICTR) have spawned a number of works fully rejecting the standard story. Peter Erlinder, in *The Accidental Genocide*, uses ICTR documents, testimony, and decisions to assert that the ex-leaders of Rwanda did not conspire to commit genocide and that the RPF was responsible for downing Habyarimana's plane, thereby triggering the spontaneous revenge that followed. In *Enduring Lies*, Edward Herman and David Peterson dissect how the Kagame regime and its allies in the West have used the charge of genocide to cover over RPF atrocities in Rwanda and Congo and justify support for the current regime. Most recently, Barrie Collins, with a foreword from an ICTR defense lawyer, ranges broadly through Central African history, the war period, and the postwar explanations of genocide in *Rwanda 1994: The Myth of the Akazu Genocide Conspiracy and Its Consequences*. His claim is that the myth of the Akazu genocide conspiracy sustains Africa's first morally constituted tyranny.

The most carefully researched study of recent date is André Guichaoua's *From War to Genocide: Criminal Politics in Rwanda, 1990–1940*. Based on long experience as a researcher in Rwanda, deep access as an expert witness for the prosecution to the Rwandan Tribunal's records, and his own long contacts with Rwandan officialdom, the book implicates the RPF in prewar terror and assassinations, while detailing the inner struggles of Habyarimana's leadership within the MRND.

My own study has been about the Arusha political negotiations, a prelude to the genocide. As regards who shot down President Habyarimana's plane, I remain agnostic; absent more affirmative evidence, I can only review the explanations others have given (see endnote 1). I do know that the assassination rekindled civil war and unleashed genocide. I was there and saw the killings begin. I also witnessed the devastation in human life and material welfare when I returned to Kigali on July 24, the first diplomat back in country after the installation of the new government. Briefly summarized, that story as I experienced it follows.

The History

Already in the evening of April 6, as news of Habyarimana's plane crash spread by word of mouth, walkie-talkie, and telephone across Kigali, military and militia set up roadblocks to seize Tutsi and Hutu partisans of the internal opposition. Shortly after midnight, tracer bullets lit the sky as machine gun and mortar fire punctuated the silence across the valley between the presidential guard and Kigali army headquarters; elements of the Rwandan army were fighting for ascendency. By morning light, reports on our embassy radio net told of house-to-house searches in residential districts with summary killings of civilians, both Tutsi and Hutu. The insecurity was such that Western ambassadors and UN leadership, who were to meet with Rwandan government officials at 9:00 a.m. at our residence, could not get past the roadblocks. The government representatives who came to the meeting turned back my plea that they make common cause with the Rwandese Patriotic Front in restoring peace.[4] The representatives rejected as well my offer of a US forensic mission to determine the cause of the plane crash, and they left shortly to deal with "rogue forces."

By midmorning, reports were coming in of ministers of the then government being hunted down and murdered. The prime minister was assassinated in the UN compound in which she had sought refuge, while Belgian paratroopers sent to protect her were stopped, told to hand over their weapons, taken to military headquarters, and brutally massacred. I learned of the whereabouts of the prime minister-designate, Faustin Twagiramungu, and was able to direct a UN armored carrier to his rescue. But shortly thereafter, UN forces that were to secure Kigali and the airport were ordered to barracks, leaving locals and expatriates to their own devices.

Most of the RPF political leadership had already departed from Kigali to their headquarters at the Mulindi tea plantation. From there the RPF, through the mediation of the UN, let it be known that the killing must stop before any truce talks could begin.[5] Meanwhile General Kagame, commander of the Rwandese Patriotic Army, released his forces from their cantonments and started a three-pronged drive toward Kigali.

Although I had recommended evacuating most US personnel but leaving behind a residual team who would work to restore peace, the State Department ordered the embassy closed; US personnel evacuated overland to Bujumbura, the capital of Burundi. Belgium, France, and Italy organized airlift operations.[6] By April 15, most expatriates had left the country. Such was the fury at the assassination of President Habyarimana that revenge massacres had started already the day afterward, and in broad daylight. But it is also true that the genocide exploded without restraint after the witnessing eyes of expatriates had left. Whether a residual diplomatic or NGO presence in Kigali would have made a difference remains an unanswered question.

The force that could have intervened to stop the violence and restore security was that of the United Nations Assistance Mission to Rwanda (UNAMIR). But UNAMIR had a chapter 6 peacekeeping mandate whose rules of engagement had been so reduced by UN headquarters as to make the troops useless in the first element of its mandate, "to contribute to the security of the city of Kigali."[7] Within an hour after the plane went down, Force Commander Dallaire called me to report that UN forces at the airport seeking to investigate the air crash had had to turn their weapons over to the presidential guard. I telephoned the State Department to advise that unless the UN force received a new mandate and the materiel to carry out that mandate, it would not be able to hold things together.

After Belgian paratroopers were brutally massacred the following day, the Belgian parliament demanded the recall of its battalion; the Bangladesh government did the same. Only the strong arguments of Force Commander Dallaire, interventions by the Nigerian and other permanent representatives at the Security Council, and active insistence from the OAU kept the UN from closing its mission. Eventually, Resolution 912 (1994) reduced UNAMIR to a mediating and monitoring role with personnel levels set at about 270 troops and civilian staff.[8] Brave forces from Canada, Ghana, Tunisia, and other rehatted OAU observers protected thousands in Amahoro stadium right across from UNAMIR headquarters, and at sites around Kigali. They also operated evacuation convoys for hundreds trapped behind hostile lines and undertook missions north and south to stop the slaughter. Of the many NGOs present in Rwanda before the violence broke out, only the International Committee of the Red Cross stayed through, often under fire, keeping two hospitals open (sometimes with staff from Doctors without Borders) and establishing liaison with both sides.

As the UN Security Council debated the mandate and composition of UNAMIR II,[9] RPF forces moved down the eastern side of the country, encircling Kigali from the south while harrying the government west to Gitarama. Under the new mandate of Resolution 918, which included protection for civilians at risk, UNAMIR was to get more equipment and more troops. But US surplus armored personnel carriers, having finally emerged from the morass of US and UN procurement procedures by June 6, got stuck in Entebbe, Uganda, without onward transportation.[10] The first reinforcements of fifty Ghanaians arriving under the expanded mandate did not show up until June 8. By June 17, when UNAMIR II plans projected forty-six hundred soldiers on the ground, troop strength was slightly over five hundred.[11] By this time, the RPF had surrounded Kigali, pushed the government out of Gitarama, and organized its own relief operations in the large areas of the country under its control.

What the RPF had not yet taken was the land along the mountainous Congo-Nile divide and on over to Lake Kivu. Thousands of displaced persons had fled before the RPF advance toward Rwanda's southwest quadrant. On the western side of the mountains, defenseless Tutsi faced roving bands of militia. France decided to carry out a short-term, multinational intervention in the area to protect threatened civilians and secure humanitarian aid, pending a takeover by UNAMIR forces. While many states questioned France's motives, the Security Council approved a two-month intervention under a peacemaking (chapter 7) mandate.[12] Opération Turquoise launched into Rwanda on June 24, confining its operations to Cyangugu and Gikongoro provinces, thus avoiding interposition between the RPF and government forces, which were now being pushed to the northwest from the government's temporary capital at Gisenyi.[13]

This Opération had several long-term effects. First, although massacres continued against Tutsi enclaves within the humanitarian zone, the

French forces, moving continuously about the zone, did save thousands of lives, both Tutsi and Hutu. Second, the presence of French forces served as a magnet to hundreds of thousands of displaced persons who found refuge and sustenance in camps within the zone. Third, although France claimed neutrality, the RPF had only grudgingly acquiesced in the intervention; government officials and partisans, however, saw the French as rescuers. Under the limitations of their humanitarian mandate, French forces did not disarm government security forces nor prohibit government officials from seeking refuge within the zone. The inability to stop all massacres of vulnerable populations, the creation of displaced-persons camps, and the harboring of government elements within the zone were to pose residual political problems both for Rwanda and for France's relations with the Rwandese Patriotic Front, which now pressed on to victory elsewhere in the country.[14]

By July 4, government forces pulled out of Kigali, leaving the capital in RPF control. Pushing toward Gisenyi, the RPF forced the government and its forces, followed by some two million refugees, across the border toward Goma, Zaire. As a humanitarian disaster loomed in Goma, the RPF declared a unilateral ceasefire on July 18 and swore in a government of national unity on July 19.[15] I returned five days later to a capital that was deadly quiet and totally secure.

Even as contingents began to deploy for a UNAMIR force of fifty-five hundred in Rwanda, the international community's focus turned from the settlement of Rwanda's civil war to the humanitarian challenge the war had created on Rwanda's borders. On the lava fields of Goma, cholera broke out, food and fresh water were hardly available, and thousands were dying each day. The United States' Operation Restore Hope opened the Kigali airport for heavy airlift, largely as a means of coping with the regional humanitarian emergency.

Having pushed the government and its forces out of Rwanda, the RPF invested all parts of the country, eventually moving into Zone Turquoise, which UNAMIR peacekeepers had taken over from the French in late August.[16] The Rwandese Patriotic Front stopped the genocide, won the war, and now set up a government of national unity, configured along the Arusha framework but dominated politically and militarily by the Front.

The MRND, the party of President Habyarimana, once politically ascendant, was immediately outlawed. By the time Rwandans got to vote in a national election, the MDR, Twagiramungu's party, was prohibited as well. Eventually, General Kagame, initially installed as vice president, withstanding challenges from without and from within the RPF, took over the presidency and then won three elections by overwhelming percentages. With democratic sanction, autocratic executive rule returned to Rwanda; the RPF dominated the legislature and co-opted the political arena, replacing both the multiparty politics of the 1991 constitution and the single-party regime instituted in 1978.

The Lessons

In the hundred days following the downing of Habyarimana's plane, eight hundred thousand innocents were brutally massacred in a rampaging genocide; thousands more died in targeted hillside massacres as the RPF asserted control.[17] The international community, which began intervening in October 1990 to reestablish peace in Rwanda, failed to stop the atrocities. Concerned states and international organizations had helped devise the Arusha Accords under which Rwandans would observe the rule of law, share power, and provide a secure life to all. But the international community was not able to establish on Rwanda's political soil the institutions enumerated in the accords. The UN mission, deployed to accompany the peace process through a transition to a new constitutional order, was not able to stop the renewal of war or the launching of genocide.[18]

In view of such disastrous failure, wherein was the international engagement for peace deficient? One must first ask whether the peace project could ever have been achieved. The RPF were determined to depose Habyarimana and transform the Rwandan polity. Habyarimana was similarly determined to preserve the institutions he helped create and to emerge in control at the end of the transition. Was this an intractable conflict? Where was the middle ground in this struggle for power? The states of the region, major donors as well as the OAU and, more latterly, the United Nations, endued with a diplomatic sense of fair play and give and take, thought that a negotiated peace was possible and sustainable.

But the international community underestimated the deep-seated complexities of Rwandan culture and the force of antagonisms fueled by Rwanda's history. Against this complexity, the classic modes of diplomatic negotiation could not prevail. A negotiated peace clearly was not sustainable, at least not under the terms of the Arusha Accords.

Moreover, as the parties came to a supposed agreement at Arusha, the Security Council conceived the role of a neutral international force in classic peacekeeping terms.[19] Of the Security Council's five permanent members, only France wanted a robust force. China was as usual ambiguous about peacekeeping intervention. The United Kingdom, Russia, and especially the United States wanted low budgets and minimal deployment. General Dallaire never got the equipment or the troops he requested for a mobile reaction force. The United States added an insistence on using the crisis in Rwanda as a training ground for OAU peacekeepers, despite the OAU's poor record in deploying and reinforcing its observer force. A minimalist peacekeeping strategy failed.

In the Arusha process, the international interveners failed to pick up on two clear warnings. On the one hand, the dominant party, the MRND, and the dominant power, the presidency, did not want to be marginalized or put in a position where they could not defend their vision for Rwanda within the government or the national assembly. Yet, absent some adjustment, the bishops' allocations for power sharing in the government spelled the end of the Habyarimana regime, as did the decision-making majorities of two-thirds in the government or three-fourths in the assembly.

Any hope that somehow it would all work out through goodwill was dashed by the attempted coup and assassination of President Ndadaye in Burundi. The lesson was clear: not to adjust the power-sharing protocol so as to have institutional guarantees for the incumbent party and president, supported by an international presence, was political suicide for the Habyarimana regime.

On the other hand, the regime persisted in allowing communal violence to erupt whenever negotiations moved toward accommodation with RPF interests. The tactic, which had worked historically, backfired, fueling RPF's determination to take control politically and to hold a position of equity in the integration of security forces. Ethnic violence in the north in

January 1993, following weeks of political stalemate in Kigali over terms of the power-sharing protocol, triggered an RPF attack that pushed close to Kigali, created a huge movement of displaced persons, and greatly weakened the government's position in subsequent negotiations. A new government, cobbled together out of political factions, ceded to the RPF's interests on military integration, thus creating an agreement that large parts of the Rwandan body politic found threatening. A durable accord needed something that all major political players could accept.

The international community considered it a victory during the negotiations when the RPF gave up its various proposals for a collective executive and accepted a formula for power sharing based on the government proposal. This proposal, in effect, expanded notions of multipartyism inscribed in the constitution of 1991. Power was to be devolved from the president to a "broad-based" government open only to parties then in government and to the RPF. The problem was that this formula allowed the self-appointed political elite sitting in government to perpetuate their power by fiat without ever testing their mandate through electoral scrutiny. Nor were members of government willing to seek a referendum on the terms of the Arusha Accords, which buttressed the elites' hold on power with international sanction.

But when those same elite split their parties in contests for position and power in the transition regime, there was no provision in Rwandan law or procedures in the accords for putting Humpty Dumpty back together. It was divisions in the MDR and the Liberal Party that kept the interim government and assembly from being installed. Governments do derive their just powers from the consent of the governed, but that principle was never given credence in the Arusha process.

The lack of institutional guarantees for the regime in power, the lack of security guarantees for the insurgent Tutsi, the shaky basis for political power built on elite parties, and the failure to ground the Arusha Accords in any popular referent left a most vulnerable and fragile peace. For the peace process to succeed, the international community needed quickly to assert strong political leadership and deploy a vigorous international force. At the time of the signing in Arusha, the Organization of African Unity was the organization on the ground. The OAU, which never had a political presence in Kigali, disengaged after the accords were signed in August, leaving its Neutral Military Observers Group in place to be integrated into an eventual UN force.[20] But the political baton was not picked up until the secretary general's special representative arrived on November 23. Minister Booh-Booh then proved ineffectual in moving the peace process forward.

The Arusha Accords signed on August 5, 1993, had called for a neutral international force to be in place by September 10. It was clear by August that the OAU Observer force could not get up to speed to support the interim peace process. That left the job to the UN. But Boutros-Ghali would not send a reconnaissance team to Rwanda until the accords were signed; after that, the UN bureaucracy moved with due deliberation in preparing the secretary general's report proposing a UN peacekeeping force. Such a force was so critically necessary that the government and the RPF sent a joint mission to leverage a quick vote. Meanwhile, the United States, which pressed hard for speedy submission of the secretary general's report, could not give assurance that it would vote for the mission. Pressure from the contenders, and at highest levels from France and Belgium, finally overcame US reluctance as the Security Council, on October 5, approved the deployment of UNAMIR. Force Commander Dallaire, already in Uganda commanding the UN border-monitoring mission, traveled to Kigali with a small staff on October 21, the day after President Ndadaye's assassination in Burundi. Although General Dallaire and his team moved with great speed in setting up the force, one wonders what might have happened if an accompanying international mission had been in place and developing confidence in the peace process before the tragic events in Burundi gave the skeptics their day.[21]

As Convener, Facilitator, or Observer at the Arusha political negotiations, the international interveners brokered political negotiations that failed to meet either side's deeply held needs. They then sought to bolster the implementation of the agreements with a lightweight, poorly equipped peacekeeping mission that did not meet the force commander's minimum needs. Moreover, the peacekeeping office in New York had rejected the force commander's recommendation for aggressive action to enforce the terms of the Arusha agreement in January and in April reduced the force's rules of engagement to the point where units could not defend themselves.[22]

The UN leadership was determined to win the peace diplomatically, but the parties were not playing a diplomatic game.

The allure of diplomatic options also beclouded efforts to stop the killing and restore peace as civil war recommenced and genocide erupted. There was an initial effort under OAU auspices to bring the parties back to Arusha, but whereas the RPF would talk to Rwandan military forces, it would not recognize or deal with the self-proclaimed government so obviously complicit in the murder of political opponents and genocidal massacres of Tutsi civilians. Accompanying Assistant Secretary of State John Shattuck on a mission to regional capitals, I was told to prepare for a return to Arusha at a moment's notice. The moment never came.

Nonetheless, interlocutors continued to insist on ceasefires and a revival of "Arusha principles" as though there were two legitimate parties and a common ground on which to build peace for a future Rwanda. Pleas for a ceasefire became a litany in contacts with the RPF, as did pleas to stop the killing in calls to the self-proclaimed government.[23] To the very end, the conceit behind these requests was that a ceasefire could be turned into a negotiation in which the various parties of the Rwandan political landscape would be accommodated. Power sharing was still the goal. The RPF were being asked to forswear victory in the interests of national reconciliation; the dream of Arusha held sway.[24]

The goal of international intervention since the RPF incursion in 1990 had been to restore peace to Rwanda and succor to its populations. When President Habyarimana's plane was shot down on April 6, the international effort for peace needed overweening force, not more diplomacy. The quickest way to assert that was to reinforce UNAMIR with a fighting mandate, adequate materiel, and battalions willing to use force.[25] There is no gainsaying the difficulty of making that happen. UNAMIR belatedly got a new mandate on May 17, but no significant materiel until late June and no reinforcements until the war was effectively over. Minister Booh-Booh withdrew, leaving his political duties to General Dallaire. Dallaire was to mediate for a truce as the first step in returning to the Arusha process for rebuilding the Rwandan state.[26] Had UNAMIR been reinforced in time, it would have confronted the discredited but vengeful presidential guard and multiple militias, on the one hand, and a disciplined RPA released from their barracks by General Kagame, who wanted no international interpositional force on the ground, on the other hand. But with timely deployments, before the course of the war was set, a reinforced UNAMIR could have stopped the genocide.[27]

Once the Rwandese Patriotic Front had won the war and established a government of national unity, international partners judged the new order by its resemblance to the Arusha pattern. International organizations and bilateral partners needed a state to deal with, but one built to their own model: cooperative, inclusive, and reconciled.[28] The new regime sought rather to demonstrate its independence by controlling movements of military and human rights observers, canceling a large international program of judicial assistance, expelling many nongovernmental agencies, voting against the International Criminal Court for Rwanda, and forcibly suppressing displaced-persons camps in the southwest, while accepting, only under intense diplomatic pressure, the continuance of a much-reduced UNAMIR mission.

The Rwandan tragedy has two distinct phases: the era of sporadic civil war and political negotiations that this study covers; and the era of genocide and all-out war that followed the downing of the president's plane. The state-centric focus of international humanitarian intervention in Rwanda poorly fit the needs of the complex humanitarian crisis generated in either phase. When faced with low-level interests in Central Africa and electorates leery of interventions in distant places, states sought out what other states might do before taking action to succor the helpless. As a matter of policy, the United States deferred to Belgium and France throughout the Arusha negotiations. But to demonstrate the "rigor" of the Clinton administration's peacekeeping stance, the United States nearly vetoed a UN peacekeeping mission. With the deployment of UNAMIR, the feckless pace of international diplomacy was in the hands of the UN, which lacked the insight, the will, or the force to lead the peace process to completion.

When the president's plane went down and the violence erupted in the capital city, the first and natural thought was of self-preservation. States that had worked lockstep in humanitarian intervention now organized their own evacuations as UN forces retreated to barracks. The international consensus was broken. Weeks of Security Council debate ensued while the killing went on in Rwanda. The tragedy here was both in the slowness of the international response and in the conceit that the Arusha process could be resurrected, that an internationally brokered ceasefire was all that was needed.

If ever there was a moment when the plight of "the least of these" should have captured the heart and driven the actions of the international community, it was after April 6, 1994, in Rwanda. But to override notions of state sovereignty and diplomatic propriety with an international rescue operation would have taken great-power leadership. No state stepped forward. By the time world leaders had resolved their differences and set their policy through the Security Council, it was too late. Rwandans settled their own accounts, with reverberations that are still heard today.

CHRONOLOGY

1600	Reign of Mwami Ruganzu Ndoori Nyginya dynasty
1894	Count von Gertzen discovers Lake Kivu
1896	Musinga supplants his brother Rutarindwa as mwami (king) at Runcunshu
1897	Germany offers Musinga a letter of protection
1907	Germany establishes civil administration by indirect rule
1916	Belgian forces push Germans out of Rwanda and Burundi
1919	League of Nations Mandate Commission approves the Belgian mandate for the territory of Ruanda-Urundi
1931	Belgians depose Musinga and install Rudahigwa as mwami
1947	Ruanda-Urundi becomes a Trust Territory under the United Nations
1959–60	Social revolution and death of Mwami Rudahigwa results in overturn of the monarchy and establishment of a republic
1962	United Nations recognizes independence of the Republic of Rwanda with Grégoire Kayibanda as president
1963, '64, '66	Exiles attempt a return to power, unleashing Hutu violence against local Tutsi
1973	April–June: National Guard is called out to quell preelectoral violence
	July 5: National Guard high command takes over power as Committee for Peace and National Unity. Guard commander Major General Juvénal Habyarimana named president

1975	Habyarimana institutes the Revolutionary National Movement for Development
1978	Referendum approves a new constitution and the single-party state
1990	July 5: Habyarimana promises multiparty democracy, refugee return
	October 1: Rwandese Patriotic Front (RPF) invades from Uganda
1991	March 29: N'sele Ceasefire Agreement
	September 16: Gbadolite Ceasefire Agreement
1992	April 7: A multiparty coalition government is sworn in with Dr. Dismas Nsengiyaremye, a leader of the opposition Democratic Republican Movement (MDR), as prime minister
	June 6–9: Ceasefire talks in Paris
	July 12: Amended N'sele Ceasefire signed in Arusha (Arusha I)
	August 11–18: Negotiations on the rule of law (Arusha II)
	September 8–18: Negotiations on power sharing (Arusha III)
	October 6–30: Negotiations on power sharing (Arusha IV)
	November 23: Foreign Minister Boniface Ngulinzira returns to Arusha without instructions
1993	January 9: Ngulinzira signs protocol on power sharing against president's wishes
	January: Ethnic violence breaks out in northwest Rwanda
	February 8: RPF attack across front lines, then offer a truce
	March 5–7: Dar es Salaam summit restores ceasefire and Arusha negotiations
	March 16: Delegations return to Arusha to negotiate military integration and refugee questions (Arusha V)
	June 9: Protocol on refugees signed
	July 23: Negotiations move to Kinihira in the demilitarized zone in Rwanda
	August 3: Protocols on military integration and final provisions signed

August 5: Arusha Accords signed

October 5: UN Security Council votes Resolution 872 establishing the United Nations Assistance Mission in Rwanda (UNAMIR)

October 21: Tutsi military assassinate President Melchior Ndadaye in Burundi

October 22: UNAMIR force commander Roméo Dallaire and staff deploy to Rwanda

November–December: Massacres and assassinations in northwest

1994   January 5: Habyarimana sworn in as interim president under the Arusha Accords

January–April: Multiple failed attempts to install the transitional government and national assembly

February 21: Minister of Public Works Gatabazi is assassinated

April 6: President's plane is shot down, killing President Habyarimana and Burundian president Cyprien Ntaryamira, staffs, and crew

April 6: Civil war is relaunched and genocide unleashed

July 4: RPF take over Kigali

July 18: Government and refugees harried into Zaire; RPF declares unilateral ceasefire

July 19: New government installed

NOTES

Documents with the notation (AC) are from the author's collection, archived at George Fox University in Newberg, Oregon.

PROLOGUE

1. The common English adjective for Rwanda is "Rwandan"; however, in their own documents, the Front keeps the French spelling "Rwandese," as in Rwandese Patriotic Front and Rwandese Patriotic Army. This study keeps to the adjective form that the Front has chosen.

2. By "international humanitarian intervention," I mean actions by states and interstate actors that abridge national sovereignty (intervene) in the interest of preserving human life and restoring peace in a particular country. Finnemore similarly defines humanitarian intervention as "deploying military force across borders for the purpose of protecting foreign nationals from man-made violence." Martha Finnemore, *The Purpose of Intervention: Changing Beliefs about the Use of Force* (Ithaca: Cornell University Press, 2003), 53. Fassin argues that natural disasters and human conflict "are now embedded in the same global logic of intervention . . . and the conflation of political and moral registers." Didier Fassin and Mariella Pandolfi, eds., *Contemporary States of Disaster* (New York: Zone Books, 2010), 10. My definition admits of any actions of "coercive inducement" that abrogate sovereign jurisdiction. See Donald C. F. Daniel and Bradd C. Hayes, with Chantall de Jonge Oudraat, *Coercive Inducement and the Containment of International Crises* (Washington, DC: The United States Institute of Peace, 1999), 21–24.

3. Throughout this study, the capitalized terms "Observer," "Facilitator," or "Convener" indicate an official status at the Arusha peace negotiations, as distinguished from other observers, facilitators, or conveners in other situations.

4. The document, formally entitled *Peace Agreement between the Government of the Republic of Rwanda and the Rwandese Patriotic Front*, is commonly called the "Arusha Accords" since it incorporates seven different protocols signed at different times in the Arusha peace process.

5. For details on the coup, see Filip Reyntjens, *Pouvoir et droit au Rwanda: Droit public et évolution politique, 1916–1973* (Tervuren: Musée Royal de l'Afrique Centrale, 1985), 506–8. Reyntjens records that Habyarimana, initially loyal to President Kayibanda, had his hand forced first by Kabyibanda's attempt to purge the administration of suspect northern elements and then by the impatience of other officers, especially Lt. Col. Alexis Kanyarengwe. The Committee for Peace and National Unity had seven of eleven officers from Rwanda's northern prefectures.

6. The manifesto and statutes for the movement were published on the second anniversary of the coup. See *Mouvement Revolutionnaire National pour le Développement, Manifeste et Statut*, Kigali, 5 Juillet, 1995 (AC).

7. Ron Rosenbaum, *Explaining Hitler: The Search for the Origins of His Evil* (Boston: Da Capo, 2014), *chap. 14*.

8. Cited in Michael Ignatieff, "The Art of Witness," *New York Review of Books* 42, no. 5 (March 23, 1995). See also Czesław Miłosz, *The Witness of Poetry* (Cambridge: Harvard University Press, 1983).

9. Joseph C. Miller, "Beyond Blacks, Bondage, and Blame: Why a Multicentric World History Needs Africa," *Historically Speaking* 6, no. 2 (November/December 2004): 7, 11.

10. Ibid., 8.

11. Hannah Arendt, *The Human Condition* (Chicago: University of Chicago Press, 1998 [1958]), 192.

12. Ibid.

13. See the epilogue for a review of this literature.

14. See the Belgian inquiry at http://www.senate.be/english/rwanda.html, and the French investigation at http://www.assemblee-nationale.fr/dossiers/rwanda/rapport.asp.

15. See "Report of the Conference," *The Rwandan Genocide: Can It Happen Again?* The Paul Simon Center for Public Policy, University of Southern Illinois, Carbondale, 1999.

16. See United Nations, *The United Nations and Rwanda, 1993–1996* (New York: United Nations Department of Public Information, 1996).

17. The majority of the documents in this study, then, have been taken from the archives of the Department of State or those of other US foreign affairs agencies. The documents are essentially of two kinds: Department of State telegraphic messages to and from embassies, and internal messages within the bureaucracy such as memoranda, background papers, and e-mails. I use in this study a simplified citation

system that identifies the document first by date, then by type, and finally by subject matter. Dates for telegraphic traffic use the abbreviated form found on the cable, that is, "28 Jun 92," or "08 Aug 92," with a six-digit number for the Department of State cables and a five-digit number for cables from embassies.

These documents can be retrieved by referencing the document number and date from the National Security archive at nsarchive.org, or the State Department's Freedom of Information Act website: foia.state.gov. In these notes, documents marked "(AC)" are available in the author's collection archived with other documents at George Fox University, Newberg, Oregon.

INTRODUCTION

1. Human Rights Watch, *Leave None to Tell the Story: Genocide in Rwanda*, written by Alison Des Forges (New York: Human Rights Watch, 1999).

2. Gérard Prunier, *The Rwandan Crisis: History of a Genocide* (New York: Columbia University Press, 1995).

3. Fred Grünfeld and Anke Huijboom, *The Failure to Prevent Genocide in Rwanda: The Role of Bystanders* (Leiden: Martinus Nijhoff, 2007).

4. André Guichaoua, *From War to Genocide: Criminal Politics in Rwanda, 1990–1994*, trans. Don E. Webster (Madison: University of Wisconsin Press, 2015).

5. Robert E. Gribbin, *In the Aftermath of Genocide: The U.S. Role in Rwanda* (New York: iUniverse Inc. 2005

6. Theogene Rudasingwa, *Healing A Nation: A Testimony* (North Charlestown, SC: Create Space Publishing, 2013). See chaps. 15 and 16.

7. Enoch Ruhigira, *Rwanda: La fin tragique d'un régime*, 2 vols. (Paris: La Pagaie, 2011), 136–50.

8. Herman J. Cohen, *Intervening in Africa: Superpower Peacemaking in a Troubled Continent* (New York, St. Martin's Press, 2000), 180.

9. Bruce D. Jones, *Peacemaking in Rwanda: The Dynamics of Failure* (Boulder, CO: Lynne Rienner, 2001); see chap. 4.

10. Compare Alexis Kagame's *Un abrégé de l'histoire du Rwanda, de 1853 à 1972* (Butare: Éditions Universitaires du Rwanda, 1975) and René Lemarchand's *Rwanda and Burundi* (New York: Praeger, 1970) with Jan Vansina's *Antecedents to Modern Rwanda: The Nyiginya Kingdom* (Madison: University of Wisconsin Press, 2004) and David Newbury's "The Clans of Rwanda: An Historical Hypothesis," *Africa, Journal of the International African Institute* 50, no. 4 (1980): 389–403.

11. Vansina, *Antecedents to Modern Rwanda*, 34.

12. Ibid., 122.

13. A succinct and contextualized treatment of this question is in Jean-Pierre Chrétien, *The Great Lakes of Africa: Two Thousand Years of History*, trans. Scott Straus (New York: Zone Books, 2006), 70–83.

14. Vansina, *Antecedents to Modern Rwanda*, 134–39. The word *kuhutuza*, from which the name Hutu derives, means "to become impoverished."

15. See Alison L. Des Forges, "Extending Court Power, 1905–1913," chap. 5 in *Defeat Is the Only Bad News* (Madison: University of Wisconsin Press, 2011), for a discussion of the expanding Rwandan Kingdom and revolts against the central court, especially in the north.

16. Or in Lord Lugard's terms, "the tutelage of nations not yet able to stand by themselves," as well as the material obligation for "development of natural resources for the mutual benefit of the people and of mankind in general." Frederick Lugard, *The Dual Mandate* (London: Frank Cass, 1965), 58, 59. These ideals, already much promoted by Lugard and his journalist wife Flora Shaw, were first encapsulated in book form in 1922 as the mandate system was being framed.

17. For a study of the league's effort to keep Belgium from merging the occupied territories directly into the administration of the Belgian Congo, see Susan Pedersen, *The Guardians: The League of Nations and the Crisis of Empire* (New York: Oxford University Press, 2015), 204–10. The Belgian formula was to establish a vice-governor general for Ruanda-Urundi who reported through the governor general in Leopoldville to the minister of colonies in Brussels, a chain of command much too close for the liking of many in the Mandates Commission.

18. Louis Franck, "Memorandum, 15 June 1920," cited in Pedersen, *Guardians*, 240.

19. European colonizers compounded their inattention to lineage and clan affiliation by isolating social constructs (Tutsi, Hutu, and Twa) largely related to status and tying them to theories of migration and race then popular in European anthropology. The colonizers (whether German or Belgian) not only accepted the traditional political and social order but believed that it was natural; Tutsi aristocrats were born to rule. See Chrétien, "An Ancient Human Settlement and Its Enigmas," chap. 1 in *Great Lakes of Africa*, and Peter Uvin, *Aiding Violence* (West Hartford, CT: Kumarian Press, 1998), 14–18.

In Rwanda, the boundaries of these categories were not all that clear. It took two years of careful study for the International Criminal Tribunal for Rwanda to decide that, based on the subjective perceptions of the Rwandan people, Tutsi, Hutu, and Twa constituted "ethnical groups" under terms of the Genocide Convention. See Paul J. Magnarella, *Justice in Africa: Rwanda's Genocide, Its Courts, and the UN Criminal Tribunal* (Burlington, VT: Ashgate Press, 2000), 97–99.

20. Pedersen, *Guardians*, 244–50.

21. See Des Forges, *Defeat Is the Only Bad News*, chap. 9, for a study of Belgian relations with Musinga as the colonial administration tried to reform the traditional social and political system.

22. United Nations, "United Nations Visiting Mission to Trust Territories in East Africa, 1948, Report on Ruanda-Urundi," T/217, 1948, 16, cited in Rawson,

"The Role of the United Nations in the Political Development of Ruanda-Urundi: 1947–1962" (PhD diss., American University, 1966), 35.

23. Reyntjens, *Pouvoir et droit*, 304, 313; see also 235–38 for a detailed chronology of events surrounding the social revolution.

24. Chrétien, *Great Lakes of Africa*, 306.

25. In Rwanda, those goals were antinomies: Hutu elite wanted representative government in which they, as representatives of the majority ethnic group, would pay the largest role. Tutsi leadership wanted national autonomy so that they might order and preserve their traditional status. Two guiding documents of the period, the *Hutu Manifesto* and the High Council of State's *Statement of Views*, reflect these polar views as drafted for consideration of the 1957 Visiting Mission. See Lemarchand, *Rwanda and Burundi*, 149–52; Reyntjens, *Pouvoir et droit*, 231; and Rawson, "Role of the United Nations," 170–89.

26. Through 1959, Tutsi aristocracy held all the positions in the High Council of State, all 55 chieftaincies, all but 10 of the 559 subchieftaincies, and all but 3 of the training slots at the Administrative School at Astrida (Butare); they also dominated the economy. Reyntjens, *Pouvoir et droit*, 107, 269; Group Scolaire figures for 1954 were 63 Tutsi and 3 Hutu, Lemarchand, *Rwanda and Burundi*, 138.

27. See Catharine Newbury, *The Cohesion of Oppression: Clientship and Ethnicity in Rwanda, 1860–1960* (New York: Columbia University Press, 1988), part 2, "Patron Client Politics," for an extended analysis of the effect of abolishing the *ubuhake* cattle clientage in southwestern Rwanda. Cattle clientage proved an encumbrance to large herd owners in a modern economy; there were easier ways to make money. The wealthiest strata of Tutsi leadership sought to have the system abolished. In a highly symbolic ceremony at the High Council of State, with the 1954 UN Visiting Mission in attendance, the councilors voted for the progressive suppression of cattle clientage. See Rawson, "Role of the United Nations," 174–79.

28. Lemarchand, *Rwanda and Burundi*, 146–53.

29. Chrétien, *Great Lakes of Africa*, 301, 303; Lemarchand, *Rwanda and Burundi*, 154, 156–57.

30. Muhutu Social Movement–MSM 1957 (later Rwandan Democratic Movement–Party for the Emancipation of the Hutu, MDR–Parmehutu); Association for the Social Promotion of the Masses–APROSOMA 1957; Rwandan Democratic Assembly-RADER 1959; and Rwandan National Union–UNAR 1959. Parmehutu had Hutu leadership and base, APROSOMA was Hutu-led with mixed base, RADER was Tutsi-led with mixed base, and UNAR was Tutsi-monarchist in several strands.

31. Casualty figures in these crises vary from double digit claims to estimates of thousands, depending on the reporter's political perspective. These figures are taken from Lemarchand, who reviewed government and church records of the time. Statistics on displaced persons/refugees were at 7,000 immediately after

the November fighting and rose to 22,000 during the preelectoral violence of April 1960. By the end of the Tutsi counterattacks in the postindependence period, some 130,000 Tutsi with some of their Hutu and Twa clients had been harried out of Rwanda into Congo, Burundi, Tanzania, and Uganda. Lemarchand, *Rwanda and Burundi*, 167, 172.

32. The UN Trusteeship Council and the UN General Assembly wanted the trust territory of Ruanda-Urundi to accede to independence as a single sovereign state. But the Belgian policy of indirect rule virtually assured separate political development for each country. A special UN commission meeting in Addis on June 15 was to urge the countries to work toward a political, economic, and administrative union. The countries would agree only to an economic union, a project that was stillborn at independence. Thus General Assembly Resolution 1746 of June 27 abrogated the trusteeship agreement as of 1 July 1962, recognizing Rwanda and Burundi as sovereign, independent states. See Reyntjens, *Pouvoir et droit*, 305–10 for details on this transition.

33. Lemarchand, *Rwanda and Burundi*, 216–35.

34. See Colette Braeckman, "Les plus anciens réfugiés du monde," chap. 2 in *Rwanda: Histoire d'un génocide* (Paris: Fayard, 1992) for descriptions of the counterpoint between the efforts of refugees trying to go home and the determined efforts of the First and Second Republics to keep them out. See also Scott Straus, *Making and Unmaking Nations: War, Leadership, and Genocide in Modern Africa* (Ithaca: Cornell University Press, 2015), chap. 9 for analysis of the virulent official reactions to the incursions.

35. Lemarchand, "The Quest for Solidarity," chap. 8 in *Rwanda and Burundi*.

36. The committee seems not to have decided much more than its name and to take advantage of the July 4 government parlay. In the early morning hours, armored vehicles were stationed in front of all strategic sites, but there were no troop movements and nothing but martial music on the national radio. The radio station across the street from the US Embassy borrowed records of Sousa marches from the US Cultural Center collection to provide variety to its martial program. The first radio announcement, without explaining why, asked that all state vehicles be turned in to the nearest military post. The announcement of the change of government was not made until late afternoon. Major General Habyarimana was named as head of the committee but not yet as chief of state. As an officer at the US Embassy from January 1973 to August 1975, I was witness to these events.

37. Guichaoua, *From War to Genocide*, 19n10. The sentences were commuted but several of the accused died in prison under unknown circumstances. It is rumored that President Kayibanda and his wife died in house arrest from untreated health problems and malnutrition. Most sources estimate around fifty

high-level officials of the First Republic were killed or died from unexplained causes in detention.

38. Diplomats, accustomed to the lackadaisical organization of state functions, showed up customarily late only to find the president already there. Civil servants would come tardy to work to discover that the president had visited and taken down their names. Hard work was symbolized by Saturday "umuganda" in which all the local population was to work on a community project, no longer a corvée of labor from client to lord but a common endeavor that all were to join.

39. For an intervener's account of these events, see Roméo Dallaire, *Shake Hands with the Devil: The Failure of Humanity in Rwanda* (Toronto: Random House, 2003), especially chaps. 10 and 11; for a detailed account of internal political maneuverings at this time see Guichaoua, *From War to Genocide*, chaps. 7–10.

40. Thus, in *The Human Condition*, Hannah Arendt states, "Men, no matter what they do, are always conditioned beings" (9); on "the sharing of words and deeds" as the essence of politics, see 197–98.

41. The final lines on the boundaries were drawn for Mfumbira in the north by the Kivu-Mfumbira Conference of 1910; see Wm. Roger Lewis. *Ruanda-Urundi 1884–1919* (Oxford: Clarendon, 1963), 259. They were drawn for Gisaka in the east by British/Belgian agreement in 1923; see Pedersen, *Guardians*, 73.

42. Rwandans hold an almost mystical attachment to the place of one's birth. Where one is from is a highly significant identifier in Rwandan political calculations.

43. See Peter Uvin, "Crisis, Elite Manipulation, and Violence in the 1990's," part 2 in *Aiding Violence*.

44. Lemarchand, *Rwanda and Burundi*, 36, defines it thus: "a highly precarious relationship between a client and a patron involving the exchange of certain commodities and services."

45. See ibid., 36–38 and 95–96 for the nature of clientage ties and the dependency complex among the peasantry.

46. For an excellent general introduction to the significance of ethnicity in conflict zones, see Warren Weinstein with Robert Schrire, *Political Conflict and Ethnic Strategies: A Case Study of Burundi* (Syracuse: Maxwell School of Citizenship and Public Affairs, Syracuse University, 1976), 1–5.

47. For an analysis of the psychological dimensions of political change in the 1950s, see Lemarchand, *Rwanda and Burundi*, 127–44.

48. For the evolution of Tutsi politics in exile, see Braeckman, *Rwanda*, chap. 2 and Guichaoua, *From War to Genocide*, chap. 2.

49. In Zartman's terms, "protracted time, identity denigration, conflict profitability, absence of ripeness and solution polarization"; William Zartman, "Analyzing Intractability," in *Grasping the Nettle: Analyzing Cases of Intractable Conflict*, ed. Chester A. Crocker, Fen Osler Hampson, and Pamela Aall (Washington,

DC: United States Institute of Peace Press, 2005), 48–58. After the October 1990 incursion, the conflict hardened through phases of "eruption, escalation, failed peacemaking and institutionalization." See Louis Kreisberg, "Dynamics and Phases of Intractability," in ibid., 68–74.

50. Or, as the Belgian ambassador remarked to me a decade after the events, "Fundamentally, we did not understand them!"

51. Formal negotiations took place in French and English with simultaneous translations (and would close down when electrical failure stopped the microphone systems), whereas both sides spoke the same mother tongue, Kinyarwanda. The language and formality of the plenary suggests that the negotiations were staged for the Convener, Facilitator, and Observers, not for real engagement with the opposing side.

52. For this insight, I am indebted to Ambassador Joyce Leader. See Joyce E. Leader, "Genocide in Rwanda and the Kigali Diplomatic Corps: Consultation, Cooperation, Coordination," in *The Diplomatic Corps as an Institution of International Society*, ed. Paul Sharp and Geoffrey Wiseman (New York: Palgrave Macmillan, 2007), 168–96. Ambassador Leader was, at the time of this study, deputy chief of mission in the US Embassy at Kigali and designated US Observer for the latter part of the political negotiations, April–July 1993.

53. Negotiating conferences, a subset of multilateralism, are a common adjunct to humanitarian intervention. Finnemore argues that, especially since the end of the Cold War, "Humanitarian intervention must be multilateral." Finnemore, *Purpose of Intervention*, 80. The difficulties of multilateral intervention are captured in Chester A. Crocker, Fen Osler Hampson, and Pamela Aall, ed., *Herding Cats: Multiparty Mediation in a Complex World* (Washington, DC: United States Institute of Peace Press, 1999), especially chap. 2, "Multiparty Mediation and the Conflict Cycle."

54. See Michael H. Cardoza, *Diplomats in International Cooperation: Stepchildren of the Foreign Service* (Ithaca: Cornell University Press, 1962), xii.

55. Anthony F. Lang Jr., *Agency and Ethics: The Politics of Military Intervention* (Albany: State University of New York Press, 2002), 204. For the dichotomy between state ethics and human rights ethics, see Hedley Bull, *The Anarchical Society* (New York: Columbia University Press, 1977), especially chap. 4. For an extended argument on the primacy of persons over institutions in analysis and policy formulation, see Christian Smith, *What Is a Person?* (Chicago: University of Chicago Press, 2011).

56. See, among others, Alan J. Kuperman, *The Limits of Humanitarian Intervention: Genocide in Rwanda* (Washington, DC: Brookings Institution Press, 2001); Rony Brauman, *Devant le mal, un génocide en direct* (Paris: Arléa, 1994); Fiona Terry, *Condemned to Repeat: The Paradox of Humanitarian Action* (Ithaca: Cornell University

Press, 2002); Adam Lebor; *Complicity with Evil: The United Nations in the Age of Modern Genocide* (New Haven: Yale University Press, 2006); Uvin, *Aiding Violence;* Donald C. F. Daniel, Bradd C. Hayes, Chantal de Jonge Oudraat, *Coercive Inducement and the Containment of International Crises* (Washington, DC: United States Institute of Peace Press, 1999); Fabrice Weissman, ed., *In the Shadow of "Just Wars"* (Ithaca: Cornell University Press, 2004); Gary J. Bass, *Freedom's Battle: The Origins of Humanitarian Intervention* (New York: Vintage Books, 2009); Michael Barnett, *Empire of Humanity: A History of Humanitarianism* (Ithaca: Cornell University Press, 2002); Didier Fassin, *Humanitarian Reason*, trans. Rachel Gomme (Berkeley: University of California Press, 2012); David Fisher, *Morality and War: Can War Be Just in the Twenty-First Century?* (Oxford: Oxford University Press, 2011).

57. Lang, *Agency and Ethics*, 19.

58. Martha Finnemore, with the benefit of historic perspective, notes the increasing importance of human rights in post–Cold War international politics, but she also argues that "intervention is thus becoming difficult (if not impossible) to separate from nation building in contemporary politics." Finnemore, *Purpose of Intervention*, 136.

59. Lang, *Agency and Ethics*, 188.

60. Nicholas Onuf, "Normative Frameworks for Humanitarian Intervention," in *Just Intervention*, ed. Anthony F. Lang Jr. (Washington, DC: Georgetown University Press, 2003), 41.

61. On the one hand, there is the story of genocide through human history; see Ben Kiernan, *Blood and Soil: A World History of Genocide and Extermination from Sparta to Darfur* (New Haven: Yale University Press, 2007). On the other hand, there is the humanitarian impulse toward peace; see Bass, *Freedom's Battle*.

CHAPTER 1: CEASEFIRE

1. There are many renditions of this invasion story with different versions of its cause and its particulars. See especially Ogenga Otunnu, "An Historical Analysis of the Invasion of the Rwanda Patriotic Army (RPA)," in *The Path of a Genocide*, ed. Howard Adleman and Astri Suhrke (New Brunswick: Transaction Publishers, 2000); Gérard Prunier, *The Rwanda Crisis: History of a Genocide* (New York: Columbia University Press, 1995); Colette Braeckman, *Rwanda: Histoire d'un génocide* (Paris: Fayard, 1994); and André Guichaoua, *From War to Genocide: Criminal Politics in Rwanda, 1990–1994*, trans. Don E. Webster (Madison: University of Wisconsin Press, 2015). This summary account is largely based on Catherine Watson, "Exile from Rwanda: Background to an Invasion," *Issue Paper* (Washington, DC: US Committee for Refugees, February 1991).

2. According to Gérard Prunier, on the third day of the invasion, Rwigyema got into a heated argument about strategy with Commanders Chris Bunyenzi

and Peter Banyingana. Banyingana pulled his pistol and shot Rwigyema. One in the group, Commander Stephen Nduguta, got away and hurried back to Uganda to inform Museveni. Museveni sent his brother to find the body and arrest the perpetrators, who were tried and executed in Uganda. Gérard Prunier, *Africa's World War* (New York: Oxford University Press, 2009), 13–14. After the RPF victory in Rwanda, Major General Rwigyema's body was repatriated and buried with highest state ceremonies in a hero's grave.

3. Watson, "Exile from Rwanda," 14.

4. Both chiefs of state may have anticipated a Tutsi-led attack against Rwanda, but perhaps neither knew just when the attack might come. In 1987, President Habyarimana told Ambassador Herman Cohen, then senior director for Africa at the US National Security Council, that "Tutsi youth in the Ugandan army were plotting to invade their ancestral homeland." Moreover, President Museveni in Washington immediately after the invasion called the French and Belgian ambassadors and asked that their respective countries not send troops to help Rwanda, thus belying his protestations of ignorance of the invasion. Herman J. Cohen, *Intervening in Africa* (New York: St. Martin's Press, 2000), 164–67. See also Guichaoua, *From War to Genocide*, 25–28.

5. Prunier, *Rwanda Crisis*, 100–101.

6. See Watson, "Exile from Rwanda," 16–17, for a comparison of the Rwandan and Ugandan positions on the invasion.

7. See Mohammed O. Maundi, I. William Zartman, Gilbert M. Khadiagala, and Kwaku Nuamah, *Getting In: Mediators' Entry in the Settlement of African Conflicts* (Washington, DC: United States Institute of Peace Press, 2006), 10.

8. See Edward N. Luttwak, "Give War a Chance," *Foreign Affairs* 78, no. 4 (July/August 1999): 36–44.

9. What Lemarchand, echoing Samuel Huntington, characterizes as the "kin country syndrome." René Lemarchand, *The Dynamics of Violence in Central Africa* (Philadelphia: University of Pennsylvania Press, 2009), 19.

10. See Paul J. Magnarella, *Justice in Africa* (Burlington, VT: Ashgate Press, 2000), 46–48.

11. Guichaoua, *From War to Genocide*, 25–28.

12. As Guichaoua notes, "Tutsi notables as well as a substantial element of the Tutsi population in Rwanda reacted to the October 1 invasions with great misgivings." Ibid., 26–28.

13. Ibid., 22.

14. Prunier, *Rwanda Crisis*, 74–90.

15. 22 Jul 92 Kigali 03002, "Newly Legalized Political Parties." For a detailed description of party origins and ideologies, see Pierre Gasore-Rukara, *Les partis politiques au Rwanda, 1990–1992: Idéologies, stratégies et pesanteurs sociologiques* (Kigali: Self-published, 1992) (AC).

16. "Protocole d'entente entre les partis politiques appelés à participer au gouvernement de transition," Kigali, 13 March 1992 (AC). Although elaborated in a different context, the insights of Littlejohn and Domenici on multiple-stakeholder systems apply. Stephen W. Littlejohn and Kathy Domenici, *Communication, Conflict, and the Management of Difference* (Long Grove, IL: Waveland Press, 2007), 179–85.

17. See Paul Collier, "Land-Locked with Bad Neighbors," chap. 4 in *The Bottom Billion* (New York: Oxford University Press, 2007), on the particular problems of landlocked countries.

18. The troops did not stay long; they were so bent on pillage and mayhem as they pushed back the Front's initial sally that Habyarimana asked Mobutu to call them home.

19. See Prunier, *Rwanda Crisis*, 81–82; and Peter Uvin, "The Image of Rwanda in the Development Community," chap. 3 in *Aiding Violence: The Development Enterprise in Rwanda* (West Hartford, CT: Kumarian Press, 1998).

20. See I. William Zartman, *Ripe for Resolution: Conflict and Intervention in Africa* (New York: Oxford University Press, 1989), 9–10, 267–68; Saadia Touval and I. William Zartman, "International Mediation in the Post–Cold War Era," in *Turbulent Peace: The Challenges of Managing International Conflict*, ed. Chester A. Crocker, Fen Osler Hampson, and Pamela Aal (Washington, DC: United States Institute of Peace Press, 2001), 434–35.

21. In this instance, Mobutu might well be characterized as an "unavoidable mediator," given his weight in the Central African Region, even though Zaire was closely tied to the Rwandan regime. As the internationalization of the Rwandan conflict expanded and other significant interests came into play, Tanzania became the "patrons-preferred mediator," a mediator carrying the least diplomatic handicaps and best positioned to deal with both sides, while unlikely seriously to jeopardize the interests of respective patrons. See Maundi et al., *Getting In*, 25–26 and chap. 2, "Rwanda, 1990–1992."

22. The preamble to the Arusha Accords lists these summits thus: "numerous high-level meetings held respectively at Mwanza, United Republic of Tanzania, on 17th October, 1990, in Gbadolite, Republic of Zaire, on the 26th October, 1990, in Goma, Republic of Zaire, on 20th November, 1990, in Zanzibar, United Republic of Tanzania, on 17th February, 1991, in Dar-es-Salaam, United Republic of Tanzania, on 19th February, 1991 and from 5th to 7th March, 1993."

23. Prunier, *Rwanda Crisis*, 119–20.

24. *The Dar es Salaam Declaration on the Refugee Problem*, 19 February 1991, http://www.refworld.org/pdfid/4dde22d22.pdf./; see also the analysis in Maundi et al., *Getting In*, 44–45.

25. "*Loi No. 60/91 du 13 décembre 1991, portant amnistie générale et voie de solution au problème des réfugiés*" (AC). The Amnesty Law, voted on November 12 and

promulgated a month later, in essence ratifies the Dar es Salaam Declaration and N'sele Ceasefire Agreement while recognizing both "the right of all Rwandans to return peacefully and without arms to Rwanda" and the right of those who chose to remain abroad to come under Rwandan diplomatic protection.

26. Prominent in this effort was the active role of prosecutor Alphonse Nkubito, who argued in and out of court for release of all those against whom there were no charges. Nkubito, a human rights activist, refused to align himself with any political party and was named as an "independent" minister of justice in the first postgenocide government.

27. See 18 Mar 92 Kigali 01152, "Democracy/Governance and A.I.D. Allocations" for a good summary of political changes in this period.

28. The limits of summitry—lack of consistent attention, high stakes bargaining, instant deal making—that characterize the early Rwandan negotiations are illustrated in many historic instances, not the least the negotiations of the Paris Peace Conference following World War I. See George F. Kennan, *Russia and the West under Lenin and Stalin* (Boston: Little, Brown, 1961), 45, 134, 146–47.

29. 27 Apr 92 Brussels 05768, "GOB Views on Possible Belgian Initiatives in Rwanda and Burundi."

30. 26 Feb 92 Paris 05531, "French Perceptions of East Africa and the Indian Ocean States."

31. Rwandan National Radio reported at least sixty-four dead in Gashora Commune alone and twelve thousand internal refugees in Gashora and Kanzenze communes. FBIS 081010Z Mar 92, "Kigali, Rwandan National Radio in Kinyarwanda," and FBIS 151823Z Mar 92 Kigali, Rwandan National Radio in French (AC).

32. 11 Mar 92 Kigali 01038, "Demarche to President Habyarimana on Bugesera and Democracy."

33. Ibid. One of the reasons for the stern demarche and the president's apparent acceptance of its points was that an Italian religious sister had been killed in the onslaught. An outbreak of violence in Byumba had also taken the life of a French nun. Anger in European capitals against Rwandan government inaction did indeed threaten aid programs.

34. "*Relevé de conclusions de la rencontre des 22, 23, et 24 octobre 1991 entre une délégation du gouvernement Rwandais et une délégation du FPR*" (AC). The delegations agreed to seek unity, democracy, right of return, equality of opportunity, freedom of information, respect for human rights, and peace.

35. "*Lettre préparante la rencontre du 06/02/92 au Centre National Pastorale St. Paul (C.N.R.) à Kigali*" (AC) sets out an agenda for the parties and the president, based on the clerics' call for unity, peace, and security. This "*Comité de contact*" would come to play a critical role in negotiations on power sharing. See chap. 4.

36. 02 Mar 92 Nairobi 00853, "The Church and Peace." For further details on early mediation by the World Council of Churches, see Guichaoua, *From War to Genocide*, 63.

37. *"Protocole d'entente entre les parties politiques appelés à participer au gouvernement de transition,"* 13 March 1992 (AC).

38. *The Inaugural Address of George Bush,* http://avalon.law.yale.edu/20th _century/bush.asp; and George Bush, *Address before a Joint Session of the Congress on the State of the Union,* 31 January 1990, http://www.presidency.ucsb.edu /ws/?pid=18095. See also The White House, *National Security Strategy,* August 1991, 10, 14, http://nssarchive.us/national-security-strategy-1991.

39. 08 Feb 91 State 041422, "A/S Cohen Telephone Conversation with President Museveni on Rwanda Crisis, Gulf War."

40. 09 Feb 91 State 043896, "Demarche to Habyarimana and Museveni."

41. See 17 Apr 91 Bujumbura 01570, "Visit of A/S Cohen to Burundi: Conclusions and Recommendations of Regional COM Program"; and 26 Apr 91 Bujumbura 01680, "Visit of A/S Cohen to Burundi: Bilateral Program." See also 03 Apr 92 Kigali 01400, "The New Government and Peace Negotiations," in which Ambassador Flaten took as central to the recommendations of the chiefs of missions "that we utilize the crisis to encourage movement on democracy and that we tell the RPF that we support their democracy and political equality goals." The chiefs of mission also concluded that power sharing in Rwanda should be achieved by democracy and not by force: "For this reason, moving the GOR toward genuine democracy is a key element in our regional strategy."

42. 24 May 91 Kigali 02257, "EC Demarche to Uganda and Rwanda."

43. 22 May 91 Kampala 02234, "Next Steps in the Rwanda Crisis."

44. 20 Jun 91 State 203263, "OAU Mediation of Rwandan Conflict."

45. Ibid. After outlining the tasks that it believed the OAU should undertake in stopping the conflict in Rwanda, the Department of State asked embassies in Paris and Brussels to be sure that the Belgian and French approach tracked with our own.

46. 29 Jul 91 Harare 06923, "GOR/RPF Meetings Make Little Progress."

47. Ibid. This was the first high-level US meeting with the RPF's commissioner for information, Pasteur Bizimungu, a Hutu from Gisenyi province, trained as a lawyer and former director of the state utility, Electrogaz. When his brother Colonel Mayuya was assassinated in 1990, Bizimungu fled Rwanda and joined the Rwandese Patriotic Front. He would be chief negotiator and spokesperson for the RPF and was named president of the postgenocide government in 1994. In 2000 he resigned and formed a new political party. He was arrested in 2002 and pardoned in 2007. He died 17 April 2017, in a California hospital.

48. 17 Apr 91 Bujumbura 01570. "Let the French take the lead," became a mantra in policy pronouncements and instructions to US diplomats. When in March 1992 Assistant Secretary Herman Cohen approved a variety of measures that would engage the United States in the peace effort, he did so with the proviso, "If France and Belgium agree."

49. 26 Feb 92 Paris 05531.

50. See for example, Roger P. Winter, "Refugees in Uganda and Rwanda: The Banyarwandan Tragedy," *Issue Brief* (Washington, DC: U.S. Committee for Refugees, 12 April 1983).

51. 21 March 1991, Memorandum, drafted by Gene Dewey; Subject: *Need for a Problem-Solving Approach to the Uganda/Rwanda Border Tensions and the Banrywanda [sic] Refugee Problem.* Mr. Dewey had formerly been assistant secretary of state for refugee affairs and then deputy high commissioner for refugees at UNHCR. His concern for the Rwandan issue had strong cachet within Washington policy circles.

52. 30 March 1992, Memorandum, to AF-Mr. Cohen; from INR-N. Shaw Smith, Acting; Subject: *Rwanda; In Search of a Settlement.* The conference actually took place on 12 March, and its conclusions immediately became grist for the policy mill. The late Warren Weinstein, who probably knew more of the Rwandan actors than anyone at the table, suggested that Habyarimana had lost control of the situation and needed to be eased out of power. I observed that the situation in Rwanda gathered all the ingredients of genocide as described in the literature on the subject: a deep-seated rivalry for power, an unstable political transition, and the capacity to inflict massive atrocities. Pressing for regime change in this context had its obvious dangers.

53. 27 March 1992, Memorandum, to Mr. Brent Scowcroft and others; Subject: *Results of the PCC Meeting on Rwanda and Burundi* (emphasis added).

54. 17 Apr 92 Kampala 02167, "AF/DAS Houdek's Visit to Kampala."

55. 18 May 1992, Memorandum, to AF/FO-Robert Houdek; from AF/C-Robert Pringle; Subject: *Rwanda: Negotiations with the RPF.* The negotiations were complex and diffuse enough that this memo was subtitled "What HJC Agreed to Do." The policy proposals were forward-leaning in terms of previous US commitments but considerably less than either the RPF or the Rwandan government had wanted.

56. See Herman J. Cohen, *Intervening in Africa,* chap. 6.

57. 13 May 92 Kigali 01978, "Habyarimana Tells Cohen Transition Government Can Govern."

58. 13 May 92 Kigali 01981, "GOR Outlines Strategy to Negotiations to End War." This was the first high-level US meeting with Boniface Ngulinzira, who was born in Ruhengeri prefecture, held two degrees in philology, worked in the Ministry of Education, and was professor at the University of Butare. As a founding organizer of the renewed MDR party, Ngulinzira was named foreign minister in the coalition government installed on 16 April 1992. Bitterly opposed by the Hutu extremists because of his negotiation of the Arusha Accords, Boniface Ngulinzira was assassinated on 11 April 1994.

59. The US role in arranging the meeting was delayed as US embassies in Kigali and Kampala asked for Washington's go-ahead and the State Department, in turn, sought French agreement to the initiative before proceeding. 15 May 92 Kampala 02699, "Uganda: Scheduling Rwanda-RPF in Kampala"; 18 May 92 Paris 13836, "No French Objection to USG arranging Meeting on Rwanda"; and 22 May 92 Kigali 02135, "Rwandan Meetings in Kampala."

60. 08 Jun 92 Paris 15752, "Rwanda Paris Talks Conclude on Positive Note."

61. The French, who were the best-informed on Rwandan military capabilities, had by early 1991 concluded that "neither the GOR nor the RPF can win militarily." 26 Feb 92 Paris 05531.

62. Ibid.

63. That the United States should have at this early date in the development of a European political consciousness suggested the European Community as a "facilitator/mediator" suggests two things: the interest of the Bush administration in looking for regional partnerships particularly in areas where the United States had little experience or interest (coalitions of the willing), and an early appreciation by Assistant Secretary Cohen of the EC's emerging potential as a diplomatic partner. This was despite a failed attempt at a joint demarche with the EC in February 1991.

64. 08 Jun 92 Paris 15752.

65. Ibid.

66. 05 Jun 92 Paris 15719, "DAS Davidow Meets Rwandan Rebel Representatives." At this early stage in the negotiating process, the RPF seems committed to a democratic openness and inclusiveness that it eschewed as the possibility of controlling power came into view.

67. 05 Jun 92 Paris 15720, "Rwanda Talks in Paris: DAS Davidow Meeting with Quai Africa Director Dijoud." Davidow also informed Dijoud that Ambassador Cohen had followed through on his pledge to work on the Uganda dimension of the issue with a letter to President Museveni urging Uganda to sign a security accord with Rwanda, to open the road to Kigali as signals of restored relations, and to pressure the RPF toward serious participation in the negotiations.

68. 08 June 92 Paris 15752. See also 01 Jul 92 State 209671, "INR/AA's African Trends-6/29/92 (no. 12)," for a helpful analysis of the Paris talks.

69. Davidow even avoided the term "observer," referring rather to the US "presence" at Paris talks, even though Cohen in his May diplomatic roundabout had agreed to be an "observer at French-led negotiations between the GOR and RPF." Ibid. and 18 May 1992, Memorandum, *Rwanda: Negotiations with the RPF.*

70. 08 Jun 92 Paris 15752. The retention of Mobutu as mediator and the N'sele Accord as founding document was apparently at the behest of the Rwandese

Patriotic Front, which saw its position as a negotiating partner internationally affirmed by the N'sele Accord and did not wish to open that question again.

71. 18 May 1992, Memorandum, Rwanda: *Negotiations with the RPF.*

72. 25 Jun 92 State 203384, "Time for Museveni to Be Serious about a Cease Fire."

73. Ibid. Regarding this confrontation, Assistant Secretary Cohen admits that "I would have gone way out on a limb here as no bureaucratic groundwork for such a threat had been established in Washington." Cohen, *Intervening in Africa,* 172n7.

74. 20 June 1992, Memorandum, to AF/FO-Robert Houdek; from AF/C-Robert C. Porter; Subject: *Rwanda: Options of Cease-fire Negotiations and Implementation.*

75. 25 June 1992, Memorandum, to AF/FO-Mr. Cohen; through AF/FO-Robert Houdek; from AF/C-Robert M. Pringle; Subject: *Rwanda: Cease-fire Negotiations.*

76. 27 Jun 92 State 206093, "Cease-fire Negotiations: A USG Niche in the Rwandan Conflict?" See Chester A. Crocker, *High Noon in Southern Africa* (New York: W. W. Norton, 1992), 401–2 for an early assessment of the Byerly-Snyder team; and Cohen, *Intervening in Africa,* 90, 108, 194 for their exploits in this time frame.

77. 10 Jul 92 State 220184, "Preliminary Cease-fire Talks with the RPF." See Guichaoua, *From War to Genocide,* 70–71 for divisions within the Rwandan government on negotiating strategy.

78. 27 May 92 Dar es Salaam 03052, "Rwanda: Tanzanians Considering Mediation and Requesting U.S. Input"; and 01 Jun 92 Dar es Salaam 03132, "Rwanda: Tanzania Will Agree to Mediate." Ambassador Mpungwe told the US embassy that Tanzania had been approached in a general way, was still awaiting specifics, and would be "willing to mediate and to host negotiations if the parties so desire."

79. 29 Jun 92 Dar es Salaam 03690, "July 10–12 Rwanda Talks: Arusha, Say the Tanzanians."

80. 13 Jul 92 Dar es Salaam 03989, "Interim Report on the Rwanda Cease-fire Negotiations at Arusha, Tanzania."

81. Ibid.

82. 14 Jul 92 Dar es Salaam 04011, "Text of Joint Communique and N'sele Amendments."

83. 15 Jul 92 State 228637, "Press Guidance."

84. 17 Jul 92 State 229789, "Presidential Letter for Habyarimana"; 18 Jul 92 State 230027, "Letter to Chairman Alexis Kanyarengwe"; and 18 Jul 92 State 229982, "Congratulations to Rwandan Foreign Minister."

85. There was agreement within the US delegation and among other Observers at the ceasefire talks that the RPF was extracting multiple concessions from the poorly prepared Rwandan delegation. The Facilitator was more interested in

emerging from the talks with an agreement than in the equity of that agreement. It was agreed that Colonel Snyder should meet informally with RPF military and point out that this was an exercise not in destroying the other side but in finding mutual ground on which to build peace. As it was, President Habyarimana might have rejected the negotiated document had it not been for highest-level intervention on the part of the US government. Snyder's informal intervention was pursuant to previous conversations Snyder had had with an RPF delegation led by RPA military commander Paul Kagame. See 10 Jul 92 State 220184, and 24 Jul 92 Brussels 09690, "Belgian Read-Out on Cease-fire Developments and Habyarimana's Visit."

86. 08 Jun 92 Paris 15752.

87. See Guichaoua, *From War to Genocide*, 25–28.

88. 23 Jul 92 Brussels 09624, "Habyarimana's Reply to President's Letter."

89. 24 Jun 92 Brussels 09690.

90. 22 Jul 92 Kampala 04092, "The Situation in Rwanda: President Museveni Acts."

91. See 29 Sep 92 Addis Ababa 04935, "Rwanda JPMC Meeting 26–28 Sep 92"; and *Report of the Third Meeting of the Joint Political Military Commission (JPMC), Arusha, United Republic of Tanzania, 22–26 October 1992* (AC). For Observer contributions to the Neutral Military Observer Group see 17 Jul 92 Kigali 02937, "French Views after Arusha."

92. 24 Jul 92 Kigali 03044, "Kigali's Reaction to Arusha Accord." The "new government" would, of course, have the CDR in it as champion of the Hutu cause.

93. Michele D. Wagner, "All the Bourgmestre's Men: Making Sense of Genocide in Rwanda," *Africa Today* 45, no. 1 (January–March 1998): 25–36. Wagner gives an account of mayhem in Nyakizu, a commune in southern Rwanda where MDR partisans forced out the former MRND administration. Wagner concludes that in the shift from single party to multiparty politics, "Rwandan citizens developed the techniques, practices and patterns of behavior that would enable genocide" (30).

94. 04 Aug 92 Kigali 03196, "Democracy Update: Insecurity Abounds But Democratization Continues."

95. See Roger Fisher, William Ury, and Bruce Patton, *Getting to Yes: Negotiating Agreement without Giving In*, 2nd ed. (New York: Penguin Books, 1991), especially chap. 1, "Don't Bargain over Positions," and chap. 2, "Separate the People from the Problem."

96. Zartman, *Ripe for Resolution*, 9–10.

CHAPTER 2: LAW

1. 14 Jul 92 Dar es Salaam 04011, "Text of Joint Communiqué and N'sele Amendments."

2. "Concluding Document of the CSCE Copenhagen Conference on the Human Dimension," 29 June 1990, cited by Neil J. Kritz, "The Rule of Law in Conflict Management," in *Leashing the Dogs of War: Conflict Management in a Divided World*, ed. Chester A. Crocker, Fen Osler Hampson, and Pamela Aal (Washington, DC: United States Institute of Peace Press, 2007), 402.

3. Boutros Boutros-Ghali, *An Agenda for Peace 1995*, 2nd ed. (New York: United Nations Publications, 1995).

4. Koffi Annan, *The Rule of Law and Transitional Justice in Conflict and Post-conflict Societies*, UN Do. No S/2004/616, August 23, 2004.

5. *Constitution of the Commonwealth of Massachusetts*, Part the First, Article XXX (1730), http://press-pubs.uchicago.edu/founders/print_documents/v1ch18.html. See also Thomas Carothers, ed., *Promoting the Rule of Law Abroad* (Washington, DC: Carnegie Endowment for International Peace, 2006).

6. See Ruth Wedgwood, "The Dilemmas of International Law and Coercive Enforcement," in Crocker, Hampson, and Aal, *Leashing the Dogs of War*, 583–84, on the limits of law, an analysis that applies equally well to domestic as to international law in this context of conflict.

7. See A. R. Radcliffe-Brown, "Social Sanctions" and "Primitive Law," chaps. 11 and 12, respectively, in *Structure and Function in Primitive Society* (New York: The Free Press, 1965).

8. See Wedgwood, "Dilemmas of International Law," 584–85, for a succinct analysis of differences in legal traditions.

9. See Hans S. Pawlish, *Sir John Davies and the Conquest of Ireland: A Study in Legal Imperialism* (Cambridge: Cambridge University Press, 2002) for a study of how the application of common law in place of Gaelic customary law not only gave rights to freeholders, thus changing landholding patterns and society with it, but also undermined ancient prerogatives of the Irish earls, eventually bringing all of Ireland under the sovereign control of the British monarch.

10. This raises the question of "whether the insistence that conflicts be waged and resolved in accordance with international law makes their resolution easier and more likely." William A. Schabas, "International Law and Response to Conflict," in *Turbulent Peace: The Challenges of Managing International Conflict*, ed. Chester A. Crocker, Fen Osler Hampson, and Pamela Aal (Washington, DC: United States Institute of Peace Press, 2001), 603. This dichotomy between internal and external norms would become critical in the founding of the International Criminal Tribunal for Rwanda. See Kritz, "Rule of Law in Conflict Management," 402, and David P. Rawson, "Prosecuting Genocide: Founding the International Tribunal for Rwanda," *Ohio Northern University Law Review* 32, no. 2 (2007): 641–63.

11. Do invocations of the rule of law really apply? John Phillip Reid has argued that the rule of law emerges out of an English curb to monarchical ambition and the evolution of the American legal system. The legal tradition sustaining the

rule of law is not transferable to other political cultures. John Phillip Reid, *Rule of Law: The Jurisprudence of Liberty in the Seventeenth and Eighteenth Centuries* (DeKalb: Northern Illinois University Press, 2002).

12. Kritz, "Rule of Law in Conflict Management," 403–4.

13. The dimensions of this issue are debated in Michael Ignatieff, ed., *Human Rights as Idolatry and Politics* (Princeton: Princeton University Press, 2003); and I. William Zartman and Victor Kremenyuk, eds., *Peace versus Justice* (Langham, MD: Rowan and Littlefield, 2005).

14. See Arend Lipjhart, *Democracy in Plural Societies* (New Haven: Yale University Press, 1977), and James W. Skillen and Rockne M. McCarthy, eds., *Political Order and the Plural Structure of Society* (Atlanta: Scholars Press, 1991), especially the introduction and part 4.

15. M. d'Hertefelt, A. A.Trouwborst, and J. S. Scherer, *Les anciens royaumes de la zone interlacustre méridionale: Rwanda, Burundi, Buha* (Tervuren: Musée Royal de l'Afrique Central, 1962), 66–67; René Lemarchand, *Rwanda and Burundi* (New York: Praeger, 1970), 28, 76; and Filip Reyntjens, *Pouvoir et droit au Rwanda: Droit public et évolution politique, 1916–1973* (Tervuren: Musée Royal de l'Afrique Centrale, 1985), 24–25.

16. According to Schabas, "the wisdom of a rigorously judicial approach [in transitional situations] remains unproven." Schabas, "International Law and Response to Conflict," 615.

17. Charles Tilly, *Democracy* (New York: Cambridge University Press, 2007), 13–14.

18. These included the political officer in Dar es Salaam, Robert Bentley; the deputy chief of mission in Kigali, Joyce Leader; and the military expert in the State Department's Bureau of African Affairs, Lt. Col. Anthony Marley.

19. 24 Jul 92 Kigali 03044, "Rwandan Reactions to Arusha Accord," and 04 Aug 92 Kigali 3196, "Democracy Update: Insecurity Abounds but Democratization Continues."

20. 21 Aug 92 Kigali 03478, "Internal Security: An Ongoing Problem."

21. 28 Aug 92 Kigali 03616, "Major Opposition Party to Choose Leader."

22. 21 Aug 92 Kigali 03478.

23. 07 Aug 92 Kigali 03298, "GOR Arusha Strategy Preserves Democratic Institutions."

24. Ibid.

25. Ibid.

26. Rwandese Patriotic Front, *The Genesis of Rwandese Patriotic Front* (Kampala: Africa Leadership Forum; Kampala Forum on CSSDCA, 19–23 May 1991), 16.

27. Ibid., 14.

28. Ibid., 9–10.

29. 08 March 1992, "Letter from Claude Dusaidi, Director for Diplomatic Affairs in the Americas, to Carol S. Fuller, Office of Central African Affairs, United States Department of State" (AC).

30. *RPF Project and Rwandese Patriotic Front Demands* (AC). See also 10 Jul 92 State 220184, "Preliminary Cease-fire Talks with the RPF"; 13 Jul 92 Dar es Salaam 03989; and 18 Aug 92 Dar es Salaam 04745, "RPF Leader on Arusha Negotiations: Holding Out for New Transitional Regime."

31. Rwandese Patriotic Front, *Genesis*, 16.

32. *RPF Project and Rwandese Patriotic Front Demands* (AC). This approach to transition governance was explained by RPA commander Kagame to the Department of State on July 7 and to the Tanzanian Facilitator (as well as to the US ambassador in Dar es Salaam) by RPF chairman Kanyarengwe on August 18. See 10 Jul 92 State 220184; 24 Jul 92 State 237711, "Planned Meeting with Kanyarengwe"; 13 Jul 92 Dar es Salaam 03989; and 18 Aug 92 Dar es Salaam 04745.

33. The very success of the refugee negotiations in the summer of 1990, as well as the absence of President Museveni that October, suggested the necessity of imminent attack before the reason for it was co-opted. See André Guichaoua, *From War to Genocide: Criminal Politics in Rwanda, 1990–1994*, trans. Don E. Webster (Madison: University of Wisconsin Press, 2015), 25–26; Gérard Prunier, *The Rwandan Crisis: History of a Genocide* (New York: Columbia University Press, 1995), 74.

34. Front Patriotique Rwandais, *Communiqué de presse*, 23 June 1992 (AC).

35. Rwandese Patriotic Front, *Press Release*, 8 March 1993 (AC).

36. Front Patriotique Rwandais, *Communiqué de presse*, 24 April 1992 (AC).

37. Front Patriotique Rwandais, *Communiqué de presse*, 2 April 1992 (AC).

38. Front Patriotique Rwandais, *Communiqué de presse* 2.901, 1 September 1992 (AC).

39. Front Patriotique Rwandais, *Communiqué de presse*, 24 March 1992 (AC).

40. London BBC World Service in English, "Focus on Africa," 1515 GMT, 15 June 1992 (AC).

41. Rwandese Patriotic Front, *Press Release*, 17 April 1992, "RPF's Position on the New Government" (AC).

42. Front Patriotique Rwandais, *Communiqué de presse*, 23 June 1992 (AC).

43. I began my duties as US Observer to the Arusha political negotiations at the beginning of these talks. Impressions of the environment and proceedings in these talks are based on my recollections and notes.

44. 14 Jul 92 Dar es Salaam 04011, "Text of Joint Communiqué and N'sele Amendments."

45. 07 Aug 92 Kigali 03298, "GOR Arusha Strategy."

46. 26 Feb 92 Paris 05531, "French Perceptions of East Africa and the Indian Ocean States." The French believed, in fact, that neither party could win the war

militarily. The Tanzanians, on the other hand, "believed the RPF capable of defeating the FAR outright." Bruce D. Jones, *Peacemaking in Rwanda: The Dynamics of Failure* (Boulder, CO: Lynne Rienner, 2001), 50n49.

47. See 08 Jun 92 Paris 15752, "Rwanda Paris Talks Conclude on Positive Note"; 14 Jul 92 Dar es Salaam 04011, "Text of Joint Communiqué and N'sele Amendments"; and 11 Aug 92 Dar es Salaam 04577, "Rwanda Peace Talks Begin Optimistically."

48. Ambassador DeJarnette set up a meeting with OAU secretary general Salim Salim, Foreign Minister Diria, Foreign Minister Ngulinzira, and RPF chairman Kanyarengwe both to introduce me and to express US hopes for quick forward progress on the negotiations.

49. 11 Aug 92 Dar es Salaam 04577.

50. Ibid.

51. Ibid.

52. Foreign Minister Ngulinzira's desire to work from general principles to particular understandings reflected his hope of getting the Kigali government on board on general ideas before engaging the RPF on particulars. What frustrated that good intent was the poor telephone communications in Arusha. As Ngulinzira got more confident in his conduct of the negotiations, poor communication became but an excuse for not checking with Kigali first.

53. 20 Aug 92 Nairobi 18628, "Arusha II—Pact on Rule of Law Concluded."

54. Commissioner Patrick Mazimpaka was born in Gahini, eastern Rwanda and, as a young boy, fled with his family (his father was an Anglican pastor) in the 1962 Tutsi exodus to Uganda. Mazimpaka took two degrees in geology at the Makerere University and became head of the department in that faculty. He immigrated with his family to Canada, where he worked in the mining field. Joining the Rwandese Patriotic Front in its early days, he was made commissioner for external affairs. As chief negotiator, along with Pasteur Bizimungu, of the Arusha Accords, Mazimpaka served in several capacities in the postgenocide government, was chief negotiator of the peace settlements in Zaire, and became deputy chairperson of the African Union. He now works as a private consultant.

55. 11 Aug 92 Dar es Salaam 04577.

56. 20 Aug 92 Nairobi 18628.

57. My remarks on being sworn in as United States ambassador to the Republic of Rwanda, 8 December 1993.

58. This relationship was buttressed by wild rides into the African bush in Belliard's Land Rover. For another view of Observer dynamics taken from soundings later in the negotiations, see Jones, *Peacemaking in Rwanda*, 74, 77. Jones's assessment based on interviews with participants accords largely with mine.

59. Ibid., 70–71.

60. 20 Aug 92 Nairobi 18628.

61. Ibid.

62. Ibid. See also "Protocol of Agreement between the Government of the Republic of Rwanda and the Rwandese Patriotic Front on the Rule of Law," signed at Arusha 18 August 1992. The text of the "Protocol on the Rule of Law" can be found within the *Peace Agreement between the Government of the Republic of Rwanda and the Rwandese Patriotic Front,* http://www.incore. ulst.ac.uk/services /cds/agreements/pdf/rwan1.pdf.

63. The *"politique d'équilibre,"* instituted after Habyarimana's coup in 1973, sought to codify and thus pacify social relations by limiting access to schools and government jobs to numeric proportions in society. For Tutsi within Rwanda, the *"politique d'équilibre"* was a constant font of frustration and animus. Given the RPF's dislike of group tags in any form, the term "sectarian" came to be used to express ethnic or social group differences.

64. Ironically and necessarily, the RPF position on individual rights changed after the 1994 genocide. Genocide is, by definition of the Convention on the Prevention and Punishment of the Crime of Genocide, in article 2, a violation of group rights, "the intent to destroy, in whole or in part, a national, ethnical, racial or religious group"; http://www.ohchr.org.

65. 20 Aug 92 Nairobi 18628, and "Protocol on the Rule of Law," articles 5 and 13.

66. Pierre Bayle, *Philosophical Commentary on These Words of the Gospel* (1686) (Carmel, IN: Liberty Fund, Natural Law Series, 2005); John Locke, *A Letter Concerning Toleration* (1689) (Amherst, NY: Prometheus Books, 1990); Thomas Jefferson, *First Inaugural Address,* 1801, http://avalon.law.yale.edu/19th_century /jefinau1.asp; J. S. Mill, *On Liberty* (1859) (New York: Penguin Books, 1984); Charter of the United Nations, "Preamble," 1947, http://www.un.org/en /sections/un-charter/un-charter-full-text/.

67. 20 Aug 02 Nairobi 18628 and "Protocol on the Rule of Law," article 2. For a review of toleration in various historical societies, see Michael Walzer, *On Toleration* (New Haven: Yale University Press, 1999).

68. 18 Aug 92 Dar es Salaam 04745, RPF chairman Kanyarengwe told the US ambassador that "RPF's goal was to do away with ethnic labeling."

69. See Milton J. Esman, *Ethnic Politics* (Ithaca: Cornell University Press, 1994), especially chap. 1, "Ethnic Solidarity as a Political Force," and 253–55.

70. This is in contrast to the opinion of the "experts" advising the Department of State in March that "constitutional arrangements that explicitly define minority and majority rights probably are required during a transitional period." 02 Apr 92 State 103597, "Rwanda: In Search of a Settlement."

71. See 02 Sep 92 State 284576, "Guidance for Arusha III Talks." In this follow-up of the rule of law negotiations and in preparation for the next round of talks, the Department of State provided "points of departure" for discussions with

the Rwandan government, the Rwandese Patriotic Front, and interested third parties. This document makes clear that the US government assumed that the "transition is to democracy via free, transparent, and fair elections."

72. "Protocol on the Rule of Law," preamble.

73. 20 Aug 92 Nairobi 18628.

74. Ibid.

75. 21 Aug 92 Kigali 03478, "Internal Insecurity: An Ongoing Problem." This remarkable analysis has in it many of the items—party militia, arms distribution, militia training, death squads, political use of ethnicity—that became the fodder of postgenocide essays. On the basis of this and other embassy reporting on insecurity, it cannot be said that the US government did not know. It can be said that the US government did not act on the information it had.

76. Ibid.

77. 31 Aug 92 Kigali 03622, "Arusha III."

78. 21 Aug 92 Kigali 03478.

79. Ibid. At this time, the MRND president's denial of cooperation with CDR may well have been true as each party was trying to establish its identity and delimit its base of support.

80. Ibid. This report parallels the findings of Belgian professor Filip Reyntjens, who uncovered in the same time frame a secret organization named "network zero" that he and Senator Willy Kuypers revealed to the Belgian Senate on 2 October 1992. The organization included many of the same personalities but was not the same thing as the "Akazu" (household), an informal group of influential persons related to the president and especially to his wife. See Prunier, *Rwanda Crisis*, 168.

81. Guichaoua, on the basis of his research in documents gathered by the International Criminal Tribunal for Rwanda, holds that much of the violence, especially terrorist attacks on civilian centers and land-mine attacks, were part of RPF strategy to destabilize the country. Guichaoua, *From War to Genocide*, 67–70. Ruzibiza, an RPF commando and intelligence operative at this time, reports on dates, places, and persons engaged in such events; Abdul Joshua Ruzibiza, *Rwanda: L'histoire secrète* (Paris: Éditions du Panama, 2005).

82. 28 Aug 92 Kigali 03596. Mugenzi even suggested bringing the political negotiations to Kigali, where the RPF could be in immediate telephone contact with their forces in the border region.

83. 31 Aug 92 Kigali 03622.

84. Ibid.

85. "Protocol on the Rule of Law," article 3 and article 7.

86. 25 Aug 92 Paris 23403, "Post-Arusha Talks with the French: Ambassador Flaten and U.S. Observer Rawson at the Quai." For the situation in Washington, see Herman J. Cohen, *Intervening in Africa: Superpower Peacemaking in a Troubled Continent* (New York: St. Martin's Press, 2000), 176.

87. 14 Jul 92 Dar es Salaam 04011, "Text of Joint Communiqué and N'sele Amendments."

88. Ibid.

89. 24 Aug 92 Kigali 03520, "Getting on with the GOMN." The Nigerian contingent, whose commander, General Opalaye, would head the NMOG, arrived in Kigali as this message was being drafted. It was another two months, however, before these officers and others were deployed to the ceasefire lines.

90. 28 Aug 92 Kigali 03596, "Arusha III."

91. Ami Mpungwe, *Crises and Response in Rwanda: Reflections on the Arusha Peace Process*, 2, http://www.iss.co.za/Pubs/MONOGRAPHS/MG%2036/crisis %26res.html.

CHAPTER 3: POWER SHARING

1. See chaps. 1 and 2 above.

2. Hans J. Morgenthau, *Politics among Nations* (New York: Alfred A. Knopf, 1967), 36.

3. Hanna Arendt, *The Human Condition* (Chicago: University of Chicago Press, 1958), 200.

4. Joseph S. Nye, *Bound to Lead: The Changing Nature of American Power* (New York: Basic Books, 1990), 15 and 26. See also John M. Rothgeb Jr., *Defining Power: Influence and Force in the Contemporary International System* (New York: St. Martin's Press, 1993), chap. 2, "Defining Power." If power is definitionally ambiguous in an interstate setting, it is doubly so when contending parties seek to establish and control a common weal.

5. Hedley Bull, *The Anarchical Society* (New York: Columbia University Press, 1977), 57.

6. Clifford Geertz, *The Interpretation of Cultures* (New York: Basic Books, 1973), 317; see also Robert H. Jackson, "A New Sovereignty Regime," chap. 2 in *Quasi-States: Sovereignty, International Relations and the Third World* (New York: Cambridge University Press, 1990).

7. 08 September 1992, "Notes on Plenary and Observer's Meeting with Diria" (AC). This and subsequent notes were personal notes (now in the author's collection) that I summarized in telephone conversations with the Department of State when an open line could be obtained. Communications out of Arusha in the first part of the political negotiations were rudimentary at best. Citations of such notes will follow the format here.

8. Ibid. The foreign minister had vetted this idea with me over an early breakfast in his suite; tea, sweetbread, and millet porridge was on the menu.

9. 10 September 1992, "Notes on Plenary Session" (AC).

10. 11 September 1992, "Notes on Plenary Session" (AC).

11. Ibid.

12. Ibid.

13. 12 September 1992, "Notes on Meeting with Foreign Minister Diria" (AC).

14. 12 September 1992, "Notes on Plenary" (AC).

15. 13 September 1992, "Notes on Plenary" (AC).

16. I had tried to broker a compromise on this issue, but the parties apparently wanted to argue this one out. The negotiations stalled again, but ultimately, discussion of specifics won through.

17. 14 September 1992, "Notes on Plenary" (AC).

18. Ibid.

19. Ibid.

20. E-mail to John Byerly, from Carol S. Fuller, subject *Arusha Update*, 16 September 1992; and e-mail to Pringle/Porter/Snyder/Marley/Byerly/Norman, from Carol S. Fuller, subject *Arusha Update PM*, 16 September 1992 (AC).

21. 12 September 1992, "Notes on Plenary" (AC). The United States was the originator of the "commissions" notion, having seen it work well in South Africa and to a lesser extent in the negotiations in Angola and Mozambique. Foremost among these commissions was the Joint Political Military Commission, adopted by the ceasefire negotiators at US urging.

22. Proposals for effective governance in crisis situations often focus on creative ideas for executive power; David Orentlicher, for example, has argued that a copresidency could break through the partisan gridlock in Washington. David Orentlicher, *Two Presidents Are Better Than One: The Case for a Bipartisan Executive Branch* (New York: New York University Press, 2013).

23. 04 Sep 92 Kigali 03732, "What Kanyarengwe Wants."

24. See also chap. 1, under "To Arusha through Paris."

25. 5 Oct 92 Dar es Salaam 05776, "Arusha IV: Opening Notes."

26. *Joint Communiqué Issued at the End of the Second Round of the Political Negotiations on Power Sharing between the Government of the Republic of Rwanda and the Rwandese Patriotic Front Held in Arusha from 5th to 30th October, 1992* (AC).

27. 18 September 1992, *Allocution du Ministre des Affaires Etrangères et de la Coopération de la République Rwandaise, Arusha* (AC).

28. 05 Oct 92 Dar es Salaam 05776.

29. 29 Sep 92 Addis Ababa 04935, "Rwanda JPMC Meeting 26–28 Sep 92." The Joint Political Military Commission, which functioned as an arena for contact and complaint in the early days of the political negotiations, withered in late 1992 when the politics of the negotiations overtook the commission's efforts to deal with what was happening along the ceasefire line. Its last meeting was in December 1992 in the middle of the negotiations crisis.

30. Ibid. The French, who were providing the transport, said that the last element from Mali would arrive in Kigali by October 3. In fact, the full complement of officers was not filled until mid-month and not fully operative in the field for another month.

31. Ibid. The Observers took reconciliation and achieving peace as the objectives of the JPMC meeting. It might well have been that the parties saw the opportunity to "score points" in front of a large Observer group as the principal objective.

32. Ibid.

33. 05 Oct 92 Dar es Salaam 05776.

34. 09 Oct 92 Kampala 05643, "President Museveni Discusses the Arusha Talks"; 13 Oct 92 Kampala 05675, "Museveni Supports Arusha: New Vision Report"; and my personal recollections of the conversation.

35. 06 October 1992, "Notes: Second Day at Arusha IV."

36. Ibid. The enumerated powers of the proposed council included the following: to promulgate laws, to initiate new legislation, to guarantee national sovereignty, to exercise the right of control over the government, to assume powers of appointment, to command the armed forces, to declare war, to declare states of emergency, to control the printing of currency, and to exercise a suspense veto over legislation.

37. Ibid.

38. Ibid.

39. 05 October 1992, "Notes: Arusha IV: First Day" (AC).

40. 06 October 1992, "Notes: Second Day at Arusha IV" (AC).

41. Ibid.

42. 07 October 1992, "Notes: Arusha IV: October 7" (AC).

43. Ibid.

44. 10 October 1992, "Notes on October 10" (AC).

45. 12 October 1992, "Notes on October 12" (AC). In this process of devolving powers from the president to the Council of Ministers, where decisions would be taken by consensus, the notion of a collective executive favored by the RPF was being incorporated within institutions of the 1991 constitution. Observers cautioned that negotiated solutions, while dealing with RPF concerns, must also satisfy the major political forces in Rwanda if they were to endure.

46. 13 October 1992, "Notes on October 13" (AC). Having shared my concern with both parties without much effect, I informally discussed the issue with the Ugandan Observer, Vice-Minister Didi. I argued that the government side had given away significant presidential powers, especially the president's authority in national emergencies. To devolve his powers as commander-in-chief as well would give Habyarimana good reason to contest the newly negotiated order. On the other hand, if the parties conceded to the president the title of commander-in-chief, they would buy maneuvering room on other issues. Minister Didi later reported that the "RPF had agreed to leave that prerogative to the president," with the implication that he had convinced them to do so. Ibid. and 14 October 1992, "Notes on Wednesday, October 14" (AC).

47. Ibid. and 15 October 1992, "Notes on Thursday, October 15" (AC).

48. Ibid.

49. This quick agreement on judicial structure shows how much the notion of civic rights had permeated the Rwandan political ethos since 1990 under the aegis of NGO human rights activists funded by Western donors, Switzerland and the United States chief among them. The US country team in Kigali led by Ambassador Flaten was one of the first to implement a democratization program under new Bush Administration guidelines. See Joyce Leader, *Rwanda's Struggle for Democracy and Peace, 1991–1994* (Washington, DC: Fund for Peace, 2001), 6–7; and 18 Mar 92 Kigali 01152, "Democracy, Governance and A.I.D. Budget Allocations."

50. 19 Oct 92 Kigali 04298, "Habyarimana on Arusha."

51. 21 October 1992, "Arusha Notes on October 20–21." For analysis of the dwindling domestic support for Nsengiyaremye, and Habyarimana's role in the process, see André Guichaoua, *From War to Genocide: Criminal Politics in Rwanda, 1990–1994*, trans. Don E. Webster (Madison: University of Wisconsin Press, 2015), 81–83.

52. "Arusha Notes" and 03 Nov 92 Kigali 04527, "Arusha Suspension and Beyond."

53. In postnegotiation analysis, presidential cabinet director Ruhigira commented that the three-tier approach and the limitations on seats per party in each tier were proposals put forward by Foreign Minister Ngulinzira and not "make or break" issues for the RPF. Some modification of formula was thus feasible. See 03 Nov 92 Kigali 04527.

54. 22 October 1992, "Arusha Notes" (AC).

55. 23 October 1992, "Arusha Notes" (AC).

56. 24 October 1992, "Arusha Notes" (AC).

57. 27 October 1992, "Arusha Notes" (AC).

58. 28 October 1992, "Arusha Notes" (AC).

59. 29 October 1992, "Arusha Notes" (AC). For all our apparent pragmatism and flexibility in encouraging forward movement in the peace negotiations, this conversation revealed two abiding elements of US policy toward the Rwandan conflict: that the will of the people be expressed over the powers of government by an electoral process, and that that process be inclusive, else excluded elements would undermine the peace process from without.

60. *Protocol IV,* signed October 30, 1992, in *Peace Agreement between the Government of the Republic of Rwanda and the Rwandese Patriotic Front,* Arusha Accord, www.incore.ulst.ac.uk/cds/agreements/pdf/rwan1.pdf.

61. 29 Sep 92 Addis Ababa 04935.

62. *Report of the Third Meeting of the Joint Political Military Commission (JPMC), Arusha, United Republic of Tanzania,* 22–26 October 1992, 1, 2 (AC).

63. Ibid., 12, 16.

64. Ibid., 17–20.

65. Ibid., 25–27.

66. Ibid., 21–25.

67. Ibid.

68. 28 Sep 92 Kigali 04031, "Habyarimana on Politics and Arusha."

69. 01 Oct 92 Kigali 04071, "Rwanda Prepares for Arusha III.B."

70. 19 Oct 92 Kigali 04298, "Habyarimana on Arusha."

71. 03 Nov 92 Kigali 04527, "Arusha Suspension and Beyond," and my personal recollections of the meeting.

72. 06 Nov 92 Kigali 04614, "Arusha Negotiations: Internal Debate."

73. Hans Morgenthau, *Politics among Nations,* 36.

CHAPTER 4: IMPASSE

1. 03 Nov 92 Kigali 04527, "Arusha Suspension and Beyond," and my personal recollections of the meeting.

2. Thus Lederach holds that "all these experiences [of impasse, blockages, retrogression, and breakdown] are normal parts of the change circle." John Paul Lederach, *The Little Book of Conflict Transformation* (Intercourse, PA: Good Books, 2003), 42–43. See also Lawrence Susskind and Jeffrey Cruikshank, *Breaking the Impasse: Consensual Approaches to Resolving Public Disputes* (New York: Basic Books, 1987); Elinor Orstom, *Governing the Commons: The Evolution of Institutions for Collective Action* (New York: Cambridge University Press, 1990); John Paul Lederach, *Building Peace: Sustainable Reconciliation in Divided Societies* (Washington, DC: United States Institute of Peace Press, 1997); or Jock Covey, Michael H. Dziedzic, and Leonard R. Hawley, eds., *The Quest for Viable Peace* (Washington, DC: United States Institute of Peace Press, 2005). See also Jacob Bercovitch, "Managing Internationalized Ethnic Conflict," *World Affairs* 166, no. 1 (Summer 2003): 62–64, and "Mediation in the Most Resistant Cases," in *Grasping the Nettle: Analyzing Cases of Intractable Conflict,* ed. Chester A. Crocker, Fen Osler Hampson, and Pamela Aal (Washington, DC: United States Institute of Peace Press, 2005), 99–121.

3. Kevin Avruch, *Culture and Conflict Resolution* (Washington, DC: United States Institute of Peace Press, 1998), 50.

4. Lederach, *Building Peace,* 35, 15.

5. See Douglas Stone, Bruce Patton, and Sheila Heen, *Difficult Conversations* (New York: Penguin Books, 2010); and Stephen W. Littlejohn and Kathy Domenici, *Communication, Conflict, and the Management of Difference* (Long Grove, IL: Waveland Press, 2007), chaps. 5 and 10.

6. For a basic human needs approach, see John Burton, "Human Needs Theory," chap. 3 in *Conflict: Resolution and Prevention* (London: Macmillan, 1990). For a critique of Burton's method, see Kevin Avruch, "Discourses of Culture in Conflict Resolution," section 4 in *Culture and Conflict Resolution.*

7. For the distorting effects of empowerment, see Avruch, *Culture and Conflict Resolution*, 51–52.

8. 28 Oct 92 Kigali 04422, "Impasse."

9. See 07 Nov 92 State 364080, "Letter to Museveni on Rwandan Negotiations."

10. See I. William Zartman, "Analyzing Intractibility," in Crocker, Hampson, and Aal, *Grasping the Nettle*, 52.

11. See Alain Pekar Lempereur and Aurelien Colson, *Méthode de négociation* (Paris: Dunod, 2004), 92–93.

12. 03 Nov 92 Kigali 04527 and 27 October 1992, "Arusha Notes."

13. Lempereur and Colson, *Méthode de négociation*, 87–89.

14. See the "Protocol of Agreement on Power-Sharing within the Framework of a Broad-Based Transitional Government between the Government of the Republic of Rwanda and the Rwandese Patriotic Front," signed 30 October 1992. The text of the "Protocol of Agreement on Power-Sharing" can be found within the *Peace Agreement between the Government of the Republic of Rwanda and the Rwandese Patriotic Front*, http://www.incore.ulst.ac.uk/services/cds/agreements/pdf /rwan1.pdf.

15. 03 Nov 92 Kigali 04527.

16. Ibid. and 06 Nov 92 Kigali 04614, "Arusha Negotiations: Internal Debate."

17. 06 Nov 92 Kigali 04614.

18. 17 Nov 92 Dar es Salaam 06591, "Arusha V: Observers Meeting in Dar."

19. Letter dated 17 November 1992 from Prime Minister Nsengiyaremye to the president of the Republic (AC).

20. 17 Nov 92 Dar es Salaam 06591.

21. 20 Nov 92 Dar es Salaam 06690, "Arusha V-Going Ahead on Nov. 23, Military Integration to Top the Agenda." Meanwhile the embassy was prepared in case the talks moved quickly to refugee matters. 25 Nov 92 Kigali 04871, "Arusha V: Refugee Discussions."

22. 25 Nov 92 Dar es Salaam 06786, "Arusha V: Political Negotiations Resume."

23. 03 Nov 92 Kigali 04527; 06 Nov 92 Kigali 04614; and 27 Nov 92 Kigali 04901, "Arusha Progress."

24. Ibid.

25. 03 Nov 92 Kigali 04527.

26. 19 Oct 92 Kigali 04298, "Habyarimana on Arusha."

27. 03 Nov 92 Kigali 04527. According to 06 Nov 92 Kigali 04614, former prime minister Nsanzimana, an MRND stalwart, "personally despises the CDR and will not even talk with old friends who have moved into that party." Yet, the same report notes that "the CDR accepts much of the Arusha Protocol. . . . What it does not accept is being excluded from the process. And by letters, statement and communiqués, the CDR has threatened to disrupt the entire life of the

country if it does not get its way." Another report points out the president's wife's strong support for the CDR. 14 Sep 92 Kigali 03782, "Political Parties in Rwanda."

28. 27 Nov 92 Kigali 04901.

29. 30 Nov 92 Kigali 04921, "A Proposition for Arusha."

30. 11 Dec 92 Kigali 05119, "Demarches to Prime Minister and President: Possible Progress Toward Consensus"; and 14 Dec 92 Kigali 05147, "Demarches to President and Prime Minister."

31. That is, Belgium, France, Germany, and the United States. Canada and Switzerland had diplomatic offices in Kigali headed by development officers who focused mainly on bilateral assistance issues.

32. 28 Oct 92 Kigali 04422.

33. 03 Nov 92 Kigali 04527.

34. 06 Nov 92 Kigali 04614.

35. 30 Nov 92 Kigali 04921.

36. Ibid.

37. 06 Nov 92 Kigali 04614.

38. 09 Aug 91 Kigali 03349, "Official-Informal," is an early assessment of Habyarimana by Ambassador Flaten correctly noting the triangular relationship between the president's family (that is, in-laws), the president's party (MRND), and the man himself. At the 1990 Francophone summit in La Baule, Habyarimana personally told Mitterrand that he would open Rwandan politics to democratic, multiparty participation, and he had reiterated that commitment in a speech on 1 July 1991. But whether the president would be able to lead toward democratic governance and keep in check the Hutu supremacists within the family while negotiating peace with the RPF was a question the ambassador could not answer. Obviously, the question and the answer remained unresolved throughout the peace process.

39. 02 Dec 92 Kigali 04972, "New Hope for Arusha Talks."

40. Ibid. The principles were the following:

- There was not to be exclusion of any major political bloc.
- Agreements reached would not be reopened, but practical measures for implementing them must be negotiated.
- Other political sensibilities should be added to the transition government in addition to those in the current multiparty government.
- Measures to govern voting formulas were to be adopted when some members are absent.
- There were to be early communal elections.
- There was to be a decision by referendum or adoption by the CND to give the accords the legitimacy of law.

41. 30 Nov 92 Dar es Salaam 06841, "Arusha V: Update."

42. 03 Dec 92 Dar es Salam 06925, "Arusha V: Briefing by Rwandan Foreign Minister and Tanzania MFA Rep on December 1 and 2." The implication of Ngulinzira's briefing was that he could press ahead in negotiating agreements while waiting for the political process in Kigali to catch up.

43. 01 Dec 92 Kigali 04936, "Arusha to Continue but Major Issues Unresolved."

44. 05 Oct 92 Dar es Salaam 05776, "Arusha IV: Opening Notes."

45. See 30 Nov 92 Dar es Salaam 06841. Three different groups in the Rwandan negotiating team—ambassadors, MRND members, and military officers—sent separate letters to President Habyarimana asking him to accept the October 30 Arusha Protocol as written, agree to a nominated transitional assembly, and not insist on inclusion of all parties in the transitional government. For the RPF view, see par. 4, 19 Nov 92 Kampala, "RPF Reps in Uganda Discuss Arusha Talks."

46. 11 Dec 92 Kigali 05115, "Visit of Tanzanian Foreign Minister Diria." Diria had always conceived the role of the Joint Political Military Committee as larger than that of a guarantor of the ceasefire and a monitor of the peace process.

47. Ibid. and 03 Dec 92 Dar es Salaam 06925. According to President Habyarimana, both Foreign Minister Diria and OAU secretary general Salim Salim had suggested that the president replace the foreign minister as head of the delegation or designate a deputy chief of delegation to represent his own views. 14 Dec 92 Kigali 05147, "Demarches to President and Prime Minister." Since the president did neither, the Tanzanians felt they could press on with the existing team.

48. 11 Dec 92 Kigali 05119; and 14 Dec 92 Kigali 05147. The latter dispatch is a detailed analysis of the demarches and their result written for "a small and select audience."

49. This is but a reiteration of Ngulinzira's strategy briefed to Observers on December 2.

50. 19 Oct 92 Kigali 04928, "Habyarimana on Arusha."

51. Marley was traveling in the region and standing by in Nairobi. The embassy in Dar es Salaam was anxious to have him join Bentley in Arusha. 20 Nov 92 Dar es Salaam 06690, "Official-Informal," "Bentley will depart here midday on the 23rd. . . . And while we hate to spoil Col Marley's Thanksgiving weekend, we suggest that he or another suitable military expert come to Arusha by the 28th or 29th at best."

52. 25 Nov 92 Dar es Salaam 06786, Ambassador Ewing urged, "Despite these problems, political talks are now underway. We hope Ambassador Brynn can arrange to come out as soon as possible following the [Thanksgiving] holiday." By December 2, Ewing was more insistent: "I strongly urge that Ambassador Ed Brynn travel to Arusha at once. . . . In addition since I will depart Tanzania on

December 8, it would be exceedingly helpful to this Embassy to have Bentley in Dar es Salaam rather than in Arusha." 02 Dec 92 Dar es Salaam 06903, "Arusha V: Renewed Optimism in Arusha."

53. Kigali quickly rejoined, "There is still a risk that if we launch Ambassador Brynn today, he will arrive in Arusha to see another postponement." 02 Dec 92 Kigali 04972. Six days later, Ambassador Flaten reluctantly concluded, "I fear it may be a few more days before Brynn's presence in Arusha will be useful." 08 Dec 92 Kigali 05058, "Arusha Process: Proposed Demarche and Possible Parties' Meeting."

54. 11 December 1992, American embassy telefax to Ambassador Dietrich Ventzlaff from Robert Bentley. "Sir: After speaking to you on the telephone this afternoon, I managed to reach Ambassador Flaten in Kigali. His understanding from highest-level officials there is that more work needs to be done in Kigali regarding necessary compromises on power sharing before the various groups in the government and within the Presidency will be ready to issue joint instructions to the delegation in Arusha. . . . In view of this, he has suggested I delay my own return to Arusha until I hear further from him or Washington."

55. 27 Feb 93 Kampala 01485, "U. S. Meeting with RPF Military Commander".

56. 27 March 1992, Memorandum, to Brent Scowcroft, National Security Affairs Advisor, The White House and others; Subject: "Results of PCC Meeting on Rwanda and Burundi." The principle of collective engagement with "legitimate European interests (notably French, British and Portuguese)" was reaffirmed in the National Security Directive 75, "American Policy Toward Sub-Saharan Africa in the 1990's," December 3, 1992 (AC).

57. 04 Dec 92 Kigali 05023, "NMOG Reports Cease Fire Violation."

58. 10 Dec 92 State 397185, "French Military Involvement in Rwandan Cease-fire Process." It is noteworthy that the architect of Franco-American cooperation in Central Africa, Assistant Secretary Hank Cohen, did not see this instruction. It was drafted and cleared at lower levels in the department and then approved by Mr. Cohen's deputy. It was, in part, the fear that the RPF would use this incident to again belabor French presence in Rwanda at the next JMPC that occasioned this direct approach to the French government and its ambassador in Kigali.

59. 11 Dec 92 Paris 34521, "French Military Involvement in Rwanda Ceasefire Process: Exchanges with the Quai." This very thorough, almost Cartesian, dissection of the US demarche shows how deeply the French were invested in their Rwandan strategy, how disturbed they were to be called to account by the United States, and how keen they were to stand their ground on this incident.

60. 09 Dec 92 Addis Ababa 06375, "Meeting with Dr. Rudasingwa."

61. 16 Dec 92 Kigali 05197, "The Politics of Peace: Internal Dialogue."

62. Ibid.

63. Ibid. This was the second meeting of these regional leaders in four months. The first was arranged at the initiation of the Arusha talks by Rudolf Decker, a member of the German State Parliament of Baden-Württemberg, and a track-two peacemaker. See Rudolf Decker, *Ruanda: Tod und Hoffnung im Land der Tausend Hügel* (Neuhausen-Stuttgart: Hänssler-Verlag, 1998).

64. See 03 Nov 92 Kigali 04527; 06 Nov 92 Kigali 04614; 07 Dec 92 Kigali 05027, "Arusha Process: Proposed Demarche and Possible Parties' Meeting."

65. 16 Dec 92 Kigali 05197.

66. 23 Dec 92 Kigali 05287, "Political Negotiations and Arusha," and 24 Dec 92 Dar es Salaam 07326, "Arusha V: Negotiators Settle on Cabinet, Move on to Transitional Assembly."

67. 11 Dec 92 Kigali 05119.

68. 24 Dec 92 Dar es Salaam 07326. The prime minister's counselor for political affairs also admitted that the proposal "had come from the Tanzanian Facilitator, not from either party to the negotiations." 23 Dec 92 Kigali 05319, "Arusha Agreement: Kigali Reaction."

69. 23 Dec 92 Kigali 05319.

70. *Contribution du Parti MRND (Mouvement Républicain National pour la Démocratie et le Développement) a l'aboutissement des négociations de paix à Arusha et au succès de la période de transition au Rwanda.* Kigali: Secrétariat National du MRND, 21 December 1992 (AC).

71. 262044Z Dec 92 FBIS, "President's Party Offers Plan for Distributing Posts."

72. For example, 171105Z Dec 92 FBIS, "RPF Details Government Effort to Disrupt Peace Efforts," and 240915Z Dec 92 FBIS, "RPF Radio on French Troops, Government Agreement."

73. 24 Dec 92 Dar es Salaam 07326.

74. 29 Dec 92 Kigali 05356, "Progress Toward Political Compromise."

75. *Contribution du Parti MRND.*

76. 23 Dec 92 Kigali 05319; and 29 Dec 92 Kigali 05356.

77. 23 Dec 92 State 413010, "RPF Chairman Kanyarengwe Visits Department." The United States saw this principle of inclusiveness as a fundamental element of the move from exclusive single party systems to multiparty democracy. As such it was implicit in the US commitment to promote democracy in Rwanda and Burundi as articulated at the Regional Ambassadors' Conference in Bujumbura in 1991 and in the Policy Coordinating Committee priorities established in March 1992.

78. 29 Dec 92 Kigali 05356.

79. Letter no. 1737/01.10 of 30 December 1992 from the Presidency of the Republic to His Excellency the Prime Minister (AC).

80. 23 Dec 92 Kigali 05319.

81. 31 Dec 92 Kigali 05381, "Impasse Again."

82. Ibid. As the MRND communiqué explained, the demonstration was intended to do the following:

- Make the prime minister understand that the negotiations in Arusha were for all Rwandans.

- Show that the alliance has the force to prevent implementation of any accords signed in Arusha without their consent.

- Demand that the government meet to decide on further instructions to the foreign minister and prime minister.

83. 04 Jan 93 Dar es Salaam 00022, "Arusha V: Talks Deadlocked on CDR Issue."

84. 08 Jan 93 Kigali 00068, "Kigali Awaits Protocol."

85. MRND *Communiqué de presse* (Traduction Officieuse), 8 January 1993 (AC).

86. 07 Jan 93 State 004773, "Rwandan Peace Talks."

87. 09 Jan 93 State 006775, "Arusha Protocol to be Signed January 9."

88. *Joint communiqué issued at the end of the third round of the political negotiations between the Government of the Republic of Rwanda and the Rwandese Patriotic Front held in Arusha from 24 November, 1992 to 9 January, 1993* (AC).

89. 08 Jan 93 Kigali 00068.

90. 19 Jan 93 Kigali 00151, "Arusha Protocol: Further Reactions."

91. Ibid.

92. Ibid.

93. 21 Jan 93 Kigali 00239, "International Human Rights Commission Completes Work; Anticipates Press Conference in Brussels 1/22," and *Report of the International Commission on Human Rights Violations in Rwanda Since October 1, 1990*, March 6, 1993, https://www.hrw.org/sites/default/files/reports/intlhrviolations393 .pdf. The report maintained inter alia the following:

- More than two thousand civilians had been massacred since the beginning of the war, mostly Tutsi. A large number of officials have been implicated in those killings, only two had been removed from office, and none had been brought to trial.

- Armed party militia terrorized and pillaged people in many parts of the country and carried out political assassinations with no effective reaction from public security.

- The Rwandan military was responsible for the massacre at Mutara of five hundred or more Bagogwe; the RPF was guilty of summary executions, kidnapping, and pillaging.

- The commission had discovered mass graves in the northwest, one in the backyard of the local mayor.

+ Local officials directed massacres at Kibilira in 1990 and in Bugesera in 1993.

+ A circle of twenty-some people around the president, called Reseau Zero, organized the confrontations and massacres. The head of state was reported to have participated in their meetings.

+ About one in seven Rwandans is a displaced person having fled the war zone and surviving in total misery in camps for the displaced.

94. 27 January 1993, Africa Watch, "Outbreak of Violence Follows Human Rights Investigation in Rwanda" (AC).

95. 31 Jan 94 State 024880, "Final (V-4) Country Human Rights Report," and US Department of State, *Human Rights Report—Rwanda*, 1993, 2 (AC).

96. Ibid.

97. 27 January 1993, *Communiqué de presse* [les parties MRND, MDR, PSD, PDC et PL], Fait à Kigali (AC).

98. 30 Jan 93 State 029560, "Arusha Negotiations."

99. 03 Feb 93 State 033201, "Arusha: On and Off."

100. 30 Jan 93 State 029560.

101. In August 1992, Prime Minister Nsengiyaremye told me during my pre-Arusha consultations that "the old man had to go." He was not clear how that would happen but obviously looked to the political negotiations in Arusha as the means to that end.

102. 03 Dec 92 Dar es Salaam 06925.

103. Habyarimana's long reign would not seem to warrant undying hostility and retribution. But he was opposed by two elite groups, both of whom wanted his power. The RPF from their clandestine radio broadcast a continuing litany against Habyarimana, personalizing their battle as a fight against a dictator and tyrant. It was as though Habyarimana had to be personally denigrated before he could be removed. On the other side were Hutu political elite from the central south who had been reduced to an inferior status in the Second Republic. Moreover, following the 1973 coup, some fifty high officials from this region died in prison or were assassinated. President Kayibanda may have died from untreated health problems while under house arrest. Former members of the Kayibanda regime and their acolytes certainly wanted revenge.

104. 04 Jan 93 Dar es Salaam 00022.

105. Kwame Bediako finds such "sacralizing of authority and power" common among traditional and postcolonial African societies. Kwame Bediako, *Jesus and the Gospel in Africa* (Maryknoll, NY: Orbis Books, 2004), 102, 105–7.

106. For analyses, see Gérard Prunier, *The Rwandan Crisis: History of a Genocide* (New York: Columbia University Press, 1995) and André Guichaoua, *From War to Genocide: Criminal Politics in Rwanda, 1990–1994*, trans. Don E. Webster (Madison: University of Wisconsin Press, 2015). As a confirmation of the analyses in Prunier

and Guichaoua, an RPF insider told me that two elements galvanized the decision to attack in October: the absence of Ugandan president Museveni in New York, and the fact that under the agreement with the UNHCR, refugees would soon be resettled in Rwanda, making the RPF's war aims redundant.

CHAPTER 5: ENDGAME

1. 06 Feb 93 State 037511, "Arusha Pause"; and 10 Feb 93 Kigali 00537, "Politics and Peace."

2. 06 Feb 93 State 037511.

3. Ibid.

4. 18 Feb 93 Kigali 00682, "RPF-Rwanda Meetings."

5. 06 Feb 93 State 037511.

6. 08 Feb 93 Kigali 00463, "RPF Attack."

7. See Hedley Bull, *The Anarchical Society* (New York: Columbia University Press, 1977), chap. 9.

8. Martha Finnemore, *The Purpose of Intervention: Changing Beliefs about the Use of Force* (Ithaca: Cornell University Press, 2003), 78–82.

9. 21 Jan 93 Kigali 002393, "International Human Rights Commission Completes Work: Anticipates Press Conference in Brussels 1/22"; and 30 Jan 93 State 029560, "Arusha Negotiations." The release of the report's conclusion was accompanied by the airing of a video on European and Canadian television. Africa Rights Watch could find no TV stations in the United States interested in the footage.

10. For notions of breakthrough strategies, see William Ury, *Getting Past No: Negotiating in Difficult Situations* (New York: Bantam Books, 1993) and William Ury, *The Third Side: Why We Fight and How We Can Stop* (New York: Penguin, 2000). For further analytical and comparative perspectives into moving beyond impasses, see Charles King, "Power, Social Violence and Civil War," in *Leashing the Dogs of War: Conflict Management in a Divided World*, ed. Chester A. Crocker, Fen Osler Hampson, and Pamela Aal (Washington, DC: United States Institute of Peace Press, 2007), 123–28; John Paul Lederach, *Building Peace: Sustainable Reconciliation in Divided Societies* (Washington, DC: United States Institute of Peace Press, 1997), 63–65; Donald C. F. Daniel and Bradd C. Hayes with Chantal de Jonge Oudraat, *Coercive Inducement and the Containment of International Crises* (Washington, DC: United States Institute of Peace Press, 1999), 30–31; Lawrence Freedman, "Using Force for Peace in an Age of Terror," in Crocker, Hampson, and Aal, *Leashing the Dogs of War*, 248–49; and Daniel Serwer and Patricia Thomson, "A Framework for Success: International Intervention in Societies Emerging from Conflict," in Crocker, Hampson, and Aal, *Leashing the Dogs of War*, 369–73.

11. French officials characterized the crisis as more serious than that caused by the initial RPF attack in October 1990 or the RPF investiture of Ruhengeri in January 1991.

12. 13 Feb 93 Kigali 00603, "RPF Attacks Again: French Broker Joint Prime Minister-President Declaration; Habyarimana Asks for Help." The president and prime minister, while taking note of the Arusha protocol of January 9, agreed to examine the modalities for implementation of the protocol, to continue the democratic process, to overcome obstacles in the government, and to come forward with an agreed program for presentation in Arusha.

13. 18 Feb 93 Kigali 00682, "RPF-Rwanda Meetings."

14. See 27 January 1993, "*Communiqué de Presse de MRND, MDR, PSD, PDC, et PL*" (AC).

15. 23 Feb 93 Kigali 00709, "Rwanda Parties to Meet RPF in Bujumbura."

16. 272205Z Feb 93 FBIS, "RPF Lists Demands Given at Bujumbura Meeting."

17. One of the big historical questions of this period is why the RPF so quickly drew back from their offensive. The most obvious answer is that which RPF commander Kagame gave to a US delegation on February 25 during this time of truce, namely, that "the RPF strongly prefers to reach a negotiated settlement to the conflict." 27 Feb 93 Kampala 01485, "U.S. Meeting with RPF Military Commander"; for a more nuanced evaluation of RPF intentions, see 27 Feb 93 State 060346, "INR Analysis: RPF Goals."

18. 03 Mar 93 Kigali 00911, "Preparation for Dar es Salaam Summit." The agreed points were the following:

- Each side should renounce a military solution to the conflict.
- The government and RPF should confirm their respective declarations on a ceasefire, with the government holding to its current lines and the RPF returning to its original positions. OAU and UN Observers, eventually to be replaced by a neutral international military force, would patrol the demilitarized zone.
- Displaced persons should return to their homes in the demilitarized zone.
- The five parties in the current government should take note of the protocols already signed and promise to bring their contributions on how to implement those protocols.
- The government would assure protection of all citizens, and cleaning up of the administration at all levels would be accelerated.
- The democratic process should continue.

19. Ibid.

20. Ibid.

21. 08 Mar 93 Dar es Salaam 01189, "Dar es Salaam Meeting Communique."

22. Ibid.

23. 092021Z Mar 93 FBIS, "Secret Clause in Accord Concerns French Troops Withdrawal," and 101936Z Mar 93 FBIS, "France Conditionally Accepts Troop Withdrawal from Rwanda."

24. 07 Mar 93 USUN 01028, "3/5 Security Council Informals on Rwanda"; and 04 Mar 93 USUN 00973, "France Wants Security Council Action on Rwanda."

25. This observation by Ambassador Robert Pringle became policy dogma guiding US approaches to the renewed civil war and genocide after April 1994.

26. 12 Mar 93 Paris 06242, "Tri-lateral Discussions in Brussels on Rwanda, March 10."

27. 101936Z Mar 93 FBIS.

28. See 20 Feb 93 State 052756, "UNHRC Consideration of Rwanda: Request for Upgrade"; 12 Mar 93 Paris 06242; and 04 Mar 93 USUN 00973.

29. 23 Feb 93 USUN 00790, "Rwanda Requests UN Military Observers." This report came a fortnight before the French tabled their request for an observing force but shows in retrospect that that strategy had been carefully worked out with French meetings in Uganda that brought both Uganda and Rwanda on board.

30. See 04 Mar 93 USUN 00973; and 10 Mar 93 USUN 01075, "Rwanda: SC Stonewalls French Buffer Idea."

31. See 06 Mar 93 USUN 01028; 04 Mar 93 USUN 00973; and 10 Mar 93 USUN 01075.

32. 18 Feb 93 Kigali 00683, "Time for the UN."

33. 11 Mar 93 Kigali 01034, "Minister of Defense on GOMN and Civil Defense." Minister Gasana told Ambassador Flaten that the Rwandan government suspected the Neutral Military Observing Group of complicity in the February RPF attack and in the establishment of ceasefire lines subsequently. He also reported the distribution of weapons to communal police in the north as a civil-defense measure. He claimed, however, that the weapons were carefully inventoried and controlled.

34. 18 Feb 93 Kigali 00683; 19 Feb 93 Kigali 00702, "Rwanda May Request UN Help"; 23 Feb 93 USUN 00790; and 25 Feb 93 Kigali 00790, "Rwandan Request for UN Observers."

35. 27 Feb 93 State 060041, "Some Thoughts on UN and OAU Involvement in the Rwandan Conflict."

36. Ibid.

37. Ibid.

38. Ibid.

39. 13 Mar 93 USUN 01250, "Rwanda-Security Council Adopts Resolution."

40. 17 Mar 93 Dar es Salaam 01408, "Rwandan Peace Talks Recommence in Arusha."

41. Ibid.

42. Ibid.

43. See 26 Mar 93 Dar es Salaam 01531, "OAU Update on Rwanda," for a fairly optimistic assessment of the OAU's operational capacity to enlarge its

monitoring force and take on new mandates occasioned by the March 7 Dar es Salaam agreement.

44. 26 Mar 93 State 090273, "Improving OAU Peacekeeping Operations in Rwanda" set forth, after a series of conversations between the US embassy in Addis Ababa and OAU officials, a stern demarche asking in effect for the OAU to get its act together, use funds already put at its disposal by the US government, and shoulder its responsibilities in Rwanda. This may have been one of the reasons OAU secretary general Salim Salim stopped at Kilimanjaro airport on April 4 on his way back from a "Frontline States" meeting in Harare to brief heads of delegations on OAU intentions. 06 Apr 93 State 102691, "Rwanda Negotiations Weekend Update."

45. 17 Mar 93 Dar es Salaam 01408.

46. Ibid.

47. 15 Mar 93 Kigali 001086, "Rwandan Delegation Heads for Arusha."

48. 18 Mar 93 State 080504, "USG Representation at Arusha Peace Talks."

49. 18 Mar 93 State 082050, "Arusha Update 3/18/83."

50. 21 Apr 93 State 121210, "Rwanda: Arusha Talks Update for 4/20/93"; and 22 Apr 93 State 122018, "Rwanda: Update on Arusha Negotiations 4/21."

51. 22 Apr 93 State 122018.

52. 26 Apr 93 State 126323, "Rwanda: Update on Arusha Negotiations 4/26/93."

53. 21 Apr 93 State 121210.

54. 07 Apr 93 State 103466, "Rwanda Tri-laterals"; and 21 Apr 93 State 121249, "Request for Demarche on Rwanda Peacekeepers."

55. 02 Apr 93 Dar es Salaam 01697, "Rwandan Delegations Meet to Discuss Roles of OAU and UN in the Peace Process." The Rwandese Patriotic Front had from the beginning been leery of peacekeeping forces that might hamstring its military flexibility—in other words, an interpositional force of any stripe.

56. 26 Apr 93 State 126323; 28 Apr 93 State 129206, "Rwanda: Update on Arusha Negotiations 4/28/93"; and 04 May 93 Nairobi 09777, "Arusha Talks: Facilitator Probes Status of Dar Communique Implementation."

57. Notes on 30 Apr 93 USUN 02145, "UN SYG Nixes Both OAU Cooperation and Border Force." In response to a joint demarche on Rwanda a month previously (02 Apr 93 USUN 01653, "Rwanda: UN SYG's Views"), the secretary had raised procedural issues: the need for a Security Council mandate, the importance of not being competitive with or subordinate to the OAU, and the need to await the report of his goodwill mission. A month later, the secretary general seemed to take the UN out of the Rwanda peace process entirely, at least until a peace agreement was signed.

58. 07 Apr 93 Kigali 01472, "Meeting with U.N. Military Team."

59. 29 May 93 Libreville 02073, "Rwanda: A/S Moose's Meeting in Libreville with Rwandan President Habyarimana, May 27."

60. See 07 May 93 State 139430, "UN/OAU Initiatives on Rwanda: What Next?"; 13 May 93 State 145911, "Rwanda: Discussion at May 11 Tri-laterals"; and 13 May 93 State 146622, "Tri-laterals-Agreed Next Steps."

61. 25 May USUN 02579, "A/S Moose discusses Africa at the UN."

62. This diplomatic dialogue is summed up in 10 Mar 93 USUN 01075; 31 Mar 93 USUN 01594, "French Want to Urge UNSYG on Rwandan Border Force"; 02 Apr 93 State 099580, "French Desire to Urge UNSYG on Rwandan Border"; 04 Jun USUN 02729, "SC Members Not Enthusiastic about Border Force"; 07 Jun 93 Paris 14665, "GOF Requests Urgent Meeting to Resolve Rwanda Impasse"; and 14 Jun 93 USUN 02899, "US/French Meeting on Rwandan Border Force."

63. 27 Mar 93 State 091736, "Update on Rwanda Negotiations in Arusha: 3/26/93."

64. Ibid.

65. 03 May 93 Nairobi 09701, "Arusha Talks: Status Report."

66. 29 May 93 Libreville 02073.

67. 29 Sep 92 Addis Ababa 04935, "Rwanda JPMC Meeting 26–28 Sep 92."

68. For example, Museveni had, as early as the beginning of the power-sharing negotiations the previous October, taken that line in my meeting with him. It is to be assumed that he used the same line with other observing states.

69. 27 Mar 93 State 091736.

70. 29 Mar 93 Dar es Salaam 01565, "Proportionality Issue Blocking Rwanda Negotiations."

71. Apr 93 State 126323, and 3 May 93 Nairobi 09701.

72. 13 May 93 Dar es Salaam 02535, "Notes from the Arusha Peace Talks."

73. Joseph Clemence Rwegasira replaced Ahmed Hassan Diria as Tanzanian minister of foreign affairs in early 1993.

74. 14 May 93 Dar es Salaam 02558, "Rwanda Negotiations: Texts from Arusha."

75. 07 May 93 State 140127, "Rwanda: Update on Negotiations 5/6/93"; 11 May 93 Dar es Salam 02474, "Arusha Talks: End of Military Talks Near?"; 21 May 93 State 155879, "Arusha Peace Talks Stalled on Pending Military Issues"; and 25 May 93 Dar es Salaam 02733, "Arusha Peace Talks." Although the RPF and the government agreed to "an enhanced gendarmerie with enhanced civilian protection functions," the question of the degree of RPF participation in that organization was still being debated.

76. 01 Jun 93 State 165200, "Arusha Peace Talks: Force Proportion Discussions Resume."

77. 02 Jun 93 Dar es Salaam 02873, "Notes from Arusha Peace Talks on Rwanda."

78. 04 Jun 93 State 169758, "Rwanda: Atmosphere at Arusha Talks Deteriorates Markedly." Joyce Leader, who was the US Observer at the time, believes that

"RPF behavior in those first weeks of June was probably linked to June 1 presidential elections in Burundi," a landslide victory for a Hutu candidate. The RPF recognized that they would not win a political contest and thus had to have parity (read "effective superiority") in transition security organizations. Joyce Leader, *Rwanda's Struggle for Democracy and Peace, 1991–1994* (Washington, DC: The Fund for Peace, 2001), 36.

79. 07 Jun 93 Dar es Salaam 02953, "Arusha Peace Talks: Tanzania Presses Both Sides towards Conclusion"; and 09 Jun 93 Kigali 02231, "Rwanda Visited By Tanzanian Prime Minister."

80. 10 Jun 93 Dar es Salaam 030366, "Subject: Arusha Peace Talks: Tanzanians Appeal for Western Support"; and 14 Jun 93 Kigali 02284, "Arusha Process: Internal Progress."

81. 22 Apr 93 State 122018.

82. 27 May 93 Dar es Salaam 02769, "Arusha Peace Talks: Facilitator Pushes for Conclusion." The minister's public statement reflected a behind-the-scenes and growing impatience with RPF's revisiting of settled issues, which made the talks "go round in circles." The Facilitator had considered a "take it or leave it" final proposal for the RPF but settled instead for a pointed plenary statement. 21 May 93 State 155879; and 25 May 93 Dar es Salaam 02733.

83. 25 May 93 Dar es Salaam 02733.

84. 28 May 93 Dar es Salaam 02852, "Arusha Peace Talks: Military Issues Continue."

85. 14 Jun 93 Dar es Salam 03093, "Arusha Peace Talks: Signing Date Set."

86. Ibid. These issues included the timing for the formation of the transition government, linked to the deployment of a yet-unidentified international neutral force; the process for integrating the gendarmerie while maintaining its security functions; the question of a fifty-fifty ratio in the command structure; and the status of Kigali as a demilitarized zone.

87. 14 Jun 93 Kigali 02284.

88. Ibid.

89. Ibid; and 23 Jun 93 Kigali 02381, "Cabinet Delays Signature, Rejects Prime Minister."

90. 24 Jun 93 Dar es Salaam 03328, "Arusha Peace Talks"; 25 Jun 93 Kigali 02406, "Arusha Talks Suspended"; and 25 Jun 93 Dar es Salaam 03339, "Arusha Peace Talks Adjourned Indefinitely."

91. 25 Jun 93 State 193841, "Briefing Paper on Rwanda Negotiations."

92. Since the February offensive and drawback to previous lines, the Rwandan Patriotic Army (RPA) had been operating out of the former government tea plantation of Mulindi, in Rwanda's central north.

93. 26 Mar 93 Kigali 01298, "Political Miscellany."

94. Ibid.

95. 12 Apr 93 Kigali 01535, "President, Government Commit to Respect Human Rights." In the Response, the president and government committed themselves to the following:

- To guarantee the security of all Rwandans
- To respect the independence of the judiciary
- To respect all the accords deriving from Arusha peace negotiations
- To reprimand and sanction individuals participating in militias, as well as the political parties that support them
- To insist that judicial authorities continue the investigations begun by the international commission
- To establish a National Commission on Human Rights

96. Ibid.

97. 26 Mar 93 Kigali 01298.

98. 19 Jul 93 Kigali 02652, "Transition Government Extended-MDR Splits." Two of Nsegiyaremye's political allies (Foreign Minister Ngulinzira and Minister of Information Ndengejeho) voluntarily stepped down. Uwilingiyimana's director of cabinet, Anatase Gasana, became foreign minister, while Nsengiyaremye's director of cabinet, J. M. V. Mbonimpa, changed alliances and accepted the Ministry of Education. A political unknown, Faustin Rucogoza, became minister of information, thus taking all MDR cabinet ministers in cabinet from outside the MDR heartland of Gitarama.

99. 25 Jun 93 Kigali 02406.

100. Trained in Quebec as an economist and the former director of a Rwandan transport parastatal, Twagiramungu posed as a businessman with no political interests other than a better future for Rwanda. For a supposed political novice, he demonstrated from 1990 to 1994 great skills in political maneuvering.

101. 26 Jul 93 Kigali 02761, "The MDR vs. the MDR"; and 30 Jul 93 Kigali 02839, "The MDR vs. the MDR: Part II."

102. 26 Jul 93 Kigali 02756, "Agreement on Peace." The original compromise proposal worked out by the Facilitator in June, in addition to force proportions that the RPF rejected, had suggested the initial convening of interim institutions in the demilitarized zone until a "neutral international force" was in place to assure the demilitarization of Kigali and that the military forces were integrated. The Rwandan government desire to keep the institutions in the capital city now required it to invite the RPF to bring its own security for VIP protection. In making this offer, the government had not expected the RPF to require a full battalion. See 22 Jul 93 Kigali 02720, "Peacekeeping and Observing in Rwanda."

103. Ibid.

104. 19 Jul 93 Kigali 02653, "NMOG/Kigali Principles on Expanded NMOG, NIF."

105. 16 Jul 93 State 216726, "French Views on Peacekeeping Operation in Rwanda."

106. 30 Jul 93 Kigali 02836, "Support for Peace."

107. 15 Jun 93 Kigali 02288, "Rwanda-NMOG Expansion"; 22 Jul 93 Kigali 02720; and 30 Jul 93 Kigali 02836.

108. 26 Jul 93 Kigali 02756. Other observers now on the sidelines, like Assistant Secretary Cohen and the Bierly/Snyder team, were astonished at the security arrangements finally conceded by the new Rwandan government team (personal interview).

109. 26 Jul 93 Kigali 02761.

110. 26 Jul 93 Kigali 02756.

111. 16 Jun 93 Dar es Salaam 03147, "Arusha Peace Talks: Negotiations Continue."

112. 21 Jun 93 Dar es Salaam 03236, "Arusha Peace Talks: Itching Toward Conclusion"; and 22 Jun 93 Dar es Salaam, "Tying Up Loose Ends."

113. 30 Jul 93 Kigali 02836.

114. *Peace Agreement between the Government of the Republic of Rwanda and the Rwandese Patriotic Front,* article 1. Article 2 accepted as documents integral to the peace agreement the following: the N'Sele Ceasefire Agreement of 29 March 1991 as amended in Gbadolite on 16 September 1991 and at Arusha on 12 July 1992; the "Protocol on the Rule of Law"; two "Protocols on Power Sharing within the Framework of a Broad-Based Transitional Government"; the "Protocol on Repatriation of Refugees and Resettlement of Displaced Persons"; the "Protocol on Integration of Armed Forces"; and a "Protocol on Miscellaneous Issues and Final Provisions."

115. 05 Aug 93 Nairobi 16758, "Rwandans Sign Arusha Accord: The First Fruits of African Conflict Resolution."

116. 16 Jul 93 State 216726.

CHAPTER 6: THINGS FALL APART

1. The events, in particular, were those in Burundi. Tutsi president Buyoya's resounding loss in the June 1993 election to the Hutu candidate Ndadaye startled the RPF into digging in its heels on military integration, and the assassination of Ndadaye by Tutsi military in October hardened Hutu identity and opposition to power sharing under the Arusha Accords.

2. See Donald C. F. Daniel, Bradd C. Hayes, and Chantal de Jonge Oudraat, *Coercive Inducement and the Containment of International Crises* (Washington, DC: United States Institute of Peace Press, 1999), 30–39.

3. Chester A. Crocker, Fen Osler Hampson, and Pamela Aall, eds., *Herding Cats: Multiparty Mediation in a Complex World* (Washington, DC: United States Institute of Peace Press, 1999), 29–33.

4. On the goal of keeping promises, see Hedley Bull, *The Anarchical Society* (New York: Columbia University Press, 1977), 18.

5. Chester A. Crocker, Fen Osler Hampson, and Pamela Aall, eds., *Taming Intractable Conflicts: Mediation in the Hardest Cases* (Washington, DC: United States Institute of Peace Press, 2004), 16.

6. The downing of the president's aircraft was obviously a game changer. In my first call to the Department of State that night, I said that the UN forces needed a changed mandate and materiel to carry out that mandate, if they were to hold the peace together.

7. Already in 1992, an academic conference convoked by the Department of State's Bureau of Intelligence and Research reviewed the situation in Rwanda and highlighted the structural relations that made genocide not only possible but likely. See 30 March 1992, Memorandum, to AF-Mr. Cohen; from INR-N. Shaw Smith, Acting; Subject: Rwanda: In Search of a Settlement. Also see chap. 2.

8. Sayre Shatz coined the phrase "naïve policy optimism" in the context of British and American efforts to stabilize the infant Nigerian state back in the 1960s and early 1970s. Sayre Shatz, *Nigerian Capitalism* (Berkley: University of California Press, 1977), 250–53. Such optimism certainly characterized the international perspective on Rwanda at the advent of the transition process.

9. "Letter dated 13 August 1992 from the Secretary-General of the United Nations to the Secretary-General of the Organization of African Unity expressing full support and cooperation for OAU efforts to achieve a comprehensive and lasting peace in Rwanda," in United Nations, *The United Nations and Rwanda, 1993–1996* (New York: United Nations Department of Public Information, 1996), 151.

10. See Bruce D. Jones, *Peacemaking in Rwanda: The Dynamics of Failure* (Boulder, CO: Lynne Rienner, 2001), 34.

11. 02 Apr 93 Dar es Salaam 01697, "Rwandan Delegation Meet to Discuss Roles of OAU and UN in the Peace Process."

12. 27 Feb 93 Kampala 01485, "U.S. Meeting with RPF Military Commander."

13. 23 Mar 93 State 008710, "French Views on International Forces for Rwanda."

14. 12 Mar 93 Paris 06242, "Tri-lateral Discussions in Brussels on Rwanda, March 10."

15. 27 Feb 93 State 060041, "Some Thoughts on UN and OAU Involvement in the Rwandan Conflict"; Apr 93 State 103466, "Rwanda Tri-laterals"; and 14 Jul 93 USUN 03423, "Possible Peacekeeping Operation in Rwanda."

16. S/RES/846 (1993), 22 June 1993, "Security Council resolution establishing the United Nations Observer Mission Uganda-Rwanda (UNOMUR), to be deployed on the Ugandan side of the Uganda-Rwanda border for an initial period of six months," United Nations, *United Nations and Rwanda*, 167.

17. 07 Apr 93 Kigali 01472, "Meeting with U.N. Military Team"; 07 May 93 State 070545, "UN/OAU Initiatives on Rwanda: What Next?"; 08 Jul 93 USUN 03326, "UN SYG Won't Send Observers to Rwanda"; and 14 Jul 93 USUN 03423, "Possible Peacekeeping Operation in Rwanda," par. 8.

18. 19 Jul 93 Kigali 02653, "NMOG/Kigali Principles on Expanded NMOG."

19. 15 Jun 93 Kigali 02288, "Rwanda-NMOG Expansion"; and 13 Jul 93 Addis Ababa 04498, "Expansion of OAU NMOG for Rwanda."

20. "Letter dated 14 June 1993 from the Permanent Representative of Rwanda to the United Nations addressed to the President of the Security Council, transmitting a joint request by the Government of Rwanda and the RPF concerning the stationing of a neutral international force in Rwanda," S/25051, 15 June 1993, United Nations, *United Nations and Rwanda*, 165.

21. 27 Feb 93 Kampala 01485, "U.S. Meeting with RPF Military Commander."

22. 29 May 93 Libreville 02073, "Rwanda: A/S Moose's meeting in Libreville with Rwandan President Habyarimana, May 27."

23. 30 Jun 93 State 197863, "Russians Voice Doubts on UN Presence in Rwanda"; 14 Jul 93 UnSUN 3423, "Possible Peacekeeping Operation in Rwanda"; 10 Aug 93 USUN 3856, "Rwanda: UN Views on PKO"; and 26 July 1993, Memorandum, to AF/FO–DAS Bushnell; from AF/RA-LTC Anthony Marley, AF/C-Kevin Aiston; Subject: "Preliminary Peacekeeping Force Options for Rwanda." The Belgian policy turnaround on providing peacekeepers was as a result of a direct appeal from UN secretary general Boutros-Ghali to Foreign Minister Willy Claes and the provision of European Union funds to underwrite the cost (personal interview with Minister Claes).

24. 12 Jul 93 State 210975, "Possible Peacekeeping Operation in Rwanda: USUN Views of Secretariat and P-5 Attitudes."

25. 23 Sep 93 USUN 4653, "UN Plans for PKO"; 23 Dec 93 Kigali 4551, "Critical Analysis of UNAMIR's Phase 1 Operations"; and S/26488, 24 September 1993, "Report of the Secretary-General on Rwanda, requesting establishment of a United Nations Assistance Mission for Rwanda (UNAMIR) and the integration of UNOMUR into UNAMIR," in United Nations, *United Nations and Rwanda*, 221.

26. 02 Oct 93 USUN 04844, "Ambassador Albright's October 1 Meeting with French Foreign Minister Juppe." The ambassador prefaced her offer of US support with a comment that while the operation met our criteria, we would work to bring the cost down. A few days before, Albright had informed the divided bureaucracy in Washington that the only way the United States could stop the Rwandan PKO was by threatening to veto; she then justified the operation in terms of the latest PRD-13 draft. 28 Sep 93 USUN 04735, "Rwanda and Criteria for New UN PKO."

27. 27 Aug 93 USUN 04167, "Liberia and Rwanda: Informals August 26"; 18 Sep 93 USUN 04553, "Rwanda: Joint RPF-Government Delegation Asks USG

Support for Quick Deployment of an NIF"; 29 Sep 93 USUN 04766, "SC Pressure Building to Approve Rwanda PKO"; and S/RES/872(1993), 5 October 1993, "Security Council resolution establishing UNAMIR for a six-month period and approving the integration of UNOMUR into UNAMIR," United Nations, United Nations and Rwanda, 231.

28. 10 Aug 93 USUN 3856.

29. 19 Aug 93 Kigali 03060, "The Rwandan Peace Process: Problems and Prospects of Implementing the Peace Accord"; 23 Aug Kigali 03107, "Controversial Ex-Burgomaster Assassinated"; and 31 Aug 93 Kigali 03224, "Preparing for the Broad-based Government." Guichaoua holds that Gapyisi, having turned back an appeal from RPF's Sendashonga for a more cooperative attitude, was assassinated by an RPF commando. André Guichaoua, *From War to Genocide: Criminal Politics in Rwanda, 1990–1994*, trans. Don E. Webster (Madison: University of Wisconsin Press, 2015), 65.

30. 19 Aug 93 Kigali 03060.

31. 31 Aug 93 Kigali 03224.

32. 13 Oct 93 Kigali 03734, "Forming the GTBE (Transition Government)."

33. Sep 93 USUN 04553, "Rwanda: Joint RPF-Government Delegations Asks for USG Support for Quick Deployment of an NIF."

34. 23 Sep 93 Kigali 03485, "GOR and RPF Military Officers Meet."

35. 06 Oct 93 Kampala 07873, "RPF Inquires about UN Peacekeepers."

36. 05 Nov 93 Kigali 03989, "MDR Fails in Effort to Exploit Burundi."

37. 15 Nov 93 Kigali 04060, "Progress on the GTBE."

38. 16 Nov 93 Kigali 04082, "Assassination Attempt on Human Rights Leader."

39. 18 Nov 93 Kigali 04098, "Civilians Killed in DMZ"; and 24 Nov 93 Kigali 04164, "Calm Still Prevails after Civilians Killed in DMZ." Another raid in the north took place on November 30 in Mutura commune, leaving some seventeen civilians dead. Guichaoua claims that these were the RPA's response to the success of the MRND and the CDR in recent communal elections and that General Dallaire deferred to an investigation commission to avoid derailing the Arusha implementation efforts. Guichaoua, *From War to Genocide*, 69.

40. 24 Nov 93 Kigali 04164.

41. 24 Nov 93 Kigali 04169, "Government to Resume Joint Sessions with RPF"; and 26 Nov 93 Kigali 04193, "UNAMIR Sidesteps Naming Culprit in Ruhengeri Incident; Parties to Explore Reconciliation."

42. 29 Nov 93 Kigali 04211, "Prime Minister Solicits Diplomatic Help."

43. 23 Dec 93 Kigali 04561, "Transition Institutions: Target Date Dec. 29."

44. 29 Nov 93 Kigali 04211; and 01 Dec 93 Kigali 04250, "Uncertainty Persists after Mutura-Kabatwa."

45. 15 Dec 93 Kigali 04440, "GOR/RPF Jointly Set Year's End as Target for Installing Broad-Based Government."

46. Ibid.

47. 15 Dec 93 Kigali 04440; and 23 Dec 93 Kigali 04551, "Critical Analysis of UNAMIR's Phase 1 Operations." About this same time, in a briefing at the United Nations, Assistant Secretary General Igbal Riza made a point of telling me that the mandate of UNAMIR did not include the security of diplomatic missions.

48. 23 Dec 93 Kigali 04551.

49. Ibid.

50. Ibid.; and 20 Dec 93 Kigali 04481, "UNAMIR Submits Report for Security Council."

51. 21 Dec 93 Kigali 04506, "Political Conundrum Continues"; 23 Dec 93 Kigali 04561, "Transition Institutions: Target Date Dec. 29"; 27 Dec 93 Kigali 04577, "Transition Institutions: The Plot Thickens"; and 30 Dec 93 Kigali, "Transition Institutions: Maneuvering."

52. 04 Jan 94 Kigali 00034, "Transition Institutions: Impasse Persists"; 04 Jan 94 Kigali 00034, "Transition Institutions: Maybe January 5?"; and 05 Jan 94 Kigali 00045, "Transition Institutions: Only President Takes Oath of Office."

53. 08 Jan 94 Kigali 00086, "Presentation of Credentials."

54. 10 Jan 94 Kigali 00111, "Transition Institutions: No Breakthrough"; and 12 Jan 94 Kigali 00155, "Transition Institutions: Still Stalled." It was in this context that I found myself seated next to the ambassador of Libya, both of us expressing in similar terms to RPF leadership the importance of moving ahead with installation of the government and assembly.

55. 12 Jan 94 Kigali 00157, "UN Special Representative Asks for Support on Security Demarche."

56. Ibid.

57. Ibid. In follow-on conversations, the ambassadors agreed to seek approval of a demarche that would urge strict conformity to the Arusha Accord provision calling for Kigali to be a weapons-secure zone; express deep concern over the continuing evidence of arms being distributed to party and civilian militia and reiterate a previous call for the militia to be disbanded; note that the only secure future for Rwanda is for all parties to leave security to the integrated security forces; and urge the president to play a positive part in breaking the impasse over installation of the government and legislature for the transition period in which the president continues to have a leading role. In regard to operations against the arms caches, I reiterated to Dallaire the US position that peacekeeping missions should operate within their terms of reference but that "UNAMIR already had a mandate to establish an arms secure zone in Kigali. . . . There was real benefit to the UN actively pursuing its mandate to make Kigali secure." Dallaire said that if he needed help with headquarters in getting operational authority, he would contact the embassy. See my message to the assistant secretary for international

organization affairs, Douglas Bennet, in 09 Feb 94 Kigali 00576, "Postscript to Your Trip."

58. 13 Jan 94 State 011254, "UN Proposal for a Security Demarche." The working-level officers of the Department of State, accustomed to the chicaneries of the Kigali political scene, suspected that the informant might be a plant. Years later, a high-level RPF official admitted that the informant had indeed been sent forward by the RPF to raise the alarm in UNAMIR about arms distribution. That fact changed in no way the realities that arms distribution within the ten-kilometer Kigali arms-free zone was a direct violation of agreements between the two parties and an immediate challenge to UN authority that needed to be addressed.

59. 14 Jan 94 Kigali 00217, "Transition Institutions: No Movement Yet." For the director of cabinet's rendition of the president's views, see Enoch Ruhigira, *Rwanda: La fin tragique d'un régime*, 2 vols. (Paris: La Pagaie, 2011).

60. 20 Jan 94 00275, "Demarches on Security Concerns."

61. 24 Jan 94 USUN 00312, "UN Concern over Rwanda."

62. Ibid.

63. In a ploy that would seem childish if it were not so serious, the high court was denying physical access to the Code of Ethics to keep the CDR from signing it, from registering its support of the Accords, and from being a legitimate candidate of a seat in government or at the assembly.

64. 23 Feb 94 Kigali 00792, "Insecurity Escalates: At Kigali and Elsewhere."

65. 25 Feb 94 Kigali 00833, "Gatabazi's Funeral: President's New Initiatives."

66. 26 Jan 94 Paris 02338, "Assistant Secretary's Discussions with the French on January 24."

67. 25 Feb 94 Kigali 00833. This is a concrete example of how having singular leadership of a diplomatic project can restrict creative approaches to problem solving.

68. 28 Jan 94 State 022910, "Tri-lateral Demarche on Forming Government." Demarche points were the following:

- The Arusha Accords must be implemented and the new government formed as soon as possible.
- All sides must show flexibility in overcoming the current impasse.
- All parties should put the national interest ahead of personal or partisan interest.
- Time is of the essence.
- The new government must be formed so that Rwanda's structural adjustment program under IMF/World Bank auspices could be put in place.
- By deploying UN Peacekeepers, the international community has shown its support for the Rwandan peace process. UNSC 893 stresses that continued support for UNAMIR depends on the full and prompt implementation of the Arusha Accords.

69. 14 Feb 94 Kigali 00634, "Observer's Demarche on Launching Government."

70. 20 Feb 94 Kigali 00784, and personal recollections of the day's events.

71. 22 Feb 94 Kigali 00786, "Weekend Negotiations Fail to Shake Impasse on Government."

72. 18 Feb 94 Kigali 00777, "Next Steps."

73. Ibid.

74. 22 Feb 94 Kigali 00786.

75. 23 Feb 94 Kigali 00792.

76. 25 Feb 94 Kigali 00833.

77. 28 Feb 94 Kigali 00843, "Calm Prevails, New Political Gambit on Table."

78. Ibid., and 08 Feb 94 Kigali 00848, "Further Efforts to Break the Impasse."

79. 01 Mar 94 Kigali 00853, "RPF Rejects Party Agreement: Kigali Calm But Tense."

80. S/26927, 30 December 1993, "Report of the Secretary-General on UNAMIR," in United Nations, *United Nations and Rwanda*, 237–40.

81. S/RES/893 (1994), 6 January 1994, "Security Council resolution reaffirming approval for deployment of UNAMIR as outlined in the Secretary-General's report of 24 September 1994 (S/26488 and S26488/Add.1), including the early deployment of a second battalion to the demilitarized zone (DMZ)," in United Nations, *United Nations and Rwanda*, 241.

82. "Letter dated 27 January 1994 from the Secretary-General to the President of Rwanda expressing concern over delays in establishing a transitional Government and national assembly in Rwanda," in United Nations, *United Nations and Rwanda*, 242.

83. S/PRST/1994/8, 17 February 1994, "Statement by the President of the Security Council expressing concern over delays in establishing a transitional Government and the deteriorating security situation in Rwanda," in United Nations, *United Nations and Rwanda*, 243.

84. 25 Feb 94 Kigali 00833; and 01 Mar 94 Kigali 00853.

85. S/1994/360, 30 March 1994, "Second progress report of the Secretary-General on UNAMIR for the period from 30 December 1993 to 30 March 1994, requesting an extension of its mandate for a period of six months," in United Nations, *United Nations and Rwanda*, 244.

86. Ibid.

87. Ibid.

88. Ibid.

89. 24 Feb 94 State 047786, "Belgians Call for Continued Pressure on Rwandans."

90. Personal conversation with the French ambassador.

91. 03 Feb 94 Kigali 00475, "General Dallaire's Comments on UNAMIR Operations to A/S/ Bennet"; 04 Feb 94 Kigali 00505, "A/S Bennet Meets Prime Ministers"; and 07 Feb 94 Kigali 00551, "A/S Bennet's Meeting with President."

92. 07 Feb 94 Kigali 00551.

93. 23 Mar 94 USUN 01187, "Discussions on the Rwanda Mandate and New SRSG to Zaire."

94. 11 Mar 94 Kigali 01063, "Establishing the Institutions: Next Steps."

95. 24 Mar 94 Kigali 01269, "DAS Bushnell and AF/C Director Render Push for Transition to Begin." See also 24 Mar 94 Kigali 01270, "DAS Bushnell and AF/C Director Render Push for Transition to Begin," for a record of the delegation's conversation with SRSG Booh-Booh.

96. 24 Mar 94 Kigali 01269.

97. 25 Mar 94 Kigali 01316, "DAS Bushnell Meets Habyarimana and RPF."

98. 25 Mar 94 Kigali 01323, "President Habyarimana Receives DASD Irvin, Promised Installation Ceremonies Aborted."

99. 11 Mar 94 Dar es Salaam 01552, "Rwanda Impasse: Tanzanian Role."

100. 28 Mar 94 Kigali 01335, "CDR Issue Proves Intractable."

101. 01 Apr 94 Kigali 01458, "Negotiations Slide into Long Weekend."

102. Ibid.

103. 04 Apr 94 Kigali 01459, "A Visit with Habyarimana."

104. Ibid.

105. Rudolf Decker, *Ruanda: Tod und Hoffnung im Land der Tausend Hügel* (Neuhausen-Stuttgart: Hänssler-Verlag, 1998), 163–71. Decker was the last Westerner to see Habyarimana alive.

106. 28 Mar 94 Kigali 01335.

107. See 23 Dec 92 State 413010, "RPF Chairman Kanyarengwe Visits Department."

108. See Roméo Dallaire, *Shake Hands with the Devil: The Failure of Humanity in Rwanda* (Toronto: Random House, 2003), 99, 173, 233, 264, and 290 for a discussion of how his forward-leaning rules of engagement were apparently accepted until conflict threatened.

109. This was what Taleb calls an "outlier" in that it lies "outside the realm of regular expectations, because nothing in the past can convincingly point to its possibility," and in that it carries an extreme impact. Since, to this day, we do not know who shot down the plane, it is impossible to point back from this improbable event to any discernable cause that would let us explain this "black swan." See Nassim Nicholas Taleb, *The Black Swan: The Impact of the Highly Improbable* (New York: Random House, 2007), xvii–xviii.

EPILOGUE

1. There are in essence three theories about the downing of the aircraft:
   - The first holds that it was the work of Belgians (mercenary or official) trying to ensure RPF victory. This claim was broadcast by RTLM radio, coincident

with the murder of ten Belgian paratroopers, as part of a plan to neutralize the Belgian contingent in UNAMIR. A variant is the claim by Braeckman that French military intelligence shot down the plane. See Colette Braeckman, *Rwanda: Histoire d'un génocide* (Paris: Fayard, 1994), 188–97. No evidence or credible argument has ever been brought forward that expatriates of any stripe were involved in the missile attack.

- The second holds that it was the work of Hutu extremists who feared that Habyarimana finally intended to put the Arusha institutions in place and deprive Hutu partisans of their privileged positions. The rapidity with which roadblocks were set up after the crash suggests a close link between the crash and the immediate launching of Presidential Guard and militia in pursuit of Tutsi and of Hutu opposition figures, as well as the seizure of power by Hutu extremists in the army. The brusque refusal by the acting minister of defense Colonel Bagasora early the next morning to accept my offer of a forensic team to investigate the cause of the crash also implicates the Hutu extremists. (This argument about Hutu instigators is put most forcefully in Gérard Prunier, *The Rwanda Crisis: History of a Genocide* [New York: Columbia University Press, 1995], 213–29). However, no Hutu partisans have ever claimed any involvement in the assassination or knowledge of its operations.

- The third holds that General Kagame, weary of the wrangling in setting up the institutions, decided that the only way to move ahead was to eliminate President Habyarimana, no matter what the consequences. Various RPF cadre have claimed knowledge of or involvement in the plot. See Abdul Joshua Ruzibiza, *Rwanda: L'histoire secrète* (Paris: Éditions du Panama, 2005), 237–51. More recently, Dr. Theogene Rudasingwa, a prominent RPF strategist now in opposition, has asserted that General Kagame planned and ordered the attack. Theogene Rudasingwa, *Healing a Nation: A Testimony* (North Charlestown, SC: Create Space Publishing, 2013), chap. 41.

The United Nations, which holds the aircraft black box, has never released a report on the causes of the crash.

2. The flow of cable traffic, and hence the documentary record from the field, stopped with the crash of the president's plane. What follows is largely based on my notes and recollections, as well as on memoirs such as Roméo Dallaire, *Shake Hands with the Devil: The Failure of Humanity in Rwanda* (Toronto: Random House, 2003); Luc Marchal, *La descente aux enfers* (Brussels: Éditions Labor, 2001); Paul Rusesebagina, *An Ordinary Man* (New York: Viking, 2006); Immaculée Ilibagiza, *Left to Tell* (Carlsbad, CA: Hay House, 2006).

3. Luc Reydams, in a detailed investigation, shows how the RPF's speedy delivery of data and narrative made it possible for Africa Watch (a two-person NGO) to publish the 742-page *Rwanda: Death, Despair, and Defiance* (London:

African Rights, 1994) within three months after the war. According to Reydams, this was not to challenge the truth of the testimonies therein but to show the report's source and bias. Luc Reydams, "NGO Justice: Africa Rights as Pseudo-Prosecutor of the Rwandan Genocide," *Human Rights Quarterly* 38 (2016): 547–88.

4. The military officers in this particular case were Colonel Theoneste Bagosora, acting minister of defense; Major General Augustin Ndindiliymana, commander of the gendarmerie; and Lieutenant Colonel Ephrem Rwabalinda, liaison officer with UNAMIR.

5. See Dallaire, *Shake Hands*, 250–52. This established a pattern that persisted until the RPF finally won on the battlefield. International pleas for an end to communal violence and a ceasefire between forces was met by the RPF with the demand that killings stop before ceasefire talks begin and with the "government" riposte that it could not use forces to get militia under control until a ceasefire was in place. On the eve of April 7, it was the extremists within the Rwandan government forces who were calling the shots; the so-called interim government was not cobbled together until the next day. For details on the efforts of Theoneste Bagasora to master the course of events after the plane went down, see André Guichaoua, *From War to Genocide: Criminal Politics in Rwanda, 1990–1994*, trans. Don E. Webster (Madison: University of Wisconsin Press, 2015), 184–91.

6. Since fighting between the RPF and the Rwandan government forces had broken out along the road to the airport, the US Country Team chose an overland evacuation to Burundi, away from the zones of conflict. Hundreds of British subjects and Kenyan and German citizens joined the US convoys on April 8–10.

7. S/RES/872(1993), 5 October 1993, "Security Council resolution establishing UNAMIR for a six-month period and approving the integration of UNOMUR into UNAMIR," in United Nations, *United Nations and Rwanda*, 231–33; and Dallaire, *Shake Hands*, 233 and 264.

8. S/RES/912 (1994), 21 April 1994, "Security Council resolution adjusting UNAMIR's mandate and authorizing a reduction in its strength," in United Nations, *United Nations and Rwanda*, 268–69. Force Commander Dallaire was finally able to hold on to about 450 troops and staff, a small but intrepid team, living under horrible physical conditions and incredible stress. Dallaire, *Shake Hands*, 221, 328. For a ground view of an NGO who stayed on, see Médecins Sans Frontières, *Populations en danger 1995* (Paris: Éditions la Découverte, 1995), chap. 2.

9. Finally voted as a Security Council resolution on 17 May 1994. See S/RES/918 (1994), 17 May 1994, "Security Council resolution expanding UNAMIR to 5,500 troops and mandating UNAMIR II to provide security to displaced persons, refugees and civilians at risk and to support relief efforts, and imposing an arms embargo on Rwanda," in United Nations, *United Nations and Rwanda*, 282–84.

10. 16 June 1994, Memorandum, to AF/C Arlene Render and others; from PM/ISP Roy Wharton; Subject: "UN—Requested Delay to June 22 on Airshipping APC's." 25 Jun 94 USUN 02628, "Rwanda-UN Willing to Accept Responsibility for APCS," reports the problem solved, but 29 Jul 94 Kampala 06026, "APC's in Entebbe—Can We Hitch a Ride," reports that thirty-six of fifty US APCs were still sitting at the airport.

11. Dallaire, *Shake Hands*, 375–432.

12. S/RES/929 (1994), 22 June 1994, "Security Council resolution, invoking Chapter VII of the Charter, authorizing Member States to conduct a multinational operation for humanitarian purposes in Rwanda until UNAMIR is brought up to strength," in United Nations, *United Nations and Rwanda*, 308. See also 20 June 1994, Information Memorandum, to the deputy secretary; from INR-Toby T. Gati; Subject: "French Intervention in Africa."

13. For summations of the French position, see 06 Jul 94 USUN 02788, "Rwanda: French Reassure SC about Humanitarian Zone"; and 09 Aug 94 Paris 22856, "Rwanda: French Pullout from Humanitarian Zone Remains on Track." For the US positions supporting the objectives of Turquoise, see 17 Jun 94 State 163273, "Support for French Initiative on Rwanda"; and 23 Jun 94 State 168777, "Support for French-led Operation, Expanded UNAMIR." For an analysis of French intentions, see Prunier, *Rwanda Crisis*, chap. 8. See also Human Rights Watch, *Leave None to Tell the Story*, written by Alison Des Forges (New York: Human Rights Watch, 1999), 654–68.

14. See Bruce D. Jones, *Peacemaking in Rwanda: The Dynamics of Failure* (Boulder, CO: Lynne Rienner, 2001), 123–27. Jones, whose overview largely tracks with the above analysis, is wrong in asserting that "Turquoise did nothing at all to halt FAR's genocidal attacks. . . . Turquoise occupied the only section of Rwanda where there were not ongoing killings." Genocide patrols were, on the contrary, still very active. See Ilibagiza, *Left to Tell*, especially chaps. 17–20, for a harrowing account of rescue by the French within the zone. For French views on the difficulties of having government personnel within the humanitarian zone, see 16 Jul 94 USUN 02940, "Rwanda: 15 Jul 94 Security Council Meeting."

15. For the confusion surrounding the final days of the RPF offensive and the Rwandan government forces retreat over the border into Zaire, see 19 Jul 94 USUN 02952, "Rwanda: 18 Jul 94 Security Council Meeting"; 19 Jul 94 State 192840, "US Efforts with RPF to Obtain Cease Fire"; and 20 Jul 94 State 194079, "A/S Moose July 19 TelCon with RPF Commander."

16. In an early assertion of state sovereignty, the RPF moved into the Turquoise zone without UNAMIR escort, as had been previously agreed, while ignoring UNAMIR checkpoints. 16 Sep 94 State 251294, "Demarche on RPA Deployment into the Southwest."

17. Analysts disagree on the numbers. A systematic but contested attempt to map out the killings, based on Rwandan government and ICTR documents, is found in Christian Davenport and Allan C. Stam, "What Really Happened in Rwanda," *Pacific Standard Magazine,* October 6, 2009, https://psmag.com /social-justice/what-really-happened-in-rwanda-3432. My own sense is that a large number of people died on both sides of the ethnic divide in a short period of time. Deaths could have exceeded eight hundred thousand. Persons identified as Tutsi were intentionally hunted down and brutally slaughtered because of who they were. Under terms of the UN Genocide Convention, this was genocide.

18. Arguably General Dallaire, with more troops and the right materiel and mandate, could have done both. Resolution 918 of May 17 belatedly gave him the mandate, but troops and equipment did not show up until the genocide flamed out and the RPF had taken over the country.

19. Dallaire, *Shake Hands,* 71.

20. 10 Aug 93 USUN 03856, "Rwanda: UN Views on PKO"; and Dallaire, *Shake Hands,* 78–79.

21. 12 Sep 94 USUN 03783, "Rwanda: Gen Dallaire Addresses Troop Contributors." Dallaire told sending states that "the inability to deploy quickly contributed to the political deterioration."

22. Dallaire, *Shake Hands,* 146–48, 233.

23. See, for example, 17 May 94 State 131212, "Department Reminds Rwandan Ambassador of Responsibility for Civilians; Calls for Immediate End to Massacres"; 24 May 94 State 138779, "Moose Urges the RPF to Agree to Cease-fire"; 06 Jun 94 State 150411, "AF/C Presses GOR and RPF Reps"; 02 Jul 94 State 177562, "Dept Urges RPF to Stop Fighting; RPF Rep Complains about the French"; 07 Jul 94 State 180391, "AF/C Urges Cease-fire in Meeting with RPF"; 15 Jul 94 State 189038, "RPF to Halt Offensive by Friday Night?" 15 Jul 94 USUN 02918, "Rwanda: Security Council Adopts Statement July 14 Calling for Ceasefire"; 19 Jul 94 State 192840, "US Efforts with RPF to Obtain Cease-fire"; 18 Jul 94 Brussels 07949, "Humanitarian Crisis in Goma: July 17 Conversations with RPF Representative Ruego in Brussels and Belgian MFA Chef de Cabinet Willems"; 18 Jul 94 Kampala 05644, "Message to Museveni for RPF"; and 20 Jul 94 State 194079, "A/S Moose July 19 Telcon with RPF Commander."

24. See, for example, 17 Jun 94 Kampala 04809, "RPF Chairman Calls on Ambassador." In this demarche, the United States and Uganda were singing the same tune. President Museveni on June 6 had issued a public statement urging the RPF to accept a ceasefire and work toward power sharing. Museveni reportedly said, "If the RPF insists on fighting, I think they are making a mistake." 09 Jun 94 State 154770, "Museveni's Constructive Statement on Rwanda."

25. My April 6 advice to the department to reinforce UNAMIR did not anticipate that the next day the two largest UN contingents, the Belgians and

the Bangladeshis, would be neutralized—the Belgians by the murder of their paratroopers and the Bangladeshis by direct orders from headquarters not to go out on dangerous missions.

26. Dallaire, *Shake Hands*, 299–301, 331, 390.

27. For a discussion of the difficulties inherent in a rapid deployment of adequate reinforcements, see Alan Kuperman, *The Limits of Humanitarian Intervention: Genocide in Rwanda* (Washington, DC: Brookings Institution Press, 2001), especially chap. 8.

28. See, for example, 13 Oct 94 State 278118, "President Bizimungu and Deputy Secretary Talbott Discuss Assistance and Benchmarks"; 22 Sep 94 Bonn 23717, "Continuation of German Development Assistance to Rwanda"; or 27 Sep 94 State 261936, "Friends of Rwanda Political Group."

SELECTED BIBLIOGRAPHY

I. STATE BUILDING, CONFLICT RESOLUTION, AND GENOCIDE STUDIES

Arendt, Hannah. *The Human Condition.* Chicago: University of Chicago Press, 1998.

Avruch, Kevin. *Culture and Conflict Resolution.* Washington, DC: United States Institute of Peace Press, 1998.

Bass, Gary J. *Freedom's Battle.* New York: Vintage Books, 2008.

Boutros-Ghali, Boutros. *An Agenda for Peace 1995.* 2nd ed. New York: United Nations Department of Public Information, 1995.

Cohen, Herman J. *Intervening in Africa: Superpower Peacemaking in a Troubled Continent.* New York: St. Martin's Press, 2000.

Collier, Paul. *The Bottom Billion.* New York: Oxford University Press, 2007.

Covey, Jock, Michael J. Dziedzic, and Leonard R. Hawley, eds. *The Quest for Viable Peace.* Washington, DC: United States Institute of Peace Press, 2005.

Crocker, Chester A., Fen Osler Hampson, and Pamela Aall, eds. *Grasping the Nettle: Analyzing Cases of Intractable Conflict.* Washington, DC: United States Institute of Peace Press. 2005.

———, eds. *Herding Cats: Multiparty Mediation in a Complex World.* Washington, DC: United States Institute of Peace Press, 1999.

———, eds. *Leashing the Dogs of War: Conflict Management in a Divided World.* Washington, DC: United States Institute of Peace Press, 2007.

———, eds. *Taming Intractable Conflicts: Mediation in the Hardest Cases.* Washington, DC: United States Institute of Peace Press, 2004.

———, eds. *Turbulent Peace: The Challenges of Managing International Conflict.* Washington, DC: United States Institute of Peace Press, 2001.

Daniel, Donald C. F., and Bradd C. Hayes, with Chantal de Jonge Oudraat. *Coercive Inducement and the Containment of International Crises.* Washington, DC: United States Institute of Peace Press, 1999.

Fassin, Didier, and Mariella Pandolfi, eds. *Contemporary States of Disaster*. New York: Zone Books, 2010.

Finnemore, Martha. *The Purpose of Intervention: Changing Beliefs about the Use of Force*. Ithaca: Cornell University Press, 2003.

Fisher, Roger, William Ury, and Bruce Patton. *Getting to Yes: Negotiating Agreement without Giving In*. 2nd ed. New York: Penguin Books, 1981.

Geertz, Clifford. *The Interpretation of Cultures*. New York: Basic Books, 1973.

Jackson, Robert H. *Quasi-States: Sovereignty, International Relations, and the Third World*. New York: Cambridge University Press, 1990.

Khadiagala, Gilbert M. *Security Dynamics in Africa's Great Lakes Region*. Boulder, CO: Lynne Rienner, 2006.

Kiernan, Ben. *Blood and Soil: A World History of Genocide and Extermination from Sparta to Darfur*. New Haven: Yale University Press, 2007.

Lang, Anthony F., Jr. *Agency and Ethics*. Albany: State University of New York Press, 2002.

———, ed. *Just Intervention*. Washington, DC: Georgetown University, 2003.

Lederach, John Paul. *Building Peace: Sustainable Reconciliation in Divided Societies*. Washington, DC: United States Institute of Peace Press, 1997.

———. *The Little Book of Conflict Transformation*. Intercourse, PA: Good Books, 2003.

Lemarchand, René. *Forgotten Genocides*. Philadelphia: University of Pennsylvania Press, 2011.

Lipjhart, Arend. *Democracy in Plural Societies*. New Haven: Yale University Press, 1977.

Littlejohn, Stephen W., and Kathy Domenici. *Communication, Conflict, and the Management of Difference*. Long Grove, IL: Waveland Press, 2007.

Lund, Michael S. *Preventing Violent Conflicts: A Strategy for Preventive Diplomacy*. Washington, DC: United States Institute of Peace Press, 1996.

Maundi, Mohammed O., I. William Zartman, Gilbert Khadiagala, and Kwaku Nuamah. *Getting In*. Washington, DC: United States Institute of Peace Press, 2006.

Orstom, Elinor. *Governing the Commons: The Evolution of Institutions for Collective Action*. New York: Cambridge University Press, 1990.

Power, Samantha. *A Problem from Hell*. New York: Basic Books, 2002.

Spector, Bertram L., and I. William Zartman. *Getting It Done*. Washington, DC: United States Institute of Peace Press, 2003.

Susskind, Lawrence, and Jeffrey Cruikshank. *Breaking the Impasse: Consensual Approaches to Resolving Public Disputes*. New York: Basic Books, 1987.

Taleb, Nassim Nicholas. *The Black Swan*. New York: Random House, 2007.

Ury, William. *Getting Past No*. New York: Bantam Books, 1993.

Zartman, I. William. *Ripe for Resolution: Conflict and Intervention in Africa*. New York: Oxford University Press, 1989.

II. RWANDA HISTORY

Berger, Iris. *Religion and Resistance: East African Kingdoms in the Pre-Colonial Period*. Tervuren: Musée Royal de l'Afrique Centrale, 1981.

Chrétien, Jean-Pierre. *The Great Lakes of Africa: Two Thousand Years of History*. Translated by Scott Straus. New York: Zone Books, 2006.

Coupez, A., and Th. Kamanzi. *Récits historiques Rwanda.* Tervuren: Musée Royal de L'Afrique Centrale, 1962.

d'Hertefelt, Marcel. *Les clans du Rwanda ancien: Éléments d'ethnosociologie et d'ethnohistoire.* Tervuren: Musée Royal de l'Afrique Centrale, 1971.

d'Hertefelt, M., A. A.Trouwborst, and J. H. Scherer. *Les anciens royaumes de la zone interlacustre méridionale: Rwanda, Burundi, Buha.* Tervuren: Musée Royal de l'Afrique Centrale, 1962.

Gasore-Rukara, Pierre. *Les partis politiques au Rwanda (1990–1992): Idéologies, stratégies et pesanteurs sociologiques.* Kigali: Imprimerie Nationale du Rwanda, 1992.

Kagame, Alexis. *Un abrégé de l'histoire du Rwanda, de 1853 à 1972.* Butare: Éditions Universitaires du Rwanda, 1975.

Lemarchand, René. *Rwanda and Burundi.* New York: Praeger, 1970.

Louis, Wm. Roger. *Ruanda-Urundi 1884–1919.* Oxford: Clarendon, 1963.

Maquet, Jacques J. *The Premise of Inequality in Ruanda: A Study of Political Relations in a Central African Kingdom.* London: Oxford University Press, 1961.

Newbury, Catharine. *The Cohesion of Oppression: Clientship and Ethnicity in Rwanda, 1860–1960.* New York: Columbia University Press, 1988.

Newbury, David. *The Land beyond the Mists: Essays on Identity and Authority in Precolonial Congo and Rwanda.* Athens: Ohio University Press, 2009.

Rawson, David. *The Role of the United Nations in the Political Development of Ruanda-Urundi, 1947–1962.* Ann Arbor, MI: UMI Dissertation Services, 1966.

Reyntjens, Filip. *Pouvoir et droit au Rwanda: Droit public et évolution politique, 1916–1973.* Tervuren: Musée Royal de l'Afrique Centrale, 1985.

Schoenbrun, David Lee. *A Green Place, A Good Place: Agrarian Change, Gender, and Social Identity in the Great Lakes Region to the 15th Century.* Portsmouth, NH: Heinemann, 1998.

Vansina, Jan. *Antecedents to Modern Rwanda.* Madison: University of Wisconsin Press, 2004.

III. THE RWANDA GENOCIDE

Adelman, Howard, and Astri Suhrke, eds. *The Path of a Genocide: The Rwanda Crisis from Uganda to Zaire.* New Brunswick, NJ: Transaction Publishers, 2000.

African Rights. *Rwanda: Death, Despair, and Defiance.* London: African Rights, 1994.

Barnett, Michael. *Eyewitness to a Genocide: The United Nations and Rwanda.* Ithaca: Cornell University Press, 2002.

Braeckman, Colette. *Rwanda: Histoire d'un génocide.* Paris: Fayard, 1992.

Brauman, Rony. *Devant le mal: Rwanda, un génocide en direct.* Paris: Arléa, 1994.

Chrétien, Jean-Pierre. *Rwanda: Les médias du génocide.* Paris: Éditions Karthala, 1995

Cohen, Jared. *One Hundred Days of Silence: America and the Rwanda Genocide.* New York: Rowan, Littlefield, 2007.

Collins, Barrie. *Rwanda 1994: The Myth of the Akazu Genocide Conspiracy and Its Consequences.* New York: Palgrave Macmillan, 2014.

Dallaire, Roméo. *Shake Hands with the Devil: The Failure of Humanity in Rwanda.* Toronto: Random House, 2003.

Decker, Rudolf. *Ruanda: Tod und Hoffnung im Land der Tausend Hügel.* Neuhausen-Stuttgart: Hänssler-Verlag, 1998.

Deme, Amadou. *Rwanda 1994 and the Failure of the United Nations Missions.* Bloomington, IN: Xlibris, 2010.

Des Forges, Alison. *Leave None to Tell the Story: Genocide in Rwanda.* New York: Human Rights Watch, 1999.

Destexhe, Alain. *Rwanda and Genocide in the Twentieth Century.* New York: New York University Press, 1995.

Erlinder, Peter. *The Accidental Genocide.* St. Paul, MN: International Humanitarian Law Institute, 2013.

Fujii, Lee Ann. *Killing Neighbors: Webs of Violence in Rwanda.* Ithaca: Cornell University Press, 2009.

Gourevitch, Philip. *We Wish to Inform You That Tomorrow We Will Be Killed with Our Families: Stories from Rwanda.* New York: Farrar, Straus and Giroux, 1998.

Gribbin, Robert E. *In the Aftermath of Genocide: The U.S. Role in Rwanda.* New York: iUniverse, 2005.

Grünfeld, Fred, and Anke Huijboom. *The Failure to Prevent Genocide in Rwanda: The Role of Bystanders.* Leiden: Martinus Nijhoff, 2007.

Guichaoua, André. *From War to Genocide: Criminal Politics in Rwanda, 1990–1994.* Translated by Don E. Webster. Madison: University of Wisconsin Press, 2015.

Herman, Edward S., and David Peterson. *Enduring Lies: The Rwanda Genocide in the Propaganda System, 20 Years Later.* Evergreen Park, IL: Real New Books, 2014.

Ilibagiza, Immaculée. *Left to Tell: Discovering God amidst the Rwandan Holocaust.* Carlsbad, CA: Hay House, 2006.

Jones, Bruce D. *Peacemaking in Rwanda: The Dynamics of Failure.* Boulder, CO: Lynne Rienner, 2001.

Keane, Fergal. *Season of Blood: A Rwandan Journey.* New York: Penguin Books, 1995.

Kuperman, Alan J. *The Limits of Humanitarian Intervention: Genocide in Rwanda.* Washington, DC: Brookings Institute Press, 2001.

Leader, Joyce E. *Rwanda's Struggle for Democracy and Peace, 1991–1994.* Washington, DC: Fund for Peace, 2001.

Lemarchand, René. *The Dynamics of Violence in Central Africa.* Philadelphia: University of Pennsylvania Press, 2009.

Magnarella, Paul J. *Justice in Africa: Rwanda's Genocide, Its Courts, and the UN Criminal Tribunal.* Burlington, VT: Ashgate Press, 2000.

Mamdani, Mahmood. *When Victims Become Killers: Colonialism, Nativism, and Genocide in Rwanda.* Princeton, NJ: Princeton University Press, 2001.

Marchal, Luc. *Rwanda: La descente aux enfers.* Brussels: Éditions Labor, 2001.

Médecins Sans Frontières. *Populations en Danger 1995.* Paris: Éditions la Découverte, 1995.

Melvern, Linda R. *Conspiracy to Murder: The Rwandan Genocide.* New York: Verso, 2004.

Odom, Thomas P. *Journey into Darkness: Genocide in Rwanda.* College Station: Texas A&M University Press, 2005.

Prunier, Gérard. *Africa's World War: Congo, the Rwandan Genocide, and the Making of a Continental Catastrophe.* New York: Oxford University Press. 2009.

———. *The Rwanda Crisis: History of a Genocide.* New York: Columbia University Press, 1995.

Rawson, David. "From Retribution to Reconciliation: Transitional Justice in Rwanda, 1994–2011." *Georgetown Journal of International Affairs* 13, no. 2 (Summer/Fall 2012): 115–23.

———. "Prosecuting Genocide: Founding the International Tribunal for Rwanda." *Ohio Northern University Law Review* 32, no. 2 (2007): 641–63.

Reyntjens, Filip. *Political Governance in Post-Genocide Rwanda.* New York: Cambridge University Press, 2013.

———. *Rwanda: Trois jours qui ont fait basculer l'histoire.* Paris: Éditions L'Harmattan, 1995.

———. *Talking or Fighting? Political Evolution in Rwanda and Burundi, 1998–1999.* Uppsala: Nordiska Afrikainstitutet, 1999.

Rudasingwa, Theogene. *Healing a Nation: A Testimony.* North Charleston, SC: Create Space Publishing, 2013.

Ruhigira, Enoch. *Rwanda: La fin tragique d'un régime.* 2 vols. Paris: La Pagaie, 2011.

Rusesabagina, Paul. *An Ordinary Man.* New York: Viking, 2006.

Ruzibiza, Abdul Joshua. *Rwanda: L'histoire secrète.* Paris: Éditions du Panama, 2005.

Sommers, Marc. *Stuck: Rwandan Youth and the Struggle for Adulthood.* Athens: University of Georgia Press, 2012.

Straus, Scott. *Making and Unmaking Nations: War, Leadership, and Genocide in Modern Africa.* Ithaca: Cornell University Press, 2015.

———. *The Order of Genocide: Race, Power, and War in Rwanda.* Ithaca: Cornell University Press, 2006.

Straus, Scott, and Lars Waldorf, eds. *Remaking Rwanda: State Building and Human Rights after Mass Violence.* Madison: University of Wisconsin Press, 2011.

Thompson, Allan, ed. *The Media and the Rwanda Genocide.* London: Pluto Press, 2007.

Umutesi, Marie Béatrice. *Surviving the Slaughter: The Ordeal of a Rwandan Refugee in Zaire.* Madison: University of Wisconsin Press, 2000.

United Nations. *The United Nations and Rwanda, 1993–1996.* New York: United Nations Department of Public Information, 1996.

Uvin, Peter. *Aiding Violence: The Development Enterprise in Rwanda.* West Hartford, CT: Kumarian Press, 1998.

INDEX